# Pioneers and Preachers:
# Stories of the Old Frontier

# Pioneers and Preachers: Stories of the Old Frontier

Robert William Mondy

Illustrations by

Albino Hinojosa

Nelson-Hall nh Chicago

Library of Congress Cataloging in Publication Data

Mondy, Robert William,
　Pioneers and preachers.

　Includes bibliographical references and index.
　1. Frontier and pioneer life—United States. 2. United States—Religious life and customs. 3. Rural clergy—United States—History. 4. United States—Social life and customs—1783-1865.　I. Title
E179.5.M58　　　973　　　79-169
ISBN 0-88229-619-1　(Cloth)
ISBN 0-88229-722-8　　(Paper)

Copyright© 1980 by Robert William Mondy

All rights reserved. No part of this book may be reproduced in any form without permission in writing from the publisher, except by a reviewer who wishes to quote brief passages in connection with a review written for broadcast or for inclusion in a magazine or newspaper. For information address Nelson-Hall Inc., Publishers, 111 North Canal Street, Chicago, Illinois 60606.

Manufactured in the United States of America
10　　9　　8　　7　　6　　5　　4　　3　　2　　1

# Contents

Preface .................................................. vii

1. From Romance to Reality ........................ 1
2. The Hard Life ..................................... 11
3. Marriage and Sex ................................. 37
4. Health and Medical Practices on the Frontier ......... 51
5. Perils of Travel ................................... 63
6. Odd Ideas ......................................... 81
7. Barbarous and Unorthodox Manners ................ 93
8. Frontier Fights ................................... 107
9. Outlaws .......................................... 129
10. Vigilante Committees ............................ 149
11. Acquiring Land .................................. 175
12. The Frontier Preacher ........................... 187
13. Emotional Religion and Frontier Sermons ........... 213
14. Conclusion ...................................... 237
    Notes .......................................... 243
    Index .......................................... 263

**In Memory of Walter Prescott Webb**

# Preface

Although society evidently evolves by impersonal forces, each individual can usually determine why his interests have developed along certain lines. This was certainly the case with me. As a lad of ten, I wondered and continued to be amazed at what it would be like to live without societal benefits to which we have grown so accustomed; advantages such as law and law-enforcing agencies, doctors, money and a market for one's produce. As a small boy, I was often in the company of my two great-grandmothers, each in her eighties. They reminisced constantly about their early years on the North Louisiana frontier and their stories remain as exciting today as they were the moment they were told. One ancestor spoke of the prevalence of snakes that crawled into poorly constructed log cabins, especially those that had only earthen floors. Another related how a neighbor, using only a butcher knife and handsaw, attempted to amputate a man's infected leg above the knee. The "patient" got drunk on home-distilled whiskey before the operation began but he died, likely from pain and shock, despite the fervent prayers of a few neighbors and the local preacher during the ordeal. The deceased was soon placed in a crudely built homemade coffin and buried the next day on a nearby hillside. My other great-grandmother, on hearing this tale, remarked, "It was the will of God."

*Pioneers and Preachers: Stories of the Old Frontier* was written to describe the adjustments that American pioneers attempted to make to their many primitive life conditions. The pioneers described in this book might have lived along the coast of Massachusetts in the 1600's, the wilds of Kentucky in the 1700's, in the red hills of North Louisiana or in the valleys of the far western mountains in the 1800's. Although the American frontier encompassed vast geographical areas and spanned three centuries, the pioneers had two life conditions in common: they had access to the land and its resources but few societal benefits. I do not intend to imply, however, that frontier behavior was uniform. Different soil and climatic conditions, diverse cultural backgrounds of the people—these and many other factors created dissimilar mannerisms of the pioneers. This book is designed to present a typical occurrence of events on the frontier. As such, a story regarding outlaws in Massachusetts in the seventeenth century may be followed by a tale concerning the same topic 100 years later in Texas. I believe that this approach is perfectly justifiable because of the similar life conditions in which the pioneers lived.

Many have asked, "Why the title *Pioneers and Preachers: Stories of the Old Frontier?*" Although there were few organized churches on the frontier, the frontier preacher, nevertheless, did play a major role in providing information which significantly assisted in the writing of this book. In order for the minister to reach his congregation, he was often required to travel over vast areas of untamed territory. Because of his travels, the itinerant preacher was in an excellent position to observe and record the primitive conditions existing on the frontier. Because of the high rate of illiteracy that existed on many sections of the frontier, the frontier minister often was the only available witness to provide written records of events. In letters written to friends and church leaders, they described the actions of the pioneers and the conditions that existed on the frontier. It was while searching through old church records and letters that many of these unusual stories of the frontier surfaced. If there was one source that made the writing of this book possible, it was the itinerant preacher who searched for "lost souls" in a most hostile environment—the frontier—and recorded the experiences of his journeys.

No person had greater impact upon the writing of this book than Dr. Walter Prescott Webb, who until his untimely death in 1962 was the distinguished professor of frontier history at the University of Texas at Austin. In the summer of 1931, I enrolled for my first graduate course, *The Great Plains*, under Professor Webb. The other two courses I had that term were by comparison dry and stale. As a lecturer, Dr. Webb swept me off my feet. William Jennings Bryan could not have been more spellbinding. I couldn't take a note for watching and listening to him relive the Great Plains frontier to seventy-six graduate students.

Webb's first world frontier course was offered in 1938–39. I was one of nine students in this study. At the end of the course, before returning to Louisiana, I asked Webb for permission to use for my dissertation the topic "American Frontier Aberrant Behavior." Without hesitation, Webb's reply was "No! Wait until you are as old as William Graham Sumner when he wrote *Folkways* before doing a topic of that magnitude!" He eventually gave me a topic that was not nearly as thought-provoking and one for which I could find little material.

Perhaps because of Webb's advice, the writing of this book did not begin until decades after my graduation and the writing and research has taken over a quarter of a century to complete. It became a ritual to leave my teaching each summer to visit some distant library in the hopes of finding letters and other documentation that would be helpful in describing life on the frontier. Four times my journeys took me to the Library of Congress, twice to the University of Texas Library, and other seemingly endless visits to archives across the country. Webb must have had fantastic insight because I was as old as Sumner when I eventually completed the manuscript.

But the time spent on the project also created a manuscript of considerable length. When told by a publisher that it was too long, I could not bare the agony of performing surgery on my life's work. As would be the case with any researcher who had spent twenty-five years living with a topic so near and dear to his heart, I was in love with every word. It was at this stage that my son, R. Wayne Mondy, a recognized writer in his own field, stepped in with scapel in hand and saved the patient. Although I did not agree with all points of incisions into the manuscript and my heart skipped a beat each time a paragraph was extracted, I must say that the end product is something of which I am proud.

I would like to thank everyone who helped in this project, but, because it spanned twenty-five years, the list would simply be too long. Some, however, must be mentioned. Professor John D. Winters provided valuable editorial assistance and moral support during a large portion of the project. Professor Robert C. Snyder, my close friend and confidant, provided me with constant inspiration in the completion of the project. Professor Morgan Peoples provided me with pleasant conversation, stimulating ideas, and encouragement. The services of Mr. Sam Thomas, Mr. Jim Hall and Mrs. Martha Reichert during the completion of this project also deserve special thanks. I wish to thank Mrs. John Winters for her efficient work helping to ensure that my bibliography was correct.

I would especially like to acknowledge the assistance of Dr. W. Tarrentine Jackson, Professor of History at the University of California, for suggesting the title of the manuscript. Professor William Long of the Department of History and Professor James Conrad, Director of the Archives, at East Texas State University deserve special mention for the support and encouragement they provided my son in the finalization of the manuscript. It would be my fondest wish for the reader to receive as much satisfaction from viewing this aspect of the frontier as I have enjoyed the writing and the research of this my favorite topic—the pioneers of the American frontier.

# 1

# From Romance to Reality

After the Great Mariner's historic discovery of the October days, bold and daring navigators and explorers made enchanting reports of new seas, of unsuspected constellations, of a cross in the southern skies, of places where the needle varied from the pole, and of innumerable continents and islands on which lived people of diverse cultures unfamiliar to Europeans. The "Admiral of the Ocean Sea," after a fourth and unsuccessful attempt to find a strait through his "Other World" did not exaggerate when he said "'Over there I have placed under the Highnesses' sovereignty more land than there is in Africa and Europe, and more than 1700 islands, not counting Hispaniola. . . .'"[1] In the history of man, there has been only one discovery worthy of name—that of the new lands beyond the western seas.

Nearly everything about the New World—from its majestic forests and winding rivers to its marshy jungles and "black pit of the Magellan clouds"—intrigued Europeans. Particularly dazzling to them was the wealth acquired in far-off places. Balboa, the first to view the "Great Main Sea," obtained a million dollars in gold and pearls from the Indians. In September 1522, after having completed the greatest voyage of all time, the *Vittoria*, the only ship of Magellan's five to sail around the world, had more than enough spices to pay for the entire expedition. A few years later, Pizarro ransomed $17.5 million in gold from the Inca Indians. In 1580, as the autumn gales blew up the English Channel, Francis Drake's *Golden Hind*, worm-eaten and weed-clogged after a three-year voyage around the world, sailed into Plymouth Harbor with the spoil of a Peruvian ship,[2] netting Queen Elizabeth and other financial backers 4600 percent profit and causing

England to look to the sea for her future greatness. Seven years later, young Thomas Cavendish bagged a Manila galleon on a similar piratical expedition: "his ships entered the Thames rigged with Damask sails; and each sailor wore a silk suit and a chain of pure gold around his neck."[3] As curious spectators in Europe stood on shore and watched a ship draw away from the familiar harbor and dip below the horizon, they wondered about the nature of the new frontiers to the west.

What Europeans learned of the new land and seas, often exaggerated but always of great interest, enabled them to soar to new heights on the wings of imagination. This is reflected in the romantic literature written during the period of discovery and exploration. On his homeward voyage from Newfoundland, Sir Humphrey Gilbert was reading a book when last seen on the quarter deck of the *Squirrel*. From what he said just before his ship was lost at sea—"We are as near Heaven by sea as by land"—the book must have been Sir Thomas More's *Utopia* (1516) describing, among other things, an ideal commonwealth on an island "set in the ocean, somewhere in the new world . . . [where the] air was soft, temperate, and gentle—and everyone was honestly employed, and no one was exploited or overworked."[4] In Luis de Camoens' epic *The Luciads* (1572), the author not only tells the story of da Gama's voyage around the Cape to India, but also relates the remarkable feats of other seamen such as Magellan, who discovered the "Strait which shall forever be honored with his name." Influenced by what he had learned of turbulent western seas, William Shakespeare described in *The Tempest* (1613) a shipwreck in a North Atlantic storm. Daniel Defoe in *Robinson Crusoe* (1719) allowed an English sailor to be shipwrecked on a tropical island and live there in comfort and ease until rescued. In *The Rime of the Ancient Mariner* (1798), Samuel Coleridge had his rugged mariner sail many strange seas before returning safely to his home port. Such was the imaginative literature written by Europeans of the seas and lands of the west.

But mariners of the period of discovery led a hard and dangerous life. Stormy winds, mountainous waves, breathless calms, and dangerous coral reefs sank many a ship and made sailing a nightmare. Because of their slow-sailing ships—the *Mayflower* was at sea for sixty-five days—sailors were often short of food and water and sometimes completely without them. The rats that infested ships were a luxury for the tables of the privileged, while others ate the leather which kept the spars from chafing against the masts after soaking it in sea water and roasting it over the embers of a fire. In rare cases starving men even fought over bodies of vermin or resorted to cannibalism. Epidemics and diseases of malnutrition made some ships floating coffins. On board one vessel, there were all kinds of miseries: "stench, fumes, horror, vomiting, fever, dysentery, heat, constipation, boils, scurvy, cancer, and mouth-rot. . . . Many voyagers died in such misery and had to be cast into the sea."[5] Of the 239 men who set forth on the Magellan voyage, only eighteen survived. In one instance, 350 of the 400 passengers and crewmen died on a voyage from England to America. A bay and a river bear Henry Hudson's name; he and his men lost their lives on the bay.

A strait is named in honor of Vitus Bering; he and thirty-eight sailors lost their lives after being shipwrecked on a polar island. Mariners who died seeking fame and fortune are legion.

Land explorers of the new frontiers fared little better than the seamen. Although Balboa discovered the Pacific Ocean and acquired vast wealth from the Indians, he was so ill on returning to the Atlantic side of the isthmus connecting the Americas that he had to be carried in a basket. Searching for a fountain of youth, Ponce de Leon discovered Florida, but he died there in the wilderness from a poisoned arrow. De Narvaez and all but four of 600 colonists perished in an attempt to establish a settlement in Florida. De Soto discovered the Mississippi River and died of a fever on the banks of the "Father of Waters." The new seas and lands were romantic mainly to those who remained at home and explored them in their fancy.

**THE PIONEERS**

Though the frontier era is past, Americans still regard it with an imaginative, romantic fervor, full of excitement, enthusiasm, and emotion. It was the land of Hiawatha and Pocahontas, of Daniel Boone and Andrew Jackson. It was the land of the dedicated Pilgrims and their first Thanksgiving, of intrepid pioneers on foot, on horseback, and in covered wagons winding their way through primitive forests, over rolling treeless plains, and across mountains and streams toward the setting sun. In part because of movies and popular literature, the frontier was the home of the cowboy. He had the courage needed to fight Indians and bad men, to break broncos and rope steers, and to deal with stampedes and prairie fires. Americans take pride in their frontier heritage, believing in a vague sort of way that the civilization hewn out of the wilderness by their forefathers to be the last best hope on earth.

Frontiersmen lived during many periods of American history. They were the people who were on the outward fringes of organized society. As portions of America became organized, the frontier disappeared in those locations but reappeared in other segments of the continent. Actually, the frontier was developing in many places at different times. As a portion of the country took on the characteristics of organized society, it could no longer be considered the frontier.

There were always those who were willing to move away from organized society. These were the pioneers, and this factor stood uppermost in shaping their lives.[6] As pioneers migrated to the frontier they left integrated society behind with such advantages as law enforcing institutions, a monetary system, a division of labor, and an organized stable religion. The early settlers living along the coast were isolated from the mother lands by the Atlantic Ocean. Even later, after society had developed in various regions, settlers often had little contact with these parts. Going to the frontier was regarded by many men and women as closing the door between them and civilization.

**FROM CHAOS TO ORDER**

Whether the frontiersmen lived along the coast of

Maine, on the red hills of North Louisiana, or on the wind-swept Great Plains, they were subjected to two forces: they had access to the land and its resources but had few and sometimes no societal benefits.

Beginning with few societal benefits, settlers knew that peace and prosperity could be most effectively attained through organization. It was imperative to maintain peace, both among themselves and with Indians. A group of men working together could increase and economize their strength; five men working in cooperation to build a log cabin or sodhouse, to construct a bridge across a stream, or to clear a tract of land were more efficient than each of them working separately. Though many settlers had never read a book and often could not read at all, they would have agreed with the basic truth—at least after it was explained to them—that a society is greater than the sum of its parts.

The evolution of institutions in response to frontier conditions came about "without rationally conceived and visualized purpose, without reflection or analysis."[7] Dodging, twisting, and turning under the pain of maladjustment, settlers, as all mankind, began with acts, not with thoughts. Their method was trial and failure.[8] As society unfolded on the frontier, old and cherished customs were often discarded or altered and new ones emerged. The time required to evolve new institutions varied. Usually it took more than a generation.

There were conditions inherent to frontier life that delayed and impeded societal growth. Without benefit of organized society, the settlers' first task was to live—to obtain food, clothes, shelter for themselves and provide for a few indispensable livestock. Having little or no means of conveying their produce to markets, they were forced to depend almost entirely upon the land for their livelihood.[9] This adaptation was particularly difficult for many settlers coming from integrated societies with a division of labor, technology, and money economy. Making an adjustment to the land itself was arduous, especially when faced with an unfamiliar climate. Scandinavians found the warm climate of the Mississippi Valley quite different from that of their homeland. Georgians learned that the wind-swept Illinois prairie was in sharp contrast to the South and its milder weather. Those who migrated to the Great Plains were forced to construct their dwellings from sod, to till the soil so as to preserve the greatest amount of moisture, and to evolve new hunting techniques.

Pioneers were from diverse cultures. During the Colonial Period, they were from England and many other parts of Europe. Andrew Burnaby traveling through the Colonies in 1759-1760 said the population was composed of "different nations, different religions, and different languages." The heterogeneous population of Pennsylvania made it alien to England.[10] Commenting on the nature of the population near Winchester, Virginia, Francis Asbury noted that the people were much divided because of different languages spoken. They agreed about scarcely anything except that they should not sin against God.[11]

For the remainder of the frontier era, people migrated to the new lands from all parts of the United States and from nearly every country. Referring to the varied cultural elements west of the Allegheny Mountains in the early years of the nineteenth century, John Bradbury, a British traveler, commented that the people were "compounded of a great number of nations not yet amalgamated, consisting of emigrants from every state in the Union, mixed with English, Irish, Scotch, Swiss, German, French, and almost every country of Europe."[12] Two missionaries, Samuel J. Mills and David Smith, asserted that frontier people could "hardly have any character," composed as they were of such different cultural elements.[13] In his *Plea for the West*, Reverend Lyman Beecher said the "population of the . . . West . . . was rushing in like the waters of a flood . . ." in need of institutions to discipline the mind. "So various were the opinions and habits," Beecher continued, "so recent and imperfect the acquaintances, and so sparse the settlements . . . that no homogeneous public sentiment could be formed to legislate into being the requisite institutions."[14] Another author compared the frontier to a melting pot in which the "shrewd Yankee, the . . . Southerner, the positive Englishman, the metaphysical Scotchman, the jovial Irishman, the excitable Frenchman, the passionate Spaniard, the voluptuous Italian, the debased African . . ." were flung into a "mighty crucible;" but, because of antagonistic elements, "no chemical agent was sufficiently potent to reduce them to a splendid unity."[15]

The church had almost every type of "character and sentiment: Baptists, Methodists, Campbellites, Christians, Episcopalians, and Universalists of two kinds, no-hellers and hell-redemptionists."[16] Reverend W. W. Hall's congregation in St. Charles, Missouri, consisted in 1833 of Yankees, Pennsylvanians, Tennesseans, Kentuckians, Lutherans, Dutch, French, Danes, English, Scotch, Irish, and others, all of whom had to be a little humored.[17] Another missionary believed the "nations of the world" had "boiled" and thrown their "scum" into his Kansas Congregation.[18] With regard to the representatives of diverse cultures that converged in San Francisco in the 1850's, Robert Louis Stevenson wrote, "I wonder about this evocation of a roaring city, in a few years of man's life, from the marshes and the blowing sand! . . . that city of God which adventurers congregated out of all the winds of Heaven."[19] When strangers met in any part of the frontier, they usually asked each other, "What part of the world are you from?"

Living among people whose culture was in sharp contrast to their own accentuated the settlers' problem of social organization; Indians had made an efficient adjustment to raw nature. Their difficulty, when the white man arrived, was not in establishing a compact organization among themselves, but in continuing their integrity and retaining ancestral lands. Though there were instances of friendly and humane relations between Indians and the pioneers, cultural differences between them were so distinct as to preclude much fusion of institutions.

The seemingly endless horde of humanity migrating to the frontier also impeded societal growth. For instance, Kentucky increased from an estimated population of 3,000 in 1782 to 100,000 in 1790. Until near the close of the eighteenth century, Ohio was a wilderness occupied almost

exclusively by Indians; by 1800 its population was 45,000, and in the next ten years, it increased five fold.[20] Traveling to the Ohio River in 1817, Morris Birkbeck was seldom out of sight of families, either before or behind him, all going to some part of the promised land. Some had nothing but a cart and horse, others only a horse and pack-saddle. There were a few men who walked followed by barefooted wives; bearing all their effects on their backs, they endured the hardships with hope of a better life.[21] So many people of diverse origins migrating to an area made for *social instability* or *social chaos* rather than order.

Vagrancy also retarded western cultural growth. Morris Birkbeck contended that backwoodsmen needed "only a slender motive" to move from one place to another. Once, while visiting a family living in a cabin, he learned that this was the third dwelling his host had built within a twelve-month period.[22] Another man, born in eastern Virginia, later moved with his father to the western part of the state. There, before he was twenty years old, he left his father, married, and moved to South Carolina, where he built a cabin in a remote area. When people began settling around him he sold his home and took his family to Kentucky where he lived for two years, and then moved to Indiana. But, as Indiana was "not healthy for cattle," he soon planned to live in Illinois.[23] Still another settler planted fruit trees in seven different places and only lived at the last place long enough to harvest the fruit. Although he and his wife had twelve children, no two were born at the same place. Unable to remember how many times she and her husband had moved, the wife felt they were finally "fix'd for life."[24]

Social relations were definitely weakened when any of the settlers who had made a partial adjustment to land and people moved away. Arrivals from other frontier areas had to make new adjustments to settlers and frequently to different geographic conditions, such as rainfall, temperature, soil, plants, and animals. Also, the influx of vagrants usually forced those who had lived in an area for some time to alter their behavior in some respects. Frontiersmen needed to "stay put" long enough to adjust to the people and nature about them.

Until people had free and easy communication with each other, there could be little societal growth. Settlers, because of their new life conditions, had to evolve many new institutions; but their culture, at least among adults, did not undergo a complete transformation on the frontier. Many institutions were eventually blended. Until the pioneers established frequent and easy contact with each other, new institutions could not evolve nor old ones be modified, because folkways and other institutions come about not of one mind, but of many. To have a consensus, unanimity, or general agreement, it was imperative that pioneers have contact and conflict of ideas to eliminate or alter old institutions and develop new ones.

In time, however, each frontier area came to possess ordinary benefits derived from a society. Ultimately the settlers organized themselves despite all barriers, but this process was slow and painful. The major influence that gave rise to societal evolution was the ever increasing communication between frontier settlers and those of older social orders. The increased contact between people of the original thirteen colonies and Europe accelerated societal

organization on the Atlantic seaboard. During the entire era of the westward movement, while settlers themselves were slowly evolving a semblance of social order, the older pattern of society of the United States was gradually working its way toward newly settled areas.

In his *Life of John Marshall*, A. J. Beveridge said that when he considered the coarse environment in which the famed Chief Justice spent his youth—heavy drinking, general indolence, coarse sports, and eagerness for physical combat—he "wondered at the greatness of mind and soul which grew from such social soil."[25] The same may be said, however, of many other celebrated Americans, born and reared under the most primitive of frontier conditions. Many people marvel at Abraham Lincoln's ability to speak and write, as exemplified in his debates with Stephen A. Douglas, in his many letters, and in his unforgettable Gettysburg Address. It must be remembered there were two Abraham Lincolns, one a product of the raw frontier and the other that of a relatively organized society.

Had Marshall and Lincoln continued to move westward with the waves of migrants they would probably have been "flowers born to blush unseen." Without doubt the frontier left a deep imprint on both Marshall and Lincoln; but it was the blessings of organized society that enabled them to win distinction.

The behavior of frontier people has been variously regarded as odd, strange, repulsive, and romantic. But it was none of these. In a sense, it may be compared to "a great restless sea of clouds, in which the parts are forever rolling, changing, and jostling as temperature, wind currents, and electric discharges vary. . . . The cloud shapes do not change in a series of any definable character and . . . they do not run forward in time towards some ultimate shape, but they change and change, rise and fall, ebb and flow, without any sequence and purpose."[26] With no idea of being perverse, pioneers were preoccupied in their struggle to live.

To evaluate the settlers' behavior is like trying to evaluate the plaintive call of the whippoorwill or the cruel crunch of the tiger's jaws. In his *Origin of Species*, Charles Darwin said that one "need not marvel at the sting of the bee, when used against any enemy, causing the bee's own death; at drones being produced in such great numbers for one single act, and being slaughtered by their sterile sisters. . . ." Such courses of actions, as he said, were only an adjustment to life.[27] So it was for the settlers who migrated to the new lands. Their character traits were nothing more than an adjustment or an attempted adjustment to time and place.

All frontier behavior, however, was not the same, because pioneers lived under different conditions. Some lived in such remote areas that they had little contact with civilization for two generations or longer, while others were not isolated nearly as long. Varied geographic conditions necessitated different responses to the natural setting. The degree of diverse or homogeneous cultural elements in various areas gave rise to dissimilar character traits. Although there were variations in individual behavior for these and other reasons, virtually all settlers were reacting to situations in which the forces of social control were lax.

From chaos, order would come. Society would evolve and the frontier would disappear.

# 2

# The Hard Life

Nearly all settlers were impelled to make new and painful adjustments to frontier life. To truly appreciate and understand why pioneers acted as they did, one must first think of the environment in which they lived. Of the "necessities" of life which we take for granted, the pioneer had few. Even the poorest and most downtrodden in our society today would have been considered well-off on the frontier. Virtually everything necessary to provide food and safety for the pioneer had to be taken from the land, and with no modern tools and implements, this was often a trying task. Food, clothing, housing, and furnishings were hard to obtain. Neighbors lived far apart and trade was difficult because of the distances and lack of means of transport to get the goods to market. These factors combined to make an extremely hard life and set the stage for odd and unusual behavior.

The pioneers, living under drab, monotonous, lonely conditions, and faced with adversity on every hand, did not lead lives of splendor and ease. Day after day, they struggled merely for survival. Contrary to popular notions, they were not healthy, robust people; their exposure to adverse weather and their lack of an adequate diet caused them much suffering. Danger was ever present in their thinking. Only the gods would know the number who died at the hands of their fellow men and Indians. Of those who lived in a state of quiet frustration and disappointment, most names are lost in silence. The romantic regard for them has been "read-in" with the passage of time.

## FOOD

Most pioneers had access to an abundance of nourishing foods, though it was lacking in variety. Corn was a staple food of many settlers. They liked bread made from corn so much that they were even known to fight if an outsider looked down on its use. While drinking bitters in a saloon in Illinois, a Yankee made an offensive allusion to corn bread set before him, stating among other things that it was only fit for hogs. Hearing this remark, an irritable native took offense, peeled his coat, squared his brawny shoulders before the surprised stranger and said, "See yer, stranger, I don't know who you are, and I don't keer a durn, nuther; but I'll have you understand that the man who makes fun of corn bread makes fun of the principal part of my living." With considerable difficulty a fight was prevented, but only after the Yankee apologized and treated all of the customers to a drink.[1]

In every frontier area the problem of keeping an abundant food supply on hand at all times stood uppermost. For instance, after having constructed an extremely crude, one-room log cabin, Reverend James B. Finley and his wife were primarily concerned about obtaining plenty of food. Wild game was abundant and easily killed, but this meat alone was too monotonous. Thus, Finley split 100 rails for a neighbor in exchange for a bushel of potatoes, which he carried home on his back, six miles away. He also cleared an acre and a half of land with an ax and broke it with a grubbing-hoe as he had neither plow tools nor a horse. Planting the field in corn, using all the seed he had, and cultivating it with a hoe, he realized a good harvest of more than a hundred bushels. As time passed, the Finleys raised other foods, all of which, with game meat, gave them a bountiful and nourishing food supply.[2]

At one place where Reverend Hamilton Pierson stopped for the night, a family served plenty of corn bread, fried bacon, potatoes, and coffee. At another place he was delighted to find that the food consisted of barbecued shoat, sweet potatoes roasted in ashes, wheat bread, honey, and coffee. The wheat used on this occasion was ground at a "horse mill" which did not separate the bran from the flour.[3] Also arriving at a log cabin late in the afternoon, Reverend John Stewart in due time was given a sumptuous supper of bear meat and corn bread.[4]

Francis Baily and several English travelers, after stabling and caring for their horses, were invited to supper by a Dutch settler. The Englishmen were served a meal such as they had never before experienced. First, the guests and family, seven or eight in number, were served warm sour milk in a large crock set in the center of the table. Each person dipped milk with a big spoon, some to their plates first, others directly from bowl to mouth. Hands were flying to and from the crock faster than one could count. Ordinarily the sour milk would have made the travelers sick, Baily believed, but, as they had fasted all day, it tasted good, even when served in this manner. After the milk, a big dish of stewed pork and pickled cabbage was placed on the table. Again everyone helped himself with his own spoon, the same one he had previously used. Once more, some spooned the food directly from dish to mouth, but most spooned it into plates; two or three people ate from the same plate, as there were not enough to go around. The pork and cabbage disposed of, the wife next put a bowl of cold milk and bread on the table which was eaten in the same "hoggish fashion." Exhausted and hungry, the aristocratic English travelers for a moment forgot they were anything but backwoodsmen during the meal. Despite the family's ungodly and unsanitary table manners, the visitors enjoyed the meal and hearty good will that the Dutch pioneers provided.[5]

Most preachers, accustomed as they were to frontier adversities, accepted settlers' generosity without complaint, knowing they were doing the best they could under the circumstances. For instance, Reverend Hamilton Pierson arrived at an isolated cabin around dinner time. Several children were parching corn in a spider, but the mother was making no preparation for a meal. The children brought the minister some brown corn, but none of it was "popped." Believing this was his dinner, he began eating with the children. Several hours later, the father returned and urged Pierson to have supper and spend the night. Knowing how far it was to the next dwelling, he gladly accepted.

The host, wanting his guest to have something better to eat than his larder offered, picked up a bag and began walking through the woods, seemingly where there was no trail, to a neighbor's house. Soon he returned with a piece of bacon and some cornmeal. The mother in a short time had supper ready, corn dodgers and bacon. The minister ate heartily. After supper, Pierson talked at length with the family, principally answering their many questions. He then conducted a devotional and went to bed. The next morning, after breakfasting on the same kind of food he had for supper, Pierson mounted his horse and bade farewell to the family with a feeling he had been graciously entertained by people living under adverse circumstances.[6]

While Reverend Cyrus R. Rice was preaching his first sermon in Kansas Territory, the landlord watched a pot of beef and turnips cooking over the fire. Twice, when the pot boiled over, the sermon was stopped while the fire was adjusted. Despite these interruptions, the roomful of settlers "heard the preaching gladly" and gave the minister a most cordial invitation to preach in their area again. After the service was over, most settlers left for their homes. But, a few remained, including the hungry minister, to eat turnips, beef, and corn bread—a most delicious meal, especially as it was served late in the day.[7]

Some ministers, however, were not so grateful for what the settlers gave them to eat. For example, a plainsman who lived in a sodhouse once invited a preacher home for dinner, believing at the time that he had coffee, cornbread, and a pound of butter in his "root-house." But, as the table was being set, he learned that the family dog, misnamed "Trusty," had eaten the butter. After grace, the family and the guest had only corn bread and corn-coffee. According to the pioneer, the minister indicated he did not appreciate the meal and never returned.[8]

Another minister revealed his dislike of frontier food, but did so with a sense of humor, evidently offending no one. Reverend George Barrett served a circuit in Illinois, known as Pecan Bottom, where the people grew and cooked many pumpkins. In his prayer one Sunday morning before a small congregation, he thanked God for the genial sunshine and rain, which helped grow corn for hog feed that would enable the settlers to have pork, but he also asked Him to "blast the pumpkin crop," for His humble servant could no longer perform his duties on a diet mainly restricted to pumpkins. The solemnity of the prayer was broken by laughter. The settlers got the idea, and thereafter the itinerant was given all the pork he wanted.[9]

As many frontiersmen did not have salt, they "jerked" their meat, that is they cut it into small strips and hung it in the open to dry. Some people ate jerked meat raw, but it was usually cooked. The most common jerked meat was beef and venison, but pork was sometimes also prepared in this manner.[10]

Settlers raised much of their meat, such as pork, beef, and poultry. After hogs were slaughtered, they were scalded to remove the hair. They were then usually cut into sections, and most of the fat was removed to be rendered into lard. Hams, shoulders, and middlings were packed in salt for several weeks, after which they were hung over a low burning hickory fire for several days. Generally, before the smoked meat was used, other parts of the hog—chitterlings, feet, liver, and head—were eaten. When a family had plenty of pork and a sausage grinder, which was not often the case, they had sausage in some form throughout the year. In many frontier areas a man was considered a poor provider unless he could slaughter enough pork to provide his family from one winter to the next.

Other methods of food preparation were used. Meat was often placed on the sharpened end of a stick and held over a fire to roast or barbecue. A wedge of wood about six inches in length was sometimes driven between chimney stones just above the arch. One end of a string was tied around the wedge and the other to a piece of meat, which was given a twirl and left to cook. This was an easy method of cooking, since the meat required little attention.

Though food was coarse, people rarely got sick from their diet. The settlers always seemed to be able to perform hard manual labor. Reverend James B. Finley said that if one had gone to the backwoods with indigestion, he would have been cured of it within a few months by eating "buffalo, venison, and good, fat bear meat, with the oil of the raccoon and opossum mixed up with plenty of hominy."[11]

## CLOTHING

Settlers wore whatever was available. In most cases they made their own hats, clothes, and shoes. Nearly all cloth was produced at home.

In warm weather, men, women, and children often wore hats made of wheat or oat straw crudely platted and sewed together. In cold weather they wore hats or caps made from furs of animals, mainly raccoons.[12] To provide warm bedcovers, a woman might weave a blanket from the hair of cows' tails.[13] In areas where wool and flax were produced, these materials were converted into clothing.[14] Wearing apparel made from such material, as well as from other products, was nearly always home-dyed; the dye was obtained from tree bark, especially butternut bark, and from indigo grown domestically.[15]

It was from animal skins, however, that settlers made

most of their clothing. Bear skins were more durable than deer skins, but bears were not found in abundance in all areas and were more dangerous and harder to kill than deer. Because of this, the deer was the most highly prized of all wild animals, not only for its meat but also for its skin.

Harvey Lee Ross, a thirteen-year-old Illinois boy, accepted an invitation from an Indian chieftain named Raccoon to go deer hunting with his sons. One day after a heavy snow, Harvey mounted his pony and rode to the Indian dwelling on Spoon River, but he found Raccoon's sons had already gone out to hunt.

While Harvey warmed by the fire, the chief brought a buckskin sinew roll, used by Indians for sewing moccasins and mittens and for making charms. He then tied one of the charms in a button hole of young Ross' vest, saying it would bring him good luck and make him a brave deer hunter.

Later, when Harvey started home, he saw a deer standing on the ice of a little lake near the trail. Realizing the deer was grazing on bushes and did not see him, Ross dismounted, tied his pony and crept to a large tree about eighty yards away. Harvey rested his gun against the tree, took careful aim and fired. The deer fell, jumped up and fell again, floundering in the snow. Ecstatically the boy ran to the wounded animal and slit his throat. To get the animal home, three miles away, young Ross tied the deer's neck to the stirrups and dragged the deer behind him through the snow.

Killing his first deer was a big event, but getting it home successfully after dark was an unprecedented achievement of his life. His parents were relieved, for they had already begun to worry about him. They were grateful for his skill; there was fresh meat and a deer skin from which to make clothes, moccasins and strings. Later, when Raccoon saw young Ross, he patted the boy on the back and said he would be a great deer hunter. Pointing to the bit of sinew, still tied in the boy's vest, the chief said it was the reason for his good luck.[16]

Butchering a deer involved several steps. First the animal was skinned. The meat was then cut into desired sections, some of which were cooked immediately, while others were jerked, or dried. Sinews, or tendons, were removed and dried; they were made into strings and used for various purposes, particularly to sew clothing together. A considerable amount of work and skill was required to convert the deer skin into usable material. The deer's brain was removed and dried before a fire, after which it was wrapped tightly in a cloth and washed vigorously in warm water, making a sudsy solution. The raw skin was washed thoroughly in the brain water and then taken out and pulled or worked over a board until thoroughly dry. It was then put through the same process a second time, using a stronger solution of brain water. The skin was eventually smoked for several hours over a fire of rotten hickory wood. The tanned, supple skin was then ready to be cut into pieces for a shirt and trousers and sewn together with deer sinews.

These buckskin suits, worn with fringed coat and laced leggins, were not only handsome but were also comfortable and durable. When saturated with deer's tallow or bear's oil, they would repel rain "like a goose's back." For brush and briers there was no better clothing.[17]

Many men wore deer skin clothes all of their lives and on all occasions, even sleeping in them. One man, after being elected to a territorial legislature of the Old Northwest, decided his deer skin suit was not appropriate to wear as a lawmaker. With the help of his sons, he gathered hazel nuts and bartered them at a crossroads store for a few yards of blue strouding, after which he asked his wife and neighbors to make him a coat and pantaloons. As there was only enough material to make a "very short coat and a long pair of leggins," he wore this garb to the legislature.[18]

The deer was not the only animal that provided material for clothes. Skins of bears, buffaloes, and cows were frequently used, often before they were tanned or processed. "Great coats" or overcoats were often made from bear or buffalo hides. Returning from an appointment at Richland, Dakota Territory, Reverend L. Bridgman was overtaken by a fearful blizzard, which detained him for twenty-four hours. While waiting for the storm to abate, a number of ladies made him a buffalo overcoat, which enabled him later to travel with reasonable comfort, except for his face and hands, many miles through a "furious north-westerly gale."[19] The moccasin was a comfortable shoe made by folding a piece of skin or hide around a foot and tying it around the ankle. An early jurist from Illinois remembered that "gentlemen of the jury" sat on a log outside the log courthouse while trying to reach a verdict. All twelve wore moccasins.[20]

## TRADE

The scarcity of money—some children grew to adulthood without ever seeing any—caused most settlers to resort to barter, exchanging one commodity for another or exchanging commodities for services rendered. While traveling through the Arkansas frontier, G. W. Featherstonhaugh and his son once stopped at the home of a settler named Morton. Here they fed their horses and procured bread, milk, and fried venison. The charge for their fare was a bit, or twelve and one half cents. This made it difficult to make change, as the smallest coin that Featherstonhaugh had was a fifty cent piece and the settler had no money at all. The settler was quite fair though and said that as he was out of lead, he would be glad to take one of the four small bars of lead that Featherstonhaugh's son had in his possession in payment of the debt. The impasse was broken, and the settler was given one of the bars, which he figured would be worth "a heap" of deer skins to him. The traveler also profited because he had paid only one bit for the four bars, giving him a magnificent return of 300 percent profit.[21]

Under the system of barter, each article bore a comparative value. With no hard currency, the people evolved a flexible exchange system. In colonial New England, Indian shell-bead money, called wampum, was used. In Massachusetts, "in 1625, musket balls were made receivable up to twelve pence on one payment; five years later maize was made current at the stipulated rate of four shillings a bushel, wheat at six, peas at six, rye at five, and barley at five."[22] A North Carolina law of 1715 declared nineteen products legal tender in payment of public and private dues and in making business deals with outsiders and between colonists. These products included beef, pork, cheese, pitch, wheat, leather, a variety of hides and skins, tallow, Indian corn, and tobacco. It was not uncommon on the frontier for acres of land to be exchanged for horses and cows; syrup for corn; coon skins for a deer skin; tobacco for potatoes; a day's work for seed; and whiskey for preachers' sermons. Even George Washington engaged in barter. On one occasion, he stopped at an inn, ordered a glass of wine and in payment he handed the landlord a beaver skin, receiving as "change" more rabbit skins than he could comfortably carry. So, rather than continue his journey with his bulky "money," he bought wine for all those in the inn.[23]

At stores in frontier Ohio there were some articles, such as tea, coffee, leather, iron, powder, and lead, that could be purchased only with cash money or, in some cases, with linen, cloth, feathers, beeswax, deer skins and furs. Most farmers conducted trade on a grain basis. A day's work, for example, was worth a bushel of wheat or a bushel and a half of corn, rye, or buckwheat. Virtually all tailors, shoemakers, and blacksmiths accepted grain in payment for services. Grain dealers along the Ohio River paid cash for wheat, usually about fifty cents a bushel, and farmers living away from the river estimated the price of grain less the cost of transportation. A farmer living thirty-five miles from the river had to pay twenty-five cents a bushel to have wheat hauled to market; it usually required four days for a team to make the trip in favorable weather.

William Cooper, a pioneer, remembered taking a load of wheat to a store where it was exchanged at the value of twenty-five cents a bushel for iron valued at twelve and a half cents a pound.[24]

Tobacco was recognized as a medium of exchange in frontier Virginia. Farmers deposited tobacco in warehouses and were given receipts. Until merchants sold the commodity, the paper passed from one person to another as money. In describing prices of different purchases, instead of saying they had given so many pounds for an article, farmers said that they paid so many hogsheads of tobacco.[25]

In some frontier areas coon skins were by common consent the basis of the financial system. The value of everything, including marriage licenses and preachers' sermons, was figured in the number of coon skins it was worth. One wishing to sell something stated that he would take so many coon skins for it. Some people counted coon skins with as much pride as others did bank bills. Thus a man's wealth was measured in terms of coon skins, and to say that he had the coon skins was equivalent to saying that he had the cash.

These skins were prepared for circulation by stretching them tight, above the reach of dogs, on outside cabin walls, where, if the weather were favorable, they dried in a few days. When a family wished to purchase anything, they simply procured the desired number of skins.[26]

In addition to coon and raccoon skins, various other pelts, such as rabbit, deer, bear, beaver, opossum, wolf, and buffalo, were used as money. When settlers needed

powder, lead, and many other essentials, they often sent bales of skins in exchange.[27] One item often difficult to procure was salt. Salt sold for a high price, the usual rate being four dollars for fifty pounds. In backwoods currency this amount of salt was worth "four buck-skins, or a bear skin, or sixteen coon skins."[28] On one occasion a pioneer from Jefferson County, Illinois, paid taxes with a wagon load of wolf skins. Later, when he made a purchase, he again offered a wolf skin and was given as change an opossum skin.[29] As money was scarce in Indiana, raccoon skins passed as money, being handed from one person to another. According to local legend, however, this type of money was once made worthless when a New Englander counterfeited them by sewing raccoons' tails to cats' skins.[30]

John Sanders, a Kentucky fur trader, accidentally established a "beaver-bank." During a flood in 1780, his boat was washed inland near Louisville and fastened to a tree. After the flood receded, he converted the damaged craft into a storehouse for beaver skins. Sanders began buying skins on time, giving settlers receipts for the purchases. Later, after selling the skins to eastern and southern buyers, he redeemed receipts for the price agreed upon in the original transaction. Until the trader redeemed the receipts they were circulated among the settlers in various business transactions as money. The last holder of the receipt cashed it in for money at Sanders' bank.[31]

G. W. Featherstonhaugh met an Arkansas settler, born in the woods, who had never been in a village and who knew nothing of the customs of society. The man was fearless and good-natured, but conceited. Possessing virtually no property except a rifle, he bore prejudice against all men not of his class, especially lawyers and those who would not willingly associate with him. After Featherstonhaugh had conversed with the backwoodsman for some time, the settler asked whether the traveler were a lawyer. When Featherstonhaugh replied that he was not and not much of a businessman either, the lonely man said, "Why then, I swear that's just what I am, and I'm glad you are not a lawyer, for the lawyers is the most cursedest varmints, I reckon." Inasmuch as there were no lawyers in that part of the country, the traveler wanted to know where the man had met any such people. The hunter explained that he once lived along a river that flowed into the Missouri. The area was organized as Franklin County and whenever a county was organized, so he said, lawyers soon appeared.

Continuing to recount his experience, the settler said that in Franklin County he had owed a farmer fourteen deer skins. Because he had not paid his debt, a constable tried to take him to the county seat. The more the officer tried to take him the less inclined the hunter was to go, so, during the conflict, the settler gave his antagonist "a most almighty whipping." Soon thereafter three men came for the hunter and hauled him before a Judge Monson, who fined him "ten gallons of whiskey for whipping the constable." Hearing the amount, the settler said to the Judge, "Why, you don't mean to say you'll make me pay ten gallons for whipping that fellow?" When the Judge said, "Yes I do and that you shall see," the settler replied, "Then, I calculate I'll whip you the first time I catch you in the woods, if I have to pull all the bees and bears in Missouri out of their holes." Nevertheless, the transgressor was locked up until a neighbor, who wanted some work done for him, paid the ten gallons. Afterwards, the pioneer, with his acquired dislike for lawyers and judges, and thinking the county was not going to be worth living in, left for the wilds of Arkansas where he could enjoy freedom and good hunting, principally for "bars," which were sometimes worth forty deer skins.[32]

Near the end of each frontier, banks, often with unstable currencies, were established. Within the bounds of one circuit, nine banks were instituted, seven in one county; one was said to have been kept in a lady's closet. Each of the newly established banks issued its own notes. Even tavern-keepers, merchants, butchers, and bakers became bankers.[33] A bank in Nebraska had little to show for its existence, except the name "Qaubeck" engraved on its bills. Its operators had no charter and owned no property, but issued more than $200,000 in notes. When a sheriff closed this bank he found that its assets consisted of thirteen sacks of flour, an iron safe, a counter and desk, a stove drum and pipe, three or four chairs, and a map of the county.[34]

Trust in frontier banks vacillated. A steamboat captain pulled into the Kansas shore and asked a wood salesman if his wood were dry. When the woodsman said that it was, the captain asked the price. Ignoring the question, the salesman demanded to know what type of money would be used. The captain replied that it was the best on earth, that of the Platte Valley Bank. With this information, the man on shore said that if that were the case he "would take cord for cord."[35]

Such banks usually did more harm than good. Their paper notes were often inferior to barter and many people refused them.

With the termination of each frontier, the people developed a monetary system, markets for their products and a division of labor. Their behavior changed. They came to depend on more developed areas for some of their food, tools, and dress. In time such articles as "bought meat and flour, store wagons, hats, shirts and shoes" were available in limited supply. However, as Governor Thomas Ford of Illinois said, "these changes in life-style were attended with grumbling ill-will of pioneer patriarchs," who "predicted nothing but ruin to a country that forsook old ways which were good enough for their fathers."[36]

## LOG CABINS

The most prevalent home east of the ninety-eighth meridian and in other regions where there was usable timber was the one-room log cabin. The house was constructed by the settler himself, usually with the aid of his family or neighbors. Generally few tools—possibly nothing but a poleax, an ax with only one blade and with a hammer-face opposite the edge—were used in constructing the dwellings. Sometimes the builder had access to an auger, a frow, used for splitting boards, or an adz, a cutting tool with a thin arching blade set at right angles to the

handle. Frontiersmen rarely had saws, nails, or metal hinges. Every part of the cabin had to be made by hand, without even the aid of a level or square.

Most log cabins were poorly constructed by men who knew little of the art, and the pressing need for immediate shelter often resulted in hasty construction. Also, a majority of the settlers were squatters with little or no money and few worldly possessions. They did not try to construct well-built dwellings, knowing that they did not own the land and that they might not be able to buy it when it was surveyed and placed on the market. Squatters did not want to build a good cabin that might soon fall into the hands of someone else. Even when a settler bought land and built a cabin on it, in many instances he did not look upon it as a permanent home. Imbued with the pioneer spirit, he was always looking for greener pastures and often harbored in the recesses of his mind the notion of selling his home in a year or two and moving to another place.

Many cabins were extremely uncomfortable in cold weather. Some inhabitants slept in their shoes "to keep them from freezing too stiff to put on." Writing a letter to the American Home Missionary Society, Reverend George Wood, a missionary in Missouri, complained of cold fingers. The fire was sufficiently large, but, as the crevices between wall logs were not daubed and there was no loft, it was impossible to heat the room.[37] The ink in one's writing pen would often freeze, even when sitting before a blazing fire in such a cabin. The inability to keep a house warm was also a deterrent to holding worship there. Worshippers sitting nearest the fire got too hot while those immediately behind shivered with cold.[38]

One missionary said that few settlers in early Nebraska had comfortable cabins. One woman who moved to Nebraska in the 1850's later wrote, "We moved into a log house without doors or windows, and we were glad to get even that. My son was born before either was secured. I was thankful we had no snow storms at that time." Another woman said that the roof of their first house was but partly finished when a winter storm struck one night, covering the floor with several inches of snow. Near morning her baby became ill and the mother and father were forced to walk through deep snow drifts in the cabin while caring for the child.[39]

Many cabins were even colder in winter because some settlers habitually left their doors and windows open. An Eastern man, visiting a friend in a log cabin on a cold, bleak day, suggested that the room would be warmer if the door were closed. Expressing surprise at the suggestion, the host decided to close the door as an experiment. A few minutes later the settler said, "Well I declare! I believe it does make a difference."[40]

Uncomfortable as these cabins might seem, backwoodsmen became inured to cold and accepted it without much complaint. However, continued exposure to the elements both in and outside the house caused many settlers to contract pneumonia and other diseases.

Frontiersmen had easy access to an abundance of free fuel. Cabins were usually built in a deep forest and the settlers proceeded to fell the bountiful trees for any needed purpose, generally for firewood. A traveler in the Michigan territory spent the night in a log structure that had an earthen floor, a large fireplace at one end of the building, and two very large doors, one on each side. After supper the settler opened one door, hitched his oxen to a log "ten feet long and three feet in diameter" and dragged it inside. He then rolled it into the back of his fireplace. Next, he drove his team through the opposite door, dragged two more logs, both "somewhat smaller" than the first, inside and rolled them in front of the back log. Observing this spectacle, the traveler realized that a cabin without a floor had its advantages and that a fire made from such large logs might burn for as long as twenty-four hours, provided it was occasionally replenished by small limbs or split wood.[41] Not all pioneers burned this much wood, but they did use a great deal, especially in the northern frontier areas.

In the woodland frontier, other types of cabins were constructed. Some were built to offer greater protection against hostile Indians. Two brothers built strong log cabins about thirty yards apart. They made their doors of white-oak puncheons, put together with such skill as to make it almost impossible for Indians to force them open. Port holes were cut between logs, and through these they could poke the muzzles of their guns. The area between these cabins was cleared so that the inhabitants of one could protect those of the other from attack.

Some cabins were different in other respects. Many had nothing but an earthen floor, usually elevated a few inches above the outside ground to lessen dampness. Contrary to popular opinion, such a floor did not cause a dwelling to be uncomfortable, provided the openings between wall logs were closed and provided the cabin had a loft floor with virtually no holes in it. A wooden floor was generally rough, even when covered with animal skins. An earthen floor, especially when covered with skins, was usually smooth and soft.

Other cabins had neither wooden floor, loft, nor fireplace. Neither did they have the crevices between the walls chinked. A traveler once stopped at one such cabin. A large fire was built near the room's center and smoke escaped between log crevices and holes around the roof boards. Everything inside the cabin—walls, joists, roof boards, and even household fixtures—were "as black as soot."[42]

All cabin roofs could be made rain-proof but few prevented snow from blowing between and around boards. This could be a serious problem unless the dwelling had a tight loft floor, one that was covered with skins or some farm produce, such as corn, which would keep snow from falling into the room. One Kansas family returning home on Christmas morning found snow a foot deep on the floor, in the fireplace, and on the beds. Though this cabin had a good roof and tight walls, snow entered the room through openings between cabin boards.[43] In his long preaching career, Reverend Elanthan C. Gavitt found few good sleeping quarters. In cold weather he was sometimes forced to sleep on a hay mattress in a cabin loft with no covering except his overcoat and an Indian blanket. Many mornings, when he awoke, he found himself buried in a snowdrift.[44]

A German immigrant, Jakob Schramm, traveling through a raging snow storm in Indiana in 1836, stopped at a newly constructed cabin late one afternoon to spend the night. He was given a bed, but his covering was entirely too light for such weather. The house let the snow enter freely through the roof and through crevices between wall logs which had been poorly chinked.[45]

In the woodland regions there were other dwellings of more primitive construction than the log cabin. One of these was the half-faced camp which was a partial enclosure of three sides. The lower end of its flat sloping roof was covered with brush but rarely ever boards and rested on a big log or the upper part of a hillside; the other end rested on a horizontal log seven or eight feet high that was supported by two implanted posts at each end. The ends of the makeshift affair were generally partly enclosed by skins hanging from the angling roof sides. The front part of the structure had no wall or enclosure, except skins hanging from a plate, placed there for partial protection against rain and cold wind. Just outside, a fire burned continuously in winter for warmth and cooking. In dry weather, the half-faced camp was reasonably comfortable, but it offered little protection against rain.

Other temporary shelters were constructed of bark, moss, or straw, though they were not as numerous as the half-faced camps. In 1820, within twenty hours after Ossian M. Ross arrived in Illinois, he and his sons completed a bark house. Poles were driven into the ground tent-fashion. Other poles were laid and secured across them and covered with bark. Long afterwards, Ross' son delighted in telling how he, as a lad of four, had carried bark to cover the shanty.[46] In 1839, an Iowa family made their house of bark from cuts of basswood trees that were from eighteen inches to two feet in diameter and seven feet long. After the bark was slipped off in one piece, it was taken to a pole house frame, unrolled and fitted to the sides and roof as was needed. To keep the bark from curling after it dried, poles were put outside the walls and on the roof. The house had a neat exterior appearance and on the inside it was "white and clean."[47]

In places where moss and straw were abundant, dwellings might be made of those materials. One German family in Texas lived for three years in a miserable doorless and windowless six-sided hut made of moss with a roof of straw. The roof was not waterproof and nearly everything in the hut got soaked during a hard rain. Settlers living in such quarters were sometimes troubled by cows nibbling at the moss. Although a chimney of logs and clay was sometimes built, the owner was often afraid to build a fire because of the hut's combustibility. Most families continued to cook and warm themselves from a fire built on the outside.[48]

## SOD HOUSES

On the Great Plains, where suitable timber was not available, settlers lived almost exclusively in sod houses and dugouts. To construct a sod house the ground was broken with a turning plow several inches deep near the building spot. From the broken turf, sod strips two or three feet in length were cut and stacked like bricks to form the walls. A dwelling only twelve by sixteen feet required an enormous amount of sod, all of which was carried by hand from the field to the house site, or hauled, if the settler was lucky enough to have a wagon. One settler and a neighbor

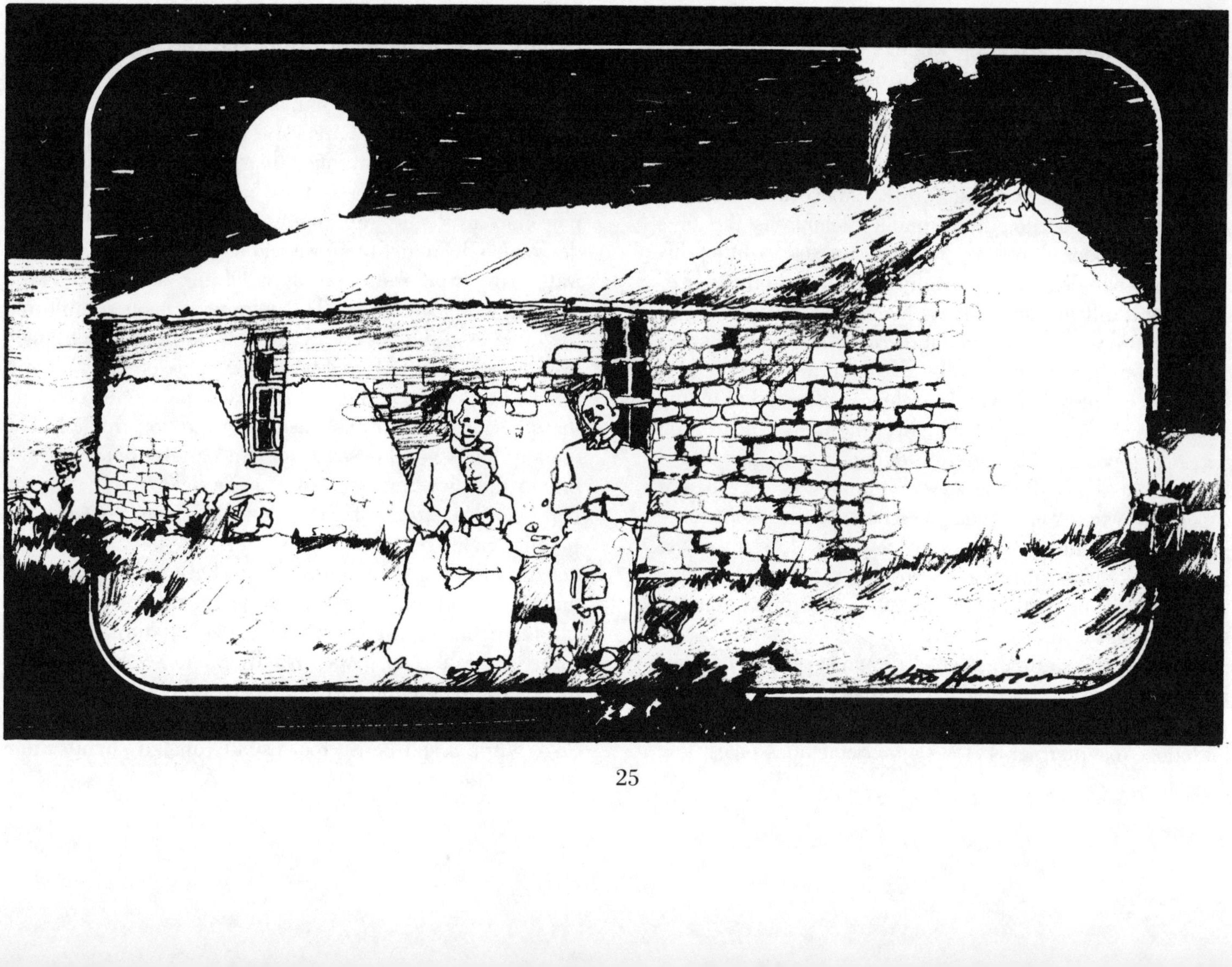

worked for more than two weeks constructing such a dwelling. One of the men laid the sod as the other brought it to him. When the strips ran out, both men cut and brought in a larger supply.

A sod dwelling usually had three openings in the walls: a fireplace, window and a door. The chimney and walls were constructed at the same time, the chimney sides being tied to the wall with sod strips. When the fireplace had been constructed to its desired height, poles, three or four inches in diameter, were laid lengthwise across the opening. The wall and chimney then rose together, the top of the chimney being about two feet above the roof. The window was constructed in similar manner as the fireplace. The door, however, was constructed a little differently. When door walls, usually at the front of the house, had been built to their desired height, several poles with forks on top were pushed into the ground so that they stood against the inside door walls all the way to its height. Lengthwise poles were laid into the opposite forks, letting pole ends extend a foot or more over the walls. One reason for putting poles at the side of the door was to give added strength to the wall, the top of which was very heavy, especially when wet. Also, poles on the sides kept those going in and out of the building from knocking pieces of sod off the sides and thus weakening the wall. The door itself was usually nothing but a buffalo hide hung from the top of the horizontal poles.

When the walls were constructed seven or eight feet high, the door end being a little higher than the back, poles or logs, though hard to find in many instances, were laid close together across the walls. Sometimes poles were laid lengthwise on top of these logs, extending only part of the distance to the opposite wall. With a sufficient foundation for the roof, brush and possibly grass, too, were laid on top of poles. On top of the grass and brush, three sod strip layers were placed. Dirt or sand was scattered over the roof to fill in any possible holes. Finally, another layer or two of sod was put on top.

Nearly all sod houses consisted of but one room, but many were divided into compartments by curtains, which afforded more privacy. Larger dwellings sometimes had sod partitions, somewhat thinner than the outside walls.[49]

Some Great Plains settlers built dugouts by digging a hole into a hillside the length of the dwelling, or at least deep enough so that there was no need to construct a back wall. The front wall and parts of the side walls were constructed of sod strips. The chimney was often built into the hillside of the back wall. This meant that the chimney front to the top of the roof had to be made of sod. When it reached this height, three sides rested on the hillside and the other on the side that had just been constructed. The roofs of many sod houses rested on parallel poles at each end of the dwelling, the poles being held by posts at the corners. The front of many dugouts also rested on a parallel pole. Some sod houses had gabled roofs but in constructing these, builders had to have nails. Many sod and dugout dwellers trimmed the inside sod walls and plastered them with a sand and grass mixture. Clay was rarely available, as it was usually found several hundred feet below the ground surface. Nearly all of these dwellings had dirt floors since there was not much available timber.

While a sod house roof usually angled slightly from

front to back, a dugout roof usually angled with the hillside. The door, window and roof of the dugout were constructed in similar fashion to those of the sod house. One woman from the East when arriving at her new home, a dugout, burst into tears. She had not realized she would have to live in a hole in the ground. Most women accepted such dwellings stoically, realizing they were the best possible under the circumstances. They had reason for hope, because both the dugout and sod houses were considered makeshift homes until better ones could be constructed of lumber.[50]

Not all sod houses and dugouts were constructed precisely as has been described. Some settlers brought doors, windows, and frames with them. Some plains pioneers brought stoves and stove pipes to their building sites and built no fireplaces.

Sod houses and dugouts had some advantages over the best constructed log cabins. In the coldest weather, when the temperature might plunge twenty degrees below zero, the well-insulated hut could be kept comfortable with a small fire burning buffalo chips, twisted rolls of grass or small tree limbs. In the summer when the temperature might register one hundred and ten degrees, they were relatively cool. No snow, even that of a blizzard, could filter inside, and the building was almost fireproof. If the surrounding ground were cultivated or the grass burned fifty yards surrounding the house, the settlers had little reason to fear even a prairie fire.

On the other hand, there were some grave disadvantages. Although the average annual rainfall on the Great Plains was usually from ten to twenty inches, prolonged rains saturated the roof and water leaked into the rooms. Reverend A. Dresser could testify to this. One Saturday night he found lodging in a sod house and retired amid a heavy thunder and lightning storm. He was awakened by raindrops falling upon his face and the voice of the good lady of the house inquiring about his clothes. After assuring her his clothes were dry, as they were under the bed, the minister spread his umbrella over his head and was soon asleep again. The next morning he learned that there was more wind than water and that harm was far less than feared.[51] The roof of a dugout was as leaky as that of the sod house. In extremely wet weather it was not unusual for water to run out of the hill into a room. Inhabitants then made trenches across the dirt floor so that water could drain through the doorway.[52]

As the rear end of a dugout roof rested on a hillside, it sometimes created problems. Once, while galloping his horse across the prairie, a rider heard a voice hail him from behind. He stopped and learned that he had ridden across the roof of a dugout, the top of which had grass growing on it the same height as on the adjoining ridge. Since no harm was done to the roof, both landlord and rider laughed about the incident—a laugh that was welcomed among the isolated people.[53] Upon another instance, a family heard a weird noise from the ceiling late one night. The entire family quickly arose. Groping in the dark toward the sound, the father felt a foot and then a horn. An instant later a heifer crashed through and landed on a bed breaking it to pieces. While entertaining Indian visitors one night, the head of the family noticed that sod suddenly began falling into the fireplace. Filled with fear, he seized his rifle, stealthily opened the door and stepped into the yard. To his relief, he discovered an ox standing on the bank next to his house hooking the chimney top, causing pieces of sod to fall.[54]

**FURNISHINGS**

Household furniture and utensils were usually few and often as crude as the one-room dwellings. A family named M'Millan moved into a cabin west of the Appalachian Mountains. They had no bedsteads, tables, stools, chairs, or buckets. They left all these things behind because there was no wagon road across the mountains. Nothing was brought that could not be carried by pack horses. The family improvised by placing one small box on top of another to serve as a table. They used two kegs as stools. After eating their supper and "committing themselves to God in family worship," they spread a bed on the floor and slept soundly. The next morning, a neighbor came to help them make all household necessities. "In a little time," M'Millan wrote "we had everything comfortable about us."[55]

In another instance, neighbors worked two days helping to construct a newcomer's cabin and on the third day they made "fixtures" for the dwelling. A dining table was made of a split slab, supported by four round legs set in auger holes. In the same manner they made three-legged stools. Wooden pins were driven into auger holes in the logs at the back of the room several feet above the floor. A piece of clap-board was placed over the pins to serve as a shelf for kitchen utensils. The neighbors then built two bedsteads which were made by first boring holes into a back log, the width of the bed apart. Holes were then drilled into two posts about three feet high, the holes being the same distance from the floor as the ones in the back log. The ends of two parallel poles, the length of the bed, were driven into the holes of the back log and the posts. To make the posts at the end of the bed more sturdy, two holes were bored on their inside surfaces into which were inserted poles the width of the bed. Across the pole railings, boards, a little longer than the width of the bed, were laid. Since the newcomers had a small baby, the neighbors split a log about two feet in diameter and three feet long. One of the split pieces was hollowed out with an ax and adz to hold the baby. To keep the cradle from overturning as it was rocked, pegs several inches long were driven into holes near the ends of the top sides.[56] These "fixtures" made life more comfortable for the family.

The conditions under which Reverend James B. Finley and his wife began their early married life were typical of that of many settlers. In the spring of the year, the young couple moved into the forest "without horse or cow, bed or bedding, bag or baggage." With the aid of his brother John, Finley built a bark cabin. The same material covered the floor. One end of the hut was left open for a fireplace, which evidently was never built. Four forks were driven into the ground to support bed-railings, across which were laid sticks that supported a layer of bark. A bed-tick, filled with leaves, was then laid on the bark. In this crude dwelling the couple lived until the end of summer, when they built a better one with the aid of their neighbors.[57]

In many log cabins, suspended above the fireplace

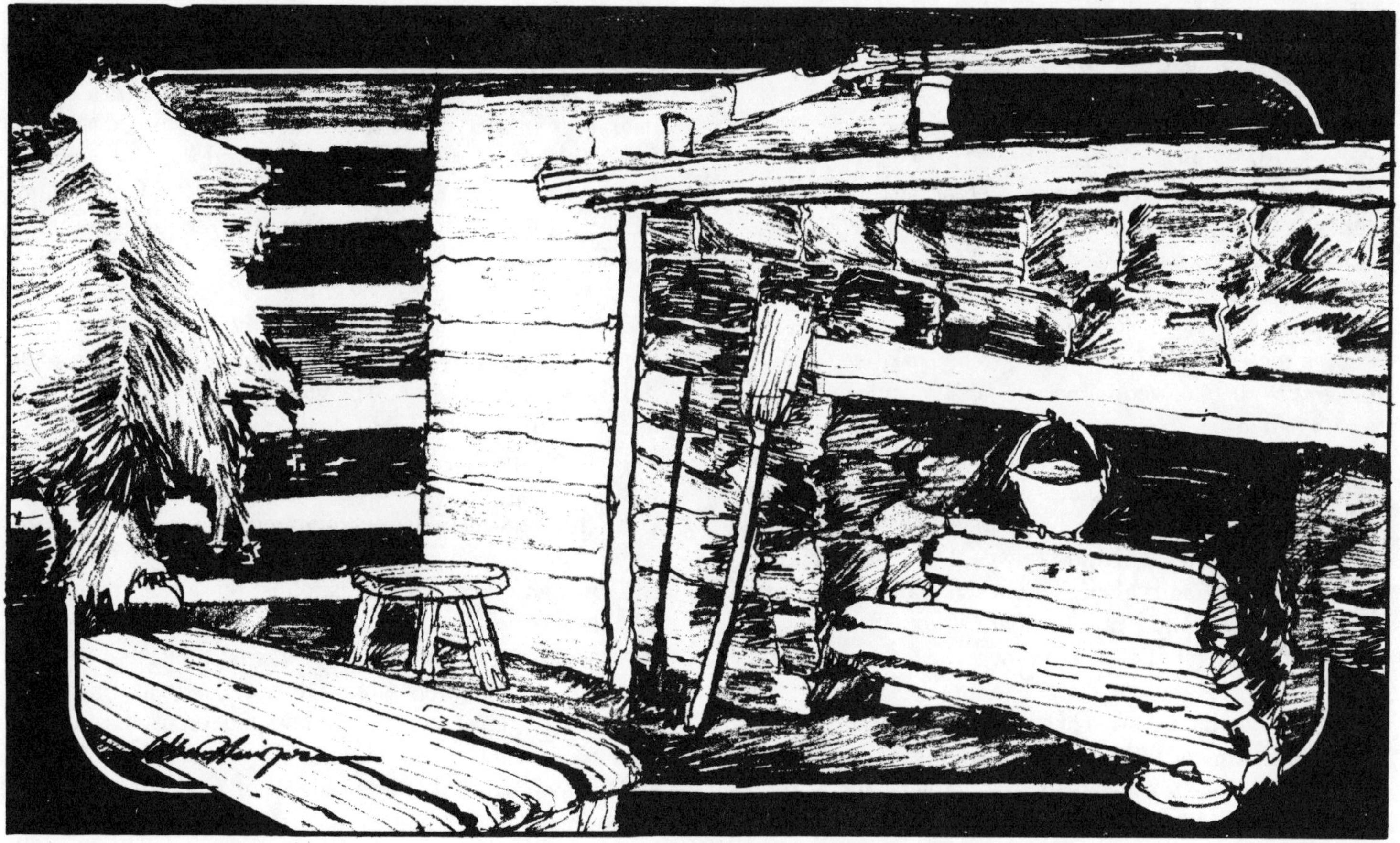

was usually a rifle, a gourd of powder, a bag of bullets, and a ramrod. In the corner of the room, but usually in the loft, were rolls of skins used as bedding and for making shoes and clothes. At one side of the fireplace there might be a kettle of "blue dye" used to color yarn for weaving. Usually the dye vat was covered with a barrel head or some flat object, on which some member of the family or even a visitor sat. One old gentleman said that "some of the best men of our country wooed and won their brides, seated on the kettle before a blazing fire."[58]

In one cabin a traveler observed that the dwelling had neither floor nor fireplace. The family had a bedstead of unhewn logs, two improvised chairs and a "low stool." A string of "buffalo hides stretched across the hovel" was used primarily to make clothes. Other items in the dwelling included a large iron pot, some baskets, a usable rifle and "two that were superannuated," and a "fiddle" that was silent only when the family was asleep.[59]

A frontier family considered itself lucky to have even a few cracked and broken plates and spoons, worn sharp at the edges, or forks that had long since lost some of their tines. Nearly every family had knives, many of which had broken handles and blades;[60] but one knifeless Texas family used a straight razor to cut "kindling, meat and leather."[61] Most families used gourds to hold water and milk.[62]

A family named Wright arrived at their dugout in Nebraska in May of 1873 with one bed, a stove, a table, a pot in which to cook meat and vegetables, and several boxes. The two children slept on the table. Guests, unless they were ministers, slept on the floor.[63] A Texas woman, called to a neighbor's house five miles away to attend a sick child, slept without a pillow on a deer skin spread on the floor. The next morning, the landlady, who had no wash basin, simply poured water over the visitor's hands. The visitor dried her hands on her neighbor's bonnet.[64]

Except on the Great Plains, cooking was done almost entirely at a fireplace, around which there was usually an assortment of pots, pans, and a Dutch oven. In a corner near the fireplace was the larder, which might include bear's meat and grease, pork and lard, jerked venison, corn meal, hominy, salt, and honey. On the Great Plains where settlers had more contact with civilization, many families cooked on stoves.[65]

Nearly all frontier dwellings were filthy, especially sod houses and dugouts, as dirt often fell from the roof and the walls. Crowded conditions in houses of only one room did not foster sanitation. The fact that dwellings were used for so many purposes—to cook, eat, and sleep, and as workshops to make clothes, shoes, harness, and other things—made them untidy.

Travelers usually encountered filth in some form when they stopped at a home. On one occasion at bedtime two travelers laid their bearskins on an earthen floor which, the host assured them, was too damp for fleas. After wrapping themselves in blankets, they slept soundly enough, although the ground was exceedingly cold and damp, smelling as though it had often been used as a place both to urinate and defecate.[66] Reverend Joseph Badger slept in one cabin that had only "half a floor of split logs, no chimney, and wide crevices between the logs, without plastering or mudding." Although a fire was kept burning throughout the night on the dirt floor, he slept uncomfortably cold. Offensive body and room odors, fleas, and bedbugs made him long for the outdoors.[67]

Two men traveling on the Wisconsin frontier stopped at a poorly built log cabin for the night. They noticed that the bedstead, which had two berths, was made with four rails inserted in wall notches and in holes in two upright posts. They were given the upper berth. Although they were treated with unusual kindness and charged nothing for food and lodging, they later agreed that they had never slept on a bed so uncomfortable and filthy. The slats and poles had not been laid evenly and the few skins spread over them did not conceal the bumps and ridges. Worst of all was the terrible odor.[68]

Filthiness of beds was proverbial. Francis Asbury often slept in the woods rather than in a frontier bed.[69] Reverend Hamilton Pierson said that his greatest privation was the want of a good bed—one that was clean and free from bugs. Once he stopped at a newly built log cabin in anticipation of a nice, clean place to sleep. His hope soon vanished when he turned down the blankets and adjusted his pillow. Thinking he saw a drop of dried syrup on the bed, he impulsively put his finger on the spot and saw it scurry away. Being very tired, he crawled into bed and kept company with numerous blood-sucking insects for the night.[70] To prevent bedbugs from feasting too freely upon his body, G. W. Featherstonhaugh slipped into a large flannel sack which was tied around his neck, leaving only his arms and head uncovered.[71]

Many missionaries and itinerant ministers wrote reports concerning the beds they slept in. Late one night, after church services were conducted in a sod house, one tired and "worn" missionary was ready for sleep; but there was only one bed. The family rose to the occasion and improvised a bedstead by setting the front of three chairs against two trunks. Here he slept well, because both bedding and sod house were clean.[72] Another missionary at bedtime noticed that hay was scattered evenly over the earthen floor, which was covered with a dirty rag carpet. A dirty carpet also was suspended through the center of the room dividing it into compartments, a kitchen and bedroom. At the end of the bedroom a bed twelve feet long was built next to the wall. Pillows were laid at each end, which made two beds, the "sleepers resting at antipodes." The minister slept "fairly well" on the floor, although he seemed always conscious of the dirty blankets which emitted "an awful odor." From the looks of the long bed, it, too, appeared to be the essence of "filth."[73]

Time eventually changed life conditions on the frontier. When a pioneer later began to live in an integrated society, his home and furnishings began to resemble those of the older settled areas.

## NEIGHBORS

Although William Shakespeare's words, "Blow! Blow! Thy winter wind, Thou art not so unkind as man's ingratitude,"[74] are generally true, particularly in an organized society, they were hardly applicable to the embryonic and chaotic social state of the frontier. There the settlers' need for neighbors was constant. They did not forget acts of kindness or good deeds of their neighbors; they could not afford to forget them. Frontier settlers were not independent of their fellowmen. They desperately needed their neighbors in order to survive.

In 1917, two aged native women of North Louisiana were reminiscing about incidents of their youth. When one of them was asked what she remembered most vividly about her early years, she replied without hesitation "We had good neighbors!" although her nearest neighbor lived "three creeks" away, or about six miles. Complaining how times had changed, she said there were many more families living "closer by" than when she was young, but "Nobody now don't care nothing about you."[75]

After living on the Minnesota frontier for a short time, a man and his family returned to their home in New York City. There they lived for two years and then returned to Minnesota. In his old age, after reading a paper before The Minnesota Historical Society, he was asked why he elected to live on a raw frontier rather than in a city. The old man snapped: "The neighbors! Would you want to spend your life where people twenty feet away do not know your name, or care whether you live or die!" During the two year period while living in the city, he said their baby had died, but none of their neighbors came to comfort them, not even when they were taking the body to the cemetery. On the Minnesota frontier, his family had good neighbors, though the nearest one lived several miles away. The elderly gentleman pined for his good neighbors of early Minnesota, but he realized that the people had changed and that they were no longer as considerate of each other as they had been in the frontier period.[76]

Today, in a relatively organized society, there is more philanthropy but less neighborliness, more love for mankind in general but less for each man. People are more independent of their neighbors, but they are infinitely more dependent on the world at large. The personal element has largely been removed from social ethics. Affectional zeal is, to a great extent, missing.

When a family gave their neighbors food and lodging for a day and night or even longer, they usually had more to gain than lose. They had an abundance of food that cost little or nothing, but, because of poor roads and distant markets, it had little or no monetary value. As most settlers led an isolated and drab existence, they were eager for the pleasures and enjoyments derived from the company of visitors. Visiting was reciprocal; it was understood that the hosts had a standing invitation to visit their guests—their neighbors—at any time. It was easy for the pioneers to have intimate, face-to-face contacts, since nearly all were uniformly poor. This fact tended to lift social barriers.

Other conditions made the settlers considerate of each other. Danger lurked on every hand. When menaced by hostile Indians and outlaws, each settler had to be his neighbor's keeper or all might perish. With few doctors and ministers, virtually no medicine, and no hospitals, each one was constrained to stand by the other in sickness and death, for, if he did not, who would help him in such contingencies? When a settler helped a neighbor husk corn, or when he gave him half of a beef or a mess of pork, he was thinking of the occasions when he, too, might need such favors. When a man worked to aid a neighbor in clearing a tract of land or in erecting a dwelling or barn, he expected to receive similar work in return.

Realizing the practical value of their neighbors, settlers usually treated each other with affectionate regard. It was not uncommon for people to give newcomers a cordial welcome, assuring them that everything they possessed, such as tools, wagons, teams, provisions, and services, were at their command. The settlers often gave a new family essential food—a bushel of potatoes, a few gallons of corn meal, a piece of meat, several combs of honey.[77] Just before the Francis Johnson family of Tennessee arrived at their new home in Illinois, they approached a church where a small congregation was assembled, listening to a sermon. When the congregation heard the bell of a colt following the Johnson wagon, they unceremoniously left the church to welcome the new family. Though complete strangers to the family, the communicants did not wait for formal introductions but greeted the Johnson family as if they were old acquaintances.[78] On the Great Plains, a mother learned that a family had settled on a claim several miles away. Early one morning, accompanied by her two small children, she began walking toward her neighbor's home. When the women met—strangers though they were—they were overjoyed. The two families became warm friends.[79]

The weather was never too severe nor the night too dark for one neighbor to help another in need. In the middle of a chilly September night, while a woman and her son born a few days before were lying in bed in a sod house on the Great Plains, rain began falling unusually hard. As the water began dripping through the roof into the room—in some places pouring—the husband stretched robes over the ceiling to keep some of the water from falling on the bed, but his efforts were in vain. But this family had a good neighbor. A woman, miles away, seeing a light in the house and fearing for the welfare of the family, walked to the dwelling to lend a helping hand. When she arrived, she and the husband placed the mother and baby in a wagon and drove to the neighbor's dry house.[80]

Neighborliness was much in evidence in Illinois in 1830 during the deep snow. The settlers endured unbelievable hardships. Had the people not stood by each other, many would have died, because food and even fuel ran short. Thomas Beard, a good neighbor, walked seven miles through the snow—a horse could not walk through the deep drifts—to the home of a widow and her small children, all of whom were on the verge of starving and freezing. Having used the last of the wood, the family was hovering over a small fire. To obtain fuel, Beard tore up rail fences from which he chopped huge piles of dry firewood. The next day he brought the family provisions.[81]

Building a church or a home was usually a cooperative effort. The people of an area in Tennessee agreed to erect a church building near a spring of water. On the designated day, a number of men gathered at the site with their teams, wagons, and axes. By the end of the day, the workers had cut and hauled logs and laid the foundation. Before they left for their homes, they offered a prayer and decided to name the church *Union*, symbolizing brotherly love manifested by the pioneers. The following day the building was completed.

After a new arrival had cut sufficient logs for his cabin, everyone for miles around rallied for the house-raising. At an early hour, teams and men with axes were on the site. Logs were hauled and dragged to the building site, where they were scored and hewed. Usually before the day closed willing hands had raised a comfortable cabin. Within a few days after his coming, it was entirely possible for neighbors to have built a newcomer a cabin, constructed his barn and lot fence, and broken his land for seed. The newcomers profited socially as well as economically; they had become acquainted with their neighbors.[82]

When a settler needed help with other work, he often rode around among his neighbors, extending to each an invitation to be at his farm on a designated day. An invitation of this kind was once given in the presence of S. A. Ferrel, a British traveler. A settler entered his neighbor's house, sat down, and after an exchange of compliments, said, "I guess I'll husk my corn tomorrow afternoon." The host replied, "You've a mighty heap this year." "Considerable of corn," said the guest. The host then said, "Well, I guess we'll be along."[83] In Wisconsin, Theodore Rodolf said that whenever a cornhusking, quilting party, or barn-raising was given, he and his family were sure of an invitation and a cordial reception on their arrival.[84]

It was well that the settlers had occasions for such social intercourse. There a man might have a chance to trade for or to buy a horse, to bargain for some seed peas, corn, or potatoes. A young lady or a bereaved widow, or a bachelor or lonely widower, might meet a mate. Most of all, the lonely settlers were able to talk to their hearts' content. They discussed their triumphs and tragedies; they swapped sympathy and advice; they suggested remedies for winter fever (pneumonia) and itch; they speculated whether a certain woman was having her baby too soon after marriage or whether the man who recently died was "saved." They commented about new neighbors or former ones; they berated or praised the effect of the weather on their crops and their health. Always there were some who told jokes, some of them off-color, which tended to bring emotional release for both the narrator and his audience. Such work assemblages helped to break the monotony of people's lonely, dull, drab lives.

Much work, such as building log cabins, sod houses and dugouts, could be done more effectively when several men worked together than when each worked separately. Some jobs could hardly be performed at all without the aid of several people. This was true of erecting a cabin, particularly when the logs were large. Building a bridge across a creek usually required the work of more than one man. Clearing land of logs was a job for many men, since the large logs had to be carried to piles where they were burned. To dig a well for water required the assistance of several workers. To fight a prairie fire was sometimes futile, even with the aid of all the settlers of an area. When the Indians were on the warpath, all men joined in tilling their fields, in harvesting their crops, in hunting game and in cutting roads through dense underbrush. Whether one liked his neighbors or not was unimportant; he cooperated for the sake of survival.

Neighborly aid was not always an unmixed blessing. It was generally understood that the family for whom the work was being done should furnish not only the food but also the whiskey. Food was usually easy to provide but whiskey generally had to be bought or bartered for, making it difficult to come by, at least enough to satisfy the thirst of many men.

One settler in Illinois built a crude cabin by himself in a remote area. When other settlers arrived later, he made plans to invite them to help him build a better dwelling. He cut and dragged logs to the desired site and hewed and notched them. He was ready for the raising—he had already attended several—except that he had no money or commodities to exchange for whiskey. The logs lay on the ground for two years until he was able to secure two gallons of whiskey. He then invited his neighbors to the much needed "working."[85]

Free labor had other disadvantages. A family's food, abundant as it usually was, was sometimes seriously depleted by hungry workers. Much feed for the visitors' livestock was also needed. The man for whom the work was done was morally obligated to help each of his neighbors when called upon, and when the crops were harvested, each of the neighbors who had helped expected a share of the produce. One Nebraska farmer, ready to harvest his five-acre field of oats, was joined by his neighbors from far and near to lend their assistance. There were sixty-one men, women, and children, all families bringing their horses and mules.

In the late afternoon, after the visiting workers had gone, the wife asked what they would do with their grain, since they had no barn. The husband replied, "Oh, I think I can manage to take care of my share of oats all right." And he could, for after feeding his neighbors' livestock and giving each of the harvesters a share of grain, he had only one and a half bushels left! Ending the harvest with such a small amount of oats did not worry the Nebraska farmer. He and his family would attend other workings where they would receive a meal and feed for their livestock, as well as a portion of the harvest.[86]

Pioneers took every opportunity to be with their neighbors. Even a murder had its rewards, for at the wake which followed, men, women, and children were given a chance to be with other people. Even when roads were formidable or dangerous, people often visited their neighbors to spend not just one night but several, possibly a week or more. The epigram, "Company, like fish, smells in three days," was not meaningful to the lonely pioneers. The Wright family of Nebraska, who had few neighbors—one living a mile and a half away, another two miles, and a third twenty miles—frequently went visiting. They usually rode in a wagon, but when the ground was covered with snow, they travelled in a sled.[87]

When the pioneers of each frontier area came to live within the framework of a society, the spirit of neighborliness largely faded. "Ingratitude," using Shakespeare's term, became more decidedly pronounced in an integrated social order. The people became more secure and had less personal dependence on their neighbors.

36

# 3

# Marriage and Sex

Economic interdependence within the frontier family would have satisfied the fondest hope of the utopian dreamer who wished to have strong marital bonds. Evidently, marriage and the family originated out of economic conditions. Whether a marriage is weak or strong is determined, to a great extent, by the economic ties within it. On the frontier, the family was a relatively stable institution in an unstable world, because all of its members were drawn together by the necessity of having to work to survive. Both husband and wife were vitally dependent on each other, as each performed indispensable work. Children relied heavily on their parents for a livelihood, and parents regarded their children as economic assets, for all of them in time could perform valuable work. In England, according to Adam Smith, a widow with five children had little chance to remarry, for where was the man who could support a family so large, each child definitely being a liability? But in frontier America, such a widow's opportunity for remarrying was excellent. The prospective bridegroom not only looked upon the widow as a bargain herself, but also regarded each child as an asset.[1] Three girls, for instance, signified three seamstresses and cooks, three soap and candle makers; two boys represented two field hands and woodchoppers, two trappers and hunters. Thus, the frontier divorce rate was extremely low.

Families were large because of early marriage and because nearly every family had an abundance of food, coarse and monotonous though it often was. Though poverty does not prevent births, it is "extremely unfavorable to the rearing of children." As Adam Smith said, "The tender plant, produced in a cold soil and severe climate, withers and dies." In the highlands of Scotland, a mother who bore twenty children often did not have more than two live, largely because of lack of food. Smith maintained that every animal species increases in proportion to its means of subsistence, but could not increase beyond that.[2] Largely as a result of a surplus of births over deaths, frontier populations often doubled every fifteen years, whereas the population of Europe doubled every five hundred years.[3]

## COURTSHIP

Most frontier parents wanted their children to marry early. Consequently, many girls married between the ages of twelve and fourteen and boys between sixteen and eighteen. The period of courtship before marriage was usually short. When a young man acquired the means of support, which was often nothing but a tract of land, a log cabin or sodhouse, and a few domestic animals, he usually popped the question to some girl, and she, apparently despising "coquetting and affection" as a waste of time, replied with a frank "yes" or "no."

This impulsiveness to marry is exemplified in the following case: Having engaged in little or no courtship, one young man promised to marry a young lady as soon as circumstances would permit. Due to a sudden turn of fortune, he resolved on a Saturday night to fulfill his word earlier than planned. With two companions, he set out in a sleigh in the midst of a snowstorm for a tavern, where, after ordering supper for the marriage feast, he requested that his friends go after the bride while he—already having procured the license—went after the minister. Within an hour the groom, accompanied by the parson, returned to the tavern, but there was no bride waiting. She pretended to have forgotten the engagement and sent back word that she would not marry any man who "wouldn't treat her to a sleighing."

Appearing not the least disconcerted, the bridegroom said, "Well, she's her own woman, and I'm my own man. I've come out for a wife, and I'm not going to be such a confounded fool, after I've ordered this supper, to go back without one." Another young woman, Mirim Bush, liked him just as well as the one he had come after. Mirim would be as good a helpmate as anyone and she was just as handy. He asked the minister and his friends to keep the supper warm, to order something strong to drink, and to wait a half-hour while he went for his second choice.

The prospective groom, though it was nearly midnight, jumped into his sleigh and started off at full gallop for the home of the young woman he hoped would be more compliant. Arriving at Mirim's house, he told his story—at least part of it—showed her the license, pointed to the sleigh in the yard, and without groveling at her feet asked that she return to the tavern and become his wife. Liking her suitor well enough and considering him a bargain, she, after a moment's pause, gave her suitor a back-country kiss to seal the compact. She hastily threw on a shawl and bonnet, and her persistent lover drove her triumphantly back to the tavern. Upon arriving there, introductions were made, and after the lovers' hands were joined in marriage, all sat down to supper.[4]

A traveler from New Orleans, while visiting Hot

Springs, Arkansas, witnessed a marriage in which the couple had never seen each other until the day before the ceremony.[5] On another occasion, when a Kansan named Bill West asked a young settler why he had not married, he replied that he was willing but that he had not yet found anyone who would marry him. Later, Bill asked a young lady the same question. She answered coyly that she had not had an offer. Bill West, seeing the need of a matchmaker, brought the two together and suggested that now was the time for them to marry. The couple talked the matter over a few minutes, walked out of the room, and "after a while came back all married up."

A fourteen-year-old girl who was walking to a neighbor's home stopped by Joe Murray's house to rest. In the course of the conversation, she remarked that she was going to marry the first man who asked her. Joe, hearing this, "cocked up one eye and looked wise." A few minutes later a young man entered the Murray home and he was told what the young woman said. Grinning a couple of times, the youth quickly said, "I am asking you right now." The girl immediately accepted the proposal and the two were married that day.[6] One desolate widower, enamored of a milkmaid on first sight, proposed marriage and, getting her approval, procured a license and "married her on the spot."[7]

There was much less flirtation among frontier suitors than in more developed societies. It was taboo for frontier men to trifle very much with the affections of girls whose big brothers were certain to reckon with the culprit. Earnest courtship usually terminated in marriage. Usually couples saw each other only a few times before they became husband and wife.[8]

The scarcity of women certainly created a special demand for wives. Unmarried women, often with more beaux than fingers on their hands, were in a quandary as to which suitor to accept. So great was the need for more women in Iowa in 1856 that the *Iowa Republican* made an appeal for women of "all lands to flock there," as they would not only enjoy the good climate, but would also have a good choice of men from which to select a husband.[9]

Both men and women tended to marry several times because of the high mortality rate. On one occasion, when a lawyer came to the bedside of a dying man to prepare his will, the man requested that the attorney be sent away because he might become his wife's next husband, a prophecy that was later fulfilled. In another instance, a German man was the fourth husband of his first wife and the third husband of his second wife.[10]

## BUNDLING

Some frontier couples did engage in regular courtship before marriage. Far into the eighteenth century, particularly in New England and the Middle Colonies, bundling or "petting" while fully clothed in bed was an accepted practice among the poorer classes. When a young man fell in love with a young lady and wished to marry her, he proposed the matter to her parents. If they voiced no objection, the man was allowed to tarry with her for one night. After the parents had gone to bed, the lovers remained up to discuss their plans. The couple, keeping

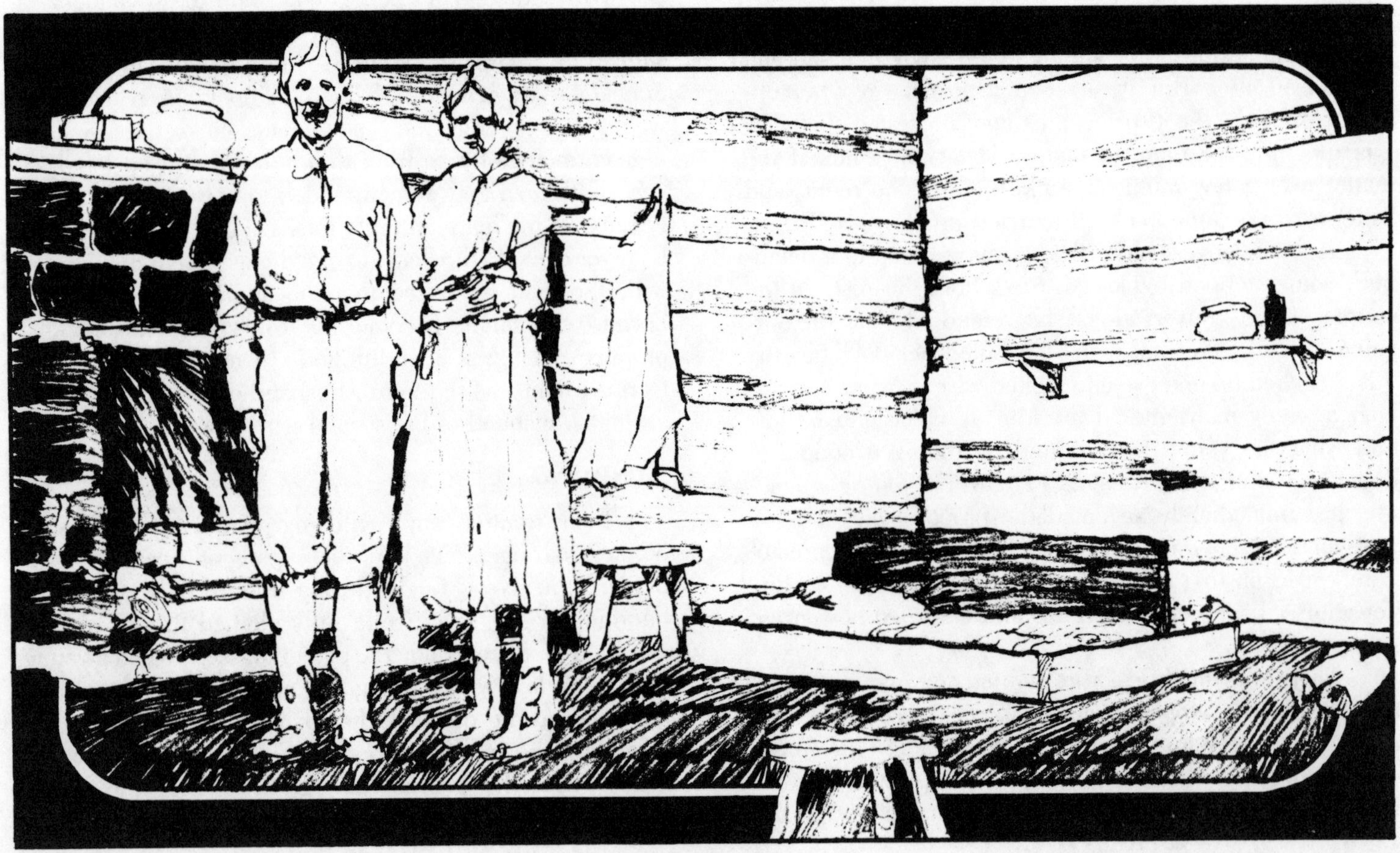

on their undergarments to avoid scandal, then went to bed together but separated by a low upright center board. If their caressing was satisfactory, they were married without delay. However, if they were displeased, they parted, possibly never to see each other again. Should the young lady become pregnant, which was not often the case, the man was obliged to marry her on "pain of excommunication."[11]

Thomas Anburey, a British traveler in Virginia, stopped for the night at a small log hut where he was first introduced to the indelicate American custom of bundling. At bedtime, the landlady said that she and her husband would occupy one of the good clean feather beds and the traveler and their daughter Jemima could sleep on the other. Shocked at such a proposal, Anburey offered to stay up all night. The head of the house replied, "Oh, La! . . . you won't be the first man our Jemima has bundled with, will he Jemima?" The pretty black-eyed sixteen or seventeen-year-old daughter replied, "No, Father, but it will be with the first Britisher." Truly, the British traveler was in a dilemma. There was a smiling invitation from the eyes and soft lips of beautiful Jemima. The Lord have mercy! What was he going to do? Even if he considered bundling, he could not do it in the same room with her parents. He could not clasp the young girl in his arms all night and do nothing. He began to apply accepted English social standards to the situation, forgetting the original proposition. If Jemima surrendered to him, she would become an outcast from the world, regarded with contempt and would be abused and perhaps left to perish. That should not be.

To Jemima's disappointment, Anburey crawled into his own hard bedroll and he would dream ever afterwards of the pleasure he had declined.[12]

In the event that an anxious mother harbored doubts as to her daughter's virtue, she sometimes placed both of her girl's legs in a large stocking before allowing her to bundle. The next morning she would examine the garment to see whether it still "were properly fixed." But, as bundling was usually followed by betrothal, such precautions were generally superfluous.[13]

To the Englishman, John Bernard, American bundling was both a shock and surprise. Offensive as it may have appeared to the European for a young woman to share the same bed with a strange man, the practice was nevertheless commonplace in many areas of colonial America. Bundling, Bernard believed, was introduced from Wales, where there was a prevalent premarital ordeal between lovers. The woman dressed in a kind of "sack tied around her throat . . . experimented with their tempers" in bed "at night as well as in day."[14]

Some clergymen, such as Jonathan Edwards, lashed out against bundling while other ministers defended it. Reverend Samuel Peters wrote that bundling was "certainly innocent, virtuous, and prudent, or the Puritans would not have permitted it to prevail among their offspring, for whom in general they would suffer crucifixion."[15] By 1785, reformers began publishing verses highly critical of bundling. In response to these attacks, supporters of bundling entered the fray with poems defending the custom:

It shant be so, they rage and storm,
And country girls in cluster swarm,
And fly and buzz like angry bees,
And vow they'll bundle when they please.
Some mothers, too, will plead their cause,
And give their daughters great applause,
And tell thee, 'Tis no sin nor shame,
For we your Mothers did the same.

If I take my sparks to bed,
A laughing stock I shall be made.
But where's the man that fire can
Into his bosom take,
Or go through coals on his foot soles
And not a blister make?

But last of all, up speaks romp Moll
And pleads to be excused,
For how can she e'er married be,
If bundling be refused.[16]

Bundling was eventually abandoned, largely because it was stripped of innocence by young men who had participated in the French and Indian War, which ended 1763. The scarcity of women on the frontier often induced men to marry quickly without going through the formalities of bundling. Marriage came to be a civil rather than a religious contract. It was possible for a justice of the peace or even a layman to perform a spur-of-the-moment marriage ceremony, often without the consent of the bride's parents.[17]

## WEDDING CEREMONIES

The lack of proper authorities to perform wedding ceremonies gave rise to extremely abnormal marriage documents. One such peculiar certificate was issued in Peoria County Illinois by Ossian M. Ross while awaiting the arrival of a justice of the peace commission from the governor. Ross wrote:

> To all the World, Greetings: Know ye, that John Smith and Poly Myers is hereby entitled to go together and do as old folks does anywhere inside of Copperas Precinct (in Peoria County, Illinois), and when my commission comes I am to marry 'em and date 'em back to kiver accidents.
>
> (signed) O.M.R., Justice of the Peace[18]

In places where there was neither gospel nor law, men and women often considered their marriage contract complete when they promised in the presence of their friends to be husband and wife. Couples married under such circumstances usually had a Bible wedding when the first circuit rider made his appearance. Unorthodox weddings of this type were sometimes abused. Some unscrupulous men went from place to place and married several women.[19]

Before Texas won her independence from Mexico, bond marriages were commonplace, although illegal. Marriages had to be performed by a priest, who charged twenty-five dollars for his services.[20] Few had so much money. Soon after Texas became a republic, a law was enacted stating that all couples who had been married by bond or who had been married by unauthorized persons could be joined in wedlock by anyone authorized to perform the ceremony. In the future "all ordained ministers, judges of the district courts, justices of the county seats, and all justices of the peace of the several counties of the republic may perform the marriage ceremony." The law further stated that all marriages so solemnized would be legal and binding "from the period the persons had previously been married agreeably to the customs of the times."[21] Reverend Z. N. Morrell said that after the passage of the law he was frequently called on to officiate in such cases. From time to time he performed marriage ceremonies in which children served as witnesses at the marriage of their fathers and mothers. One day after preaching a sermon, Reverend Morrell performed a marriage ceremony in the presence of the congregation while both the man and the wife had a child in their arms.[22]

In various places in the Mississippi Valley where Protestant ministers were few, Jesuit missionaries sometimes spoke marital vows for non-Catholics. Couples objecting to Catholic services used a justice of the peace, often of doubtful validity. When none of these authorities were available, the bride's father usually played the role of justice of the peace or minister.[23]

Many people along the Tombigbee River in Alabama during the early years of the nineteenth century lived together without matrimonial rites. Couples often paired and cohabited with the mutual promise to marry when a minister or magistrate made his appearance. One girl of the area, whose parents objected to her marriage, paddled down river with her lover in the company of other young people to Fort Stoddard, Alabama. Here the lovers begged the commandant to marry them. When the officer stated that he had no such authority, he was reminded that the government had placed him in charge of the general regulation of affairs. Seeing the predicament of the lovers, the commandant finally relented, saying, "I, Captain Shanneberg of the Second Regiment, U.S.A., and commandant of Fort Stoddard, do hereby pronounce you man and wife. Go home! Behave yourselves, multiply and replenish the Tensaw country." And they did.[24]

Late one afternoon in the Kansas Territory, friends and neighbors met at a home for a wedding. The expected circuit rider failed to arrive. Under the circumstances, with no minister and few prospects of having one, the guests persuaded the sheriff to perform the ceremony, much against his and the bride's mother's will. After the marriage, all partook of a sumptuous feast, consisting mainly of turkey and pig. The guests and young married couple danced on the rough wood floor of the log cabin till daylight. Two days later, the minister arrived and learned how the young couple had been married. He insisted that they be married in accordance with church regulations. The couple complied with his request.[25]

One justice of the peace in Illinois lived along the bank of a stream which in flood stage presented a problem for couples who wished to be married. Being a conscientious man, the justice of the peace insisted that lovers ride far enough out into the stream for him to distinguish their features by the light of a torch, and then he shouted their vows across the noisy waters.[26]

In Wisconsin, a justice of the peace accepted five bushels of turnips as his fee for performing a marriage.[27] When James B. Finley was a boy, he saw a man and woman come to his father's home to be married. The bride and groom rode separate horses, each having a bell and a horse collar made of corn-husks on its neck. Upon entering the house, the groom asked if the parson was at home. When Finley replied that he was the minister, the groom said, "May it please you, Mary M'Lain and I have come to get married. Will you do it for us?" When Finley replied that he would, the groom, who was in a hurry, seemed pleased. After the ceremony, the groomsman offered a bottle of whiskey to treat the company. He then went outside and took the shuck collars off the horses and brought them to the minister—his pay for performing the marriage.[28]

While riding his horse toward Ft. Scott, Kansas Territory, Reverend Cyrus R. Rice met a merry group of young people who paid him little attention as they passed. Having traveled only a short distance further, the minister was halted by a young man who rode after him at a full gallop shouting, "Hold on. Are you a preacher?" When Rice replied that he tried to preach sometimes, the stranger said, "There is a young couple in the crowd that wants to get married. Can you marry them?" Reverend Rice proposed that they go to a nearby village to conduct the ceremony. By this time, the couple had ridden up and the prospective groom stated, "No, we don't want to go to the post if you can marry us here. We were hunting for a squire, but if you can marry us, it will be all right."

As no marriage license was required in those days in Kansas, Rice began to question the couple about their age. The fiancee abruptly remarked, "I don't want to be married on horseback," and all of the young people dismounted. The minister arranged the lovers side by side and proceeded to unite them. The ceremony completed, Rice handed them a sheet of paper on which he had written a certificate of marriage. The wedding party mounted their horses and rode away shouting and happy.[29]

Just before a wedding in Fort County, Arkansas, a group of women, including the bride, were in a log cabin picking wool. The men were out near the woods, standing around a log fire, telling yarns. When the preacher and the groom arrived, all went inside. With the bride and groom arranged in front of the fireplace, their backs to the fire, the ceremony began. The minister asked the bride, who continued to pick wool, whether she would care for her husband "in sickness and in health and be his wife for the remainder of her life." She stopped picking, studied for a moment, took a snuff stick out of her mouth, turned around, spat a stream of tobacco into the fire and said, "I reckon." When a similar question was satisfactorily answered by the groom, the couple was pronounced man and wife.[30]

On rare occasions, cruel and practical jokes were manifested at a wedding. A man jilted by the bride or one who bore a grudge against the family for some other reason might seek revenge by cutting off the manes, foretops, and tails of the wedding party's horses. Also, when the chastity of a bride was suspect, frontiersmen sometimes mounted a pair of horns on a pole or tree along the wedding party's route. This was a "hint to the groom that he might expect to be complimented with a pair of horns himself."[31]

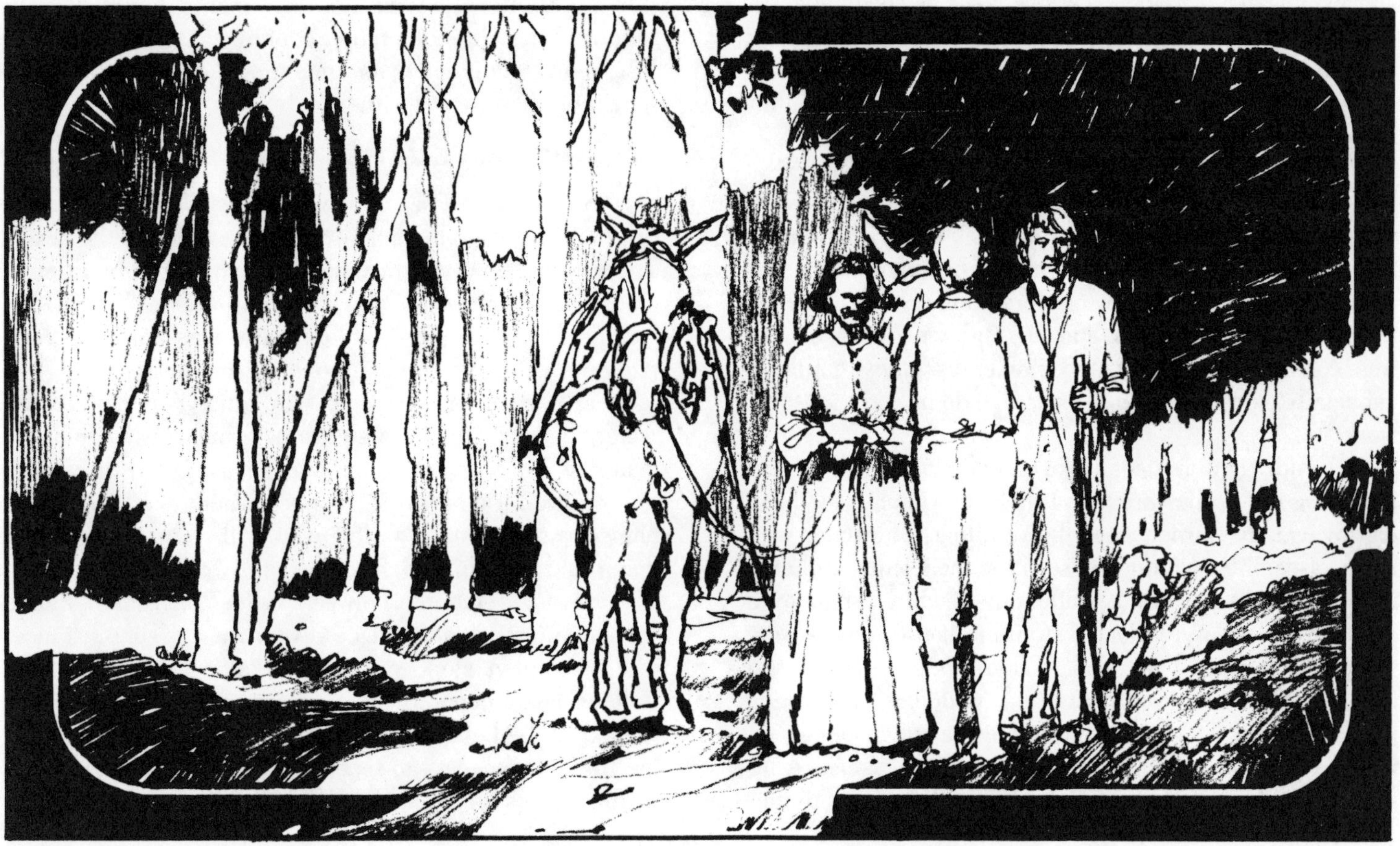

As newly marrieds usually had to spend the first night of married life either at the home of the bride or nearby, their neighbors often gave them a charivari. Men, young and old, milled around in the yard shouting crude suggestions. They made excessive noise by shooting guns, ringing cowbells, beating pans and plows, hallooing and whistling. Usually the boisterous group would leave after being invited in for refreshments, but sometimes they lingered until real trouble developed.[32]

Other forms of crude behavior were encountered at some frontier weddings. A guest wishing a drink of whiskey, might shout, "Where is black beauty? I want to kiss her lips." When given the bottle, he might hold it and say, "Health to the groom, not forgetting myself. Here's to the bride, thumping luck and big children!" Such a toast was considered friendly and proper as many children, especially sons, were needed to perform indispensable work.[33]

Weddings were usually joyful occasions, with settlers attending from miles around. If held in winter, a log-heap or two usually burned near the dwelling. The men, with rifles, assembled around these fires; the women gathered in the house. A few minutes after one wedding ceremony, a number of dogs were ejected from the house, chairs were pulled back against the wall, a fiddle began playing and dancing got under way.[34] At some weddings, the young people danced so long on the ground or rough puncheon floors that they wore holes in their moccasins. After another wedding, the women served a sumptuous dinner consisting of venison, bear meat, roast turkeys, and an abundance of other foods. After eating, the guests began to dance, but as the building was too crowded, many went outside and danced around a big fire. Merry-making on this occasion continued until long after midnight. The following day the celebration continued, while the penniless young couple left for their new home—a cabin the neighbors had built for them.[35]

## SEXUAL IRREGULARITIES

Since almost everyone was married, a "general decency" prevailed almost everywhere between the sexes. There were, however, instances of sexual irregularities.

A frontier traveler observed that white men frequently "adopted" Indian girls as their mistresses and that these alliances brought as much contentment as marriage.[36] In the early days of Texas, it was quite common for an American man to take a squaw as a mistress.[37] Upon the death of his wife, William Johnson acquired at various times several mistresses, one of whom was an Indian named Molly Brant. Molly lived with Johnson until his death and bore him eight children.[38]

Sexual relations between white men and Indian women were commonplace everywhere. For instance, when boatmen stopped overnight along western rivers, Indians often honored their guests by giving them their women as bedfellows. These bed-services were not free; the Indians expected to receive shirts, blankets and other useful articles in exchange for their hospitality. One such boatman returned to his flatboat one morning entirely naked. The Indian women during the night had stolen his shoes and every stitch of clothes.[39]

Sexual relations among the Indians were so easy and natural that they never understood why white men found it necessary to connive and lust for its pleasures. A traveler, seeing an Indian chief in a thoughtful mood, asked him if he were worried. The chief replied, "I was wondering whether you white people have any women amongst you." Assured they did, the chief replied, "Then, why is it that you people are so fond of our women? One might suppose that your men had never seen any before."[40]

Other evidence of loose frontier sexual morals is preserved in a poem from *Poor Richard's Almanac:*

When Rubin now three days had married been,
    And all his friends and neighbors gave him joy,
This question to his wife he asked then,
    Why till her marriage day she proved so coy?
Indeed, said he, 'twas well thou didst not yield,
    For doubtless then my purpose was to leave thee;
O, Sir, I once before was so beguil'd,
    And was resolved the next should not deceive me.[41]

Franklin himself was of an extremely amorous nature. As a young man he often consorted with fallen women. He fathered at least one illegitimate child and probably more. Eventually he married a respectable, uninspiring housewife and managed thereafter to keep his passions under control. As an authority on women, he is best remembered for two writings. The first was *The Speech of Polly Baker*, in which the fictitious Miss Baker, hauled before a court for having given birth to her fifth child out of wedlock, pleads for a husband. In his *Advice to a Young Man*, Franklin tells his correspondent that if he must take a mistress rather than a wife to take an old one. In his *Almanac*, he makes various observations concerning sex, such as "Neither a fortress nor a maidenhead will hold out long after they begin to parley;" "Let thy maidservant be faithful, strong, and homely;" "Old boys have their playthings as well as young ones; the difference is only in the price;" and "Keep your eyes wide open before marriage, half shut afterwards."[42]

Marital difficulties sometimes developed when men remained away from home for long periods of time and they were thought to be dead. When they eventually returned home, these men sometimes found their wives living with new husbands. In such strange circumstances, neighbors might form a court and decree that the wife choose between husbands, with the rejected husband being forced to leave. In most instances, the women returned to their first mates.[43]

A Tennessee man named Bean once took a flatboat to New Orleans and remained away from his wife and children for two years. When he returned home, he saw that his wife was nursing a child, and left without saying a word. Later, while drunk, he seized the child and clipped off its ears so that it would not "get mixed up with his own children." For this atrocity, Bean was arrested, punished, and branded. His wife was granted a divorce and she remarried her second husband. After the death of her

*Neither a fortress nor a maidenhead will hold out long after they begin to parley. —— Let thy maidservant be faithful, strong and homely. —— Old boys have their playthings as well as young ones; the difference is only in the price. —— Keep your eyes wide open before marriage, half shut afterwards.*

second husband and her "marked" child, she remarried Bean.[44]

Far West mining areas usually had a number of camp followers who came there to sell their charms to the successful miners. Some men, lonely and far from home, fell hopelessly in love with these tarts. Rivalry for the prostitutes' favors resulted in blackened eyes, broken noses, and even death. "Yes, he was killed over a damn woman" was a common expression.

In one instance, two men peacefully settled their rival love for a prostitute. Soon after Bill Mayfield, his mistress Cynthia, and Cherokee Bob arrived in a mining town, Mayfield became jealous of Bob's attentions to Cynthia. Bob made no effort to conceal his desire for the woman; she possessed many charms of person and considerable intelligence, and she had an eye for the one who had the most money. As the richer of the rivals, Bob began receiving many encouraging smiles from Cynthia.

Goaded by jealousy, Bill decided to bring matters to a head. Either he or Bob would gain undisputed possession of Cynthia. He thought she would decide in his favor when forced to decide between the two. With a hand on the butt of his revolver, Bill confronted Bob in the presence of Cynthia and said, "Bob, you know me." Bob replied, "Yes, and you know me." Explaining there was no need for the two to make fools of each other, Bill said the woman should decide which of the two she loved more. If she decided in his favor, Bill said, no one ought to come between them, and, "if that woman loves you more than me, take her."

The terms of the proposition being agreed upon, the prostitute was asked to make her choice. To Bill's surprise, Cynthia said, "Well, Bill, Bob is settled in business now, and don't you think he is better able to take care of me than you are?" Bob forced a generous purse on his rival and Bill "left him with the parting injunction to take good care of the girl."[45]

Although frontier mating was sometimes conducted in an atypical manner, settlers were merely responding to the peculiar conditions of time and place. The frontier was ever and always in a state of flux, but the family remained a relatively stable institution because there was a need for all its members to cooperate with each other in order to survive. However, any particular family's stability rested on shifting sand. A mother, a father, or several children might die or be killed in quick succession. Daughters and sons married early, often leaving for parts unknown and losing contact with their parents. Economic bonds were strong; family life was a frontier necessity and the married state was preferred.

HE DIED.....
STRUGLING
FOR FOOD, SHELTER
AND CLOTHING
FOR HIMSELF AND
HIS FAMILY.
AGE 31

# 4

# Health and Medical Practices on the Frontier

The active outdoor life of frontiersmen did not necessarily make them a healthy people. Contrary to popular belief, their health was often bad. Diseases were often diagnosed incorrectly, making it difficult to tell what disorders people had. Epidemics scourged the people and they suffered the ravages of itch, smallpox, typhoid, malaria, pneumonia, tuberculosis, bronchitis, and countless other ailments. The mortality rate among children was especially high; half died before reaching the age of four. Edgar Lee Masters in his *Spoon River Anthology* wrote:

> We were married and lived together for seventy years
> Enjoying, working, raising the twelve children,
> Eight of whom we lost,
> Ere I had reached the age of sixty.[1]

Gravestones in old cemeteries of the midwest indicate that men and women also had relatively short life expectancies. Without doctors and other medical aid, a snake bite, a broken limb, a wound, or a disease was often fatal.

## DISEASES ON THE FRONTIER

In his *Three Episodes of Massachusetts History*, Charles Francis Adams made note of several common diseases. Delirium tremors, ulcers, and other stomach disorders, Adams said, resulted from the intemperate drinking habits of the people. Many died in middle life from kidney and bladder troubles, and others were crippled by rheumatism and running sores that could not be cured. Visitations of smallpox were periodical, and in 1735 and 1751 terrible epidemics of diphtheria swept through the colonies. During 1751 in Weymouth, Massachusetts, more than a hundred and twenty of its twelve hundred inhabitants died. In 1761, seventeen elderly people from a neighborhood near Braintree, Massachusetts, died during an epidemic. In Boston in 1775, chronic dysentery became so deadly that three, four, and even five children were lost in single families. Mrs. John Adams wrote that fear of the disease was almost as great as if it were smallpox.[2]

According to Noah J. Major, the two healthiest months in Indiana were April and May, and the most unhealthy were August and September. Deaths caused by apoplexy and heart disease were rare, and there was virtually no insanity or suicide.

There were a great many rheumatic disorders and liver complaints. Itch was prevalent in the back country and, while not fatal in itself, often left victims so weak that they readily contracted other diseases. Itch also caused other infections. A man named Pete Whetstone stopped while crossing Arkansas at a log inn for the night. Two guests were already there and a mail carrier soon arrived, making four in all. There were only two guest beds available. The mail carrier was a little shabby, dirty, lousy-looking wretch, with whom none of the others cared to sleep. Pete Whetstone eyed him closely and asked, "Where do you sleep tonight, my lad?" The youth replied, "I'll sleep with you, I reckon, or one o' them fellars, I don't care which." The two men who first arrived crawled into one of the beds, leaving the other for Pete and the youth. As Pete got into bed, hoping to rid himself of his undesirable sleeping companion, he said, "My friend, I'll tell you before hand, I've got the itch, and you'd better not get in here with me, for the disease is catching." Unruffled by what he had heard, the young mail carrier pulled back his side of the covers and crawled in. "Wal I reckon that don't make a bit of difference—I've had it now for nearly three years," the youth drawled. Pete pitched out of bed as though he were in a hornet's nest. The men in the opposite bed roared with laughter. Their mirth was short lived, however, for the boy quickly added, "Why you must be a thet o' darned fules,—Mam and Dad got the eatch a heap wurth than I is, and they slep in that bed last night when they was here at the quilting party." The two men bounced from the bed as though the house was on fire. Though it was nearly ten o'clock, Pete and the two men immediately dressed and rode several miles away to the next inn, leaving the mail boy to sleep and scratch in solitary bliss.[3]

During their journeys through the frontier, travelers often encountered entire families who were ill. G. W. Featherstonhaugh and his party once came upon a family of ten members who had been so completely prostrated by malaria that not one of them had been able to draw a bucket of water for two days. The father and five of the children were still in bed, suffering extreme pains and nausea from an excessive use of calomel.[4]

"Bilious fever" was often found in the backwoods area. Martha Jackson, reminiscing in her old age about frontier life in North Louisiana, said "We was sick with fever every fall regular."[5] Reverend James Finley reported "bilious fever" took a large toll in lives. Some families "were so severely stricken that one could not help another." In some instances, Finley said, the dead lay unburied for days, as there was no one fit to bury them or able even to report their death.[6] Reverend J. Wilcox, a missionary in Illinois, said the fever was particularly bad among the settlers in 1839. For a ten-day period Wilcox visited and administered to the sick. He traveled many miles from one cabin to another consoling and nursing his patients.[7] Both Reverend Finley and Wilcox had pet theories for the cause of bilious fever: Finley attributed it to the "effluvia arising from the decomposition of the luxurent vegetation which grew so abundantly everywhere," and Wilcox thought that the hot summers, which exposed stream beds and marshes to the rays of the sun, caused them to emit "deadly miasmata."

Other diseases also ravaged the frontier. Pneumonia and tuberculosis, known as "that old breast complaint," were fatal to many.[8] Cholera took a heavy toll of life, particularly in Wisconsin in July 1850. While tending cholera victims, one physician contracted the disease himself. Having used all his medicine on his patients, the doctor jumped on his horse and made a run for his life toward his home eighteen miles away. He died a few hours after reaching his family. Riding through the valley of death itself, Reverend J. D. Stevens saw numerous roughly made coffins which contained the remains of people who, only a few hours previously, had been strong and healthy. As corpses were hauled past homes on the way to the cemetery, occupants fled into their dwellings or ran out into the fields for fear of contracting the disease. Cholera victims were often so numerous that they went long unburied.[9]

## MEDICAL TREATMENT ON THE FRONTIER

Limited knowledge of hygiene and diet coupled with insufficient clothing, inadequate bedding, poorly constructed housing, and limited medical aid made for an unhealthy frontier populace. With too few doctors, most people diagnosed and treated themselves. Everyone took calomel without hesitation. An ordinary dose of the drug was from fifteen to twenty grains. With the first warning of an approaching disease such as nausea, pains in the limbs, excessive yawning, or a chill, one took calomel at night with a little apple honey, or other suitable substances. As a follow-up the next morning, one took a dose of castor oil or salts to produce a brisk purge. Reverend Peck believed that the settlers made a mistake by not taking tonics after "evacuation medicine which left the system under some debility." He asserted that a few doses of "sulphate of quinine or Peruvian bark in its crude state would restore the body to its natural tone."[10]

Pioneers liberally dosed themselves with bitters made from barks and roots and drank much whiskey. A favorite remedy for snake bite was a large quantity of whiskey—which did more harm than good. Remedies for chills and fever included tonics made from dogwood, wild cherry bark, and boneset. Many mothers raised garden herbs from which they brewed health teas for both old and young. Plump rattlesnakes furnished another popular remedy. The snakes were skinned and oil was boiled from their carcasses. Both glistening skins and snake-oil were deemed "a wonderful specific" for chronic disorders such as rheumatism.[11]

Many cures for cancer, tuberculosis, milk fever, and other diseases were avidly purchased by gullible frontiersmen. One Indiana newspaper ran an advertisement stating that Fontain & Son, chemists from the Royal University in

Paris, had after long experiments found a cure for tuberculosis called the "Restoration Francaise." Any person could purchase an eight-franc bottle by leaving his name with the local preacher. The sales of "Restoration" were brisk.[12] Charles Latrobe, a French traveler, reports that the frontiersmen were "open to the trickery and cajoling of innumerable quacks" who traveled through the country with their vile medicines under the name of fever and steam-doctors, ruining the health of many people. One zealous quack, after steaming a person to death in fourteen minutes, was forced to run for his life.[13]

Obstetricians were badly needed, but there were none in most areas. Self-trained midwives delivered the babies and cared for mothers and infants as best they could. A midwife named Mrs. Jacob Niman was present at nearly every birth in and around Lewiston, Illinois, during a three-year period. Attending Mrs. Hugh R. Coulter during a harrowing and difficult birth, Mrs. Niman saw that the child was well, but not the mother. In despair the midwife sent for an Indian doctor living in the area. The Indian examined the patient and informed her husband that his wife was dying. The Indian refused to prescribe anything for her, since he might be blamed for her death. He intimated, however, that had he been called earlier he might have saved her life.

Thomas Ross, a neighbor, mounted a fleet horse and began a "ride for life" to Springfield, fifty miles away, to bring back a doctor. Ross rode without stopping and eventually brought the doctor to the sick woman's bedside. The doctor remained for twenty-four hours, but he could do nothing. Mrs. Coulter died two days later. This woman, as well as millions of others before and after, probably died of puerperal, or childbed, fever. It was not over until 1843 that Dr. Oliver W. Holmes discovered how to prevent childbed fever, but its use trickled slowly out to the frontier.[14]

Excessive childbearing impaired the health of many women and caused them to be old at thirty-five; a Mrs. Easely of Greenville, South Carolina, was the mother of thirty-four living children. Having a large number of children often prevented parents from looking after them adequately.

Upon the death of her husband, one woman was left in frontier Minnesota with six children between the ages of six months and twelve years. Alone with her children on a small farm, she found the first winter to be a terrible ordeal. The children frequently suffered from attacks of chills and fever. Rigors followed by burning fever came on alternate days. The mother worked hard in between to get ready for sick day. During this time the youngest child was so ill that she was not expected to live. Even if she did, the mother feared she "would not have good sense" because of her high fever. This dire prediction proved untrue; after a long and vigorous life, the child wrote her memoirs at the age of eighty-three.

Most medical practice in older settled areas was bad, but it was even worse on the frontier. Frontier doctors were usually classified as "botanic, herb, or calomel doctors." Called to see a patient, the self-made, uneducated doctor—often a jack of all trades—would examine the tongue and feel the pulse of the patient. Next the "doctor" often bled the sick. One of the patient's sleeves was rolled to his shoulder and he was instructed to hold his arm in a horizontal position by grasping a broom-stick resting on the floor. A cord was tied around the arm half way between the elbow and shoulder, a blood vessel was stabbed, and a pint or more of blood was let. The amount drawn depended upon the mood of the doctor and the age and sex of the patient. Following the bleeding, the patient was given a powerful emetic, a dose of calomel and jalap, and a "walloping dose of castor oil."

The treatment was sometimes continued with "a course of blisters." Blisters measuring six by ten inches were induced on the breast and smaller ones on the arms and legs; if very sick, the patient's head was sometimes blistered after a patch of his hair had been shaved. To produce a blister the "doctor" placed a piece of canvas over the desired body area. Tallow was then spread on the canvas, and atop this he placed pulverized Spanish flies. The plaster was left on the patient's skin from six to eight hours, and it caused great pain. After removing the canvas, the inflamed area was dressed with cabbage leaves or tallowed muslin. At the end of two weeks, the blisters began healing and a white substance known as "proud flesh" formed. This was removed by sprinkling powdered roasted alum on it. Again the patient suffered extreme agony.

Enduring the ordeals of bleeding, purging and blistering, all of which reduced the patient to the very last extremity, he was allowed to take little food or drink. From time to time he was given a small amount of thin gruel, chicken broth, or toast and tea. Even though racked with a burning fever and tortured with thirst he was given no water.

If the patient was strong enough to survive, the doctor usually claimed that it was his skill that had snatched the victim from the grave. If he died, the doctor often asserted that he was not called soon enough, but he most frequently attributed the death to an act of God.[15]

A few doctors used vomiting to cure the sick. To induce vomiting the patient was given a dose of pure tartar, followed by copious drinks of warm water. Within the space of about five minutes "everything took the back track from the bottom of the stomach upward." When the stomach calmed, the patient was fed corn gruel to reverse the order of things. For twenty-four hours the patient was denied what he craved most, cool water. During this period he might have "visions of bubbling springs and moss-covered buckets." With few clocks or watches, time seemed to lag during the day and the patient often felt that God had commanded the sun to stand still. When the long night began, the insane craving for water made the dehydrated patient sometimes "see" the flaming inferno or "hear" sounds like the "wings of bats, the caterwauling of cats, the jeering of owls and nighthawks, and monotonous quarrels of katydids."[16]

Calomel doctors garnered a following on the frontier. Calomel, it was believed, would kill almost any disease, but too much of it often killed or seriously crippled a patient. One father, after his four-year-old son became seriously ill from exposure to a cold wind, called a doctor to his home. The doctor gave the sick lad a large dose of calomel; soon after the physician departed, the boy lost the use of both legs and one arm. The next morning the father went to see the doctor, telling him of his son's condition. The doctor laughed loudly and said in a pitiless tone, "The old White Horse will do mischief sometimes." The White Horse in this case meant calomel. Fortunately, the paralysis was temporary and the child eventually recovered.[17]

Root and calomel doctors often competed for patients. In one Indiana community, Dr. Joseph S. Burr, a stranger to the people, nailed an "enormous swamp lily root, almost as large as a man, with head, eyes, nose, ears and mouth nicely carved, arms and legs with feet stuck on," to the weather boarding of an inn. Just above the root was the inscription, "Joseph S. Burr, Root Doctor: No Calomel." News of his arrival soon spread around the country like wildfire and hundreds came to see the big root and to seek the root doctor's services.

Before long the new "doctor" was the focus of a serious dispute. The resident physician, Joseph Moffitt, regarded Burr as a quack who intended to gull the people, and spoke of him with utmost contempt. The root-doctor countercharged that Dr. Moffitt killed many of his patients with calomel. The people were divided in their opinions; some favored roots and others calomel. It was now the sickly season of the year and many of Moffitt's patients died. The root practitioner in each case attributed the death to calomel and his claims were believed by many.

Driven almost to despair, Moffitt sued Burr for slander. The trial dragged on for more than a week. Each contestant was represented by the best available lawyers. When one of Burr's attorneys called the widow of a man who had recently died to the witness stand, Moffitt whispered, "I have him now; I can prove by a witness in court that her husband died before I got there." Subsequent witnesses failed to convince the jury that calomel was a killer. The case resulted in a mistrial. Burr, the root doctor, soon afterwards left the area.

Elsewhere in Indiana, Burr began to train a number of other root doctors. Burr, for a fee, freely issued diplomas to anyone who took a three-week course under his supervision. One of his graduates, Thomas T. Chinn, a former constable who was hardly able to write his name, "sallied forth to the 'New Purchase' as 'Dr. Chinn, Root Doctor and No Calomel.'" A short time after beginning his practice, he was asked how his business was progressing. Reluctantly he answered, "Only tolerable; I lost nine fine patients last week, one of them an old lady that I wanted to cure very bad. She died in spite of all I could do." As a last resort, he tried, "Calamus," meaning calomel. He followed this with a strong tea made from a root. The old woman drank the tea with great difficulty and then turned over in the bed and died. "Still," as Chinn claimed, "I don't think it was the Calamus that killed her, as all the Calamus doctors are giving it in heavier doses than I did."[18]

Other doctors enjoyed a greater success with their medicine. While Reverend Jacob Young was riding to a quarterly meeting in his circuit in Ohio, he was attacked with fever and ague. He pushed on to Warrentown where he stopped to see a doctor. Not wanting to miss his meeting, Young requested the physician break the fever as soon as possible. The doctor administered a large dose of calomel, followed by much jalap. The next morning the doctor mixed four ounces of Peruvian bark in a quart of wine and instructed the minister to take it as prescribed. Purged and weakened, Young mounted his horse and started the thirty-two mile ride to the meeting. Every two hours he drank a large portion of the compound. That night, according to the minister, "God was with us." His fever broke and he was bothered no more that year with chills and fever.[19]

A Doctor Shuler was another successful practitioner of the medical arts, especially with one patient. When an Indiana settler needed surgery in 1824, a messenger was dispatched for a doctor, Lawrence S. Shuler, who lived a hundred miles away. The messenger found the doctor away from home campaigning for Congress in an adjoining county. The messenger tracked down Shuler and brought him to the stricken man. Shuler was not a specialist in surgery. Like most other doctors, he did what he thought had to be done at the moment. He was at times a surgeon, a dentist, an obstetrician, a bone-setter, a drug-giver, a bleeder, a blisterer, and even a psychologist. The operation was performed and Dr. Shuler returned to his politicking. The doctor lost his congressional bid, but his patient lived.

Since most frontiersmen had access to no dentists at all, they performed many of their dental operations themselves. Nearly every settled area had a tooth puller who used heavy pinchers made in a blacksmith shop of rough iron or steel to extract aching teeth. The "specialist" grasped the tooth with his pinchers and then gave a twist. Usually this removed the tooth, but sometimes it broke just beneath the gum. In this event, the tooth doctor cut the gum on each side of the root and dug it out piece by piece without a painkiller.

Other techniques of extracting teeth were used. In one remote area, a man tortured by an infected tooth, went to a neighbor's house and begged him to remove it. Lacking any tooth pulling instruments, the neighbor fashioned a collar from a piece of hard seasoned wood. He fitted the device around the tooth and struck the front end with a hammer. This loosened the tooth and the amateur dentist pulled it out with his fingers. Such neighborly deeds were usually performed without charge.

Most professional and amateur dentists had learned by trial and error that it was well for the patient to wash his mouth with strong whiskey after a tooth was pulled. This made the gums heal quicker. They did not know the reason for this, as they knew nothing about germs and viruses. Tooth extractors also learned that continued application of alcohol to the gum was bad. It prevented blood clotting and thus induced excessive bleeding.

Most settlers on the frontier had bad teeth, particularly women. Excessive child bearing, the lack of proper diet, and the lack of dental hygiene, caused most women to lose all their teeth by the age of thirty-five. The men kept their teeth slightly longer. False teeth were hard

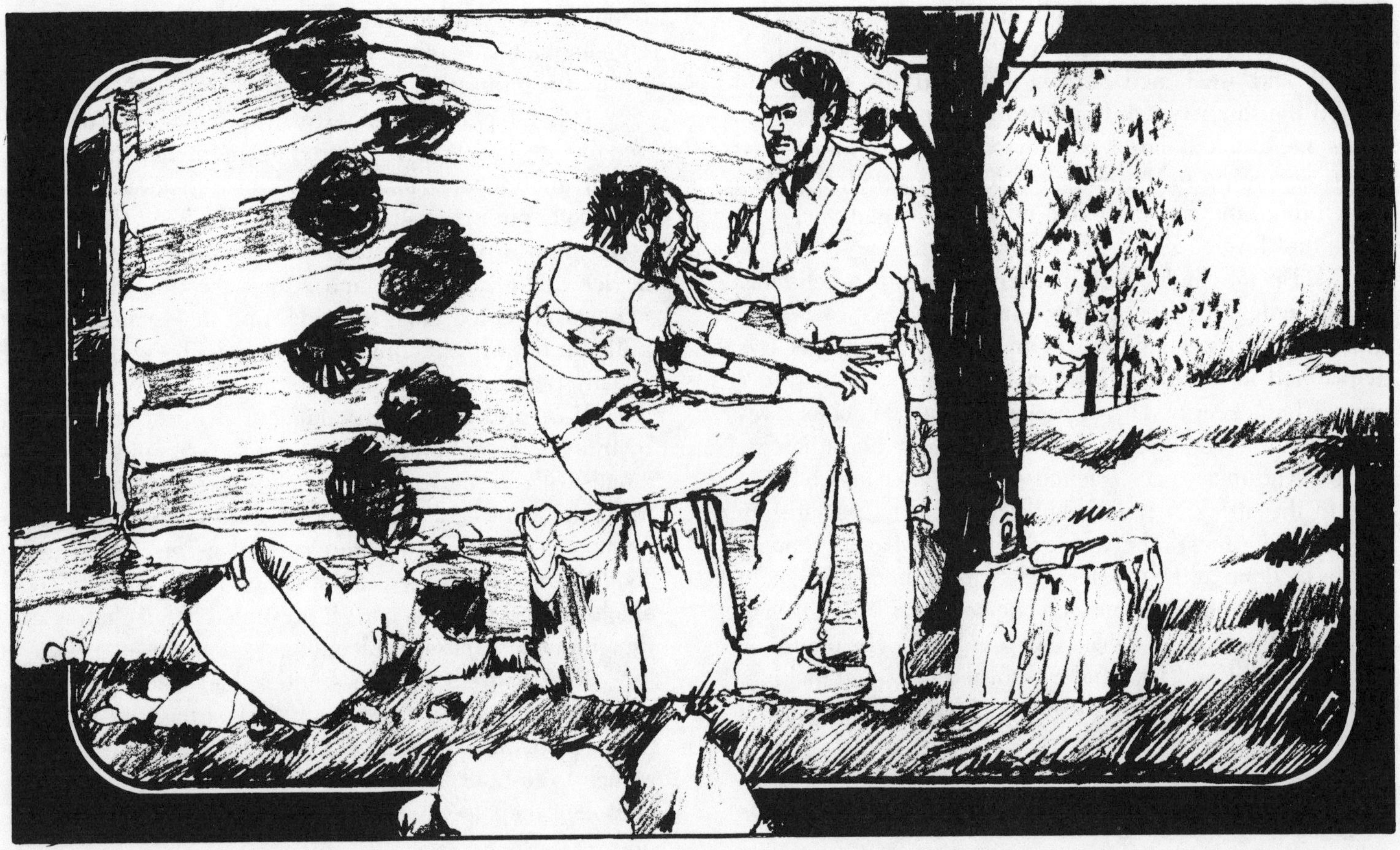

to get, and many relatively young people were toothless.[20]

Indian doctors, or "medicine men," were often consulted on the frontier. In the early days of Nashville, Tennessee, when Andrew Jackson was shot in the upper part of his arm, a white doctor decided to amputate to save Jackson's life. Jackson refused and called in an Indian medicine man. Within a few weeks Jackson recovered.[21]

More and more the Indian doctors earned the respect of the settlers. On the early Illinois frontier, one Indian doctor who was about fifty years old and only able to speak a little English had gained not only the confidence of his own race, but also that of whites. He carried his medicines—consisting of herbs, barks, root extracts, various oils from beasts, birds, and reptiles, particularly from rattlesnakes—in a bag and rode a "fine looking" black pony, rendering his services to both Indians and whites. One of his treatments was to "sweat or steam his patient." This was done by wrapping the patient in blankets and then placing him over a bed of live coals in a wigwam until he perspired profusely. At other times he steamed the patient from a vessel of boiling water placed over live coals. Once when he was treating a white boy suffering from a severe cold, the Indian gave the youth a white powder to snuff up his nose. This produced such a dreadful sneezing attack that his parents became alarmed. The doctor assured them, however, there was no danger, and when the sneezing ceased, he made a poultice of herbs and barks which he bound around the boy's forehead. The next day the boy was well.[22]

Ministers, particularly circuit-riders, were often the best physicians. A number of them were more literate than the average frontiersman, and they read medical as well as religious literature. In their extensive travels they saw sickness and death in every form. The services of Francis Asbury, one of the most revered of ministers, were often sought to treat the sick.[23] Another minister, Reverend Henry Baker, after suffering a physical breakdown brought on by his rough and toilsome life as a minister, "took the lead of Providence and commenced the study of medicine." He rose to such prominence in his new profession that he became the favorite physician of many Methodist bishops. When Baker's health began to improve, he again became an itinerant, serving people as both minister and doctor for the remainder of his life.[24] Another circuit rider, Joseph Badger, wrote that on a Friday he rode to a place where he preached a sermon, after which he gave medical aid to a child.[25] Minister, doctor, politician, and farmer, Reverend Edward Tiffin often cared for the sick in his itinerancy. One day he was asked to treat a man who had cut his foot badly with a scythe. Tiffin examined the man's foot and found it highly inflamed and mortifying. The only recourse was immediate amputation. Steeling himself for the dangerous operation, Tiffin tied a handkerchief tightly around the foot above the inflamed part and quickly cut the flesh from the bones with his pocket knife. He then sawed into the bones with a common handsaw. Though the surgery was crude and excruciatingly painful, the man's life was saved.[26]

Frontier preachers were often forced to practice medicine. Reverend James B. Finley once saw a man

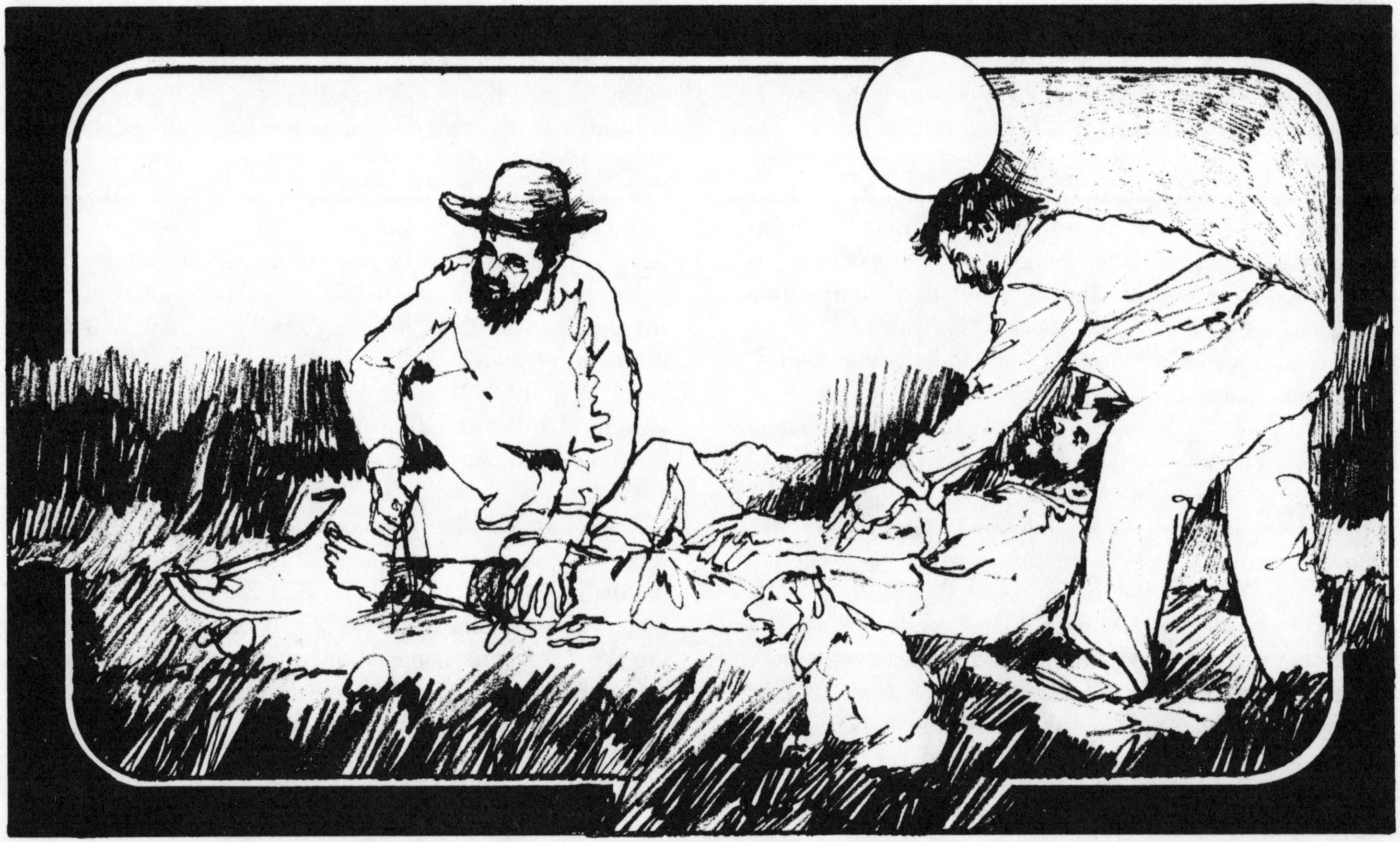

struck on the head by a falling limb. The injured man might die if nothing were done, and Finley was the only one in the area to do it. Finley quickly bled the injured man and, providentially, he lived.[27] Preaching in an area heavily infested with fevers and where there was no doctor, Reverend Charles Giles felt compelled to read medical books to acquaint himself with the human body and find remedies for prevalent diseases. What he learned enabled him not only to preserve his own health, but also to help other people he met in his "ministerial labors."[28] According to Reverend A. Jones, a Missouri missionary, visiting the sick was a matter of course, and settlers often depended upon him for medical aid.[29]

The fact remains that nearly all frontier doctors, ministers included, were both ignorant and superstitious. Faith in a doctor's skill and faith in God often wrought near miraculous cures, whatever the actual treatment. Reverend Jacob Bower, suffering untold misery from an ugly wound that would not heal, sought help from Dr. B. F. Edwards. The doctor advised, "You will never fully recover to be able to follow the plow. But God has a work for you to do, and you will be able to ride and preach. You had better go at it as soon as you can, lest the worst thing come to you." Reverend Bower pushed his infirmity into a remote recess of his brain and for many years successfully spread God's word.[30]

Certainly, medical attention on the frontier was sadly inadequate. Surgical techniques were often improvised and crude. Treatments were sometimes more harmful than the disease. The idea of psychosomatic medicine was unknown, but it was practiced. In older, more highly civilized areas, medical attention was hardly more advanced. Diagnosis and treatment of certain ailments remained primitive and regressive everywhere until the middle of the nineteenth century when many "breakthroughs" in medical science were made. These discoveries seeped slowly out to the remote frontiers and eventually medical practices began to improve.

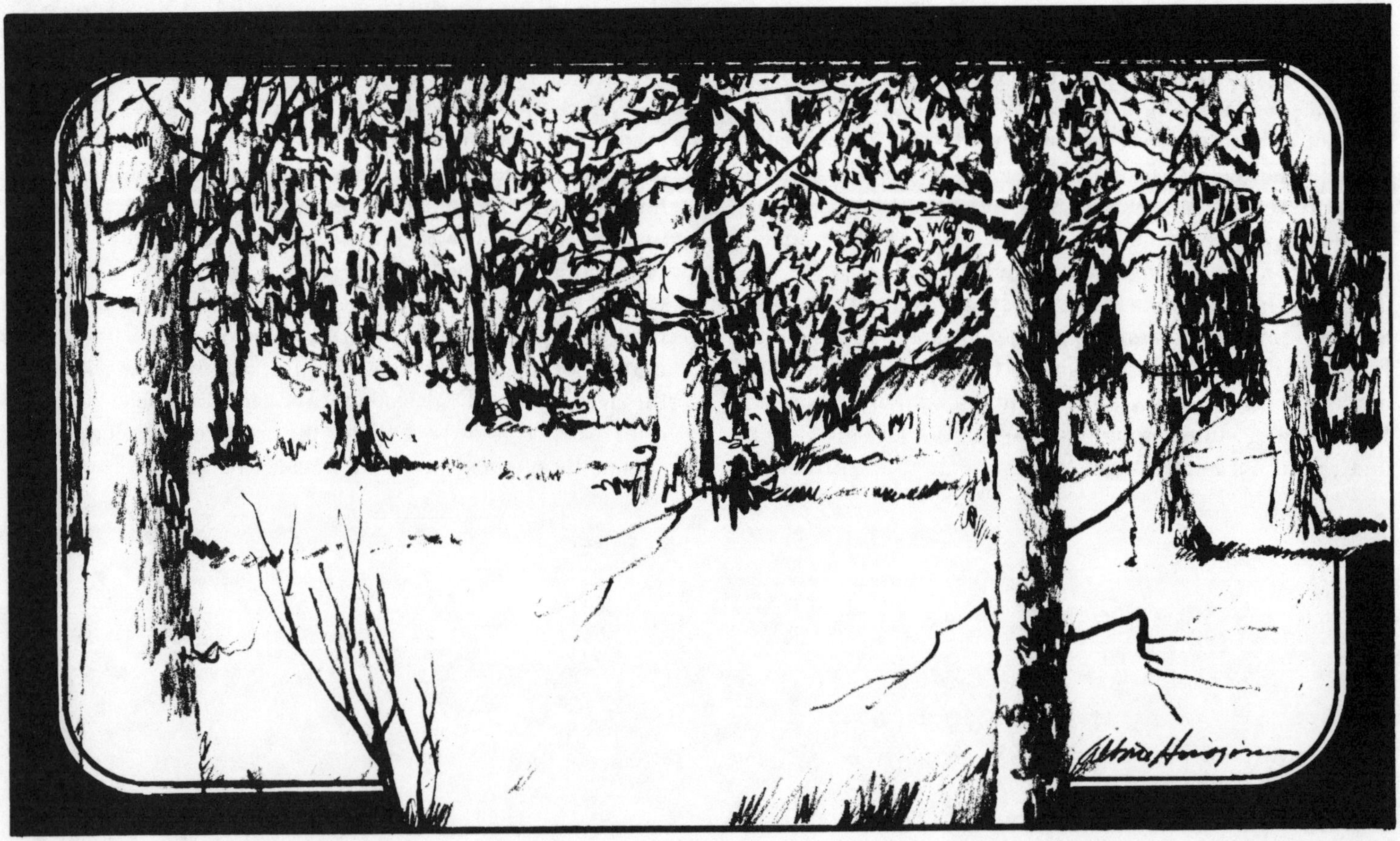

# 5

# Perils of Travel

American pioneers were no special breed. Usually poor, down-trodden and even outcast members of civilization, they went to new lands with the hope of securing a better life. Whether their dreams were ever realized or not, their lives were conditioned by the forces brought to bear on them in their new setting. A basic influence on frontiersmen was their access to a bountiful supply of fertile land and its available resources. At the beginning of the frontier era, an untapped continent was waiting for the white man to exploit. Fertile soil, forests, springs, lakes and streams, edible plants and animals, and other resources enabled them to live. Without land and its resources, there would have been no American frontier, but these in themselves do not give sufficient explanation for the people's behavior.

Barriers to travel and communication prevented the settlers from realizing much aid from either the European societies at first or the more developed parts of America at a later period.[1] During the Colonial era, the colonists were isolated from Europe by stormy seas. Governor Bradford of Plymouth wrote, "If they looked behind them, there was the mighty ocean which they had passed and was now a main bar and gulf to separate them from all the civil world."[2] With regard to the Atlantic as an impediment to contact between England and her American Colonies, as late as March 1775 Edmund Burke, a British statesman, said, "Three thousand miles of ocean lies between you and them. No contrivance can prevent the effect of this distance in weakening government."[3] In winter time it was not unusual to be "fourteen, nineteen or more weeks coming from Gravesend, England, to Philadelphia."[4] Thus, billowing seas greatly limited the contact between the settlers along the Atlantic coast and their homelands in Europe.

For the vast majority of pioneers, however, it was not the sea that isolated them, but land barriers that stood between them and the rest of America. In time, areas along the seacoast evolved relatively integrated social orders. These expanded in a general westerly direction, until around 1890 or 1900, the entire United States had a comparatively homogeneous social organization and the frontier passed out of existence. But the perils of travel the pioneer confronted were numerous and ranged from extreme isolation to Indian atrocities.

## LONELINESS AND ISOLATION

The new lands were occupied in an extremely haphazard manner, without order or plan. Settling the continent has generally been called the "westward movement," but the vanguards of civilization did not always go west. Many areas were bypassed for a time and occupied later by people moving into them from all directions. This was exemplified in the settlement of the Great Plains near the close of the frontier era. Free to go in any direction—up and down river valleys and across mountains and plains—settlers usually found themselves many miles from the confines of the American society when they arrived at their new homes.

To the pioneers the distances between themselves and civilization were formidable and harsh realities. Loneliness was ever present on the frontier. Riding his horse day after day among trees one hundred or more feet in height that obliterated the sight of distant hills fading into the clouds, Andre Michaux, a French traveler, had a feeling of seclusion such as he had never before experienced. Sitting in his saddle near the summit of a mountain in the Appalachian Range, he viewed the gloomy, verdant tops of trees below him and saw no trace of human habitation.[5]

The quietness of the day, however, was in marked contrast to the sounds at night; owls hooted, wolves howled, and panthers and tiger cats gave piercing cries. Other forest inhabitants, the most remarkable being the whippoorwills, made known their passions, wants, and appetites in different tones and modulations. On some nights, as the moon dipped below the horizon, multitudes of fireflies made the atmosphere even more melancholy. So awesome were the forest sounds and scenes at night that dogs sometimes refrained from barking. While traveling through deep woods, fifty, a hundred, or five hundred miles from civilization, some people became so lonely, melancholy, and overawed that they stopped and retraced their steps back to the old homes.[6]

Travel on the treeless plains was equally as solitary as in the deep woods. While riding his horse on the prairies, Reverend William W. Goode had a depressing sense of loneliness. To view the vast unbounded expanse with no trees or houses—nothing but the broad horizon—gave him a feeling of insignificance in the scale of creation. Though he knew such experiences induced worthy reflection, he preferred to ride over areas where he could get food and lodging and have the pleasant association of people.[7]

Politicians canvassing for office in such remote areas

were often able to gain a few votes, but at the end of a day's ride they sometimes had to sleep on the ground. As a candidate for Congress in early Indiana, Oliver H. Smith, riding through an isolated region at night, stopped his horse, hitched, and unsaddled him. Using the saddle blanket for a bed, he went to sleep near the road. The next morning he rode to Fort Wayne, where he ate dinner—his first meal since early breakfast of the preceding day. He made a speech and met a few people, but for his effort he received only three votes.[8]

## LOST ON THE FRONTIER

Another obstacle to frontier travel was the danger of getting lost, partly because of lack of roads, but mostly because of the difficulty of following established lanes of travel. As there were no roads in some places—not even horse-tracks—settlers had to chart their course in the general direction of their desired destination as best they could by the sun, a star, or a pocket compass. In many instances, roads intersected, crossed, and criss-crossed each other without any apparent plan or purpose. Travelers went around marshes and steep hills and up and down streams to the places easiest to cross. Detours were made around fallen trees, some of which were twelve feet in diameter. If one asked the distance to a place, he was often told by a native that it was many miles and would involve a "heap of turnouts."[9]

A traveler could expect to receive little and at best complicated road information. This was exemplified in the case of Reverend Alfred Brunson who stopped at a house and inquired of a woman about landmarks along the road before entering a fourteen-mile prairie. Unable to give any worthwhile information, she said that eighteen months ago a wagon had gone over it, and since that time only a few horsemen had crossed.[10] A traveler might be told to follow a rail fence until he arrived at a barn, where he should take the trail to the left, leading him across two creeks and over hills and through valleys to a cornfield six miles away. At the cornfield he was to take the dim road to the right and follow it several miles to an intersection. Here he should be careful not to miss his road.

Having received such instruction, countless travelers took the wrong path, leading them many miles from their desired destination or even back to the place where they had started. Once on a trail, a traveler was likely to be alone. He sometimes became uneasy and a little afraid, even at midday under a clear sky. If only he had a map indicating the rail fence, the barn, the road to the left, the two creeks, the cornfield, and the intersection he should not miss!

The need for road maps caused some eventually to be made. Crude though they were, they proved serviceable. While attending a Methodist conference where the bishop assigned circuits to various itinerants, Hamilton W. Pierson, a minister and Bible salesman, observed that one minister gave another a map of the circuit he was to serve. Not only did it indicate the preaching places and the homes of families where the minister would be most comfortably received, but it also showed landmarks along the roads to keep him from losing his way. Pierson also

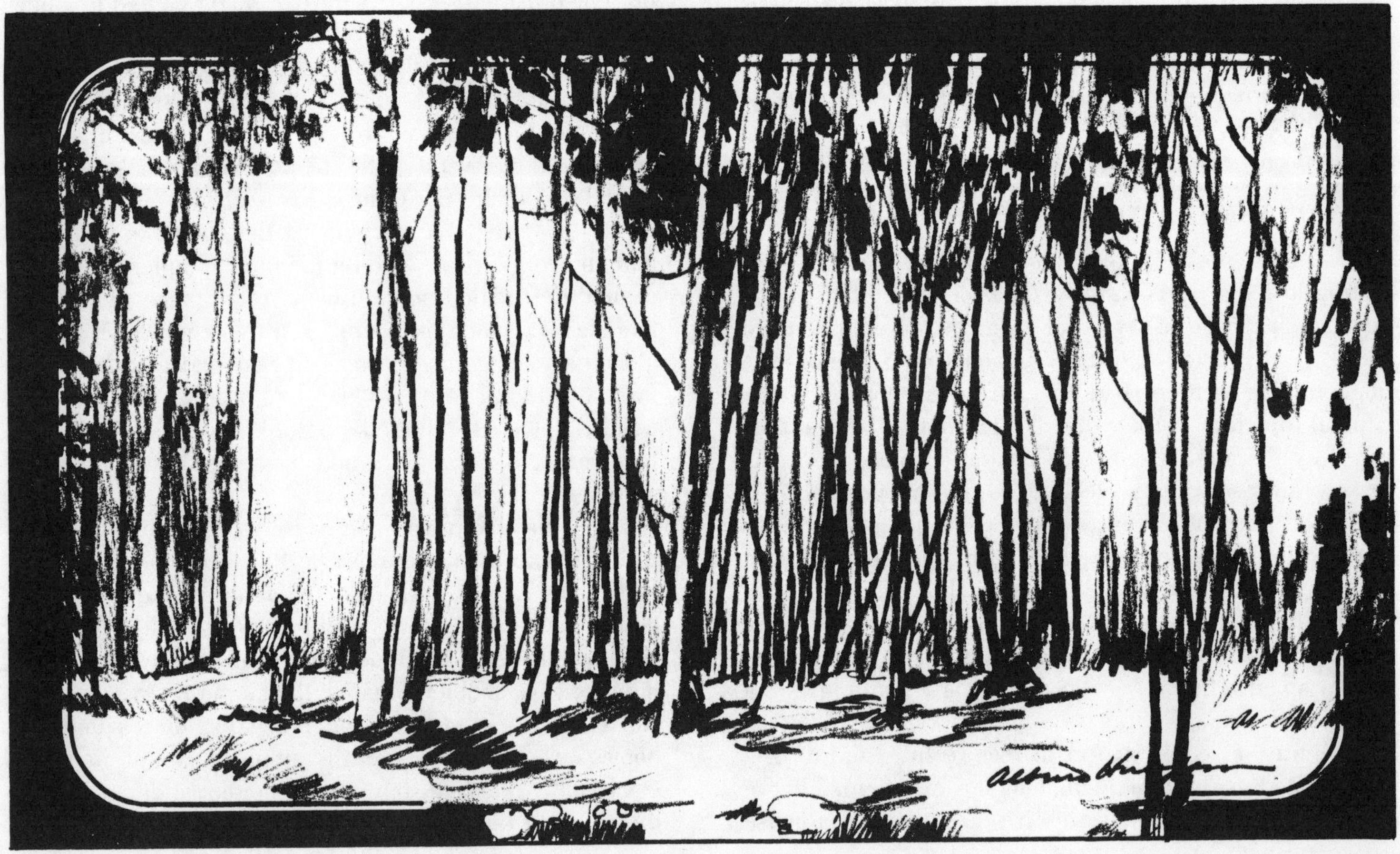

learned that it was the custom for an itinerant, if he did not have a map, to prepare one, not only for himself, but also for his successor.[11] But, as maps remained rare, many travelers faced the possibility of losing their way on the sparsely settled frontier.

One circuit rider, without a map late one afternoon came to an intersection of three trails near the top of a mountain. Exploring one of the trails, he decided it was headed in the wrong direction and he returned to the intersection with the intention of trying one or both of the others. Darkness, however, prevented him from doing so. He put on his bearskin overcoat and lay on the ground to await dawn. The incessant scream of wildcats, however, made sleep impossible. At daybreak, the sound of roosters crowing in a distant valley was audible and the minister mounted his horse and rode in that general direction.

Eventually he arrived at a cabin where a family received him cordially and expressed a desire to hear him preach. When he agreed, messages were sent to residents of the valley inviting them to attend. By nightfall a congregation was assembled at the cabin. Everyone sat on the floor. At the conclusion of the sermon, the preacher was asked about his home and other personal matters. Having finally satisfied the curiosity of the people, the exhausted minister lay on a bed and went to sleep.

Late in the night, he was awakened by a terrific rainstorm. Knowing his horse was without shelter, he arose to care for him. He felt his way to the door through a mass of humanity. The entire congregation was asleep on the floor. The next morning the visitors began leaving for their homes, and the itinerant preacher resumed his journey, always realizing the possibility of getting lost.[12]

Many travelers did lose their way. While three men were driving a flock of sixteen sheep to market over a dim road in dense woods in Indiana, one left to stalk a deer. Although he was gone for only a few minutes in his unsuccessful pursuit, the other drovers allowed the sheep to stray from the trail. In their attempt to round up the animals, one became lost and even lost his sense of direction. Though he called to his companions at the top of his voice, he received no response. Walking aimlessly in a daze, he chanced to find the trail by nightfall, which to him was as valuable as a "bar of gold of the same width and length." By following the road, he eventually found his companions, but the sheep had been lost to the mercy of the wolves.[13]

On the Great Plains it was also easy to lose one's sense of direction, even in daytime, and especially in cloudy weather. On such days, when one knew the general direction in which he wished to go, it was well to sight a sod house or a stovepipe and travel toward it. However, it was at night when directions were most commonly confused. Then, when one did not have a trail or road to follow, he generally used the light of a dwelling or a star as his guide.[14]

On one occasion, however, such a star failed to help a man go to his desired destination. Hours before dawn, a plainsman started from his home traveling by wagon for the post office miles away. As was his custom, he used a certain star as his guide. But on this particular morning, his star of hope became changed around; and he continued his journey with the belief that he was going in the right direction. At daybreak he recognized in the distance not the place where the post office was located, but his own home. His horses, with aimless guidance, had meandered on the prairie until they made their way back home.[15]

Some people became so completely turned around that they not only lost all sense of direction but were even deranged with fear. One evening, J. Hathaway, a plainsman, visited a neighboring family, the Babcocks, who lived about a mile from his house. Within a short time, Hathaway left for home, but soon returned to the Babcock dwelling, where, without recognizing the house, he asked for directions. Babcock, astounded, replied, "Why, what's the matter with you, Mr. Hathaway? It was only fifteen minutes since you left here!" The confused neighbor replied, "You are mistaken. I was never here in my life." Realizing that Hathaway had become lost in the dark and was afraid, Babcock conducted him home.[16]

According to Richard Dodge, getting lost on the Plains was an awesome sensation. He told of a case where two lost hunters once decided their compasses must be wrong, or locally attracted. They quarreled with each other and each went his own way. One of them by accident returned to camp. The other became hopelessly lost and had to be found and brought back. On another occasion, Dodge related that a soldier became lost while walking back to a military post from a small village in Texas. When a search party found him on the second or third day, he was almost naked in a little thicket. The party subdued the soldier after a wild chase, but only after he had climbed a tree. Struggling, striking, and biting like a wild animal, he was taken back to camp and carefully attended for more than a month; but in Dodge's opinion, he never fully recovered from the shock, although he was an excellent man and possessed unusual intelligence.

Dodge himself became lost one day while hunting with the surgeon of his military post. The two rode into a heavy fog, which obscured all landmarks. Finding they had left their compasses at the post, the doctor became so frightened that he had to keep riding. To calm his companion, Dodge explained that they were in a triangle formed by two streams and a road, which would make it possible for them to return to camp as soon as they could see the sun. This explanation had no effect on the doctor. He continued to ride. Believing his horse would lead them out, he gave him his head. To save his friend from himself, Dodge followed until they came to fresh horse tracks. Knowing that hostile Indians were in the area, Dodge dismounted to examine the tracks and found that they were made by their own horses, indicating that the horses had been wandering aimlessly in a circle.

Since the day was drawing to a close, the surgeon reluctantly agreed to make camp. The men were uncomfortable, having had neither food nor water the entire day. By morning the doctor was virtually insane with fear. He should have known there was no safe way out as fog still enveloped everything, but ride the doctor must, and Dodge followed.

Later in the day, Dodge killed and partly skinned a

fine buck. The doctor ate big chucks, warm and raw. Taking large slabs of meat with them, the hunters continued to ride at random through the fog. About three o'clock in the afternoon they found a water hole, made camp, and cooked some of the venison. By dark, Dodge was asleep.

The next morning around three o'clock the doctor, with unrestrained joy, awakened Dodge and showed him the glittering stars. The fog had lifted and the doctor could no longer be restrained. By noon the lost hunters rode back to the military post, having covered about twenty-five miles through glades of chaparral thickets. The doctor fortunately recovered his sanity.[17]

Even Indians sometimes became lost on the Great Plains, as is exemplified in the following incident. After dark on a Sunday evening, a group of western Nebraska settlers, having killed all the game they could haul home, heard unnatural noises. Knowing there were not only hostile Indians on the Plains, but also numerous herds of buffaloes, the hunters had reason for fear. Their apprehension became more intense when, within a few minutes, a band of yelping, howling Indians came toward them. When one of the hunters asked the Indians what they wanted, he was told that they had lost the direction to their wigwams. The ungodly noises were their method of making this fact known to their tribe.[18]

## CAMPING ON THE FRONTIER

Scarcity of dwellings and the absence of inns forced many travelers to camp beside trails rather than continue their journey over unfamiliar terrain. In December 1799, three lawyers—St. Claire, Burnett, and Morrison—set out on horseback from Cincinnati, Ohio, to Vincennes, Indiana. At the end of the first day's ride over snow and ice, they procured a "brand of fire" from friendly Indians to make their campfire. After eating supper, each man wrapped himself in a blanket and lay down on a spot cleared of ice and snow. But, they were uncomfortably cold throughout the night and slept little. At the end of the second day's journey, they made camp in a "valley of fallen timber" which provided a good supply of dry wood for their fire. This enabled them to get more sleep than the night before. On the third night, the lawyers slept in a deserted log cabin after ejecting a wildcat from it. The following day they went on to Vincennes.

Within a week, the lawyers bought supplies and started for Louisville, Kentucky. The weather was not bad the first day. On the second, while riding through a snowstorm, they stopped at noon and dined sumptuously on frozen chicken, biscuits, and some old peach brandy. Upon reaching Blue River, they selected a campsite in the woods, though the snow was from six to eight inches deep. Here they scraped a spot large enough for their camp. The next morning, they proceeded to Louisville, arriving on Christmas Eve.[19]

Itinerant ministers left the most vivid descriptions of camping along trails. Two mounted ministers, finding it impossible to continue their course through a deep, dark woods, decided to make camp. Having tied and fed their horses, they started a fire and constructed a small wigwam of tree branches. They then offered a prayer, ate the food they had brought with them, drank water from a nearby stream, and went to bed. About three hours later, one of the preachers awoke and found his companion shivering over the dying fire. After rebuilding it, the campers spent the rest of the night in conversation. With the approach of dawn, the men proceeded on their way, arriving at a house in the afternoon, hungry, thirsty, and exhausted. After eating supper, the travelers went to bed—thankful they were not in their uncomfortable wigwam.[20]

On another occasion, while riding in a buggy drawn by two horses across an open prairie between Ft. Scott and the Missouri River, two other ministers despaired of finding a dwelling and stopped for rest at midnight. They were chilled by a cold and fierce wind, and they kindled a fire from wood brought with them. They spread a buffalo skin under the carriage for a bed. Around the skin they arranged their luggage for protection against the wind. The next morning they saw only a short distance away a grove of trees which would have given much better protection against the weather.[21]

Another minister, Joseph Piggot, became chilled while riding his horse through a snowcovered forest of stunted and gnarled trees and decided to stop for the night. Clearing a spot in the snow, he started a fire. But, because of the intense cold he could not sleep; the part of his body away from the heat nearly froze. At daybreak he began walking, leading his horse until he came to a squatter's cabin where he found warm shelter.

Learning of Piggot's experience, still another minister, John Mason Peck, was amazed—not because of Piggot's discomfort but because of his inability to make a satisfactory adjustment to sleeping out in extremely cold weather. Peck maintained that camp life by the side of the road could be made bearable by using a little common sense. The traveler should select a good place, preferably beside a giant tree in some hollow or ravine for protection against the wind. Then he should arrange his bed so that his head and shoulders were near the tree trunk and his feet toward the fire. If one kept his feet warm, his whole body would be warm, according to Peck. It was foolish to lie on the cold, bare ground, because a bed could easily be made of grass, leaves, or small brush. To Peck, eating was not so important; he believed that any man, particularly a minister of the gospel on the frontier, who could not go without food for twenty-four hours should be put in the kind care of friends. When available, a piece of jerked venison or a bit of pone and water made a good supper, provided one told oneself so. Peck believed that a traveling companion made travel easier, but whether alone or not, an itinerant could wrap himself in a blanket, use a saddle for a pillow, ask the Lord for protection, and then get the sleep of the innocent under the guiding hand of Divine Providence.[22]

Knowing they would not pass a dwelling where they could get food, some itinerants carried with them small amounts of food, such as parched corn and sugar. Others relied almost wholly on food they could forage along the way. Once when several ministers stopped to make camp, one of them, Elnathan Gavitt, reached into his saddle bags

71

for a pound of parched corn and a cake of maple sugar which he proposed to divide with his colleagues. Declining his offer, the other ministers went to search for roots or something else to eat. They soon returned, not with roots, but with turtle eggs found on the banks of a stream. The eggs were roasted and eaten, but not by Gavitt, since many of them were about to hatch. Later however, after a few years on the frontier, he ate turtle and snake eggs, fertile and infertile, as the Indians did.[23]

## WEATHER CONDITIONS

Unfavorable weather was a deterrent to travel. In northern frontier regions, it was usually dangerous to start even a short trip in winter because of the possibility of a rapid drop in temperature. One such sudden change occurred in Illinois on the morning of 20 December 1836. While rain was turning the snow covered ground into slush and mud, a "cracking, roaring wind" started blowing from the north and caused the temperature to drop forty degrees within a few minutes. Running water was quickly frozen into ice. Even the feet and wings of chickens and geese froze into the slush. On this particular morning, a few men were rounding up hogs. When the temperature began to drop, the animals crowded into a mass to escape the cold. The hogs near the center smothered to death and those on the outside froze. The drovers themselves were nearly dead when they arrived at a nearby dwelling.[24]

Many other travelers had close calls due to quickly changing weather.[25] A frontier doctor returning to his home realized the mud and slush on his overcoat had frozen within a few minutes and that he himself was becoming unbearably cold. He stopped at the first house on his way to warm, after which he mounted his horse and started in a gallop toward home, miles away. Within sight of his house, the horse dropped dead. The doctor then began walking home as fast as possible, but when he arrived, he had to be assisted into the house.[26]

Another horseman, going from Sugar Creek to Springfield, Illinois, was also caught in a "sudden change." As the temperature dipped lower, the rain dripping from his reins was changed almost instantly into jingling icicles. When he arrived at his destination, he could not dismount. He was frozen securely to his saddle, his overcoat holding him as firmly as though it had been made of sheet iron. Unable to release himself, he called for help, but those who came to his assistance discovered that they could not separate man from saddle. Seeing that the rider was fast freezing to death, the rescuers took the man frozen to his saddle inside to let the warm air release him.[27]

Another man was not as fortunate. Before he arrived at a place to warm, he evidently fell from his horse and froze to death. When found, his body was so stiff that it was buried in his traveling clothes, without even wrapping a sheet around it. Some time after the burial, his wife realized her husband must have had a considerable amount of money on him. His body was disinterred, and ten dollars and twenty-five cents were taken from his pockets.[28]

Heavy snows also made travel extremely hazardous. In frontier Illinois, several men were returning home with

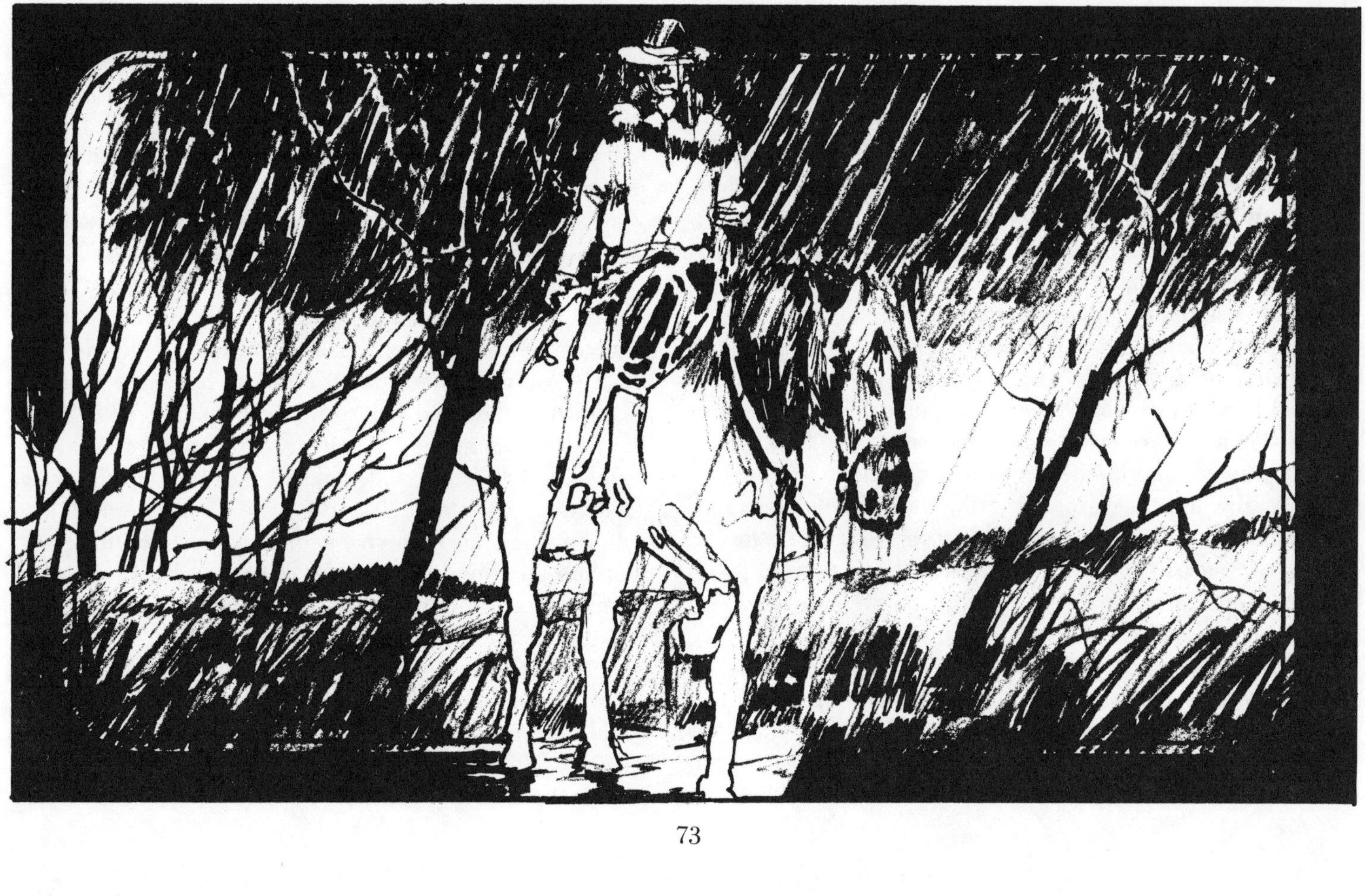

game one day in a steer-drawn wagon when snow began falling "as if thrown from a scoop-shovel." Unable to see or determine directions, the men unhitched the steers, caught hold of their tails, and trusted the homing instinct of the animals to guide them to safety. During this same storm, others who were caught in it were not as fortunate as the hunters. Some were found in drifts weeks later, their flesh eaten away by famished wolves. Others were not found until the late spring thaw uncovered their bodies.[29]

Cyrus R. Rice, a young minister, wrote of his experiences in a terrible December snowstorm in western Kansas. While visiting in a log cabin with a family named Thomas, plans were made to hold religious services that night and the next day. The young minister had begun to work on his sermons before the fire, when suddenly a gust of wind slammed against the cabin, ripping out many of the twisted rolls of grass which had been wedged into crevices between the logs. The temperature fell rapidly.

Soon, it was snowing hard, and snow was blowing through the roof and the openings between the logs of the walls. As the snow began to cover the floor and the beds, Mrs. Thomas cried and reproached her husband for moving to Kansas. Thomas then suggested that they go to bed to keep warm. In a little while all were in bed, covering both head and ears against the cold.

During the night, as the temperature dropped lower and lower, the snow continued to fall. By morning, it had covered the beds and floor to a depth of three inches. While Thomas piled wood on the fire, his wife cried as she raked the snow into large mounds in the corners. Within a short time, the husband, son, and preacher went outside to shovel snow away from the house, where in some places it had drifted nearly to the eaves, and to clear a path to the haystacks to give the horses feed. Then at one o'clock, the family and guest ate their breakfast, dinner, and supper. That night again the family and minister went to bed early. It was a better night for rest, as the wind did not blow as hard, and less snow blew into the cabin. The next morning snow was still falling from leaden skies. Mrs. Thomas managed to do her work without weeping while the men performed the necessary tasks of shoveling snow, getting wood, and caring for the horses. By noon, the snow had stopped falling, but the weather remained bitterly cold.

While sitting by the fire with the Thomas family during the afternoon and evening, Mr. Rice and Mr. Thomas concluded that the cold prairies would never be thickly populated and that it would be better for everyone to return to their old homes in the East. Later the young minister began singing "Home Sweet Home," causing the hostess to cry again and demand that he stop the song. That night, Christmas Eve, Rice and Thomas went to bed with a prayer but no merry gathering, no Christmas tree, no plum pudding, and no hope of the neighboring settlers coming to hear the young minister preach until the weather improved.[30]

A blizzard was even worse on a traveler than heavy snow. During a blizzard, snow lashed by a strong wind could become as fine as flour. So fine were some powdery particles that they penetrated the clothing as well as settlers' houses. Icy fragments also got into the eyes and nostrils, making it difficult to see and breathe.[31] It was easy to lose one's way in a blizzard, and even walking between a house and barn sometimes resulted in death.

Lack of water was another deterrent to the traveler. In areas where the annual rainfall was from ten to twenty inches or less, availability of water had to be taken into account before starting a journey. In an unusually dry season, a traveler might go hundreds of miles without finding water. Indians, angered by white intruders, sometimes added to the problem by inducing settlers to go in a direction where they would almost certainly die of thirst.[32]

Scarcity of water was usually accompanied by intense heat, at least during the day. Andy Adams, a drover, tells of the effects of intense heat and lack of water on a herd of cows along a western trail. If the morning had been cloudy, he said, the drive might have continued normally for several more hours or even until the next day. But, the cattle had not had water for more than three days and became feverish and ungovernable. The drovers threw ropes in the faces of the lead cows and fired their guns so close to them as to singe their hair. Defiantly, the cattle passed completely out of control. When wild steers walked against the drovers' horses, the cowboys realized a fact that chilled the marrow in their bones; the herd was going blind from lack of water.[33]

Even in humid areas, lack of water was often a problem to man and livestock during a dry season.[34] A group of travelers encountered this problem while making a journey in Indiana on a warm afternoon. After looking in vain on both sides of the road for a spring or stream, they continued on their way and camped that night without water. It was not until the next day that they came to a stream.[35]

A traveler on horseback usually swam the animal across a swollen stream. In the fall of 1810, Judge Burnett was forced to swim his horse frequently due to heavy rains, while returning from General Court at Marietta, Ohio. When he reached White Oak Creek, the stream was unusually high and the bottom of his side was entirely flooded. After taking valuable papers from his saddlebag and putting them in his coat pocket, he waded his horse through the flooded bottom to the edge of the stream. Here he stopped to calculate the velocity of the current so he could determine the angle at which he should swim his horse to reach the road on the opposite bank. The horse was a good swimmer and easily carried the rider across the dangerous stream. About two miles farther on, the judge's horse swam another creek, and later in the day he crossed the east fork of the Miami River opposite Williamsburg in the same manner. Judge Burnett had chosen his valuable horse well. As did most prospective horse buyers, he invariably asked, "Is he a good swimmer?"[36]

Not all horsemen used the same technique in crossing a stream. Once Peter Cartwright, a renowned Methodist circuit rider, rode to a creek too deep to ford. He walked a log across it, taking his "traveling fixtures" with him. After undressing, he walked back across the stream, mounted his horse, and swam him over. When Cartwright had dressed himself, he knelt in prayer and offered sincere thanks to God for his providential care.[37] When Reverend

Elnathan Gavitt came to a deep creek, he too took off his clothes and tied them and the saddlebags to the pommel of the saddle. Then, after turning his horse into the water, the preacher took hold of his tail and let his steed pull him safely to the opposite bank. Gavitt said he had followed this procedure as many as three times a day.[38]

There were other means of crossing streams when there were no bridges or ferries. A group of men living about five miles from the village of Shelbyville, Minnesota, sometimes went to the post office to hear the postmaster read the news from a St. Paul newspaper. One such day they arrived at Blue Ear River, adjacent to the town, and saw that the stream was not only swollen to the top of its banks, but was also freezing. To their disappointment, the canoe which was used to traverse the stream, was on the opposite bank. To determine who would swim across and retrieve it, they drew lots. The unfortunate man who swam the icy river to fetch the canoe complained he "had chills ever afterwards."[39]

## INDIAN ATROCITIES

Fear of hostile Indians also ranked high as a deterrent to frontier travel. In the vicinity of Pittsburgh, Pennsylvania, during the period between the French and Indian War and the close of the American Revolution, Indians were a constant threat to the traveler. Every farm house was a fortress. Some homes still standing in that area in the 1790s were, according to Francis Baily, a British traveler, a "monument of usurpation on the one hand and of predatory warfare on the other." Baily also reported tragic stories of settlers being killed within a few yards of their homes while they followed the plow or tended their cattle. Indians would sometimes lie in wait for weeks for an opportunity to strike. There were few early settlers in the area who did not feel the effects of Indian revenge in some form. In one family, all members were killed and scalped. In another, a father and son were found dead, their bodies mutilated beyond recognition. In still another, the children were taken into captivity.[40]

Near the close of the American Revolution, a Georgia mother testified in court that a party of Indians forced their way into her home and took what articles they wanted. They then seized her baby and dashed it to death against a stump in the yard. A few years later in the upper part of the state, a man named Bridges started on a hunt. His granddaughter began crying to go with him. To pacify her, the grandfather picked up the child and walked toward a mulberry tree a short distance from the house. Before he reached the tree, Indians, hidden in a nearby wheat field, shot him dead. Taking the child just beyond the range of gunfire from the house, but within view of those inside, the Indians disrobed her, opened her chest with a knife, removed her heart, and threw it toward the fear-stricken parents and relatives.[41]

In his *Journal*, Francis Asbury told of a group of Indians who broke into the home of a family named Scott. As the startled father jumped out of bed, several Indians fired at him. Mortally wounded, he staggered from the house and was promptly killed. The Indians murdered and scalped the children before their mother's eyes. They then plundered the house and took Mrs. Scott as prisoner to their campfire where they shouted and danced for the remainder of the night. For several days, the murderers walked toward their village with their prisoner. Each day, Mrs. Scott was forced to walk behind an Indian who carried on his back the scalps of her dead children.[42]

During the Black Hawk War, Indians forced their way into a dwelling where three families were assembled. Some of the whites were shot, others gored with spears, and the remainder tomahawked. All victims were scalped and their bodies mutilated. Gleefully, the murderers told of how the women, left tied up by their heels, "squeaked like geese" as the spears penetrated their bodies.[43]

Indians used ingenious methods of inflicting pain upon their white or Indian captives. In staging a raid into Mexico, a party of Comanches attacked a large but poorly defended ranch house and soon captured the women and children. The outnumbered men fought bravely, but all were soon killed except a giant man who defended himself with an ax. He was eventually subdued and bound hand and foot. After a ruthless violation of the women, the Comanches locked the children in a room and set fire to the building. With the giant Mexican their only prisoner, the Indians set out for an area in Texas known as the Staked Plain. Along the way they treated the Mexican well and told him that because of his bravery they were going to adopt him into their tribe as a great chief. When they arrived at a water hole on the table land of the Staked Plain, they instructed the Mexican to dig a hole in the ground three feet in diameter and five feet deep while they engaged in a religious ceremony. After the Mexican dug the hole, the Indians tied his feet together, wrapped a rope around his legs and body, and attached it to his neck, while binding his arms firmly to his side. Next, they stood him upright in the hole like a post and packed dirt around him so that only his head was above ground. They then scalped him and cut off his eyelids, nose, ears, and lips. After dancing around their prisoner and taunting him, the Comanches left, believing he would live at least eight days. The hot sun blazing down on his scalped head and defenseless eyes would drive him mad during the day and flies would fill his wounds with maggots. The cool air of the night would revive him for another day of torture.[44]

Other Indians were as adept in inflicting suffering upon their captives as the Comanche. A party of Tonkaway Indians captured two raiding Comanches in their territory in southwest Texas. One Comanche warrior was wounded. While the Tonkaways were sitting around their campfire that night, one of them went to the wounded man and cut a slice of flesh from his thigh and placed it on the coals to broil. One after another of the Tonkaways followed suit. When an artery or large vein was cut, it was seared with a firebrand to stop the flow of blood. Each Indian, while eating, talked to the Comanche, complimenting him on the tenderness of his flesh. When nearly all the flesh of his thighs and loins was consumed, the Comanche began a death song. His life and feast ended together. The other captive managed to escape while the Tonkaways slept.

There were other atrocities commonly inflicted by Indians on their captives. Having a surprisingly accurate

78

knowledge of anatomy, Indians knew how much pain the human body could endure without causing death. Corpses on their backs, arms and legs spread out and tied to bushes, trees, or stakes indicated the victims had died from starvation, thirst, rays of the sun, the sting of a thousand ants, or from other causes. Bodies of Indian victims displayed dislocations, artistic dissections, and split and broken toes and fingers. These victims had endured all imaginable horror, pain and fear.[45]

When Colonel William Crawford, a friend of George Washington, was captured, Indian women "pelted him with live coals, [and] jabbed him with burning poles. . . ." After a warrior had torn Crawford's scalp off with his teeth, the women poured live coals onto his exposed skull while he was still alive.[46] Indian women sometimes brought female captives into camp, staked them down, and invited all the men, even their sons, husbands, and lovers, to molest them sexually. They watched the sexual orgy with the liveliest of interest.[47]

While traveling on the frontier or while sitting by their firesides, settlers discussed their fear of Indian atrocities. Crying children were often quieted by the mention of a dreaded chieftain's name. Once, when Richard Irving Dodge and a Mexican were hunting, they nearly lost a bear when the Mexican failed to fire his gun. After killing the bear, Dodge reprimanded his companion. The Mexican replied, "I could have killed the bear, but I had only one shot. We may be jumped by Indians at any time. I will never be taken a prisoner, and I always save the last shot for myself."[48]

With so many perils of travel confronting the pioneers, one might wonder why the frontiersmen forged on against such hardships. The fact that they did so is amazing, and reflection on the difficulties they encountered makes a person wonder how they did it. We must remember that pioneers were usually poor, down-trodden, and even outcast members of civilization. With so little going for them in society, they were willing to face loneliness and hardship in their attempt to achieve a better life.

80

# 6

# Odd Ideas

Living apart from organized society and innocent of most formal education, frontiersmen developed many strange beliefs. Illiteracy was common. Experience was the main teacher on the frontier; book learning did not tell how to plow the farm or hunt for food. But the pioneers were curious and wanted answers to questions they could not solve through their experiences. This brought about many odd superstitions and even occasional belief in witchcraft. Many of their ideas appear strange today, but to the pioneer they provided rational and reasonable explanations of day-to-day occurrences.

## ILLITERACY

Frontier life did little to promote literacy. People were poor, there were few educational opportunities available, and there was little incentive to gain an education. Formal education was not a prerequisite for obtaining food, clothes, shelter, and protection against Indians and lawless neighbors, the immediate needs of life. Survival was the most important consideration.

Illiteracy was ever present on the frontier. A majority of the people could not even write their names. Court records of Wilkes County, Georgia, for the period 1777-1783 bear no signatures on five of the sixteen wills recorded, only the makers' marks. Of those who died without a will, the percentage who could not write was even higher.[1] Writing in Illinois in 1831, John Mason Peck reported that an unbelievable number of adults, especially women, could neither read nor write and that most who could read a little had an improper understanding of what they read.[2] A peddler of religious tracts in Arkansas estimated in 1845 that not more than half of the population could read.[3]

Illiteracy was even more prevalent among children of school age. A Presbyterian minister who hoped to establish a common school in a remote area examined fourteen families on a creek and found that only six of forty children were able to read or write.[4] A newcomer to Illinois, Mrs. Christiana Holmes Tillson, noted that many children did not know their ages.

During a song session preceding a sermon, one young lady stood out as a singer of great skill and clarity, and Reverend Hamilton Pierson requested that she lead the congregation in singing a new hymn. She politely refused saying that she did not know the particular song. Reverend Pierson opened his songbook and handed it to her saying, "Here is the hymn with the tune. Perhaps you can sing it." The young lady blushed with embarrassment and cried, "Oh! Sir, I can't read." Pierson was amazed. The many songs the young woman had sung with such consummate ease she had learned by rote. Not far from this church, Pierson remarked to a young lady that he understood that a number of the young women could not read. The young lady replied, "Oh! There are only two ladies that can read." When visiting any church thereafter, Pierson considered it as usual to ask a young lady whether she could read as it was to request a drink of water.[5]

Many people even believed that a minister of the Gospel need not have an education. All that was required of him was convincing evidence that he had been called to preach. Instead of exalting education, settlers and ministers often denounced it as a "species of infidelity . . . toward God, and a sinful exaltation of human wisdom against divine power and spiritual guidance in the ministry." Since many pioneers considered the ability to read a "heresy," many ministers made boisterous assertions of their illiteracy from the pulpit, one even saying that "grammar and dictionary words" were difficult for the people to understand. The preachers wanted to be accepted by their congregations.[6]

Since there were few if any newspapers in the backwoods, it was common for political candidates to circulate handwritten handbills among the electorate extolling their qualifications and exposing the shortcomings of their opponents. One candidate wrote the first person pronoun on his handbill with a small dotted "i." Ridiculed for not knowing better, the politician quickly replied that since his opponent had "used up" all the large "I's," he had no choice but to use the small ones.[7]

Jesse Bozan, a settler in Illinois, had no books except an old and dirty almanac hanging on the wall. He did not want any books; he "did not think it was of any use to be allus readin, didn't think folks was any better off for readin, and books cost a heap and took a power of time." Jesse moderated his statement by saying that it "twant so bad for men to read, for there was a heap of time when they couldn't work out, and could jest set by the fire." In "slack" times a man "mought" read books if he had them. But he felt women had no business reading "away their time, cause they could allus find something to do." Jesse asserted that much trouble had developed in Kentucky because "rich men's gals that had learned to write" wrote letters to their beaux. "Bles your soul, they got matches fixed up before their fathers and mothers knowed a hait about it."[8]

Rank ignorance, like illiteracy, existed everywhere. A mountaineer who was casting his ballot was asked his name by a precinct judge. When the mountaineer answered "Johnson," the judge added "Yes, but what is your other name?" The settler indignantly declared that he had but one name. "Yes, but what is your Christian name?" the judge insisted. The backwoodsman replied, "My Christian name? Why, if you want to know that, why, I am a Baptist." So the Judge recorded the man's name as "Johnson the Baptist."[9]

In Wayne County, Georgia, after the prosecution had clearly proven that a man had stolen a broad-ax, a jury composed of ignorant backwoodsmen brought in a verdict of murder in the first degree. Upon hearing the outrageous verdict, the judge reprimanded the jury and sent it back to further deliberate. The jury returned a second time and informed his honor that it had not changed its opinion. The judge angrily dismissed the jury and declared a mistrial.[10] In this same area, Wilkes County settlers were so isolated from the fighting at the beginning of the American Revolution and so ignorant of the causes of the war that many were indifferent as to its outcome. After the British extended their military operations to Georgia, the people became divided in allegiance—some becoming Whigs, others claimed Tories, though few seemed to have good reasons for their patriotism or lack of it.[11]

Early French settlers in the remote Illinois Territory became so isolated that they lost track of the days of the week. They fixed dates by such events as the time of the great waters, the period of the strawberries and the harvest of maize and potatoes.[12]

Most pioneers were simple, credulous, and unsophisticated. Rarely could they detect falsehood. Unless an idea violated some known principle of their experience or conflicted with some fact of their own observation, they usually accepted all that they were told.[13] Thus, they were easy marks for charlatans, fortune-tellers, and magicians. Between 1820 and 1830 Illinois settlers were plagued by clock peddlers who used ingenious methods to induce families to buy clocks. When a salesman asked a settler whether he wished to buy a clock the answer was usually "No." The huckster would then ask for permission to leave a clock and instruct the family to keep it running until he returned in a week or so. The family, having become accustomed to the ticking of the timepiece, often felt that they could not do without it and bought the clock. Backwoods folk usually lacked money and often gave the salesman a "twenty-five or thirty dollar note," payable in several months. Such a clock was hardly worth five dollars, but they were durable and often kept time for many years.

Clock peddlers rarely returned, but sent someone else to collect. These collection agents pretended to know nothing of any promises or guarantees that had been made, but they rarely failed to collect the amount specified on the note. Clock peddlers became extremely unpopular, and, as most of them were from New England, Illinois settlers developed a strong prejudice against Yankees.[14]

Ignorant and provincial in their thinking, many pioneers refused to accept new ideas, no matter how good. One young man who lived in the Shenandoah Valley returned home from college and told a group of settlers many things he had learned in school. He had learned, for example, that the sun did not go around the earth. An old German settler listened to the student and remarked, "You dink so, pecause de peebles at the college tells you so, but I doesn't dink so, pecause I knows petter and aught to know petter."[15] Another educated man felt that such people lived in a state of mental darkness and had about as much use for a pair of spectacles as a dead man.[16]

## SUPERSTITIONS

When something out of the ordinary occurred, the usually stoical frontiersmen sometimes became quite emotional. For instance, when a series of earthquakes shook the central Mississippi Valley beginning at 2:00 A.M. on 17 December 1811, the pioneers were frightened out of their wits. In one area where the quake was strongly felt, a Baptist minister named Reverend McConica was preaching in a log church. A cry instantly went up that the building was sinking into the ground. Some members of the congregation shouted for joy: "He is coming! He is coming!" Others screamed for mercy. In the mad rush to escape, one man thought he saw a short-cut and tried to go through a large hole between the logs. He became wedged in the crack and had to be pulled out bodily.[17]

This series of quakes lasted intermittently for a period of two years and gave rise to other humorous and pathetic behavior. On a dark night in the heart of the quake zone, a group of mischievous boys began rolling large rocks off a bank in the path of a "large, strong, wicked" man. The sinner thought that a new quake was upon him and he became exceedingly frightened. He cried for mercy and instantly became a staunch Christian.[18] When the earth began to rumble and shake, the settlers sometimes became so afraid that entire families ran helter-skelter, grasping each other in their arms. One terrified mother with five children ran hysterically up to a stranger and begged him to pray for them. For days on end the terrified people ate little and refused to work except to feed their stock. They spent their time visiting from house to house, praying, singing, and exhorting. Their principal topic of conversation was the quakes. During the quaking time, religious meetings were overcrowded and the number of conversions was high. The might of the earthquakes so strongly impressed Jacob Bower that he not only found the Lord, but soon after became an outstanding Baptist minister in Kentucky and Illinois.[19]

The unlettered and unlearned pioneers held many erroneous and superstitious beliefs. They often noted that certain events produced certain results. When the event reoccurred, it was not unusual for one to say, "I'm superstitious, for what happened before is likely to happen again." When a bird lighted on a window sill, some ignorant frontiersmen believed that death would come to the family, because sometime in the past, death had occurred after a bird had lighted in a window.[20] The croaking of a raven, the howling of a dog, and the screeching of an owl were all interpreted to be carriers of disaster. Past misfortunes had been associated with the same noises.[21]

The origin of frontier superstitions is hard to determine. It was believed that underground water was "whimsical, unreliable, run by luck." Oblivious of water tables, they never knew when a good well would go dry. A witch hazel stick was used to point out the best places to dig a well. As potatoes grew underground, they had to be planted in the dark of the moon or they would get nothing but vines. Since beans grow above the ground, they had to be planted on days followed by moonlit nights. If fence posts were not set in the dark of the moon, they would sink into the ground. To skip a row in planting corn would bring bad luck and might cause a death in the family. If one killed the first snake he saw in early spring, he would be able to defeat his enemies that year. Rheumatism could be cured by rubbing skunk grease or red worm oil over the aching parts of the body. To get rid of warts it was essential to steal a dishrag and hide it in a tree stump. Or, one should tie as many knots in a string as he had warts and bury the string under a stone. If a dog crossed a hunter's path, the man should immediately hook his two small fingers together and pull until the dog was out of sight. Failure to do this would bring bad luck. A dog could be made more fierce by feeding him gunpowder. Sighting a white mule at the start of a journey was a signal of bad luck. If a horse breathed in a child's face, it would give the child whooping cough. To carry buckeyes in one's pocket helped ward off diseases.[22]

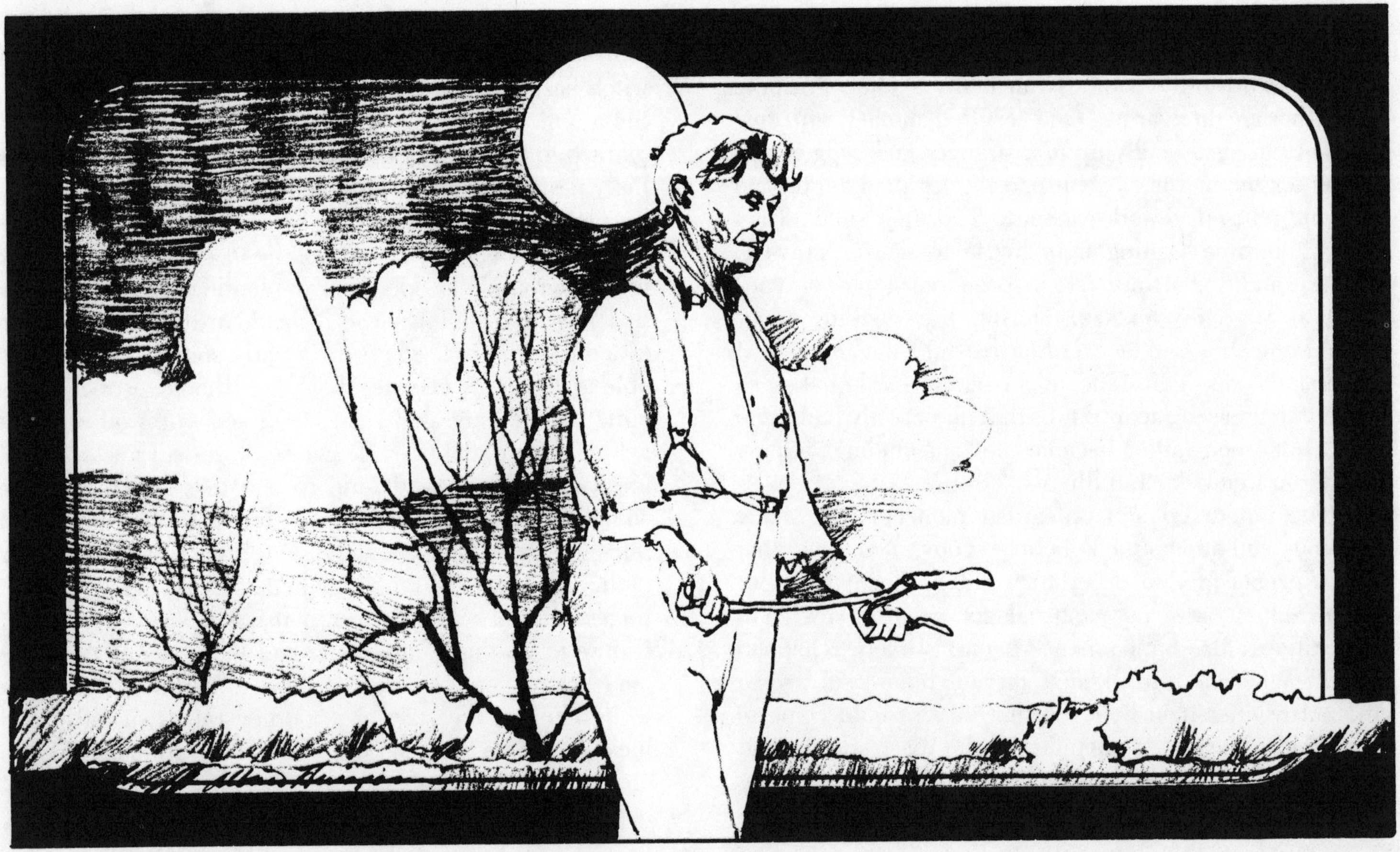

Frontiersmen lived close to nature and were directly influenced by snow and rain, warmth and cold, sunshine and clouds; hence they were ever on the alert for changing weather conditions and developed many superstitious beliefs about weather. Their crops had to have rain and they were convinced that various phenomena could herald rain or other climatic occurrences. Sunshine during a rain signified rain the next day. If hens or birds sang during a rain, there would be fair weather. The crowing of a rooster when he went to roost was a sure sign of rain. The first thunder of early spring awakened all snakes from their long winter slumber. Clear weather would follow if one's chickens got on a fence during a rain and picked themselves. If rain became "heavy, similar to a mist," cold weather could be expected. For a bob-white to "bob" only once indicated rain. Rain moving in from the east signified that it would rain for three days. Rain before seven in the morning meant that the weather would clear before eleven. Lightning in the north prophesied rain within twenty-four hours, but lightning in the south would bring dry weather. Aching corns and rheumatic pains meant a change in weather. A pale, red, setting sun portended a plague, likely smallpox or yellow fever. A crackling back log burning in the fireplace warned of an approaching snowstorm. The approach of a cold winter was indicated by thick corn shucks, low hanging hornets' nests, and busy woodpeckers and squirrels.[23]

Dreams much affected the people. Tom Lincoln once told his son Abe of a vivid dream in which he clearly saw a wayside path leading to a strange house. Sitting by the fireside was a woman with eyes, lips, and face all quite clear. This woman was paring an apple. He knew instantly that she was to be his wife. Night after night the dream reoccurred. One day he went up a path to a house similar to the one he had seen in his dreams, and he found a woman paring an apple before the fire. Her eyes, face and lips were the same, and he later married her. Tom Lincoln's son Abraham also dreamed often. He cherished "sweet" dreams, but his bitter ones haunted him. Some dreams he could not understand, and they caused him to spend much time in trying to analyze them.[24] The mystic and often moody president in his last cabinet meeting "told of dreaming the night before of sailing in a strange ship toward a dark and undefined shore." Lincoln said that he had had this same dream prior to every important battle of the Civil War.[25]

## WITCHCRAFT

Witchcraft was present and real. Frontiersmen maintained that a witch was usually a woman who had given her soul to the Devil in exchange for supernatural power. Witches were usually detected by their "Devil's pinches," by their ability to weep but three tears (all out of the left eye), and by having "predilection for black cats and broomsticks!" They were largely confined to the "most ignorant, decrepit, and ugly old women . . . , who had scarce more brains than the broomsticks they rode." Other witches might be beautiful women who enjoyed having sex relations with the Devil. Some of these witches drained nourishment from the breasts of recent mothers and left the newborn to starve.[26]

In early Massachusetts, Reverend Cotton Mather presented "undeniable" evidence of the misdeeds of witches in the colony. Another New Englander vowed there were "witches too many—bottle-bellied witches," who produced strange aspirations. Many people living near the sea were convinced that a strange shallop handled by a single woman witch lay just off the coast. There was also another witch ship anchored in a cove to the eastward. A great red horse was seen standing near the mast. This ship vanished suddenly, manned as it was by a woman witch with strange supernatural powers.[27]

Fighting against the evil influences of a witch was a serious problem. If neither "exhortation, sound reason, nor friendly entreaty" had an effect on a hardened witch, the pious people of New England resorted to more drastic measures. Confessions were wrung from the accused through the use of torture, whereupon she was burned at the stake to purify her soul of her heinous crimes. Some witches were stubborn to the end and protested their innocence until dead. Pious observers believed such characters were so possessed of the Devil that they should have lived longer to suffer even greater pain.[28]

Witchcraft beliefs were quite common in the western parts of Virginia and Pennsylvania during the period 1763-1783, according to Joseph Doddridge. Witches had the power of inflicting "strange and incurable diseases on people, particularly children. They could destroy cattle by shooting them with hair balls. They could even change men into horses," after which they were ridden at full speed to a witches' frolic.[29]

Unaccountable diseases, particularly those of children, were attributed to witches. In the home of a sick child, a poor old woman was sometimes both surprised and heartbroken when she was refused requests that had formerly been granted without hesitation. The family believed the aged woman was a witch.[30]

Various contrivances were used to cure a bewitched child. One device was to draw a picture of the suspected witch on a stump or board and then shoot the image with a bullet containing a bit of silver. It was believed that the silver would inflict mortal pain on the part of the witch corresponding with the part of the portrait struck by the bullet.

In writing about witchcraft in the western part of New York, a frontier traveler said that people "entertained strange notions respecting supernatural agencies." He thought solitude strengthened the mind of the well-informed but caused the ignorant to be timid and superstitious. Backwoodsmen believed that witches were the source of most diseases of both men and animals. A traveler once stopped at a cabin near Lake Ontario where a man was suffering a convulsive fit. Two young women were standing near the bed talking. One woman said that if a garment of the victim were removed and thrown into the fire, the man would recover immediately. The other young woman agreed, but neither of them made any attempt to execute the prescription because they feared that they would become bewitched themselves. The traveler also asserted that most of the men in the area believed that if one shot an owl (a witch's confederate), the bore of the rifle would become so crooked that the gun would never shoot true again.[31]

G. W. Featherstonhaugh wrote that, with few exceptions, all settlers of the Shenandoah Valley believed in witchcraft. The people there became afraid to take their eggs and other farm produce to market because a strange evil hung in the air. A "strange dog, with a wild look, had been hunting in the area for many days and had driven some cattle into the Shenandoah." The dog was of course bewitched. One hunter swore that he had met the Devil, who had two eyes of flaming fire, each larger than a man's head. As long as these unholy spirits were around, the settlers would not venture far from their cabins.[32]

Men who were supposedly possessed of supernatural powers were regarded by frontiersmen as wizards who performed miracles for the good of mankind. Their primary function was to counteract the "malevolent influence of witches." Joseph Doddridge was acquainted with several witch masters who made a profession of curing diseases caused by witches. He also knew a number of respectable physicians who were wizards as well as medical practitioners.[33]

## CURIOSITY

The pioneer's mind was a duality, the two parts in a state of war against itself. On one hand, pioneers were illiterate and had little desire to learn to read; on the other, they had an abiding curiosity to hear the news not only of their narrow environment but also of the world beyond. To glean local news as well as to receive emotional stimuli they attended wakes, funerals, marriages, hangings, workings, and religious meetings. Settlers were naturally curious and questioned their neighbors carefully. Their inquiries were direct and often very personal. Strangers traveling through their territory brought news of areas where they had once lived in and from exotic lands of which they had never before heard.

New Englanders living far from a town were extremely inquisitive. While Lord Napier was visiting a local inn, a number of people flocked to see him. They imagined that, being a "lord", he must be something more than a man. Most of the people stood outside and peeped through the front window. The curious said: "I wonder which is the Lord." Four women who were intimate friends of the landlord entered the common room and one of them asked, "I hear you have got a Lord among you; pray now which may he be?" Napier, who was covered with mud and wet from a sudden rainsquall, was amused and whispered something to another Englishman in the room. This English gentleman arose and pointed to his Lordship; in a manner and voice of the Herald at Arms, he not only introduced Napier as Lord but listed all of his other titles. When he had finished, one of the women lifted her hands and eyes and exclaimed, "Well, for my part, if that be a Lord, I never desire to see any other Lord but the Lord Jehovah." She immediately left the inn in disgust.[34]

Washington Irving asserted that whole gangs of Connecticut pioneers sometimes penetrated New Netherland settlements and threw entire villages into consternation by their inquisitiveness. Dutch burgers were bombarded with questions.[35] In other colonies when a visiting stranger stopped at an isolated public house he was often given a glass of whiskey and asked a "thousand questions: Where do you come from? Where are you going? What is your name? Where do you live? What profession? Were there any fevers in the country you came through?" These questions became tedious when repeated in each new area. The fusillade of questions could easily be shortened, the traveler soon learned, if he would give a speech in which he told everything he knew immediately. This would gratify the curiosity of the frontiersmen and the visitor would be left in peace.[36]

In his *Travels Through North America*, Isaac Weld, an Englishman, found the curiosity of all westerners boundless. He traveled on solitary roads and was frequently subjected to many imprudent questions. Without any social graces the settlers demanded to know his name, where he was from, where he was going and whether he were acquainted with any "news." Weld was appalled with the crude lack of manners. Once, after parrying a settler's questions for several minutes, he prepared to resume his journey. The inquisitive settler yelled, "Stop, Mister! Why, I guess you be come from the new state." Told he was not, the curious man speculated, "Why, then I guess as you be coming Kentuc." After the traveler evaded several more questions, the backwoodsman said, "Aye, aye, I see, Mister, you be not one of us." Weld, an English aristocrat, had little sympathy with frontier curiosity.[37]

Strangers who refused to satisfactorily answer all questions were usually regarded with suspicion. Reverend Alfred Brunson and his preacher friend were bone-weary from their travels and immediately went to bed in a cabin without answering the usual questions of the family and several guests. Soon the other men began surmising as to who the strangers were and what they were doing in the area. One thought that they were land speculators and should have been sent to the open prairie to spend the night. Such men claimed the best lands and compelled poor people to give double prices for a home or move farther into the wilderness. Another man believed the ministers were either doctors or merchants, seeking a good location for their trade. A third concluded correctly that the men were preachers. He based his opinion on their retired and subdued manners. By this time the sleepless ministers began to feel sorry for the curious men and identified themselves. Brunson explained that he and his friend usually announced their profession and prayed and preached at each home, but the night before they had "fallen among thieves" and were robbed. Brunson learned that there were Baptists, Methodists, and Campbellites in the room and that all of them would be glad to hear a sermon.[38]

George Gilmer, a recruiting officer, reports in his *Sketches of Some of the First Settlers of Upper Georgia* that while he was addressing a group of settlers on the advantages of enlisting in the army he became the object of frontier curiosity. The people formed a circle around him and "gazed at him as if he were a bear or an elephant." When they found that he talked as other men did, they came even closer—so close that some of them began to finger his sword and epaulets. A few had the audacity to feel his long whiskers. Gilmer says that he was forced to summon all his self-command to bear up under such indignities.[39]

Traveling through Texas in 1836, A. A. Parker said he would wager that the settlers were the most inquisitive of all people. He grew weary from answering so many questions. While passing a house near a road, the homeowner ran out and asked Parker where he was from. Instead of answering, Parker asked a question himself. The Texan said that, as he was from Kentucky, he thought Parker might be from the same state. Parker said that he was not, but he refused to say where he was from. The settler seemed frustrated when Parker rode off without imparting any information.[40]

The Tillson family living in frontier Illinois found their neighbors quite curious and inquisitive. A neighbor named Mrs. Jesse Ruzan especially enjoyed a daily visit with the Tillsons. One day the hostess offered her a piece of "Yankee Pie," which startled Mrs. Ruzan. The visitor quickly said, "I didn't think you would say the like of that. I allus knowed youens were all Yankees, but Billy said don't let on that we know it kase it'll just make them mad." Mrs. Tillson said that she was proud to be called a Yankee and that she wanted everyone to know it. Again, the neighbor looked incredulous and said, "Billy and I have always found you jess so, but some folks say they have been here when Yankees come in, and you talk a heap of things that you don't say to us." The hostess asked whether the neighbors said she ever talked against anyone. "No, not that," replied Mrs. Ruzan, "but you use a heap of words to Yankees that you don't when you talk to us. They say, too, you put a lot of nasty truck in your bread. It is what you keep in a bottle, purlass, I believe is the name, and they say it is full of dead flies and bugs and cricket legs." Mrs. Tillson, to reassure her neighbor, showed the woman a small bottle of dissolved pearl ash, which was clear and pure. Mrs. Ruzan could hardly believe her eyes.[41]

The Tillsons were bothered in other ways by their curious neighbors. On Sunday Mrs. Tillson preferred a quiet day at home, but the neighbors would not have it that way. By the time breakfast was over and the morning work disposed of, there was usually a tremendous knocking at the door, "accompanied by a sonorous demand of 'who keeps the house?' or 'housekeepers within?'" One Sunday morning when Mrs. Tillson opened the door, a backwoodsman with a baby on his arms walked in followed by his wife carrying a younger baby. The guests let it be known that they had come for a day's visit to become better acquainted.

Every Sunday, during the Tillsons' first months in Illinois, they were forced to entertain their neighbors. The curious came to inspect the house and its fixtures. They asked such questions as, "What's this 'ere fixin?" After opening the china closet, they wanted to know whether the Tillsons had any plates to sell. Informed there were none, they expressed amazement in seeing so many dishes: "Never seed so many together, reckon they cost a heap." Just before the noon meal was served to a visiting family, the father said to his older, hungry child: "Hush up, honey, and be good. See thar, see thar, Aunt Tillson is gwin to have dinner right sure. Reckon she'll have some sweetened bread, cake and all them pretty dishes!"

When their appetites were satisfied and after taking their final smoke, the guests prepared to leave. On departing, they always invited the Tillsons to spend a Sunday with them. Mrs. Tillson gradually stopped the

Sabbath visitors from coming by thanking them for their invitation and saying that it was her practice not to visit on Sunday but only on weekdays. With only one exception, none repeated a Sunday visit to the Tillson home. Mrs. Tillson believed that although some of the neighbors remained jealous and suspicious, none were offended by her refusal to visit on Sunday.[42]

Many travelers were impatient with the curiosity of the frontiersmen. Margaret Van Horn Dwight, an American who toured many parts of the thinly settled areas, said it was nobody's business where she was going, yet everybody—even tool takers and children—asked impertinent questions.[43] In an attempt to extract every possible bit of information from a traveler, Bishop Whipple said, the settlers asked many questions "about matters and things of no consequence to them. . . ."[44] Even the renowned Asbury, while in Georgia, was nonplussed over the inordinate curiosity aroused by his wig. "Why did he wear it? How much did it cost?" The wig was as exotic to the settlers as a giant animal from Africa or India would have been.[45] Reverend Cyrus R. Rice stopped in a small Kansas village to have his boots repaired. He was immediately besieged by the usual frontier questions of "Who, where, when, how come and how much?" One fellow in particular was inquisitive and pressed hard for answers. Reverend Rice skillfully evaded each inquiry. He was tired from his long ride and even more piqued with the question askers. The settler angrily blurted out, "Well, you are not ashamed to tell your name, are you?" Rice calmly answered that it was none of his concern. The thwarted man began cursing as he walked rapidly away.[46] Some travelers were not willing to be examined by every "fool they met," and some even delighted in confusing and haranguing the overly curious frontiersmen.[47]

Benjamin Franklin, with his keen understanding and sympathy for people, evolved a unique and effective ploy for dealing with his questioners. When stopping at an isolated inn he knew that he would be questioned and that there would be no possibility of procuring any service until he imparted the desired information. The moment Franklin entered an inn he asked for the "master, the mistress, the sons, the daughters, the men servants and the maid servants." When all were assembled, he said in substance, "My good people, I am Benjamin Franklin of Philadelphia. I am a bachelor and a printer by trade. I am on my way to see some of my relatives in Boston, where, after a short visit, I intend to return home to my business, as any prudent man should do. As this is all I can possibly tell you, will you please have pity on both me and my horse and give us some refreshments."[48]

As each frontier ended, the people there acquired different character traits. Schools were established, and this lessened the number of illiterates. People became more sophisticated and placed less emphasis on dreams, portents of sickness and death, and weather signals. The prevalence of witches and evil spirits disappeared. Increased literacy and greater contact with the civilized world tended to obliterate both superstition and inquisitiveness.

# 7

# Barbarous and Unorthodox Manners

Although frontiersmen were usually kind, hospitable, neighborly, and cooperative, they were occasionally rude and barbarous in their conduct. Much of their behavior was unorthodox compared to that of organized society. Crude reactions were manifest in many frontier situations. Behavioral patterns were molded by two conditions—monotonous and drab life styles and loose bonds of social control. Travelers and missionaries who tried to improve frontier manners seldom made any impression. Conditions did not improve until the settlers came to have the benefits of a more integrated social order.

## PRACTICAL JOKES

Frontiersmen often indulged in prankish and sometimes dangerous practices. They would shave a horse's mane and tail, paint and disfigure it, and offer it for sale to the owner. While drunk, they had no compunctions against nailing another drunken man in a hogshead and rolling him down a high hill. They would run down a lean and hungry wild pig, heat a stove furnace hot, and cook the animal while dancing a merry jig.[1]

Instances of crude and bizarre conduct are numerous. When the western part of Virginia was just beginning to emerge from the frontier, a young man once drove his newly varnished and handsomely built carriage through the area. While he stopped at a small inn for refreshments, a wild fellow went to the carriage and with a nail scratched all sorts of ridiculous figures on the carriage doors. The well-dressed traveler caught the culprit engaged in this occupation and reprimanded him sharply. The backwoodsman offered no apology for his conduct. Instead he said, "Look here, Sir, don't be saucy; me make no ceremony.

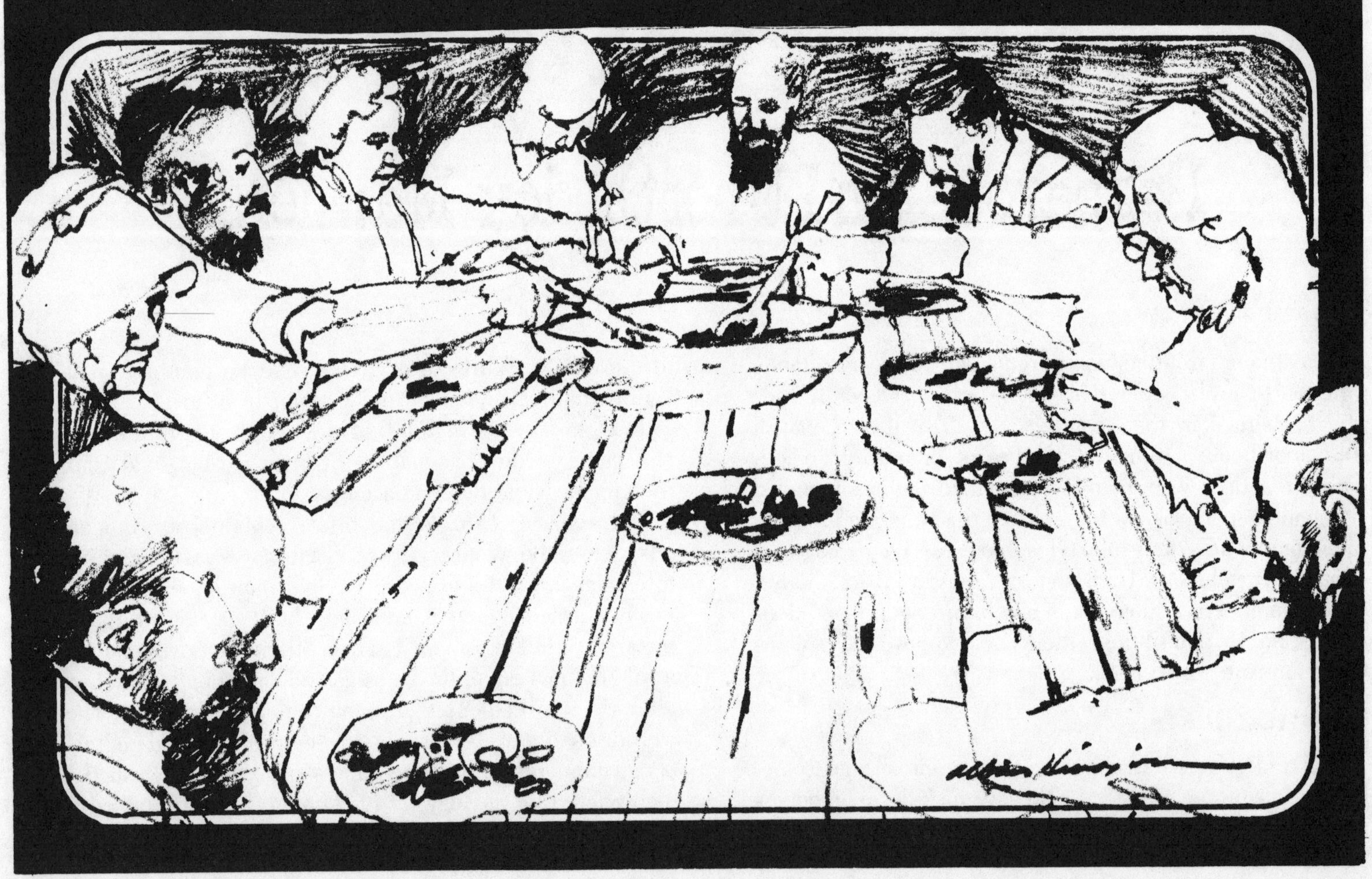

T'other day we had a European fellow here, like yourself, who was mighty saucy, so I pulled out my pistol and shot him dead, right on the spot." The traveler sarcastically asked, "And did you scalp him too?" Feeling the sharp reproach, the rude fellow gazed at the stranger for a moment and exclaimed, "By God! Sir, you must be a clever fellow! Let's shake hands!"[2]

At a prayer meeting held one night in a small log cabin, the solemnity of the occasion was broken when a man caught a calf and threw it through the only window in the building. The animal knocked over the lone candle lighting the room. The sudden darkness and the clamor of the falling calf caused women to be "terrified nearly to death, as they supposed the 'Old Boy' had jumped through the window to seize them for their sins." When the congregation discovered what had happened, they began to laugh. The calf was removed and the congregation resumed worship, as though nothing out of the ordinary had occurred.[3]

Other crude practical jokes revealed the frontiersmen's desire for novelty. A family traveling to their new home through Michigan in the 1830s lodged with a family living in a cabin with no floor. Near their house another log cabin was being built where the carpenters, who lived several miles away, had elected to spend the night in the partially constructed dwelling. The migrant family slept little that night, for the carpenters continuously entertained them by howling like wolves. The next morning the host apologized to his guests, saying that the carpenters had been fed wolf soup so long that they had taken on some of the animals' characteristics. The travelers, however, saw no humor in the situation and believed that the carpenters had been unnecessarily rude.[4]

One joke was staged for the benefit of a judge who frequently dismissed court with the command, "Mr. Sheriff, adjourn court, and let's all go take a horn." Early one morning the people living near the courthouse could hardly believe their ears; they thought that they heard calves bleating in the courtroom. To satisfy their curiosity they went to see. When they opened the door, a number of calves ran out to join their loving mothers. An old billy goat tied hard and fast to the judge's stand could not leave until released.[5]

In the early days of Sangamon County Illinois, Judge John York Sawyer sentenced an attorney named Mendel to a few hours in jail for violating the rules of decorum. Arriving at the log courtroom the next morning, the judge was surprised to find the court already in session. On the platform customarily occupied by the judge was a calf, and in the jury box was a flock of sheep. Mendel was inside the bar, addressing at one moment the calf and at another the sheep, "May it please the court and you, gentlemen of the jury." The proceedings were so ridiculous that Judge Sawyer could not suppress his laughter. He did nothing to Mendel.[6]

Some pranks were not only crude but also painful. At some frontier gatherings contests were held to see who could kick a hat the greatest distance with his bare feet. At one such frolic a man secretly placed the hats over small iron pots in the shade of the house. At a given signal, the laughing, boisterous, young fellows ran forward and kicked the hats as hard as they could. To their astonishment their toes met not only the soft woolen hats but also the hard iron of hidden pots. In a moment they were hopping around with broken and bruised toes. The audience roared with laughter and even some of those who were injured joined in.

At another social gathering held on a moonlit night, three drunk young men began a diversion that nearly killed two of them. Near a house site at the top of a hill sat several large barrels filled with wet ashes from which lye had been collected. One of the men persuaded the other two to help him roll two of the heavy barrels down the hill. When the barrels gained momentum, the drunk who had originated the idea pushed the other men in front of them. One rolled over the first man's head and body and bruised him seriously. The other drunk was more fortunate; he was able to get all of his body except his feet and legs out of the way. Although both were hurt, the prank was greatly appreciated by the other intoxicated guests.[7]

## POLITICS

Politicians and voters went to much trouble to enliven political campaigns. While one office seeker was delivering a long address on his qualifications, several local wags cut his horse's tail as short as shears could clip it. While another candidate was speaking in behalf of temperance, rowdies placed four bottles of whiskey in his saddle bags, led the politician's horse before the crowd of spectators, removed the liquor, and drank until they were roaring drunk; they completely disrupted the political rally. Another fun-loving voter placed dry gum burs under the saddle blanket of a politician's horse. At the end of his speech, the candidate mounted his gentle horse and shortly found him transformed into a bucking steed. The rowdies roared with laughter when the man was thrown to the ground, although the candidate's left shoulder and neck were severely sprained. Politicians who traveled by carriage often found that pranksters had removed all the bolts holding the wheels on the axles so that when the carriage started up, the wheels went spinning off and the carriage bed dropped with a thud in the road. Such behavior was not regarded as "bad," but as a good practical joke.[8]

Politicians sometimes went to extremes to destroy the reputation of their opponents. The second speaker at a political rally mounted the platform and said that he did not have a chance to win, particularly if "his worthy opposition" let all his mulatto children vote for him. Although this remark was made in jest, it infuriated the first speaker, who rushed forward and knocked his accuser "to kingdom come." This precipitated several fights among the spectators. They all knew that Negroes could not vote, and, although many people did not consider it disgraceful for a white man to father mulattoes, others did not share this view. The maligned first speaker won the election.[9]

Other candidates were equally as rude. While Reverend Pierson was preaching in a courthouse, a half-drunk candidate for the position of commonwealth attorney entered the room, walked around, and remarked "There is a fine crowd here, and I am going to make a speech on temperance." After Pierson restored order, the politician took his seat. Later, when the minister was about to take up a collection, the candidate sprang to his feet and exclaimed with vehemence "There is a fine crowd here, and I am going to make a speech." This time the boorish intruder was dragged out of the courtroom and thrown into jail.

## TEACHERS

Teachers as well as preachers were often subjected to ridicule and crude jokes. A New England singing-school master stood before his class and began a tune in a low melodious voice. He kept time with his hand as he moved gracefully over the floor. His students, young men and women, paid little attention. They loudly began to sing tunes of their own and drowned out the instructor. Pleased with their performance, they concluded that the teacher was not needed. The singing-school disbanded and the young people continued to sing in the community without the aid of an instructor.[10]

Many frontier students were rowdies. Peter Cartwright became a preacher while still a school boy. Often the boy preacher was made the butt of crude jokes. Two of his classmates persuaded him to go with them to a nearby creek to offer a prayer in their behalf. At the creek bank "the sinners" seized the young preacher and tried to throw him into the water. Cartwright jerked loose and threw one of the boys into the creek. The other more powerful lad grabbed Peter and after a hard struggle both boys fell and rolled over the seven-foot-high bank into deep water. Cruel practical jokes were a daily occurrence at the school, and the teacher was unable to prevent them. Cartwright soon ceased to attend.[11]

A teacher often had little social standing in a community and was sometimes barred from the school building by his students, who demanded a "treat," or vacation, or both. To execute such a plan the students would supply themselves on the evening before with enough provisions—food, water, corn whiskey and fuel— to last through the night. The children, and sometimes a few of their parents, would gather inside the school, bar the windows and the door, and proceed to enjoy a night of merriment. The next morning the sleepy students began to have nervous anxieties. If the schoolmaster succeeded in breaking in, the pupils' hopes for a vacation vanished and they would become the butt of public ridicule. It sometimes happened that the boys who had been loudest in proclaiming their courage became meek as lambs when the instructor arrived. Occasionally the teacher was happy to be barred out; he too could enjoy a short vacation from his unruly charges. If he were in this frame of mind, he pretended to yield reluctantly to their demands. A more obstinate teacher was sometimes ducked in cold water, rolled in mud, and dragged with a rope by his pupils until he conceded. A prudent teacher sensed that it was better sooner or later to make some concessions than to suffer the consequences.[12]

One morning Reverend Maxwell Gaddis arrived at his one-room log schoolhouse and found the door and window barred with long benches. Gaddis demanded admittance but was refused. One of the students shoved a crudely written note through a crack which stated that if he would "treat" them to three bushels of apples and a keg of cider he could enter. When the preacher replied it was not a part of his contract to furnish such items, the students roared with laughter. Gaddis turned abruptly and started for home. One pupil suddenly cried, "There! There! Look out! He is coming down the chimney!" This remark was made to frighten the smaller, more naive students.

Before the schoolmaster had gone far, he heard the benches being removed and in a moment the whole student body rushed after him like a pack of well-trained bloodhounds. Unable to get home before being overtaken, Gaddis took refuge in the nearest house with the students howling at his heels. When the pupils arrived, the landlady informed them that her home was open to both teachers and scholars. The cheering students stormed into the house. A few larger boys informed Gaddis that unless he met their demands, he would be tied hand and foot with a rope. Gaddis stood defiantly behind a chair and he would not yield. At the end of an hour of disrespectful harangue from his students, the schoolmaster was rescued by some passing school patrons. A compromise was arranged. The pupils were given some apples, but no cider, and a recess for the remainder of the day. The children were satisfied and for the remainder of the term they gleefully recalled the incident. Gaddis elected not to teach in this school another term.[13] This school teacher and others like him were like "birds of passage"; they came and they remained only a short time. They hardly ever returned to the same settlement again.

Teachers were sometimes as illiterate, crude, and

uncouth as their fellow frontier citizens. George Gilmer wrote in his *Sketches of Some of the First Settlers of Upper Georgia* that his first schoolmaster was a deserter from the British navy. Although the teacher wrote a good hand and could read, he was accused during the school term of attempting to steal money. Since the schoolhouse had no chimney, during cold weather the instructor "warmed his scholars by having them join hands and run round, whilst he hastened their speed by the free use of the switch." At other times he paired the boys in wrestling matches to keep them warm. To amuse himself in the afternoon he often threatened to fasten the students in the schoolhouse until the next day unless each one could give him a good reason for going home.[14]

Reverend John Johnson vividly recalled his first teacher, an Irishman named Hugh McClellan. Rough and passionate, he would knock a boy down if he were in the least impertinent. When not enraged, he was kind, particularly to the younger children. The teacher had a "parcel of types" with which he amused his pupils by showing them samples of printing. At the close of school, he presented each pupil a short booklet entitled *Eddy Grove Songster*. Like most teachers of his day, McClellan pretended to be a profound scholar and frequently quoted from Latin, Greek, and Hebrew. Though most of his quotes were delivered in his native Irish brogue, his ignorant students were much impressed with his learning.[15]

Parents had no real guarantee of an instructor's fitness to teach. Apparently most teachers came from the unemployed and drifter population. If a man knew or convinced the people that he knew a few words of Latin, he was regarded as a wizard, although he might not know how to read simple English very well. While attending the services of a foot-washing denomination, Reverend Pierson met the local teacher who regarded himself as something of a poet. The poet-schoolteacher was asked to write some new hymns for the services. The teacher could hardly write; his knowledge of words and the construction of poetry was the worst Reverend Pierson had ever seen. Afterwards the visiting minister met the school commissioner at the county seat and laughingly asked him why he had authorized the poet to teach in the foot-washing community. The superintendent replied, "Oh, I only certified that he was competent to teach in that neighborhood."[16]

In the opinion of Reverend John Mason Peck, three-fourths of all the teachers of Missouri were a public nuisance. They were not only unqualified to teach but were also of low character. Many, the Irish in particular, loved their whiskey and often gave it to their pupils when they demanded a treat. A schoolmaster named O'Flaherty procured a supply of cherry bounce, a mixture of whiskey and honey, to treat himself and his pupils. O'Flaherty drank his fill and then distributed it generously to his scholars, causing "half of them to become 'orful sick." Some pupils had to be taken home, and the professor, who required a wide path for his zig-zag course, was dismissed by the indignant parents.[17]

Few schoolmasters had any professional training and their technique of instruction was very poor. Many made use of the so-called "loud method." When this system was employed, every scholar studied at the very top of his voice and tried to drown out the others. The noise from such a school could be heard a half mile away. After becoming accustomed to the bedlam, one pupil contended that he made rapid progress. He learned the alphabet, spelled fairly well, and learned to read a little in the New Testament.[18] A. A. Parker wrote in his book *Trip to the West and Texas* of a visit to a log school where the students learned by rote. The technique was new to him and he asked the schoolmaster whether this method was customary. The teacher replied that it was widely used with much success. He admitted to his visitor, however, that his pupils were hollering a little louder than usual.[19]

## CHEWING TOBACCO

The excessive and careless use of chewing tobacco was another mark of frontier crudeness. Ministers who did not chew tobacco thundered against those who did on moral as well as health grounds. Frequently congregations were forced to listen to long sermons in which the minister said that money spent for the filthy weed could be used to build homes, schools, and churches and to pay ministers.[20]

Seeing the reckless use of tobacco, especially "amber" spat in careless abandon, some editors denounced its use in all forms. *The Christian Index* stated in 1833 that in the day of "improvement upon subjects generally" it was surprising that the evil use of tobacco—"chewing in church, filthy business this"—was permitted to remain untouched. The editors said that gentlemen of good character chewed the weed voraciously and made wretched work in the house of God. If such gentlemen served their dwellings as they did their church, they would have to reckon with their wives and daughters. Sad indeed it was, they said, that men would regard the "sacred court" as a tramping ground where showers of tobacco spittle were considered proper. Mourners who knelt in prayer to beg for grace were often forced to get on their knees in puddles of filth.[21]

Charles Dickens, on a tour of the frontier, saw no objection to the use of tobacco, provided one was not offensive with it. One morning while traveling aboard a steamboat, the Englishman was seen brushing dried spittles from his fur coat. The other passengers seemed surprised that Dickens bothered to do so. It turned out to be a losing battle, for on the next night Dickens put his coat on a stool beside him, but there it lay under a crossfire from five men—three opposite, one above, and one below.[22]

Another Englishman, John Melish, recorded his disgust with the intemperate use of tobacco by American backwoodsmen. Once as he sat before a fireplace in a small roadside inn trying to record the day's occurrences in his journal, a man came in and lighted a cigar. He puffed away, intermittently squirting a mouthful of saliva through the room. A second man and then a third entered the keeping room and lighted cigars. Melish was enveloped in a dense cloud of smoke. His eyes began to water and smart, and he was forced to stop his writing.

The situation worsened when three other tobacco users came to sit by the fire. One of the newcomers took an immense quid of tobacco, rolled it around in his mouth, and squirted saliva in all directions without regard to whom it might hit. The second smoked a pipe and the third a cigar. Melish wrote that he had witnessed many singular scenes, even rough ones, but this one of smoking, chewing and spitting was too much for him. Gasping for breath, Melish, despite the cold night, moved his chair to the farthest corner of the room and sat by a broken window.

Luckily, supper was soon announced. Eating sparingly, Melish was the first to finish and he returned to the fireplace to finish his notes. Shortly two new men came to the public room and began to smoke and spit. One of them noted that the stranger was making a wry face and said, "I am afraid the smoking disturbs you." Melish nodded and replied, "A little." For once the smokers were civil enough to withdraw, leaving the room entirely to Melish.[23]

G. W. Featherstonhaugh, while on a Mississippi steamer, discovered the passenger list included a number of base frontiersmen. These rough men, "red-hot with whiskey," would rush into the main saloon, crowd around the stove, and push aside other passengers. Armed with pistols and knives, the ruffians spat, smoked and cursed while swapping vulgar tales. One old man complained that there was too much smoke in the cabin and he was told, "If any man tells me he don't like my smoking, I'll put a knife into him." Hearing this, Featherstonhaugh was just on the verge of reproving the rude man when he realized the futility and danger of such action.

Instead, Featherstonhaugh complained to the captain that the printed rules of the boat were not being enforced.

The captain angrily replied that he had no intention of enforcing the rules, since the conduct of the men represented the customs and manners of the country. If he enforced the rules, he would never get another passenger. The captain informed the Englishman that it was customary for the majority of passengers to form their own by-laws—a statement Featherstonhaugh found to be true later.

Featherstonhaugh returned to the main cabin a defeated man. With no police on the boat, the situation on board had grown worse. One villain stood with his back to the stove, spouting vulgar invectives at another man with whom he had recently quarreled. Another ruffian walked up to the angry man and calmly reached inside the brute's waistcoat, drew forth a knife, unsheathed it, felt its edge and lavishly praised the weapon. Despite the gentle goading, the angry, cursing man shed no blood.

When the steamer later arrived at Vicksburg, Featherstonhaugh was relieved to see eight or ten gentlemen, some of whom were planters of great respectability, board the boat. After supper, the traveler was astonished and horrified to see the Mississippi gentlemen hob-nob with the rabble, gambling, drinking, smoking and blaspheming with them. When the cabin became so filled with smoke that Featherstonhaugh could not breathe, he wrapped himself in a blanket and retreated to the open deck for the night. The captain came by, expressed his sympathy for the traveler's suffering, and suggested that it would be best for him to leave the boat in Natchez. The captain explained that he could not afford to "disoblige the planters, for . . . they would never send any more freight by him." Competition among the steamers was so great that every man was obliged to look out for his own interests. He told Featherstonhaugh that recently a captain had put a disorderly fellow off his boat at Vicksburg. When the boat stopped there (on its return), fifteen men armed with knives and pistols boarded the boat and proceeded to spit in the captain's face and to kick him.

## TABLE MANNERS

Rude behavior was often paraded before Eastern visitors who traveled by steamboat. One fastidious passenger aboard a steamer in Alabama said that scarcely a man took off his hat when entering the main cabin. They sat and whiled away the time chewing and spitting in the brass boxes along the floor. When the gong announced dinner, the men rushed to their places, waited until the women were seated at the head of the table and then sat down, bolted their food, and left in almost as much haste as in going to it. The traveler observed that the women as well as the men ate with the blades of their knives rather than with the two-pronged steel forks.[24]

Bishop Whipple said that in the main cabin of a Mississippi steamboat men smoked, spit showers of tobacco juice on the carpet, talked loudly, laughed heartily, and acted as though the saloon was nothing but the lowest type of bar room. When the bell for dinner was sounded there was a grand race to the table; if a "luckless wight" got in the way, he stood the chance of being crushed to death. Immediately after being seated a game of knives and forks began. According to Whipple, the crude behavior looked for all the world like one great scrimmage.[25]

The lack of good table manners astonished Frances

Trollope. She said food was seized and devoured with voracious rapidity, while those at the table engaged in strange uncouth phrases and pronunciations. The people's method of feeding themselves with their knives was frightful, but she found their practice of cleaning their teeth with a pocket knife even worse. The dinner hour was not an occasion for polite conversation and relaxed dining.[26]

Bad food mixed with bad manners made the travelers' lot most difficult. G. W. Featherstonhaugh and his fellow travelers stopped at noon one day at a small inn at a crossroad in Arkansas. The landlady brought to the table what she called beef—tough, stringy, and cooked in such a manner that one was unable to tell whether it had been roasted or boiled. Her guests tried in vain to chew and swallow the greasy mess and left the table. The landlady's child ran into the kitchen and told her mother that the company "wouldn't touch the beef no how." The mother in true "cyclopian spirit," rushed to the dining table and said, "I ain't agoing to work myself to death to please nobody. I reckon, if you are so nice, you know where to get better . . . for you shan't stay here no longer." Featherstonhaugh and his party quickly departed, but they fared little better at various cabins where they stopped during the days ahead. The food was all bad and the service crude.[27]

## RELIGION

The conduct of religious congregations remained highly unpredictable. Reverend Eli Lindsey was preaching in a log cabin in Arkansas in 1816 to a group composed mainly of hunters. The men had stacked their guns against the wall and had left their hounds outside. During the sermon the dogs cornered a bear in the woods. The hunters bolted without ceremony from the building, and the minister promptly adjourned the service so that the entire congregation might join in the pleasure of killing the bear. When the bear was shot, the congregation returned and the minister calmly continued his sermon.[28]

Frequent were the interruptions and diversions at frontier religious services. Dogs often interrupted worship. Sometimes there were more dogs at church than there were people. Every family owned one or more dogs who followed their owners everywhere. Some of the dogs slept, but others barked and howled and disturbed the service. When a dog fight broke out, all religious activities had to be stopped until their contest was over or until the snarling beasts could be driven away. At a camp meeting women had to be on their guard to protect the food from dogs. At one camp meeting, when James Berry's dozen hounds and other dogs became unmanageable, T. G. Onstot appointed himself the chairman of dog behavior. He pelted the unruly beasts with hard, green walnuts. Despite continued complaints from their owners, Onstot continued to discharge his duties as chief dog-chastiser.[29]

Crying babies also interrupted the flow of the sermon and the solemnity of the services. In the days before birth control, nearly every family had one or more babies. There were no nurseries nor babysitters, and mothers had no choice but to bring their children to church. It was inevitable that the infants would cry during long services; sometimes dozens at a time would bawl at the top of their voices. The minister had to exercise utmost patience, for it was taboo for him to ask the mothers to take their children from the congregation. He could do nothing but raise his voice and pray that some of the babies would go to sleep or begin taking nourishment from their mothers.

There were other disruptive factors that diverted the communicants' attention from the religious services. On one occasion a beautiful young lady of queenly bearing arrived late and began searching for a seat. The preacher had just begun his sermon, and when the congregation focused its attention on the young woman, the preacher became angry. He believed that the young lady was trying to attract undue attention to her beauty, and he rudely ordered her to sit down. Stung by the crude command, she retorted, "So I will, Sir, if you will bring me a seat." The affair caused great commotion in the congregation; some of the worshipers even hissed the preacher.[30]

During his opening prayer, Reverend James Quinn observed that one flirtatious young woman was acting in a most irreverent manner. The minister rose from his knees, reminded the congregation of the significance of prayer, and castigated the people for their lack of decorum during the occasion. He pointed a finger at the young lady and said, "It is that young woman with the leghorn bonnet and artificials, who sits on the second seat beyond the stove adjoining the partition in the seats. I point her out publicly as a warning to other transgressors." The minister's stern reproof had its desired effect; there was no further disorder during the service.[31]

A Quaker once created a scene when he entered a Methodist church without removing his hat. The preacher abruptly stopped his sermon and said, "Pull your hat off and sit down!" The Quaker replied, "I intend no disrespect for thee, friend, nor for anyone; but I wear my hat because it is the principle and practice of the Society to which I belong." The minister sneeringly retorted, "Well, we must bear the infirmities of the weak." The embarrassed Quaker rose and said, "I wear my hat in the presence of God Almighty, and I shan't take it off to such a creature as thee." With tears streaming down his cheeks, the Quaker rushed from the building. Many people in the congregation began to talk loudly and to accuse the minister of being unduly rude.[32]

Even baptismal rites suffered from rowdy conduct. At one baptizing, a Baptist minister took the hand of a lady while in the act of leading each of his twenty-five candidates into a gliding stream to be immersed. Her husband, standing in a crowd on a nearby bridge, cried out that he would prosecute the minister if he baptized his wife. Confused by the threat, the preacher asked the lady whether she wished to be baptized. When she nodded "yes," the preacher immediately immersed her. The irate husband then declared that "he had a yoke of oxen and he would spend their value in money to execute vengeance" on the preacher as he departed.[33]

Abraham Bale, a tall, powerful man with the voice of a lion, enjoyed unusual success with his preaching in Illinois. He baptized converts in the River Sangamon, even as John the Baptist did in the River Jordan. On one occasion he led as many as fifty converts into the water.

Rowdy men and boys often attended the sacred ceremonies and threw dogs and logs into the stream and whooped and yelled like Indians. Just as Reverend Bale was about to baptize one woman, her husband cried out, "Hold on, Bale! Hold on, Bale! Don't you drown her! I wouldn't take the best cow and calf in Menard County for her!"[34]

During another ceremony, a lady "much affected" presented her child to a Methodist minister to be baptized. Suddenly a man jumped on a bench and demanded in a loud and angry tone, "That is my child and you must not baptize it; and if you do, I will whip you nearly to death." Members of the congregation tried without success to restrain the protester as he rushed forward to attack the preacher. Suddenly a large grey-haired man stepped in front of the enraged father and turned to the minister and said, "Baptize the child, Sir. It is not his child, for he told me so himself the other day. I will see that you are not harmed." The preacher, thus reassured, sprinkled the child, and he was never whipped.[35]

Another disturbance at a church was caused by "a religious nut." It had been announced that a Methodist class meeting was to be held behind closed doors. Only church members and those who had expressed a desire to join were to be admitted. At previous class assemblies an "old lady, a New Light by profession," usually attended in violation of the rules and no one had ever made an issue of her presence. At the beginning of the class, the pastor asked the leader whether any nonmembers were present. Informed there were three, two who wanted to join the church and "the old lady who had expressed disdain of Methodists," the minister asked the elderly woman to leave. When she refused, the preacher said he would put her out. The woman was livid with rage. She sprang to her feet, clapped her hands, and shouted her defiance. The preacher tried without success to push the struggling woman through the door. Suddenly he picked her up, took her outside, and stood her on her feet. She began to shout again. The pastor reprimanded her and said that her shouting was prompted by the Devil rather than by God. He slammed the door and stood against it while he taught.[36]

Shortly after the Civil War, while bitter animosities still raged between the North and South, a Methodist minister was presented with a child to baptize. He said, "Name of child?" He was startled when the mother answered "Jefferson Davis." The minister held the child in his arms, paused, and pondered whether he should baptize one by that name. To him Jefferson Davis was a traitor to his country and had helped cause the death of thousands of good and brave men. The preacher reasoned that to baptize a child by this name would render it odious throughout life, for Davis should have been hanged for "committing a crime of the highest degree." He refused to dedicate a child to God bearing this hated name and he handed the child back to his mother. Early the next morning, the minister, after a sleepless night spent in solemn thought and prayer, received a message from the mother and father of young Jefferson Davis, stating that they wished to change the child's name and have it baptized. The preacher was jubilant and shouted, "Glory to God, Who still reigneth." At the home of the parents, he happily baptized the child, for its name had been changed to George Washington.[37]

What might appear to be crude and rude to a person in organized society was quite acceptable on the frontier. The practical jokes that often characterized the frontier-people provided emotional release to a drab and sometimes hostile environment. The manner in which politics were conducted and schools taught on the frontier would be unthinkable today. Independent of spirit, they were not attempting to impress anyone with fancy table manners. Eating was a means of survival and not a social undertaking. As the frontier gradually disappeared, pressure from society was exerted to conform to accepted practices, and much of the barbarous and unorthodox manners disappeared.

# 8

# Frontier Fights

Although the pioneers were usually kind and considerate of one another, they had a natural tendency for fighting. Believing they were masters of their own fate, they permitted little interference in their independent way of life. Living in a disorganized social state, their behavior sometimes degenerated to a level of savagery and barbarism, and in the absence of law enforcement a fight was often the only means of resolving a controversy. Courage was a mark of manhood and a coward was held in disgrace, and neighbors and bystanders often encouraged fights to enliven their monotonous lives. Bloody conflicts with Indians also contributed to this frontier behavior and made many people more cruel and vicious.

Frontier fighting tactics amazed and horrified travelers new to them. A British subject, J. E. Alexander, said that although the ladies of England continued to denounce the cruelties of the prize ring, they should just once witness a backcountry American fight. Alexander hoped that someday prize ring supporters could tour the frontier and teach the rules of Queensbury to the Americans and wean them away from their "cowardly knife, gouging, and biting techniques."[1] Thomas Anburey, a British traveler who found the English boxing match a disgrace to a civilized nation, decided it was humanity itself when compared with the Virginia mode of fighting. When two men quarreled in England, they settled their dispute with a "stand-up fight." Bystanders formed a ring and a contestant was not permitted to strike a fallen opponent. Anburey found frontier fighting worthy only of the most ferocious savages. The object of each combatant was to fell his opponent and then to choke and mutilate him by any means.[2]

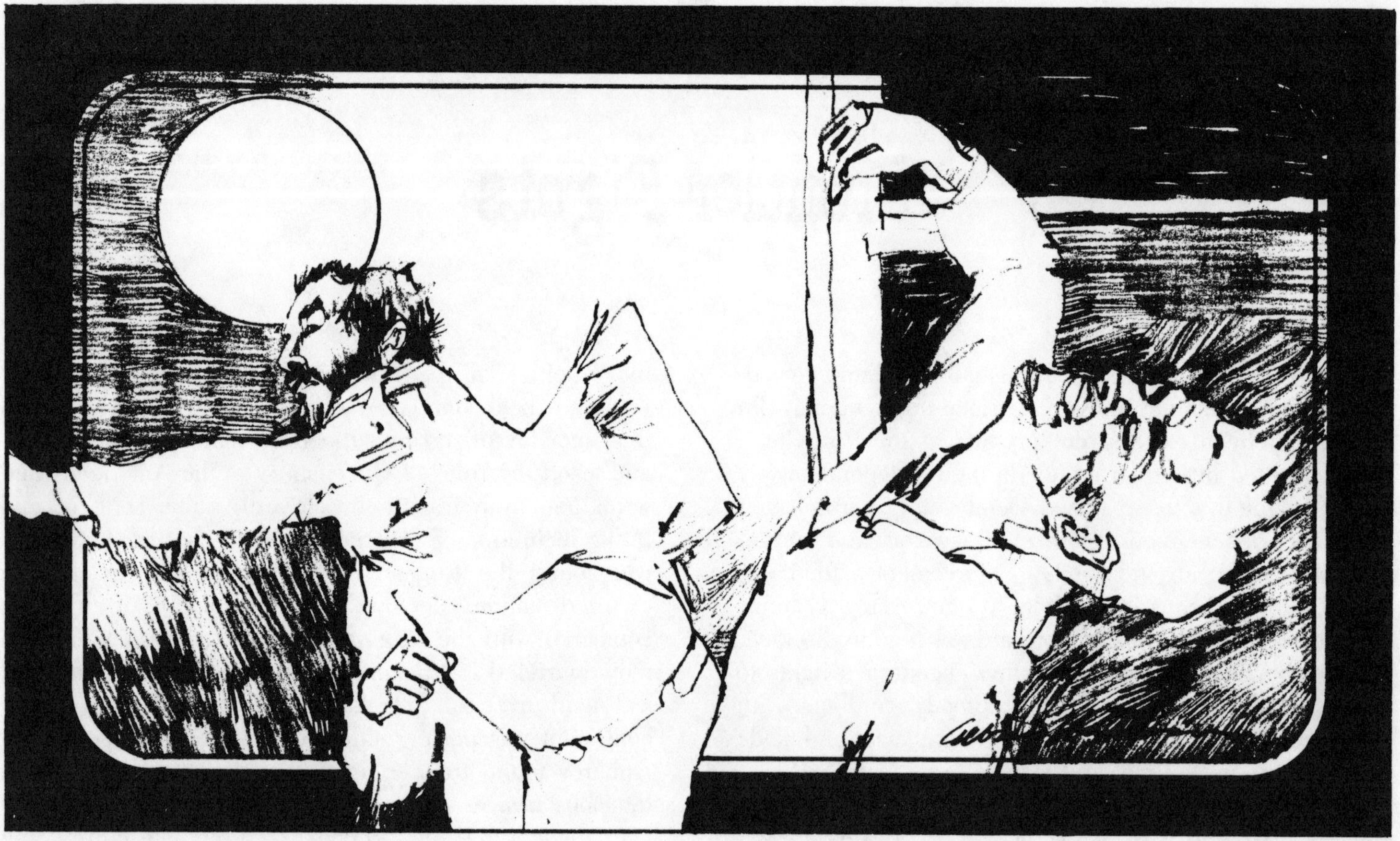

The vast majority of fights were fought with bare fists and usually produced blackened eyes, bloody lips and noses, and dislocated teeth. To call a person a liar was an insult to one's honor which had to be defended. If one refused a challenge, he was considered a coward. The insulted person usually struck the first blow and a battle royal then ensued. An old settler recalling a fight he had seen in his father's fort said that one opponent was smaller and younger and knew he "would get the worst of the battle." But if he refused, he would be dishonored. He entered the contest and received a whipping, after which the two combatants shook hands and became good friends.[3]

Many travelers in the back country were forced to fight or make a quick apology for what they had said or done. One young man, while visiting the Montana Territory, wrote to his mother and described the odd behavior of the people. After listening to a Westerner tell a "large story," the young traveler remarked that the tale was a "whopper." The angry storyteller snapped, "Lay there, stranger." In the twinkling of an eye the Easterner found himself sprawling in a ditch. On another occasion, the young man unwisely remarked to a Westerner, "That isn't a specimen of your western women, is it?" The Westerner eyed him coldly and said, "You are afraid of the fever and ague [malaria], stranger, aren't you?" When the Easterner replied that he was, the Westerner said, "Well, that lady is my wife, and if you don't apologize in two minutes, . . . I swear these two pistols shall cure you of the disorder entirely—so don't fear, stranger." The young man apologized as quickly and profusely as he could.[4]

The prevalence of fighting among male settlers gave rise to much speculation. Who was the strongest? Who was the best fighter? Who could whip all others? Many who grew up on the frontier would fight at the drop of a hat when insulted. Backwoods boys were brought up to "knock down" and "drag out." To avoid a fight, it was well to keep calm and never reveal any trace of fear.

## COURTS, POLITICS, AND ELECTIONS

In today's organized society, physical violence in the courts, the political arena, or at election places is usually unknown. Physical fighting has been replaced by lawyers who are skilled at doing battle with words. But on the frontier, a powerful arm or a good fighting reputation was often looked upon with more respect than skill with words.

Fighting sometimes even brought political rewards. In 1827, the State Legislature of Illinois elected a treasurer. One of the defeated candidates, a giant of a man, entered the assembly hall just before the Legislature adjourned and soundly thrashed four of the members who had voted against him. The members of the Legislature ran toward the exits like sheep from a wolf and soon vacated the chamber. After a hurried discussion outside, the Legislature reassembled and named the bold warrior "Clerk of the Circuit Court."[5]

Willingness to fight depended in part on the physical fitness of the parties involved. During an election in Illinois in 1840, Abraham Lincoln learned that a man named Radford, a Democrat, had taken possession of one polling place and would not allow the Whigs to vote. Lincoln loped to the precinct and immediately challenged the bully. "Radford! You will spoil and blow if you live much longer." The Democrat sized up Lincoln and wisely decided to leave. Lincoln later told his law partner, Speed, that he was disappointed when Radford surrendered so easily. He desperately wanted to fight the Democrat, knock him down and leave him kicking.[6]

Andrew Jackson is a good example of the fighting frontiersman. When he was described to President Jefferson in 1804 as being "a man of violent passions, arbitrary in his disposition, and frequently engaged in broils and disputes," the President refused to appoint him Governor of the New Orleans Territory. Jackson lived up to his reputation during the next decade. Intervention of friends prevented him and Governor John Sevier of Tennessee from doing each other personal violence as a result of a heated quarrel. Because of a disagreement, Jackson severed amicable relations with his old patron, Judge McNairy, and at a later period, Jackson caned Thomas Swan in public.[7]

A fight between Jackson and the Benton brothers, Thomas Hart and Jesse, was of particular severity. When he learned that his brother Jesse had been wounded in a duel with Major General William Carroll in which Jackson had served as a reluctant second for Carroll, Senator Thomas Hart Benton took out his wrath on Jackson without bothering to learn the facts. He wrote abusive and insulting letters to Jackson and had others published in the Nashville newspapers. The Senator accused Jackson of treachery and dishonesty. Consumed by anger, Jackson swore he would horsewhip Tom Benton the first time he saw him.

The showdown occurred about a month later. Senator Benton came to Nashville about the same time as did Jackson. With whip in hand, Jackson walked toward the City Hotel where Benton was staying and saw the Benton brothers standing on the sidewalk. He approached Thomas Benton and ordered him to retract the scandalous statements made in his letters or take a horsewhipping. Benton reached for his gun but Jackson beat him to the draw. Jesse Benton, standing only a few feet away, quickly fired his double-barreled pistol at Jackson. One ball went through Jackson's arm and the other lodged in his shoulder; Jackson fell to the ground.

News of the fight raced throughout Nashville. Within ten minutes a thousand men had gathered at the hotel. Fights erupted between friends of the two parties. A Jackson supporter knocked Jesse Benton down, stabbed him, and nearly pounded him to death. In the confusion, Thomas Benton fell through an open doorway into the basement of the hotel, which probably saved his life and at least kept him from getting a severe beating.

Jackson recuperated in about three weeks, but the bullet in his shoulder remained there for twenty-five years. Thomas Benton soon moved from Tennessee to Missouri. Sixteen years later both men were elected to the United States Senate. When they came face to face in the Capitol, they shook hands and remained good friends for the remainder of their lives.[8] Late in life Thomas Benton was asked about his early difficulty with Jackson. Benton's only reply was that "a fellow was hardly in fashion then . . . who had not had a fight."[9]

Kentucky elections seemed to be especially violent

and dramatic. One of them lasted three days, during which time whiskey and apple toddies flowed freely. Circulating among the crowd were a number of runners, each with a whiskey bottle poking its long neck from his pocket. Their task was to bribe and intimidate the voters. Each political faction hired a half dozen bullies, as mean as Kentucky alligators, who stood ready to flog anyone who dared vote "illegally." One runner slapped a bystander on the shoulder with his right hand and waved a whiskey bottle in the other, asking him if he were a voter. When the stranger replied that he was not, the runner said, "Ah, never mind." The bully pulled the cob from the bottle and said, "Jest take a swig of the creature and toss in a vote for Old Hickory's boys. I'll fight for you, damn!" Alternately eying the whiskey and the rowdy's sledgehammer fist, the traveler prudently took a drink and agreed to vote for Andrew Jackson.[10]

During another election in Kentucky, fights were numerous and cracked skulls were many. A giant of a man with arms like a pair of cables knotted at the ends and a round black head that looked like a forty-pound cannon shot walked to the polls to cast his vote. As he was walking away, a Salt River Roarer challenged, "Stop, friend! Are you a voter?" When the voter with a burst replied, "Yes," the Roarer shouted, "That's a lie and you must just prepare yourself to go home an old man, for I'll be damned if I don't knock you into the middle of your ninety-ninth year." The voter calmly agreed to fight. "Ah, ay, come on then. I'll ride you to hell, whipped up with the sea sarpint!"

The two men walked to an open space to begin the contest. Shaking his fist for a moment like a wild man, the Salt River Roarer dropped his chin and with all of his force pitched himself head first at the midsection of his adversary. The voter dodged and struck his opponent a stinging blow that sent him staggering into a table loaded with whiskey bottles, mugs, and tumblers. The stunned man regained his balance and again faced his foe. Both contestants then exchanged blows of telling effect. The Roarer, biding his time, finally succeeded in slamming his head into the stomach of the voter and knocking him down with such force that it did not appear that he would rise again. The Roarer asked, "Is the scoundrel done for?" but the voter quickly bounded to his feet and grappled with his enemy. The combatants twined around each other like serpents; they tugged, strained, and foamed at the mouth until at length the voter's reserve strength enabled him to top his struggling opponent. A dozen voices then shouted, "Gouge him! Gouge him!" It seemed like a good suggestion. The voter seized his victim by the hair and began dislodging an eyeball. Exerting superhuman strength, the Roarer locked his fingers around his assailant's throat. In a few minutes the voter's face turned black, his tongue lolled out of his mouth and he lay still, apparently dead. A spectator turned away, a confirmed believer that he had witnessed total depravity.[11]

Elections, especially in the South, occasioned many a fight. Some of these, according to the noted historian John B. McMaster, were "worthy of an Irish fair." Voters of the entire county met in one place to cast their ballots openly before the sheriff and the respective candidates. On election day rival candidates came to the polls with their followers. Each group was determined to drive their opponents away, even if they had to resort to physical violence to do it. Such a situation was described to a committee which was investigating a contested congressional election in the South. One member of the delegation said that violence and intimidation at election time was quite common. At the Montgomery County Virginia court house he reported, an election was held to choose a representative to the lower house of Congress. One of the candidates was fortunate enough to have a brother who commanded sixty or seventy Federal troops encamped nearby. On the morning of the election the troops paraded to the court house, marched thrice around it, and then lined up before the door. They threatened to beat anyone who voted against their candidate. A protesting drunken magistrate was knocked down and soon after the soldiers posted a guard at the court house door, bringing all voting to an end. A number of indignant voters retaliated by stoning the troopers and succeeded in driving them away.

Some of the committeemen were so shocked in hearing the report that they agreed that the candidate from Virginia should lose his seat. One member of the committee from Maryland objected, saying he had never heard of an election in a southern state where so little mischief was done as in this Virginia contest. He recalled another election in which the Chancellor of the court instigated a riot in his own courtroom to assist his party candidate. Several committeemen said much about a man who went to the Montgomery Court House with a club hidden under his coat, but the Maryland representative said this was a minor incident. On the day of his own election, five hundred of his constituents hid clubs under their coats. A South Carolina member of the committee was reminded that a riot had occurred during his election. The riot began in a church and was precipitated by a magistrate who knocked a voter down and dragged him into a nearby road.[12]

One of Andrew Jackson's encounters in his court suggests the attitude which prevailed on the frontier. Holding court in a shanty in a little village in Tennessee, Judge Andrew Jackson was dispensing justice in large and small doses, as seemed appropriate in the cases at hand. A hulking fellow with pistols and a Bowie knife suddenly began parading before the court house cursing the judge, the jury, and all assembled. The ruffian was disturbing the court procedure and Jackson ordered the sheriff to arrest him.

The sheriff left the court room but soon returned saying it was impossible to take the offender. Jackson then ordered the sheriff to form a posse and bring the man before him. The bully threatened to shoot anyone who came within ten feet and the posse also failed. Jackson said, "Mr. Sheriff, since you cannot obey my orders, summon me; yes, Sir, summon me!" Reluctantly the sheriff deputized the judge to make the arrest.

Jackson adjourned court for ten minutes and with pistols in hand, walked into the yard and confronted the culprit. Jackson coldly ordered, "Now, surrender, you infernal villain, this very instant, or I'll blow you through!" Eying the deputy sheriff for a moment, the rowdy replied, "There, Judge, it's no use, I give in." Jackson led the cowed man into the courtroom.

A few days later the bully was asked why he

knuckled under to one man but had refused to let the posse arrest him. "Why, when he came up, I looked him in the eye, and I saw shoot. There wasn't shoot in nary other eye in the crowd, and so I says to myself, says I, 'Hoss, it's about time to sing small!' and so I did."[13]

## GANG FIGHTING

Brawlers often organized into gangs for greater security. In New Salem, Illinois, a group of ruffians known as the Clary Grove Boys met together once or twice a week to drink, fight, and engage in brutal horseplay. When a stranger entered New Salem, he was immediately initiated into the boisterous social life by the savage young men. The gang might nail him up in a hogshead and roll him down a hill, or insult him into a fight and maul him black and blue. The Clary Grove Boys had pretentions of chivalry, but they had little regard for fair play.[14]

However, large numbers did not always bring security. In building the western railroads, gangs of workers—mostly "Fardowns" and "Corkonians" of Ireland—loved nothing more than to fight each other. Engineers found it necessary to employ on each section of the road none but Fardowns or none but Corkonians. This precaution, however, was occasionally overcome when gangs numbering three or four hundred of one party would unexpectedly stop work and walk several miles to attack the other. These brutal encounters resulted in the death of some and left scores badly wounded.[15]

Flatboatmen on the Mississippi were a wild and reckless set, ever ready for a fight or a frolic, though they were patient and courageous under conditions that would have daunted less resolute men. Flatboat crews often awarded to their most brawny and able fighter a feather or some other emblem to wear on his hat. The emblem denoted that the wearer had beaten, or, to use the Kentucky expression, "whipped all the rest."[16]

Boatmen often numbered from thirty to forty men on each river barge. When a flatboat tied up at a town, a riot usually followed. Citizens, often as dissolute as the bargemen, willingly began a fight. If the rivermen outnumbered the townsmen, they were allowed to indulge without restraint in every species of debauchery, outrage, and mischief. Law-abiding citizens withdrew behind locked doors until the flatboatmen departed.[17]

Thomas Anburey met a group of bargemen in New Orleans and soon learned how to conform to their code. He was invited to drink with them and was treated with a great deal of civility. Fraternization was not easy as these characters regarded themselves as being half horse and half alligator, with a cross of wildcat; they were the terror of the peaceful inhabitants of New Orleans. When drunk, the boatmen boasted that they owned the best rifles, horses, and had the prettiest sisters in the world. Whoever denied their claims must fight, and anyone who attempted to act as a peacemaker was soon in trouble. The ruffians might challenge by saying, "Stranger, I see you want a quarrel; I am your man." Anburey let them fight to their heart's content; he stood by as a peaceful observer.[18]

River town roughs and toughs along the Mississippi often plagued steamboat captains. On one occasion three men who boarded a steamboat at Natchez tried to leave without paying their fares. The captain collared the rowdies and swore that he would collect their fares. The riverman rammed a hand into the captain's face, shoved his middle finger into his left ear and started his eyeball from its socket with a thumb. But before the brute succeeded in gouging the eye out, the captain capsized his antagonist, fell on him, grabbed his throat, and shook him until he was black in the face. One of the ruffian's companions pulled a knife and ran the blade through the captain's arm. The third tough seized one of the captain's hands and gnawed one of his fingers to the bone. The steamboat operator was in danger of being blinded, maimed and probably murdered. At this critical point, the mate came to his aid. He knocked out the two assailants and then he and the captain, cut and bruised, dragged the three ashore. It is not known whether the captain ever received his pay for the men's passage.[19]

On another occasion in 1830 three ruffians came on board a Mississippi steamboat just before it pulled away from a dock. One of them tied his skiff to the boat's stern without consulting the captain. The captain gave a signal to steam away, but the stern-wheeler could hardly move because of the skiff. The officer, seeing the trouble, ordered "That boat must be cut adrift."

The owner of the skiff bellowed, "By God, the first man that tries to cut adrift my boat I'll cut his throat!" He shoved his hand in his pocket and drew out a large knife with a French spring to prevent its shutting. Brandishing the weapon he roared, "My name's Tom Merriman; I'll make mince-meat of ye." By this time his two companions also had knives in their hands.

The captain, a prudent Scotchman, stepped into his cabin and returned to the deck with a pair of drawn pistols. He sang out, "Cut away, if you like, my lads! Damn your knives; I've seen more of them than ever you did! Ashore you must go! Pilot, steer for the landing." As the boat approached the shore, the captain ordered, "Cast off the skiff, and put the men ashore."

The skiff owner, now humbled, replied, "I wanted to get along a bit. You wanted to cut adrift my skiff. I didn't say I would cut your throat. Let's have a horn, captain, and shake hands." The skipper growled a little, but finally accompanied the three men to the bar where they had a sling and became friends.[20]

## EYE GOUGING

Eye gouging—the tearing out of an opponent's eye by forcing the thumb deep into a person's eye socket and popping the eye out—was deeply embedded in frontier thought. The term was once used in a speech to the Kentucky House of Representatives. The member said, "We must have war with Great Britain. War will ruin her commerce. Commerce is the apple of Britain's eye. There we must gouge her."[21]

The art of eye gouging was seriously practiced. On 10 June 1809 a man named Hall, while riding through an isolated part of Georgia, was startled by loud, profane, and boisterous voices, coming from heavy undergrowth off to the side of the road. Hall surmised that he saw two men struggling with each other in the thicket. One of the fighters lunged forward, made a sudden plunge with his thumbs, and the other cried out, "Enough! My eye's out!" Hall stood transfixed with horror. He saw a young fellow about eighteen years old rise from the ground behind a bush and heard him shout, "Now, blast your corn-shucking soul, come cuttn'n shines bout me agin, next time I come to the court house, I will get you! Get your owl-eye in again if you can!"

The youth saw Hall for the first time and became exceedingly embarrassed. Hall shouted to the retreating ruffian, "Come back, you brute! Assist me in relieving your fellow mortal, whom you have ruined forever!" With a curl of the nose, the youth replied, "You needn't kick before you're spurr'd. There ain't nobody there, nor ha'nt been nother. I was just seein' how I could fout." The gouger then stalked off to a plow about thirty yards from the mock battle ground. Hall dismounted and examined the field of battle. He found two thumb holes poked in the soft earth corresponding to the distance between a man's eyes. The ground around the holes looked as if two stags had been fighting. The youth was only practicing for a possible future fight.[22]

Gougers often conditioned their hands for more effective execution of the act. Some men grew long thumb and finger nails and hardened them over the flame of a candle to make them more deadly weapons. Even in fights where gouging was attempted but no eyes lost, the contestants' faces were usually cut horribly.[23]

Journals of frontier travelers are filled with notes concerning gouging. John Palmer recorded that he had seen one white man who had lost an eye in a rough and tumble fight with a free Negro who was already nearly sightless as a result of gouging.[24] Thomas Anburey saw several men who had lost one eye and another who had lost both.[25] John Melish, a British traveler, saw a vagabond in the penitentiary at Frankfort, Kentucky, who was serving time for having picked out his neighbor's eyes.[26]

One traveler suddenly encountered a gouging match while riding along a road in Georgia. Two men were standing and clutching each other's side hair in an effort to drive their thumbs into the other's eyes. Excited spectators were loudly betting which one would be first to pop the other's eye out. Two men wrestled to the ground and suddenly one contestant arose with his enemy's eye in his hand! While the savage crowd applauded, the traveler, sick with horror, galloped away from the infernal scene.[27]

Would-be gougers were sometimes successfully interrupted. While staying at a filthy inn in Georgia during the American Revolution, Elkanah Watson and his friends were greatly annoyed by a quarrel between two plantation overseers. The overseers rushed at each other with the fury of bulldogs and tried to blind the other. Watson and others fortunately were able to separate the ruffians before they did any real damage.[28] Later in Virginia, Watson helped to liberate a fellow traveler who had been assailed by a barbarian who threatened, as he put it, "to try the strength" of the traveler's eyeball strings.[29]

In his *Travels* Thomas Anburey tells of a surgeon named Fauchee who had the misfortune to have an eye gouged out, although happily it was quickly replaced and showed some promise that it might remain useful. The surgeon was playing billiards when a local gouger entered the room and provoked a quarrel with him. The tough insisted upon settling the matter with a fight. The doctor refused, saying he knew nothing about fighting. The brute assured him he would fight like a gentleman and rushed at the physician. In an instant he popped one of the doctor's eyes out of its socket. While it was hanging on his cheek, the barbarian attempted to pluck it out entirely. A sympathetic bystander intervened and helped the doctor reseat the eye.[30]

The Englishman Thomas Ashe described a biting and gouging match that occurred at a Virginia horse race. A circle was formed around the combatants, a Virginian and a Kentuckian. The contestants agreed to fight "rough and tumble." Bulk and bone favored the Kentuckian, science and craft the Virginian.

The wiry Virginian rushed the Kentuckian and knocked him flat. The crowd roared its approval as the aggressor jabbed his knees hard into his enemy's body. The wild betting of the spectators favored the Virginian. The Kentuckian, roaring with pain, began to squeeze his prey to death like a snake. He locked his arms and legs around his opponent in a death-vise. The Virginian, choking for breath, released the hair and eyes of his opponent and embraced him tightly as the two men went rolling over each other. The bets of the rowdy people continued to favor the Virginian as the Kentuckian had by then lost both eyes, both ears, and his nose. The final result of the gruesome battle did not entirely please the spectators. The bone and muscle beast suddenly maneuvered his antagonist under him and snapped off his nose so close to his face that no manner of projection remained. With renewed effort, the

Virginian fastened his teeth to the upper lip of his mutilator and "tore it off over his chin." The Kentuckian finally quit and the elated mob carried off their hero, who preferred to taste the triumph of victory rather than receive the care of a doctor. The Kentuckian, who lost both eyes and whose lips refused to close, begged for a doctor.[31]

A particularly vicious spur-of-the-moment fight occurred one day between two strangers. In the rush to board a steamboat which had just tied up to a floating wharf, a young man wearing coarse homespun clothing and a coonskin cap was the first to start up the gangplank. He was overtaken and accidentally pushed into the water by a gigantic fellow wearing a bear skin coat. As the young man arose from the muddy waters, he stuck a clenched fist into the air and sputtered, "Hold on there—you thin mild-livered skunk! Hold on till I get on shore, and may I cut up for shoepacks if I don't make your skillet-faced phizcymahogany look like a cabbage made into sour krout!" The offender explained that the incident was accidental but warned his opponent, "If you want a tussel I am har— just like a fin on a catfish's back!"

The thoroughly drenched and angry younger man waded ashore where he was met by his opponent. With clenched fists and eyes gleaming like an enraged panther, the older man loudly bragged of his ability as a fighter. The younger man seemed unimpressed and challenged, "You pushed me off the plank and you must fight."

The two men removed some of their heavier clothing and prepared for battle. The wet ruffian drove his fist into his adversary's chest but in quick order received a blow that left his cheek bone bare. Wearing a pair of iron-bound knuckles, the older man struck the younger one in the face bringing a gush of blood from his mouth and leaving two teeth hanging by the gums. A mighty blow to the temple knocked out the wet fighter. "Thar," said the older man, "I hope he is got enough," and he took a long, deep swallow of brandy from a flask handed him by a companion.

But the younger man was not through. Friends revived him with brandy. He sprang up and shouted, "Enough! Yes, when I drink your heart's blood, I'll cry enough, and not till then. Come on you wired s.o.b."

The contest resumed. The younger brute managed to thrust a thumb into one of the eyes of his opponent and left it hanging by a few tendons on the cheek. The older fighter, seething with pain, lifted his adversary in the air, threw him to the earth, clutched his throat with both hands, and squeezed until his enemy's face was almost black. The dying young man managed to draw his knife and thrust the blade deep into his opponent's heart. The mortally wounded man staggered to his feet but soon fell dead in the arms of his companions. His battered young enemy, shielded by his friends, made good his escape.[32]

Eye gouging was also used as means of defense against beasts. One Kentucky pioneer saved his life by gouging out the eyes of a bear. According to a report of the incident written by Reverend James Finley, the pioneer spotted a bear while cutting a broomstick. He believed he could kill the animal with his only weapon, an ax. The backwoodsman crept noiselessly behind the bear and swung with all his strength. Instantly the bear turned and one of his huge paws deflected the ax and sent it spinning to the ground. The angry bear then mauled and disabled the man's left arm and began to claw his face. The Kentuckian was thrown to the ground but he succeeded in sinking his teeth into the bear's nose. Next he gouged both of the beast's eyes out of their sockets. The blinded animal began to scream piteously. Suddenly a neighbor appeared and killed the bear.

Later, when some of the bear-gouger's friends came to Kentucky, one of them asked, "How do you and the bears make it?" He quickly replied, "They can't stand Kentucky play. Biting and gouging are too hard on them."[33]

But not all pioneers accepted the practice of eye gouging. Efforts were made in various parts of the frontier to counteract gouging and other primitive forms of fighting. The clergy, various politicians, and the citizenry as a whole lashed out against the practice. Virginia passed an act forbidding eye gouging, but the law was rarely enforced because the officers, fearing for the safety of their own eyes, made little effort to arrest a gouger.[34] A Georgia legislature stated that nothing evinced a country's barbarity more than the savage gouging custom. According to Georgia law, a person convicted of his first gouging offense would be fined, locked up, and publicly scorned for not more than two hours. If the offender could not pay his fine, he was given one hundred lashes on his bare back and set free. A second gouging offense was deemed a felony punishable by death without benefit of clergy.[35]

A law of the Northwest Territory stated in 1798 that whoever "voluntarily, maliciously, and of purpose, pulled or put out an eye while fighting . . ., would be sentenced to confinement in the jail of the county in which the offense occurred for not less than one month or more than six and would have to pay a fine of not less than fifty dollars or more than one thousand. If the offender were unable to pay, he was to be sold into slavery." This probably marked the last time in the United States that a white person could be reduced to the "status of a slave" by governmental process.[36]

## OTHER PRIMITIVE FIGHTING TACTICS

Other modes of fighting were just as bestial and probably more common than gouging. Some men attacked body parts that even beasts of the field hardly ever did. This style of fighting generally terminated in serious injuries—ruptures, mutilated noses, indented cheeks, and castration. One fellow proudly boasted that he could kick any man six feet high under the chin and break his jaws.[37]

J. E. Alexander learned while traveling through the wild western country not to stop for food and lodging at inns where the landlord had lost an ear, a lip, an eye, or a nose. Such a man belonged to the brawling class and might cause trouble.[38]

A brutal fellow living in Bettie County North Carolina sharpened his front teeth with a file to make them more effective for biting. He boasted of the cheeks he had torn off and of noses and ears he had severed with his teeth. Thomas Penrise of Edenton, North Carolina, was caught cheating while playing cards with six sailors. The sailors attacked the card-shark, and in the melee Penrise knocked out the candle, gouged out three eyes and in quick succession bit off an ear, tore several cheeks and slipped away unscathed. Near the same place, Jarvis Lucas, a schoolmaster, was bitten, gouged and kicked unmercifully and left for dead. When the ruffians were tried for the brutal assault, the punishment was only a small fine.[39]

In Pitt County North Carolina lived the singularly wicked Dupray family. The male members of the family earned their living by stealing and crooked gambling. One evening in a public house, the Duprays began a fight with an Irishman who refused to play cards with them. The Irishman quickly snuffed out the candle and crawled under the table. In the dark the younger ruffians mistook their father for the Irishman and they gouged, bit, butted and kicked their parent to death. This outrage and their many crimes of the past caused the more peaceful citizens to drive the entire family from the state.[40]

Frontier fighting might have been lessened had not some of the more malicious and barbarous settlers encouraged it. In a frontier area of Georgia, Billy Stallions and Bob Durham were regarded as the best fighters in their county. Stallions was six feet, one inch tall and weighed one hundred and eighty pounds; Durham was an inch shorter and ten pounds lighter. Although Stallions was probably stronger, the lighter man had no equals in running, jumping, and wrestling. The champions were friends and would have probably remained so had not some of the more base settlers goaded them into a fight by spreading malicious lies about them.

The moment of the contest finally arrived. A ring was formed and seconds were appointed. The shorter and more agile fighter quickly threw his assailant to the ground amid shouts from spectators that could be heard for miles. Although pounded almost senseless, Stallions managed to rise, but he had hardly done so when he was leveled again. The fall this time, however, changed the fight's course, for, as Stallions fell, he managed to loop his arm around Durham's neck, preventing him from crawling on top. Struggling head to head, the men seemed to be doing no special harm to each other. Suddenly, they both rose to their feet and it could be plainly seen that Durham had lost his left ear and a large portion of his left cheek. His right eye was discolored and blood flowed freely from his wounds. Stallions' face was also a hideous spectacle; a third of his nose was bitten off and his face was swollen beyond recognition.

Within moments the combatants crashed to the earth but remained there only momentarily. Durham unfortunately stuck his middle finger into Stallions' mouth. Stallions gripped the finger firmly between his teeth and began to pummel his opponent with a series of bruising blows. Stallions' friends shouted encouragement. The fight seemed to be nearly over since Durham had the use of only one hand with which to defend himself. In desperation Durham jerked his left hand free, leaving the largest part of his middle finger in Stallions' mouth. Durham wrestled Stallions down and maneuvered himself on top. Lying in this position for a few moments, motionless, and panting for breath, Durham gathered a handful of sand and began grinding it in his adversary's eyes. Screaming with pain, Stallions cried "Enough!" Thus ended the fight amid shouts, oaths, frantic gestures, taunts, replies, and fights among the spectators.[41]

David Crockett was also known for his rough an' tumble ways. In describing his fight with a "salt-river-roarer," Crockett said his assailant gave him a "real sockdodger" which made his "very liver and lites turn to jelley." Crockett lost five teeth and one eye. The river-fighter found Crockett a "real scrounger," who broke three of the man's ribs. In the opinion of the Son of the Alamo, this river horse was the "severest colt he ever tried to break," but, after Crockett got a "bite that could not be shaken off," the two were parted by other boatmen. The two men were so weakened from the brutal combat that they were not able to engage in another fight for more than a month.[42]

With the invention of the Colt revolver fighting became a more deadly game. Rough and tumble encounters continued, but using the Colt was quicker and less brutish. George Carrhart and George Ives, two friends in a mining camp in Montana in the winter of 1862-63, had a violent disagreement. Ives, seething with rage, exclaimed, "You d----d son of a b---h, I'll shoot you!" Immediately he ran for his revolver which he had left in a nearby store. Carrhart stepped into his cabin and brought out his own pistol, which he held by his side with the muzzle pointing downward. When Ives returned, he turned his back on Carrhart and looked for him in the wrong direction. Standing very still, Carrhart watched intently. As Ives turned, he saw his antagonist, swore and fired but missed his mark. Carrhart returned the fire, but his bullet also went wild. Blinded by anger, the two men continued to blaze away at each other without effect. Ives emptied his revolver but Carrhart had one more shell, which he fired into the back of his helpless foe as he attempted to walk away. Although badly wounded, Ives requested another pistol and he cursed Carrhart for shooting a man in the back. Ives was too weak to continue and there was no more shooting. Eventually Ives' wound healed and the two men became reconciled. Ives even continued to live at Carrhart's ranch as though the two had never had a shoot-out.[43]

In Cyrus Skinner's saloon in Montana sat two men, Benefield and Sapp, the first a gambler, the second a miner. They were playing cards. During the game Sapp saw Benefield slip a card from the deck, giving him a flush hand. Seething with anger, Sapp accused him of cheating. Benefield instantly jumped to his feet, drew his revolver, and leveled it at the head of his accuser, who was not armed. Jack Russell, another miner who was watching the game, intervened and order was restored. Moments later Sapp again accused his card partner of cheating. Benefield shot at Sapp but missed. Dr. Bissell, another saloon patron, thrust a pistol into Sapp's hand. The two men then engaged in a wild and inaccurate pistol fight. They fired at each other while dodging around the posts supporting the roof of the bar until their guns were empty. They clinched and Russell restored order.

Two men named Moore and Reeves who were sleeping in one of the bunks fastened to the saloon's wall arose to the noise. Moore, groggy with sleep, immediately placed the muzzle of his pistol in Russell's ear and pulled the trigger. The cap failed to explode and he again pulled the trigger. The piece again failed to fire. Russell yelled at his assailant and asked what he was doing. Moore dropped his arm and asked, "Oh, is that you, Jack?" Russell explained the situation and added, "These are friends of mine and I want them to stop quarreling." Russell, assisted by Moore, succeeded in separating the combatants.

Moore suggested, "Let's all take a drink and be friends." The idea suited both Sapp and Benefield. While standing there drinking, they heard a tortured gasp. Moore went to the end of the bar and found a wounded dog lying there. Moore shouted, "Boys, you've killed a dog." Much relieved, Benefield ordered another round of drinks. The silence was again broken by another groan—this time from one of the bunks. They investigated and discovered a man named George Carrhart writhing in agony. Dr. Bissell made a brief examination and pronounced, "He is dying."

Moore yelled angrily, "Boys, they have shot Carrhart." With an oath he struck the counter with his fist and shouted, "Let's kill 'em!" Moore raised his gun and fired at the two "murderers." The shot went wild because Russell hit his arm. Reeves joined in and shot Benefield in the knee. The wounded man ducked under a table and crawled out the back door. Bullets continued to fly and after Sapp received a wound in his little finger he retreated. Another miner, Goliah Reilly, who had rushed to the aid of Sapp, escaped with a bullet in his heel. The bizarre shooting fray thus ended.[44]

## DUELING

Dueling, a more formal type of fighting, was also popular on the frontier. American duels were quite different from those of Europe, since most American contestants would not accept any apologies on the ground or allow the seconds to arbitrate a peaceful solution.[45] In Europe duels were fought by rigid rules, each duelist having a second. On the frontier some duels were fought without seconds and without rules.[46]

Two families in Illinois who had been feuding for years finally resolved to fight a duel. The heads of the two families met one day in a Salem saloon and one of the men suggested that they go across the river and settle their differences once and for all. His opponent accepted. The contestants crossed the river leaving the disappointed spectators on the opposite shore. Arriving at the battle ground, they removed all their clothes to fight like naked savages. After a decent interval the crowd decided to intervene. They crossed the river and parted the naked, sweating, bloody rivals. The two antagonists shook hands and became friends for a time, though one of the contestants died within a year from wounds received in the duel.[47]

Diverse weapons were used in fighting duels, ranging all the way from stones to guns. Two men in Illinois who were embroiled in a disagreement decided to preserve their honor by fighting a duel with stones. Their seconds placed an equal number of stones, all about the same size, in two piles ten yards apart. On signal, the combatants began hurling the stones at each other. One of the men, stronger and expert in stone throwing, so battered and bruised the other that he took to his heels in a hail of stones.

Duels were sometimes fought with ordinary pocket knives. On signal, the two men advanced toward one another with open knives. Each tried to slash or stab the other. To avoid undue parrying and wasted motion in some knife fights the left hands of the fighters were tied to each other. A knife was then placed in each man's free hand and the contest began. Both combatants tried to pull or swing the other to the ground so that he could more easily slash the downed man's arm or wrist, cutting veins and arteries. By constantly throwing his opponent off balance, the more agile fighter continued to back away and gradually saw his foe weakened from the loss of blood. The stronger and quicker fighter, if his honor were sufficiently vindicated by the abundant flow of blood, often asked to have his hand cut free and the fight ended. However, if it had been agreed that it would be a duel to death, the stronger would administer the coup de grace by slitting his opponent's throat or by stabbing him repeatedly in his vital organs. Duels with knives were far more inhumane and barbarous than those fought with pistols.[48]

Bullwhips were infrequently used as weapons of honor. These long plaited leather whips, when expertly used, seemingly exploded in the air by breaking the sound barrier. Some men were so accurate in the use of them that they could hit a fly fifteen feet away. When used in duels, each contestant stood behind parallel lines that were from ten to twenty feet apart, depending on the length of the whips to be used. Each time the whip's end found its mark a hunk of flesh was torn away. Whip duels usually ended when both men became completely exhausted and both were covered with blood seeping from numerous cuts on their bodies. There were instances in which a whip-duelist lost one or both eyes.[49]

A most unusual acceptance to fight a duel was issued by James Humble to Bernard Marigny in Louisiana. James Humble came to Louisiana from Georgia to open a blacksmith shop, but he later became a member of the legislature. While making a speech to the assembly, he somewhat injured the reputation of the Frenchman, Marigny. Marigny promptly challenged Humble to a duel. Since the Frenchman was skilled in the use of swords and pistols, Humble declined the challenge, saying he knew nothing about this dueling business. Humble's friends reminded him that he would have to fight, as no gentleman could refuse a challenge. Convinced that he would be ruined politically and socially for refusing, Humble sent his adversary a message of acceptance after learning that the challenged party was given the choice of weapons. He stipulated that the duel would be fought in six feet of water in Lake Pontchartrain with sledge-hammers as weapons. Marigny, realizing that his opponent was nearly seven feet tall and that he himself was a little less than five feet eight inches, declined the fight. His friends urged him to stand on a box in the lake and make the best of a bad situation. Afraid of the box and seeing the humor in his opponent, Marigny apologized to Humble. The two men later became warm friends.[50]

The mind often goaded a man suffering from hurt pride to fight a duel he would rather have avoided. Following a grand ball in Virginia, two young men remained with their host and other male friends to drink and gamble. The two young men—referred to as H and B—were intimate friends. On the following Sunday H was to marry B's sister. At the post-ball celebrations the two friends began to argue and they elected to settle their differences with dueling pistols.

Marie, B's sister and H's betrothed, learned of the impending encounter and rushed to the dueling ground to stop the fight. She arrived just in time to hear the fatal shot and watch her wounded lover die. The tragedy was too much for Maria. She became deranged and henceforward rarely ever spoke.[51]

A young attorney in St. Louis was insulted and challenged to a duel by a bully. Fearing that he would be accused of being a man lacking courage, he consented to fight a duel with rifles. The attorney's friends, wishing to avoid bloodshed, plotted to load the rifles with blanks. The attorney was informed of the plan but not his opponent. Feeling secure, the young attorney proceeded to the contest, hoping to watch the eyes of his opponent and enjoy the joke. When the signal to fire was given, the attorney fell mortally wounded; two bullets had pierced his heart. The bully's second, who had consented to the ploy, had deliberately removed the blanks and reloaded his friend's rifle with real bullets. After the duel, both the duelist and his second were arrested and thrown into jail. Both soon broke out and fled. Three years later the murderer returned to the community and was arrested, but his ultimate fate was not recorded.[52]

One of the strangest of all duels was fought with pistols and bowie knives on the Arkansas frontier. A stranger armed with a pair of pistols and several bowie knives entered a tavern that was occupied by several men.

The man was ignored, and, feeling neglected and uncomfortable, he boasted, "I don't know whether you are the very beginning of men or not, but I've got 3,000 acres of prime land, two sugar cane plantations, 150 Negroes, and I reckon I can claw up the best man in this room." When no one bothered to dispute him, the stranger enlarged upon his importance. "I've killed eleven Indians, three white men, and seven panthers, and it's my candid opinion you are all a set of cowards."[53]

Angered when the other men remained silent, the blusterer walked over to one man, a doctor, and deliberately jostled him. When the doctor shoved the man aside, the rowdy drew one of his bowie knives and prepared to carve up his enemy. The other men intervened and the two men agreed to settle the affair of honor with a duel. They would fight with pistols and knives in a totally dark room. The two men, stripped to the waist with their arms and shoulders greased with lard, entered the pitch black room with pistols and two bowie knives. The seconds sounded the signal for the contest to begin. For a quarter of an hour neither made a sound. Hearing a faint sound on the opposite of the room, the doctor fired his pistol but missed his mark. The braggart fired in the direction of the flash of light and a ball struck his opponent in the shoulder. Fearing that he would faint from the pain and be carved up, the doctor fired aimlessly in the dark. A return shot cracked in the room and a bullet tore into the fleshy part of the doctor's thigh. Wracked with pain and loss of blood, the doctor fell with a thud to the floor. Silently the apparent victor, bowie knife in hand, stalked his fallen victim. Fear of death sent the doctor's adrenalin soaring; he arose to a crouched position and drove his knife into his would-be assassin's heart. The victor yelled to the seconds to open the door. "They found the doctor weltering in his blood, but still holding his knife up to the hilt in the dead man's body." The doctor eventually recovered.[54]

One of the most publicized western duels of the nineteenth century was one between Andrew Jackson and Charles Dickinson. A feud between the two men grew out of personal and political differences. Eventually Dickinson and his followers plotted to kill Jackson.

While Jackson was speaking to a crowd, Dickinson rudely interrupted and reminded the General that he had lived with another man's wife—a statement that was technically true in that Jackson and Rachel Donelson had unknowingly married a short time before Rachel's divorce was final. Jackson, who adored his wife, started toward Dickinson to "clean his scooter" then and there. But Dickinson's friends saw to it that no fight occurred at this time. They knew that Dickinson was a crack shot with a pistol and they wanted Jackson to challenge him to a duel. Jackson did just what they expected. Dickinson was given the choice of weapons and he chose pistols as anticipated.

On the road to the dueling ground Dickinson cut a string with a pistol shot at twenty-four paces. The marksman then said, "If General Jackson comes along this road, show him that," The night before the duel, Jackson stopped at an inn with his seconds where he ate a hearty supper and then smoked a corn-cob pipe. Jackson, asked what he thought might happen, replied, "I shall swing him! Never fear!"

At the dueling ground paces were stepped off and

Jackson's second, General Overton, shouted, "Fire!" Instantly a shot rang from Dickinson's pistol. Jackson was hit, but he managed to remain steadily on his feet. Slowly and deliberately Jackson raised his arm. Dickinson, badly shaken, stepped back a pace or two and cried, "Great God! Have I missed him!" Overton ordered him back to the mark. The General raised his arm and pulled the trigger, but the hammer jammed at half-cock. Jackson examined the pistol and recocked it. Once more he took dead aim, and this time there was no misfire. The bullet tore into Dickinson's chest, striking vital organs.

When Jackson learned that Dickinson was fatally wounded, he sent him a bottle of wine. The General kept his own serious wound a guarded secret; he did not want Dickinson to die with the knowledge that he had hit his opponent. Despite several shattered ribs, Jackson remained standing and refused an examination.

Jackson's life had been saved by two things. The General had a steel determination to kill the man who plotted to kill him in cold blood. "I would have killed him if he had shot me through the brain," Jackson later said. Jackson had dressed properly for the duel, wearing an oversized overcoat. Just as Dickinson raised his gun, Jackson, tall and slim, twisted his body. Dickinson failed to detect this and his aim at Jackson's heart was thrown off.

Although Jackson won this duel, it did him great political harm in Tennessee. Many people questioned his right to recock his gun. Only his great victory in the Battle of New Orleans would erase the stain from his name.[55]

Politics caused other duels. In Northwestern Louisiana in 1839 a political controversy between Francois Gaiennie and General E. Bossier led to an affair of honor. To avoid publicity the contestants rode with their seconds to a secluded spot several miles away from their plantations. General Gaiennie left word with his wife that if he survived, his second bringing the news would be riding a white horse; if he did not, the second would be riding a black one. Gaiennie fired his rifle first but missed his mark. Bossier shot and killed his opponent. Across the prairie near Chopin a messenger rode a black horse carrying the death message to Gaiennie's widow.[56]

A bitter election race for Sheriff of Concordia Parish Louisiana, unfortunate gossip, and business differences between the two men—these and other causes—gave rise to an unresolvable hatred between Dr. Thomas Maddox and Samuel Wells. A challenge to a duel was given and accepted. The weapons were pistols to be fired at eighty paces, and the contestants, with three seconds each, rowed out to a sandbar in the Mississippi River. Maddox and Wells exchanged two shots each, all missed and the antagonists exchanged apologies. All might have gone well from this point had there not been such deep-seated hostilities between their respective supporters. Harsh words were exchanged and soon a melee broke out. When the Concordia Sandbar affair ended, two men were dead and two seriously wounded, but neither Wells nor Maddox was injured.[57]

Although various states and territories enacted laws forbidding dueling, the practice was difficult to stop. The anti-dueling law of South Carolina made the duelists liable for murder, though most juries treated the offense as manslaughter. The trial of a man who had killed another in

126

a duel usually centered around an investigation of the fairness of the contest rather than the breach of the law.

To secure a more effective antidueling law various societies petitioned the South Carolina legislature. Clergymen were requested to preach against dueling and most of them did. Various county grand juries expressed their dissatisfaction with the ineffective dueling law.

In answer to the protests, the legislature established a legal tribunal to decide points of honor that might lead to a duel. The legislature next enacted a new law which imposed penalties affecting the honor, character and civil privileges of the duelists, their seconds, aiders and abettors. This statute affected the life of the survivor only insofar as his estate could be used to support the family of the deceased. The efforts to outlaw dueling in South Carolina were to no avail and the barbarous practice continued.[58]

Plagued with the custom of settling disputes by duels, the first Illinois Territorial Legislature Assembly made the practice a crime for both principals and seconds. Dueling continued, however, as though there were no law against it. Following the death of a duelist near the Kaskaskia River in 1808, the territorial judges and governor adopted an ordinance banning any person from public office who had participated in a duel. It further provided that if either principal were killed, his antagonist would be prosecuted for murder. In the future, if any person were insulted, he was to present the matter to a jury which had power to award damages, rather than resort to a duel.[59]

It is a principle of society that any effective law is a crystallization of the mores of its members. This explains why the early laws against dueling were so flagrantly violated; they were not sufficiently reinforced by public sentiment. The common sense of any age changes constantly, and by the end of the frontier era dueling had come to be regarded as a barbarous and ridiculous means of settling disputes between men. When that happened the practice ended.

Because of the environment in which pioneers lived, frontiersmen had a natural tendency for fighting. Their tactics might seem rough to a person living in today's society where law and order is generally accepted, but on the frontier there was little law to assist in settling a grievance. Men were taught at an early age that to fight was manly and that only cowards avoided fights. Fighting was as much ingrained into the attitude of the frontierspeople as eating and sleeping.

A fight generally took place with weapons that were accepted at that location on the frontier. Sometimes bare knuckles were used; in other instances knives and pistols were the order of the day. It depended upon the time, the place, and the people who were engaged in the fight.

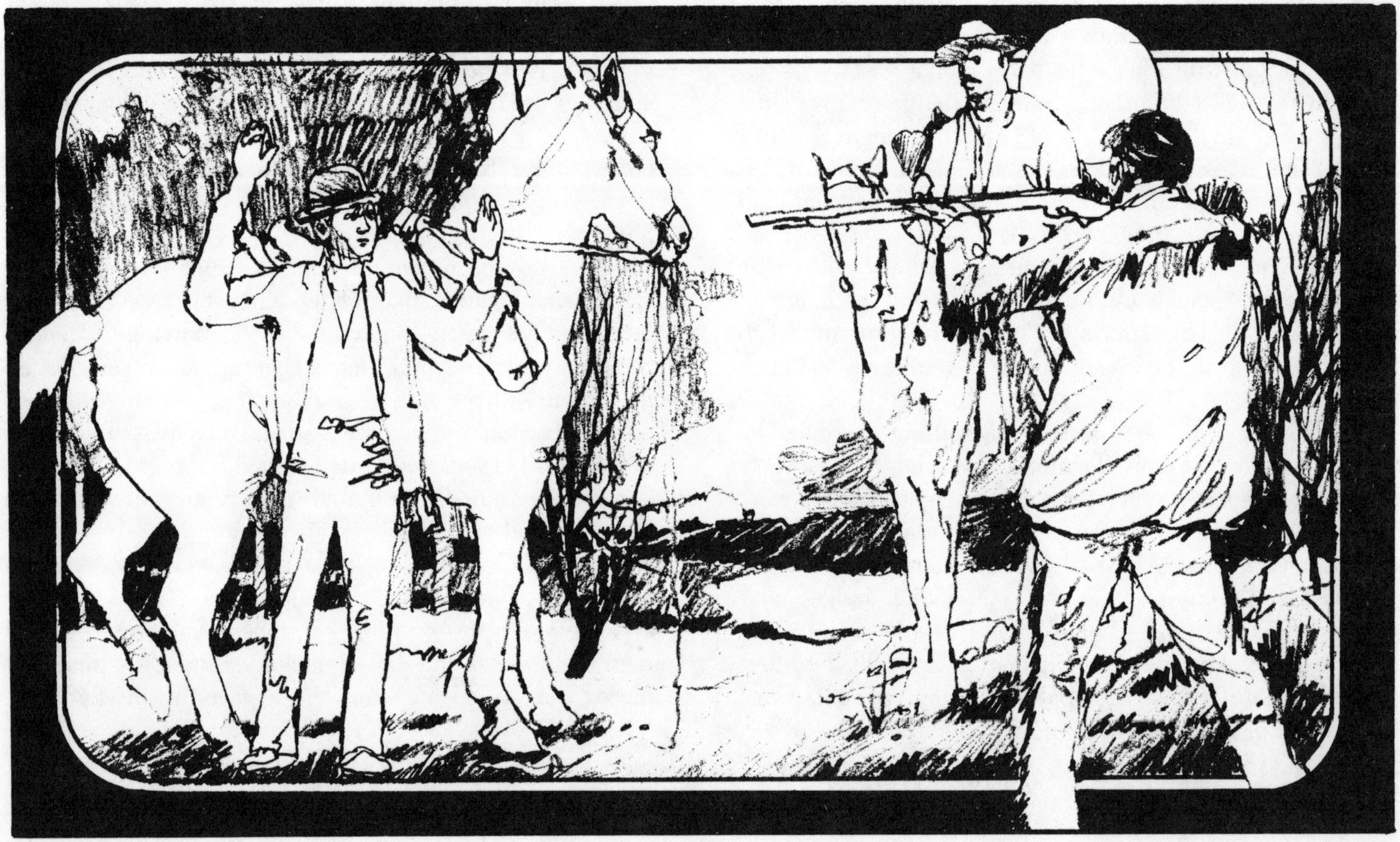

# 9

# Outlaws

Technically, there were no outlaws on the frontier, at least in areas where there were no formal laws to break. However, concepts regarding theft and murder were essentially the same in the wilds as back in the East. Robbing a stagecoach or a flatboat or a person, murdering someone, or jumping a miner's claim were reprehensible acts on the frontier just as they were in organized society. Law or no law, when individual conduct clashed with public welfare, it was considered lawless behavior.

## UNENFORCEABLE LAWS

Some frontier areas did have laws, but because of the chaotic state of societal development the laws could not be effectively enforced. Men sometimes violated the law because of lax social controls and at other times because they considered a law unfair.

An example of a law the pioneers considered unfair can be found in western Pennsylvania in 1794 when a group of pioneers rose in rebellion against Alexander Hamilton's excise tax on whiskey. The primary crop of western Pennsylvania was corn, but because there were no roads across the mountains they could not convey their bulky produce to the eastern markets. They solved this problem by converting the grain into whiskey which was transported to trading posts by means of pack horses over tortuous mountain trails. There they exchanged their whiskey for money or for necessary supplies. To these frontiersmen, the excise tax of seven cents a gallon was crushing and unfair. What is more, the whiskey tax appeared unconstitutional to them since liquor was used as a medium of exchange, and this then was a tax on money.

Revenue collectors who came among them received

harsh treatment. Their commissions were destroyed and many were forced to promise to publish their resignations in the *Pittsburgh Gazette*. A farmer who gave information to the officials as to where stills could be found had his barns burned, and any citizen who observed the law was visited by a masked mob, who might destroy his grist mill and his still, or carry away a piece of his sawmill. One man who dared rent a house to a collector was visited during the dead of night by an armed mob of angry men with blackened faces. The renter was seized and carried into the woods. There they cut off his hair, tarred and feathered him, and tied him to a tree.

Violent opposition to the hated whiskey tax increased. A party of armed men waylaid a revenue officer at Pigeon Creek, Pennsylvania; they stripped, tarred and feathered him, cut off his hair, and took away his horse. Although they had worn disguises, the victim recognized three of them and preferred charges against them in the District Court in Philadelphia. The federal marshal ordered his deputy to serve warrants. The deputy became frightened after being threatened and returned without serving the warrants. The deputy next convinced a half-witted cow driver to deliver the writs "under the cover of private papers." The distillers refused the warrants and robbed the bearer of his horse and money; they then whipped, tarred, feathered, and blindfolded him and tied him to a tree.

On another occasion, the whiskey tax violators went to the home of a revenue officer and demanded that he surrender his commission papers. They were informed that the man was not at home. The mob demanded entrance to search for the records. When their demand was refused, the women and children were ordered out of the house and the intruders began firing their rifles into the dwelling. The fire was returned by someone still in the house. A call came from the house and all firing ceased. One of the bootleggers stepped from behind a tree; suddenly a shot rang out from the house and the man fell dead. In revenge, the angry mob set fire to straw in the barn and the flames soon spread to the dwelling. Both were completely destroyed. None of the whiskey rebels captured were harmed, mainly because of their large numbers. Eventually, a number of them were imprisoned, but soon after a wild mob broke into the jail and set them free.

The rebellion was not crushed until President Washington sent thousands of Federal troops into the area to uphold Federal authority. The rebels, like most pioneers, thought that they were beyond the reach of the law and that they had the right to do as they pleased about the tax.[1]

In the early days of Illinois, politicians and members of the legislature were exceptionally careful to curry the support of the "Butcher Knife Boys." These desperate characters represented a large portion of the original pioneers, many of whom were ignorant, illiterate, and vicious. They dressed in hunting shirts, buckskin trousers, raccoon caps, and leather moccasins, and they wore long butcher knives at their waists. These ruffians were hostile to any form of government which interfered with their freedom. Since the more civilized members of the territory were divided among themselves, these lawless elements represented the balance of power in politics. Any candidate who could claim that he had the Butcher Knife Boys on his side was almost certain to win.[2]

Even as late as 1837, society was still highly disorganized in Illinois. Several Congregational Churches adopted resolutions stating that the insubordination to the restraints of law were so prevalent as to cause every patriot to be alarmed. If something were not done, anarchy would supplant authority. All law-abiding citizens were urged by the churches to support the civil authorities and help suppress the spirit of riot.[3]

On the Louisiana frontier, particularly in Attakapas County—later subdivided into parishes—there were many outlaws. Here the courts functioned slowly or not at all. At first the crimes were restricted mainly to petty thievery, but they gradually became more open and serious—house burning, rustling entire herds of cattle, and murdering people who crossed the criminals' paths. Virtually all of these crimes seemed to have been directed by some central organization, which made it almost impossible to convict the offenders.[4]

A planter in the Attakapas prairie missed his favorite cow and rode in search of her. He arrived at a roadside store kept by a Frenchman and to his astonishment, he saw the skin of his cow hanging on a fence. He asked the storekeeper where he got the skin. The Frenchman said that he had just bought the skin, but he would not disclose the name of the vendor. The planter then threatened that the grand jury would investigate the matter.

The storekeeper was indicted for larceny, but, although he was urged by his attorney during the trial to disclose the name of the man who had sold the skin, he refused and showed no concern for his own fate. The evidence against him was conclusive, but the jury acquitted him.

After the trial, the counselor asked the storekeeper why the jury had rendered its particular verdict. The Frenchman answered "I can speak now, although I will give no names. The man who sold me that skin was on that jury, and there were, besides him, five others who belong to his gang. I was sure of an acquittal." If he had dared to disclose the name of the vendor, his store would have burned down and he would probably have been killed.[5]

With so many murders and fights, and so much general lawlessness in Belmont, Nevada, the editor of its paper was impelled in 1867 to write a scathing denunciation of the town police. He wrote: "Events that have transpired in our midst during the past few days prove conclusively that our police amount to nothing at all." He accused the police of allowing outrages of the grossest character to be committed against quiet and unoffending citizens and of allowing bands of drunken men to defy the "status of decency, and justice and right" until their outrages culminated in murder. These lawless characters, for hours after they had committed their crimes, were allowed to walk the streets without arrest. Only after popular feeling rose against them were they apprehended, and then they were frequently allowed to escape. The editor found the apathy of police officials as strange as it was unaccountable, and he demanded a speedy and radical change. He pointed out that one alert officer could have stopped a quarrel that had occurred only a few nights earlier before it terminated in a murderous affray.

The editor acknowledged that the law-enforcing agents were sorely handicapped by inadequate jail facilities. The responsibility for erection of a suitable prison rested upon the shoulders of the citizens and they should do their duty. Lack of respect for the law would prevent businessmen from locating in Belmont. Stern enforcement of justice would cause those disposed to lawlessness either to become peaceful or to seek a new home in some other locality, the editor said.[6]

## Murderers

Though the James Brothers, Jesse and Frank, achieved unprecedented fame as frontier badmen, they were no more debased than many others.

Richard Lee Mason, a frontier traveler in Illinois in 1819, said that the area only a few years before was inhabited by Indians who were crude and uncivilized and often used the scalping knife and tomahawk in the most inhumane manner. The Indians were replaced by whites who were little less barbaric than the aborigines. He could hardly recognize the fact that one human being could be so depraved as to murder a defenseless and unoffending traveler while pretending to give him a meal and shelter in a storm.[7]

In 1824, a wounded Mexican rode into a settlement on the Colorado River in Texas and reported to W. B. Dewees that his employer and all his associates had been ambushed and killed at a creek twelve miles away while driving horses and mules to Louisiana. Dewees organized a posse and immediately set out to hunt down the murderers. The men rode to the creek, found the corpses and buried them in a deep ravine. Then they went in pursuit of the outlaws. The murderers were overtaken just as they were about to cross the Brazos River. The posse fired and killed all but three. The survivors jumped into the river and began swimming to the opposite bank. Two were killed in the water, but one made his escape.

The posse, in gunning down the murderers, was following the advice of Stephen F. Austin. Austin had long before learned that bringing an outlaw to justice was next to impossible and that uncertainty seemed to magnify crimes rather than decrease them. Austin realistically advised that it was better to follow the thieves, recover the stolen property, and then kill the outlaws. There were no real courts of justice. As a warning to others, the head of one of the murderers was cut off and placed on a pole by the wayside.[8]

One writer, Richard Mason, compiled a list of known cutthroats and murderers in Illinois. The names included were: Gatewood, Rutherford, Grimberry, Cain, Young, and Portlewaits. To satisfy his curiosity, Mason set out to learn all he could about the cutthroats. He rode to Gatewood's home, the first on his list, but he found that the outlaw was absent. The villain's young, beautiful wife was uneasy to have an armed man come to inquire about her husband, and she gave no information. Mason later joined a Dr. Hill and two strangers from Kentucky to cross the "Twelve-Mile Prairie" to Rutherford's tavern, the second on the list.

Arriving at the tavern, the travelers were met by a

man dressed like a Quaker who pretended to be a hostler so that he could examine the quantity and quality of the guests' baggage. Mason recognized this man as a counterfeiter from Philadelphia who had been a candidate for the penitentiary. The travelers asked for the landlord; Mrs. Rutherford said that her husband was away, but she assured her guests that they would be comfortable and well entertained.

A little later the guests were startled to hear a shrill Indian warwhoop emit from a thicket near the house. In a short time, Rutherford and three companions, all armed and half drunk, burst into the tavern. They did not molest the guests but concentrated their attention on the baggage piled on the floor.

That night Mason went outside the inn and heard two strange men whispering in the chimney corner. He spoke to them and they immediately went into the inn. Now there were six bandits in the place, one of whom was Rutherford in disguise who swore that he did not live there. The ruffians were an ugly lot. All were armed with rifles and butcher knives. Their beards were long and greasy and their faces were black with ingrained soot and grime. To frighten the guests, the outlaws began to whisper and slyly pinch each other. They winked and suspiciously eyed the travelers; they poked one another in the ribs and exchanged strange signals. They began to mention certain cutthroats familiar to Mason. They discussed two men who had been murdered the day before. They claimed that the unfortunate fellows had eaten their last meal in this very house. The murderers laughed heartily when discussing the manner in which one man's throat was cut.

Convinced beyond a doubt that these were the bandits that had been described to them, the travelers now realized that their safety was a matter of serious consideration. The night was uncommonly dark and cloudy, and the psychological tensions continued to mount. One of the ruffians went into the yard and gave three lusty warwhoops. Then all of them took their rifles and each one snuffed a candle at forty yards. The guns were reloaded and the flints were picked. One of the ruffians blew a hunting horn three times as a signal of some sort.

The visitors, armed with pistols, dirks, knives and guns, resolved that if they were to be murdered the act would take place in the house rather than in the woods. At midnight the murderers took a huge swig of liquor and lay down on the floor of the main room, while the guests occupied the small back one. The rooms had no solid partition between them, only logs set about six inches apart. The guests lay down fully dressed with their dirks unsheathed, the guards off their pistols and three extra bullets for their guns. The travelers remained on the alert throughout the night. When the desperadoes coughed or moved, the guests did the same. Fear that some of their members might be killed prevented the brutes from attacking Mason and his companions.

When the hosts arose at daybreak, so did the guests. Three of the outlaws departed with their guns and proceeded up the road that the guests had to take. The travelers lost no time in paying their bill and in placing their baggage in the carriage. As they were ready to drive away, one of the outlaws begged Mason to bring some medicine into the house and treat one of the men who had suddenly become ill. Mason refused and told the man to call on one whom he knew better. The guests then bade adieu to Rutherford, his family, and Twelve-Mile Prairie, and started on their way. They had gone only a short distance when they overtook four other well-armed travelers. Thus reinforced, Mason knew the outlaws would not dare to attack.[9]

Other men who toured the frontier often feared that they might encounter debased and dangerous characters. While traveling in the Arkansas territory, G. W. Featherstonhaugh listened intently to a harrowing account of what had happened to a Mr. Childers several years previously. While on the south side of White River, the old bachelor Childers was murdered while sleeping in his bivouac. His body was left to rot and his bleached bones continued to mark the spot. Featherstonhaugh expressed surprise that Childers had not been given a decent burial. The native replied that he had often thought of "this matter," but had done nothing about it.

The next morning dawned bright and clear, after a night made miserable by a leaky roof. Featherstonhaugh expressed a desire at breakfast to bury Mr. Childers, and the host sent his son to point out the spot. Featherstonhaugh and the boy looked among dead leaves and finally found the remnants of the murdered man's skeleton: two shoulder blades, two thigh bones, two leg bones and one arm bone. The missing parts had probably been carried away by wild beasts or flood water. Featherstonhaugh collected the bones and buried them near the spot where the man had slept on the night of his murder.

He then placed a stone over the grave and gave the boy a dollar not only to take care of it, but also to bury any other bones he might happen to find.[10]

One of the most heartless wretches that ever lived was Boone Helm. He was born in Kentucky, but he migrated at an early age with his parents to Missouri. Helm loved the rough and tumble life on the frontier. He possessed great physical strength and loved to provoke fights with anyone. One of his feats of skill as a horseman was to throw his bowie knife into the ground and then to ride at full speed, swoop down and regain the weapon. Once while the Missouri circuit court was in session, he brushed aside the sheriff, who was trying to arrest him for drunkenness, rode up the steps of the courthouse, and made several demands upon the judge. This wild young man married in 1848, but his respectable wife and infant daughter did not influence him to renounce his profligate habits. Helm continued to abuse his wife, and she eventually divorced him.

One of his neighbors, Littlebury Shoot, was frightened by Helm when he was roaring drunk and agreed to go to Texas with the outlaw. Helm later learned that his neighbor had no intention of going off with him, and he rode to Shoot's house and roused him from his bed. "So Shoot, you have backed down on the Texas question, have you?" Helm asked. Shoot, in great fear, grasped for words, but Helm interrupted him, "Well, are you going or not? Say yes or no." When the neighbor answered "No," Helm, without saying another word, coldly drove his bowie knife into Shoot's heart killing him instantly. Helm was tried and convicted for this murder, but because of his odd behavior the authorities doubted his sanity and confined him to an asylum. He later escaped and went to California.

After committing several murders in California, Helm was forced to flee first to Oregon and then to Fort Hall, Utah. Helm boasted to one of his new associates, "Many's the poor devil I've killed, at one time or another, and the time has been that I've been obliged to feed on some of 'em." Some time later while holed up with another outlaw, Helm and his companion were faced with starvation because the frigid winter made the procurement of food impossible. To escape the agonies of starving, Helm killed his friend, hacked off one of the dead man's thighs, ate what he wanted, and put the remainder in a sack to keep him alive until he could find help.

Helm broadened his scene of criminal activity. In Salt Lake City he murdered two leading citizens; he then hurried to San Francisco and from there to Oregon where he engaged in fresh villainies, including murder and horse stealing. From Oregon he went to Florence in the Idaho Territory where he soon provoked a fight with a powerful giant named Dutch Fred. Bystanders disarmed the two men and gave their pistols to the barkeeper. The brutish fight ended when Helm apologized to Dutch for his conduct. Helm asked for his pistol and promised to leave and cause no more disturbance. He took the weapon, walked over and fired at Dutch Fred, but his shot missed. The unarmed man threw his arms protectively over his chest as Helm fired a second shot. This time the bullet pierced Dutch Fred's heart. Helm glared at the stunned witnesses and snarled "Maybe some more of you want some of this!" Again, the murderer escaped.

In the autumn of 1862, Helm was arrested for a new crime, the mysterious disappearance of a fellow traveling companion. Weakened from lack of food and rest, he made no resistance. When asked what became of his "friend," he replied, "Why, do you suppose that I'm a damn fool enough to starve to death when I can help it? I ate him up, of course." The man was never found and it was believed that he had done just what he said. Once again the repulsive, cannibalistic murderer escaped, but he eventually met his fate on the gallows.[11]

Another murderer had the reputation of having killed ten men in unfair fights. As a school boy J, as he was called, was noted for his infernal temper and diabolical disposition and was feared by his fellow students. Once he whipped and threatened to kill the schoolmaster. A Negro boy was J's first victim. During a ballgame, the Negro, because of his skill as a player, incurred the jealousy of his white opponent, and J split the skull of the Negro boy with a paddle in a fit of rage. At the age of thirty-six, J had already killed several men and he walked about with a rifle on his shoulder, a dagger at his waist, and a belt full of pistols. J was a walking arsenal because he feared reprisals from the relatives and friends of his many victims.

The murderer J had never been convicted, because he was able to pay a lawyer large sums of money to keep him from being brought to trial. When he was arrested and imprisoned, his friends and relatives set fire to the jail and released him.

One young man foolishly boasted that he was not afraid of this bully. J learned of this remark and followed the young man into a room and shot him dead. J became a political enemy of Andrew Jackson and once, when the general was on his way to Washington, the murderer and several other desperadoes waited in ambush to kill Congressman Jackson. The miscreants' murder plot might have succeeded had not several of Jackson's friends intervened.[12]

A few characters were even more vicious than J. In the late 1790s two brothers named Harpe came to Kentucky. The brothers were accompanied by three women—apparently their wives—and several children. These malevolent brothers soon spread death and terror on the frontier.

In the autumn of 1799 a young Virginian named Langford set out to explore Daniel Boone's Wilderness Road into Kentucky. He traveled the mountainous and sparsely settled area on the border of the two states and stopped to eat at a public house. While breakfast was being prepared, the Harpes made their appearance. They were squalid and miserable and seemed to be objects of pity rather than fear. As was the custom, the innkeeper invited all persons assembled to sit down and partake of the meal. The Harpes declined the invitation, apparently because they had no money. Langford, filled with compassion, asked the Harpes to eat at his expense. They accepted and ate voraciously. While paying the bill, Langford imprudently displayed a handful of silver.

Langford left the public house accompanied by his seemingly grateful new acquaintances, the Harpes. A few days later a group of men driving cattle over the same road found a corpse behind a log which was soon identified as that of Langford. The Harpes were immediately suspect; they were pursued and jailed to await trial. However, before the court could convene, the Harpes escaped and fled into a new area of Kentucky which was just beginning to be settled.

In Henderson County, Kentucky, the Harpes acquired an even more dastardly reputation. Sometimes a father would return home and find his cabin burned and his family slaughtered. Plunder was not the murderers' object; they took only what would have been freely given and murdered for pleasure. For example, the Harpes murdered a Negro boy who was riding to a grist mill but did not bother to take either his corn or the horse he was riding. Fear of the Harpe brothers grew so strong that women and children dared not stir from their homes, and unarmed men feared to meet one of them anywhere. Hunters trod the solitary forest ever wary of any stranger they met; they picked their flints and stood on the defensive.

One night two travelers stopped at a home owned by the Stegal family and were given lodging. The Harpe brothers appeared a short time later posing as Methodist ministers. Each Harpe was assigned to bed with a traveler; one bed was in the loft and the other in the main room of the cabin. The Harpes coldly murdered their sleeping companions during the night. To conceal the evidence against them, the Harpe brothers murdered Mrs. Stegal and fled. Their tracks were covered by a heavy fall of snow. Late the next day, the Harpes halted in an isolated spot and built a fire. While warming themselves and preparing for the night, a man who had lost his horses walked up. The brothers murdered him on the spot, thinking he was pursuing them.

The crimes committed by the Harpes so disturbed the governor of Kentucky that he was led to offer a reward for their heads.

To avenge the murder of Mrs. Stegal, a neighbor named Leiper formed a posse and went in pursuit of the Harpe brothers. Wiley Harpe escaped, but the other brother cruelly spurred his jaded horse in a wild flight to escape. Leiper overtook the desperado and shouted for him to surrender. Micajah Harpe refused, but a short time later his horse stumbled and sprained its foot while crossing a ravine. Leiper shot and severely wounded the outlaw. The desperate man returned the fire, but his shot missed. Harpe angrily dashed his rifle to the ground, vowing that this was the first time his weapon had ever deceived him. The cornered, wounded desperado then drew his tomahawk and waited. Leiper advanced toward his foe carrying an unsheathed long hunting knife. He disarmed Harpe and threw him to the ground. Harpe plaintively asked if Stegal were a member of the posse. When told that he was, Harpe said, "Then I am a dead man."

While waiting for his associates, Leiper questioned Micajah Harpe about his latest crimes. Harpe did not hesitate in admitting various murders and said that they were motivated by a hatred for mankind, which he wished to destroy in retaliation for a fancied injury. The brute showed no remorse for any of his murders except the death of his own child. He said: "It cried and I killed it. I had always told the woman I would have no crying about me." He boasted that he had acquired a large sum of money and told where it was hidden. It was a lie; the money was never found.

When Stegal arrived, he advanced to the wounded outlaw and severed his head with a hunting knife. They carried the bloody trophy to the nearest magistrate where they learned that it had belonged to Micajah Harpe. The grisly head was mounted in the fork of a tree where it remained for a long time as a revolting object of horror and a strong warning to other outlaws. This spot in Union County Kentucky came to be called "Harpe's Head" and the road running by it was called "Harpe's Road."

The other Harpe brother fled to the vicinity of Natchez, Mississippi, where he joined a gang of robbers led by a man named Mason. Mason's criminal behavior became so notorious that a reward was eventually offered for his head. The Mason gang occasionally plundered flatboats descending the Mississippi, but they usually allowed them to pass, preferring to rob the men of their sales money when they returned northward by land on the way home. Harpe began plotting against his leader. Catching Mason alone, Harpe slew his chief, cut off his head, put it in a bag and took it to Natchez to claim the reward. The dead man's head was acknowledged to be Mason, but Harpe was recognized by one of his recent victims, arrested and executed.

After the death of the Harpe brothers, their wives—all three of them—asked for protection from the irate Kentucky settlers. Two of the women were wives of "Big" Harpe or Micajah; the other, of his brother. Wiley's wife was apparently a decent woman, and she claimed that she had married her husband without knowledge of his real character. When she learned that Wiley was a murderer, she tried to escape but was held a prisoner by her husband. The woman wrote to her father in Virginia to explain her plight, and he immediately came to Kentucky and took his daughter home. The two wives of Micajah remained in Kentucky.[13]

**RIVER PIRATES**

Many outlaws preyed upon the flatboatmen along the Mississippi River. They first enticed the keelsmen to land, then provoked a fight and killed the flatboatmen. The cutthroats then seized the boats, floated them down to New Orleans, and sold their produce as their own.[14]

Flatboatmen who managed to escape being ambushed sold their produce in Natchez or New Orleans and then began the long journey homeward, walking or riding horseback. They usually carried their money sewed in a red hide bag. The road from New Orleans to Kentucky was hardly more than a bridle path, but from New Orleans to Natchez it was fairly well policed. From Natchez to Memphis—a distance of about 550 miles—the trail was known as the Natchez Trace. Along this path, through an unpopulated wilderness, a traveler was in grave danger. The bloody history of the trace with its many robberies, ambushes, and murders has become part of American folklore.[15]

Flatboatmen learned to their sorrow not to tie up at

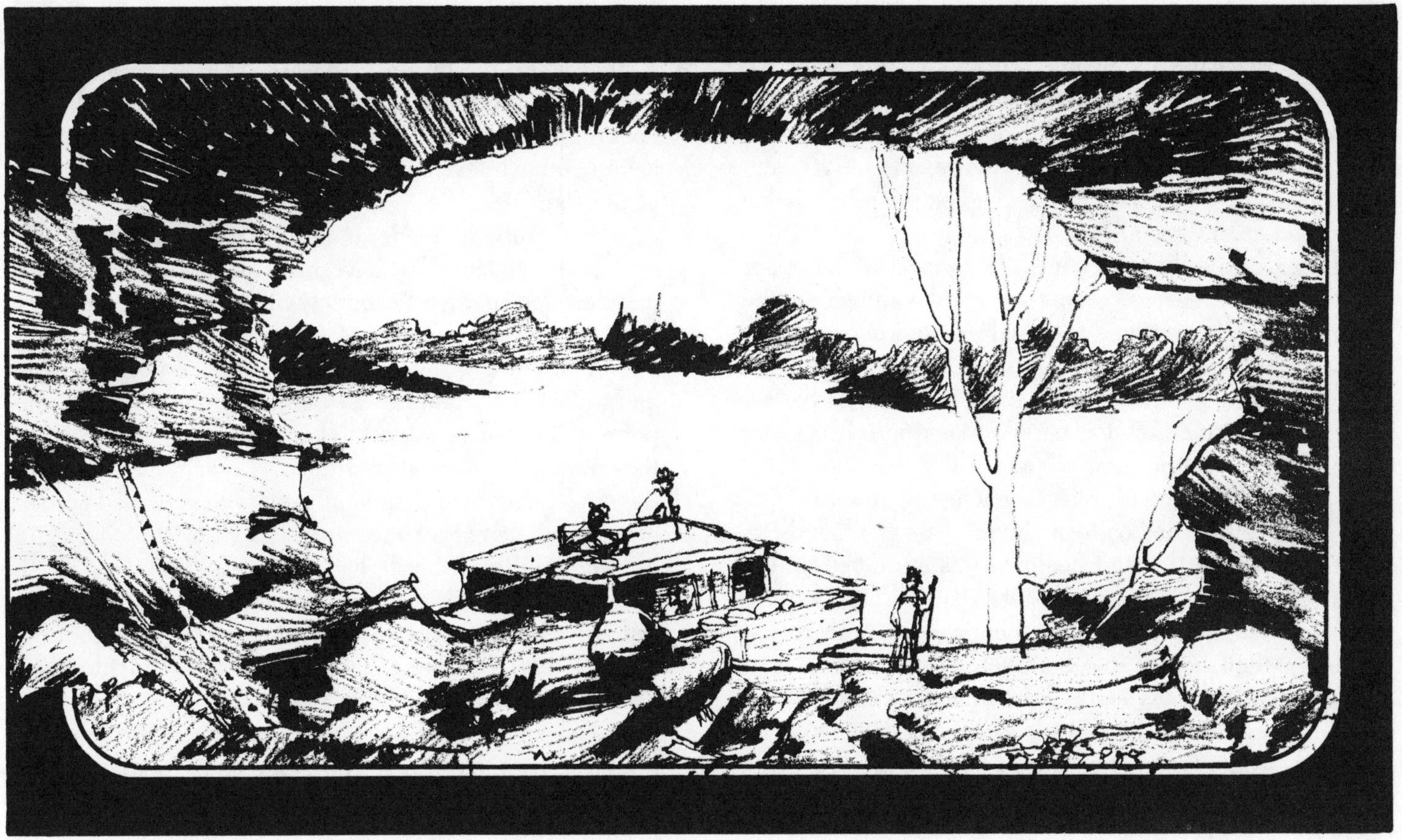

"Cave-in-Rock" on the Kentucky side of the Mississippi River. A specious house operated by a man named Wilson and his gang of desperadoes bore a sign at the waterside reading: "Wilson's liquor vault and house of entertainment." After weeks of lonely travel, the river men could not resist the temptation, and lawless, scummy characters made the place ring with the "clamour of riot, and the blasphemy of gamblers." The nefarious Wilson gang murdered the flatboatmen and floated their cargoes down the river to market. Wilson instructed his men to rob and murder anyone they found on the road on the return home from Natchez or New Orleans.

After a time the merchants and farmers of the upper country became alarmed when they heard nothing from the boatmen or of the produce they had sent down the river to sell. They offered liberal rewards for the capture of the outlaws, and this soon ended their piratical activities. Some of the gang left for parts unknown, others were captured and Wilson himself was killed by one of his associates who wanted to collect the tempting reward.[16]

Many other flatboatmen suffered at the hands of lawless men. One crew of boatmen was murdered on the Arkansas side of the Mississippi River. The robbers disemboweled the dead, filled their cavities with rocks, and threw their bodies into the river. The murderers then appropriated the boats' stores. The infamous Murrell Clan was held responsible for the deed—though this was not their first crime—and the citizens of western Tennessee called a public meeting to stamp out the gang. An expedition of eighty fully armed men floated down the Mississippi River to the place where the murders had been committed. They tied their boat securely and marched single file towards Shawnee Village, Arkansas, where they expected to enlist the aid of the sheriff in apprehending the murderers and in bringing them to trial. While moving along a narrow, tortuous trail, hemmed in by towering, matted cane, the citizen posse was startled to hear sharp whistles at the head of the column followed by clicks of cocking rifles. Hidden by the thick cane, the outlaws had set an ambush less than a dozen yards from the right flank of the file.

Suddenly the leader of the gang jumped out onto the trail and shouted: "We have man for man; move forward another step and a rifle bullet will be sent through every man under your command."

The murder gang granted the citizen posse a parley and, after the outlaws saw how strong the group was, permitted them to depart. Had the citizens been fewer, they would have been murdered. Upon returning home, the citizens learned that members of the gang had actually attended their earlier meetings. They also heard that the Shawnee Village sheriff had been well informed of the punitive expedition planned against them. Not long afterwards, another citizens' committee captured John A. Murrell, and the arrest of the ringleader brought a rapid decline of the Murrell Clan.[17]

During the keelboat era and even after the coming of the steamboat, crewmen and passengers found a visit to Natchez-Under-the-Hill to be extremely dangerous. Flatboatmen who stopped off there on their way to New

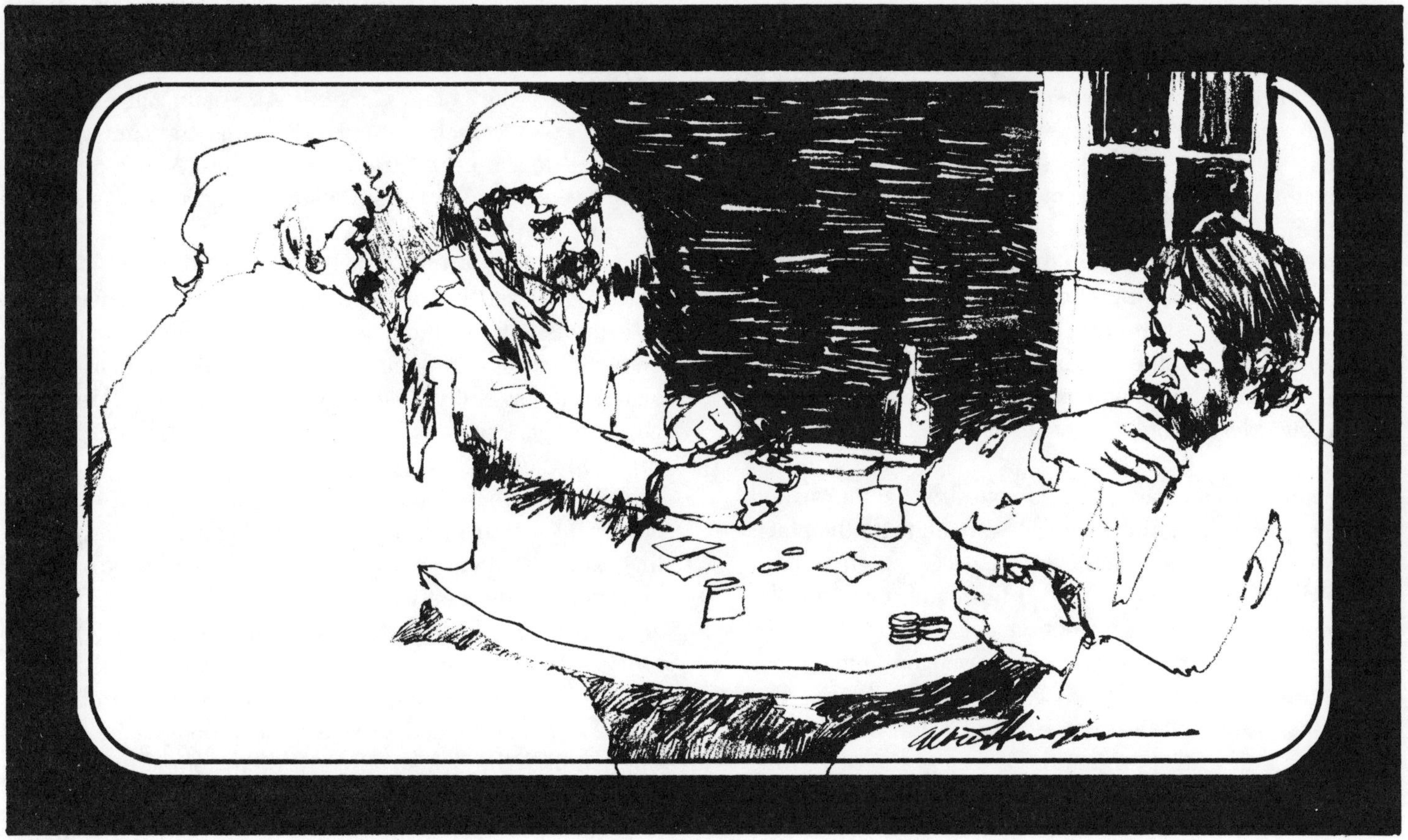

Orleans often lost their lives and their boats. During the steamboat era, Natchez-Under-the-Hill remained a raucous, brawling sink-hole of iniquity, peopled by robbers, lewd prostitutes, and lawless barkeepers.

The place was most dangerous at night. Male passengers with hours to kill before their steamboat departed observed lights in various places of business, heard the sounds of fiddles and merriment, and were often induced to venture into lower Natchez, to their sorrow. Once there, card players stripped many of their money. Loose women enticed them to drink too much and then had them dragged into an alley and robbed. When the bell of the steamboat rang the signal that the boat was about to leave, all lights in the gambling and liquor dens were instantly extinguished. Brutish ruffians seized the passengers, beat them, and robbed them. Passengers lucky enough to hobble back to the steamboat before it left were often bruised and bloody, and they never saw those who attacked them.[18]

When Tyrone Power, the famous Irish actor, visited Natchez-Under-the-Hill in the 1830s, he thought the place the worst "pit of sin" he had ever seen. He reported that it was perilous for strangers to stroll there even in the daytime. A rifle shot rang out just as Power's boat was pulling away from the wharf, and a passenger on the upper deck slumped over dead, shot through the brain. The captain carefully laid the corpse on the wharf and gave an account of the death to the authorities and he steered his ship toward New Orleans. Power learned that the dead man had in some manner "excited a spirit of revenge amongst some of the desperadoes."[19]

Of all the pirates, Jean Lafitte and his gang top the list. He himself was a "strange mixture of magnanimity and ferocity." Before the War of 1812 this desperado placed himself at the head of a band of outlaws from all nations under heaven and established his abode on the Island of Barataria, southwest of the mouth of the Mississippi River. They called themselves Baratarians and lived under the colors of South American patriots. They pirated every vessel that came their way and smuggled the captured loot up the various bayous into New Orleans.

Eventually the United States Government dispatched an armed expedition against Lafitte and his men and drove them from their stronghold, but the government ships had hardly departed before the outlaws were reorganized and re-established on their island. The United States was engaged in war with Britain and could take no more action against the brigands. They scoured the gulf at will until the governor of Louisiana, William C. C. Claiborne, set a price on the head of Lafitte.

Events then took a curious turn. A British naval officer appeared at Barataria and began negotiating with the Lafitte brothers who knew "all the secret windings and entrances of the many-mouthed Mississippi." The pirates could have made the planned invasion of New Orleans much easier. The Baratarians were offered rewards calculated to tempt their cupidity and flatter their ambitions. Jean Lafitte pretended to relish the proposals he artfully wormed from the British officer without committing himself and immediately dispatched one of his men to the Louisiana governor to inform him of the British plot and to offer assistance in exchange for a pardon for the pirates' offenses. The inflexible Claiborne was touched by Lafitte's proof of loyalty to the United States, but he was also convinced that he should not compromise with crime and refused to accept the bargain. As the danger to New Orleans became more eminent, Lafitte continued to report the British plans while he kept himself open to an offer from the Louisiana governor. Urged by Andrew Jackson, Claiborne finally granted Lafitte and his followers "life and pardon," provided they gave their undivided assistance in the defense of New Orleans. Lafitte and his pirates served with valor, fidelity, and good conduct not surpassed by the best volunteers of the republic.[20]

Other outlaws were not as honorable as the Lafittes. In Giles County Tennessee in 1808, two law officials named Reynolds and Rarden arrested a nephew of the notorious Bolin brothers for a felony. The lawmen tied the young man's hands behind him and took him to Columbia, Tennessee, for trial; there were no civil authorities in Giles County.

On the way, the two men and their prisoner stopped at the home of a family named Ford and asked for breakfast. Ford was a friend of the Bolins and asked the men not to eat there, as he did not want any trouble with the Bolins. The officers insisted that they be fed, and Mrs. Ford took them into the kitchen. Suddenly the Bolins rode up and advanced toward their nephew. Reynolds saw one of the men begin unfastening the rope that bound the young man's hands, fired, and mortally wounded him. But, before the man collapsed, he shot and instantly killed Rarden. The other Bolin shot Reynolds and broke his arm, making it impossible for the officer to reload his rifle. He managed to pour the powder down the barrel, but with only one arm he was too weak to ram the ball into its proper place. As the young prisoner began to ride off, Reynolds in desperation offered the Fords fifty dollars if they would ram the ball down so he could stop the escapee. They refused, and because of the absence of civil authority in the area, nothing was ever done about the altercation.[21]

## BADMEN

According to Theodore Roosevelt, some of the so-called badmen were "quiet, good fellows" who had been pushed into a career after being forced to kill a man in self-defense. They then became targets for others who wanted to enhance their reputation by killing them. Having acquired such a role, they had to be constantly on the alert and ready to draw quick and shoot straight. Too often they had to take lives to save their own. Brave only because of their skill with a gun, some men turned into "abject cowards" when convinced they were overmatched. Other gunmen with nerves of steel were ready to face any odds, even death itself, and did not waver or flinch.

Many badmen had been reared in respectable families, but their moral codes were slowly dulled by frontier conditions as they gradually drifted into careers of crime. Harsh frontier life often had a strange effect in changing a man of morals into a badman.

One man from Arkansas anticipated trouble from his two Irish partners. The rival parties lurked about the saloons and boardwalk streets for days, each trying to get the drop on the other. The citizens regarded the rivalry with excited curiosity and had no intentions of interfering.

One day as the Arkansan walked into a gambling hall, one of the Irishmen shot him and broke his back. Despite his mortal wound, he twisted himself into position and killed his assassin. Aware that he had only a few minutes to live, the injured man was determined to kill his other enemy. He anticipated that the other Irishman would be drawn to the gambling den after he heard the shooting, and with super-human effort the wounded man dragged himself out into the street in order to have a better shot. The second Irishman did come and was killed instantly. The wounded man died a few minutes later. In most such deadly encounters, Roosevelt said, the victims "deserved their fate," and people were usually glad to hear of their death.[22]

Nearly all fast-growing railroad towns had their quota of badmen. Abilene, Kansas, became an important cattle shipping point by 1867 and was a boisterous place. For several years it was regarded as the wickedest town of the west, but this title was soon awarded to Dodge City, Kansas. Under the supervision of A. A. Robinson, chief engineer of the Atchison, Topeka and Santa Fe Railroad, Dodge City was laid out in July 1872. One of the leading citizens reported that Dodge was entirely without law and order. The nearest point of justice was Hays City, ninety-five miles away. Citizens therefore settled their differences with the "rifle or six-shooter on the spot."[23]

Teddy Roosevelt was a rancher on the Great Plains for a short while; he wrote that many men had renounced their businesses and worked for men who needed bravos. This was the case in Arizona and New Mexico, where land claims were jumped and cattle stolen all the time. He knew of one or two outfits where the men were good ropers and riders but were also a gambling, brawling, hard-drinking set, too quick to anger and shoot each other or strangers. Too often their rancher boss had risen to power through unblushing rascality. His neighbors knew he was sure to try to shift calves to his own cows, to brand any blurred animal with his own mark, and to attempt to alter perfectly plain brands.[24]

Nowhere on the frontier did the taking of human life carry less stigma than in the gold mining areas. Travelers unfamiliar with the turbulent life of gold mining areas acquired indelible impressions of these places. Lodging in a hotel in San Francisco in the summer of 1859, Horace Greeley found life there most interesting. One morning he was shaved by a nervous barber who pretended to be a nephew of Murat. The main drinking room was also a gambling hall frequented by "blacklegs" who constantly called "Who'll go me twenty? The ace of hearts is the winning card. Whoever turns the ace of hearts wins the twenty dollars." They fired their revolvers at random for the most part but sometimes at each other. This type of conduct was inconvenient for a quiet guest with only a leg and a half, and Greeley, believing he was not too good at dodging bullets, soon departed.[25]

Badmen of the gold regions were as cold-blooded and vicious as any that ever lived. Jack Cleveland, a desperado in Idaho, often drunkenly boasted that he was going to the town of Bannick to get Henry Plummer. Cleveland arrived in Bannick completely broke but soon thereafter robbed and shot William Bates. Later in a saloon in Bannick, he boasted that he was "chief" and that since he knew every damn scoundrel in the area, he would take care of them. Cleveland began a dispute with Jeff Perkins concerning money Perkins owed to one of Cleveland's pals. Perkins assured the ill-tempered ruffian that the debt had already been paid, and Cleveland pretended to accept the statement but at the same time placed his hand on his gun as if to draw on Perkins. Henry Plummer, one of the best shots in the area, warned Cleveland to behave himself or he would take him in hand. Jeff Perkins slipped out of the saloon and went home to get his pistol. Cleveland, his courage fortified by liquor, continued to boast that he was not afraid of anyone present.

At this Henry Plummer grew angry; he jumped to his feet and said, "You damned son of a b---h, I am tired of this." Then he drew his gun and began firing at Cleveland. His aim was bad and the first bullet lodged in an overhead beam. His second bullet struck Cleveland below the belt and he fell to his knees grasping wildly for his gun. He cried "Plummer, you won't shoot me when I'm down!" Plummer replied, "You d----d son of a bitch, get up." After the wounded man staggered to his feet, Plummer shot him a little above the heart, but the bullet struck a rib and the wound was not fatal. Plummer's next shot was more accurate; the bullet entered one of Cleveland's eyes and caused instant death.[26]

Henry Plummer was a man of mystery. Some people claimed he came from Boston and others said he was from England. He had migrated to California in 1852, and a short time later he established a bakery in partnership with Henry Hyer in Nevada City. Plummer seemed to be a gentleman under ordinary circumstances. He had polished manners and an attractive and magnetic personality, but he became a demon possessed by his passions when excited. He built up a circle of friends and was elected marshall of Nevada City in 1857. He did this job well for a time and won a second election. He was eventually nominated by the Democratic party for a seat in the California legislature but then suddenly seemed to lose his balance and was bypassed; the Democrats elected another man.

Just before the end of his second term as marshall, Plummer began an affair with the wife of a man named Vedder. One day while Plummer was visiting Mrs. Vedder, her husband unexpectedly appeared. Marshall Plummer rushed outside and ordered the husband not to enter. The irate husband refused the order and continued to walk toward his door. Plummer drew his pistol and shot him dead. Plummer was tried and sentenced to ten years in the penitentiary, but he remained in prison for only a few months because a group of his friends claimed that he had tuberculosis and successfully petitioned the governor for his release.

Plummer returned to Nevada City and quickly made a bargain with a man named Thompson who was running for marshall. Thompson agreed that if elected he would resign in favor of Plummer, but the citizens learned of the plot and defeated Thompson in the election.

Soon after this, Plummer visited a house of prostitution and while there became irate with another patron and struck him on the head with the butt of his pistol. The ex-marshall left town for a few days but returned when he learned that his victim had not died and made friends with him. He was seen walking the street arm-in-arm with him. The man died about a year and a half later, apparently from brain damage he had received.

Plummer then began a new career as a road agent. His first efforts were aimed at a Well and Fargo's bullion express. Plummer halted the wagon, leveled his gun at the driver and pulled the trigger. The rifle failed to fire and the barrel fell from the stock. The frightened driver escaped and reported the identity of his would-be assassin. Ex-marshall Plummer was tried for this crime but was acquitted for lack of sufficient evidence.

His checkered crime career continued. Plummer killed another man and was thrown into jail. He soon escaped, probably by bribing the jailer. Soon after, a man named Mayfield killed the sheriff of Nevada County. Plummer helped the murderer to escape, and the two men fled to Oregon. Arriving there, they sent word to the California newspapers that they had been hanged in the Washington Territory. While in Washington, Plummer seduced a man's wife and later killed the operator of a dance hall. He then returned East. Plummer was eventually tried and executed for his crimes.[27]

Some outlaws known in the mining areas as road agents operated in small groups. Each man was armed with a pair of revolvers, a sawed-off large bore shotgun, and a knife or dagger. The men were usually disguised with blankets and masks, and their horses were fleet and well trained. They stalked their prey along the roads and sprang from their places of concealment with leveled shotguns to order their victims to stop. Sometimes they yelled: "Halt! Throw up your hands, sons of b-----s!" Any driver failing to obey their command was instantly shot. If he obeyed—which was the usual reaction—the bandits disarmed the travelers, relieved them of their purses and valuables, and swiftly disappeared.[28]

Most outlaws met a violent end; only a few died a natural death. They were either killed in a fight or hanged. "Are you going to the hanging?" was a commonplace question on the frontier. At one execution a large, noisy crowd of men, women and children gathered long before the appointed hour. A squeaking cart bore the condemned man up "gallows" hill. A hushed silence fell over the people. The criminal mounted the scaffold and was asked to sign a paper commuting his sentence to life in prison. He refused and cried "Hang me!" At midday the sheriff stood ready with a watch in one hand and a knife in the other. Just as the officer raised his hand, the murderer screamed "I will sign!" The people packed around the gallows began boisterously shouting and laughing as the cart drove the murderer back to prison.[29]

A man was sentenced to death in Springfield, Illinois, for the murder of his wife during a drunken spree. Thousands of people gathered to watch the execution. Reverend Hargrove climbed up on the roof of the jail and delivered one of the greatest sermons of his career to the large crowd below. This time there was no last minute commutation, and the killer was hanged while the appreciative audience watched.[30]

A more gruesome hanging took place in Sangamon

County Illinois, where a large number of citizens witnessed the execution. The murderer had previously sold his body to a physician, and the doctor began dissecting the body immediately, in full view of the crowd. Law officers halted the revolting spectacle and forced the doctor to complete his work in private.[31]

Public executions were so important in the lives of the pioneers that they often dated important events such as marriages, births, deaths, and the arrival of new settlers by saying they occurred about the same time that some infamous outlaw was hanged.

Life conditions make all people what they are. No one is "to the manner born." Because of personal pride, Americans like to think that they are making America, and in a sense this is true. But in reality America shapes the lives and destiny of its people. So it was on the frontier, where the loose bonds of social control spawned outlaws. When the frontier came to have the discipline of an integrated society, the day of the outlaw was at an end.

# 10

# Vigilante Committees

Life was precarious on the frontier. In periods of extreme chaos settlers had one of two choices, either to abandon the community to the criminal element or to join together to establish more orderly human relations. Their organizations were designed to act swiftly and to preserve order. They were pragmatic and stoical in dealing with lawless elements, and their attempts to maintain peace followed no set pattern. At times their action was high-handed and unjustifiable, but the settlers had to choose between peace and chaos and continued to organize.

## RULES AND ORGANIZATIONS

There is ample evidence of how quickly pioneers might enter into an agreement against lawlessness. In the 1760's the people of the back country of South Carolina despaired of redress through legal channels since the courts of justice were often two hundred miles away. They organized themselves to solve their dilemma with a speed common on the frontier. Several men signed a document stating that they would cooperate with each other in arresting and punishing horse thieves and other criminals. After catching a criminal, the organization quickly tried him; if he was found guilty, he was given "stripes" on his bare back in proportion to the seriousness of his crime. The criminal was then ordered to leave the area with the threat that if he dared return his punishment would be doubled.[1]

Other evidence of how readily frontiersmen entered into a vigilante compact comes from the little settlement of Clarksville, across the Ohio River from Louisville. In the absence of a real government, the settlers here called a convention on 27 January 1785 of eleven men—a majority of the adult males of the town—to make laws that were not

150

repugnant to the Articles of Confederation or the Resolves of Congress. They established a tribunal of four magistrates with judicial authority and elected a sheriff to carry out their decisions. This organization maintained its existence until November 1787.[2]

Soon after the American revolution many disbanded colonial soldiers began to commit lawless acts in the Carolinas. Area citizens lacked police officers and were inconvenienced by having to take prisoners and the necessary witnesses great distances to a seat of justice; they delegated judicial powers to an individual named Lynch. Lynch's decisions were regarded as both impartial and effective and were looked upon as having the force of law. In time, when any extra-legal organization took law into its own hands the process was called *Lynch Law*.[3]

When vigilante compacts were written, they usually adhered to the style and phraseology of the *Justice Form Book*, one of the few legal documents some settlers had access to. The constitutions often began: "Know all men by these present," followed by statements that the men would work in cooperation to rid the area of criminal elements, peacefully if possible but by force if necessary. Constitutions usually ended with the date and the signatures of those entering the agreement.[4]

There were various names given to such extra-legal organizations; Regulators, Vigilante Committees, Vigilante Societies, Vigilantes, Law-and-Order-Men, Citizens Associations, Claim Clubs, and Claim Associations all operated at various times—sometimes secretly and sometimes openly—to apprehend and punish criminals. Usually the organizations gave accused criminals some type of trial, but they hardly ever rendered a verdict of "not guilty." They believed that firmness was the only way to maintain discipline in a chaotic situation. It was always futile for the accused to make a plea for change of venue; the associations were courts of last resort and their verdicts were final.

It was useless for anyone to ask for clemency in behalf of the accused on the grounds of insanity, though this was sometimes done, particularly before legalized juries and in rare instances before citizens' committees. It was deeply imbedded in frontier thought that an insane person was in league with the Devil and had to be done away with.[5]

Each unit of Regulators or Vigilantes was organized like a military company. They most often operated at night and rode out to strike at some criminal hideout armed and equipped, as if going to war. They arrested, "tried," punished, and banished the lawbreakers from an area.

Once a criminal was apprehended, he was guaranteed a speedy trial. There was the danger that elected officials—if there were any—might intervene to give the accused a legal trial or free him for lack of evidence or other reasons. Witnesses were too often unwilling to be absent from their homes for long periods of time, and there was always the danger that the prisoner's friends or accomplices might interfere with the citizens' committee, particularly if they were slow in their deliberations. Even more important, the frontier had few jails and these so poorly constructed that escape was easy.

Insofar as extra-legal associations were directed against criminality in general rather than against particular criminals, the organizations were different from mobs. Vigilante societies operated in areas where there were no courts of justice or where the courts were too weak to maintain order. The associations generally ceased to exist as an area became more orderly and stable. Although many injustices were committed by these organizations, they did hasten the establishment of law and order.[6]

Although vigilante committees usually captured and punished criminals, they sometimes tried to force outlaws to leave an area by posting printed warnings. An example of such action occurred in Texas in 1873:

> Warning to Thieves in Hill Country
> (The names of the thieves were given here)
>
> We give you choice between two things: You can take which you please. Many of your companions in thieving have gone to another country. The ropes and six-shooter balls are also prepared for you by the same one. If you wish to preserve your lives, leave this country in thirty days. Get clear away. If any one of you are found in this country after the fifteenth of April, you will meet with the same fate that (here giving the names of two reputed outlaws), and others have met with.
> 
> Yours respectfully,
> Death to Thieves[7]

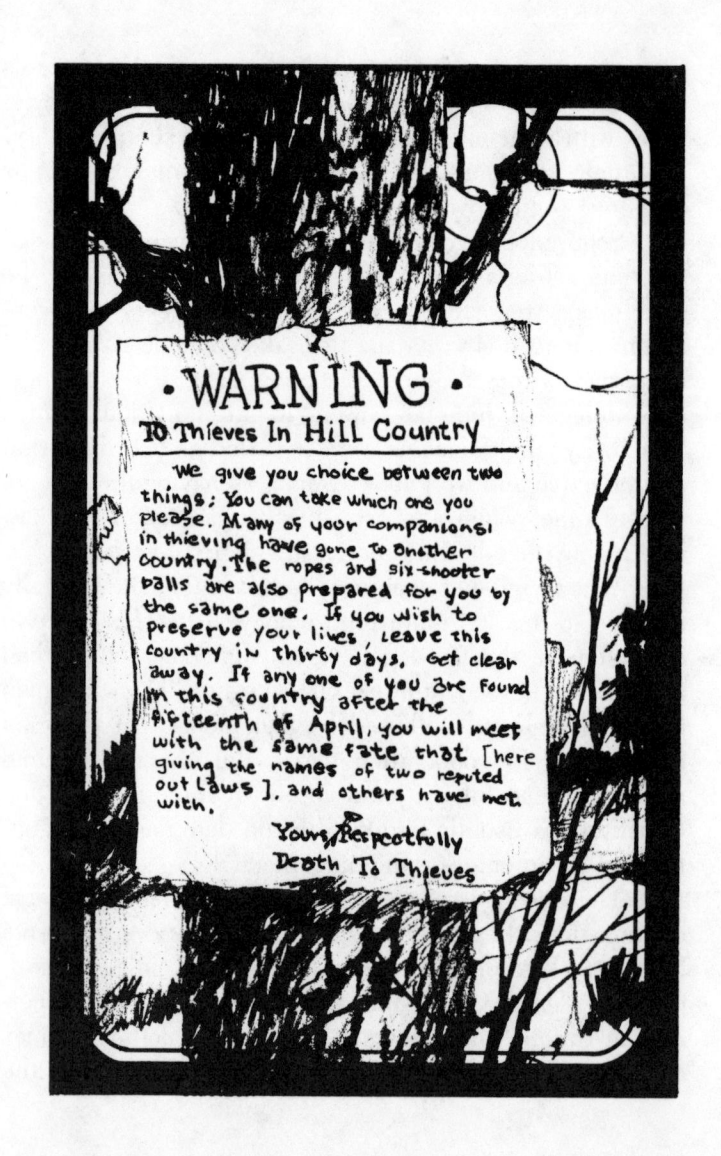

When criminals ignored a public order to leave, more drastic action was called for. In one backwoods community, vigilantes rode to a recalcitrant outlaw's cabin one night, seized him, and tied him to a tree. The vigilantes took turns beating him with a stiff leather strip. Even after the severe beating the culprit remained in the region, and the regulators paid him a second visit. The second penalty was more severe; they cut off his ears. The mutilated man delayed his departure no longer, and his punishment served as a warning to all other undesirable characters to leave the area.[8]

## GOLD FIELD COURTS

Of all the frontier people, miners probably made the most use of extra-legal associations. Life conditions in the gold mining areas were similar in some respects to those on other frontiers and quite different in others. Gold miners had free use of the land and its available resources—water, wild game, and all the gold they could find. Fortune seekers, mostly men, flocked to the gold fields from all parts of the world. After a strike in a locality, it was not uncommon for the population to increase by several thousand within ninety days. Gold miners lived further from an organized society than most pioneers, but they were able to procure most supplies (at highly inflated prices) from the civilized world. However, most other influences of the American society were lacking.

Miners found it as necessary as other frontiersmen to establish vigilante groups for protection. In parts of California where Spanish culture still remained, the miners chose an *alcalde* and gave him the power to hear complaints, settle disputes, summon juries, and enforce the unwritten by-laws of the camps. In most mining towns, however, courts were formed by calling a mass meeting and electing a temporary chairman to handle the immediate business. If the town was large a jury was drawn; if small, a decision was rendered by those present. When a horse thief, a claim jumper, a sluice robber, a thief, or a murderer was tried, the chairman delivered the charge and the offender was defended and prosecuted by men who had studied at least some law. In personal matters relating to debts, quarrels, and individual differences, the courts took little or no action, since it was believed that each man should settle such matters for himself.[9]

A mining court in its earliest form was an assembly of the freemen in open council. Men of all ages—whether sixteen or sixty—who swung a pick or held a claim participated in its deliberations. The citizens elected a presiding officer and judge, impanelled a jury of six or twelve men, summoned witnesses, and proceeded with the trial. In some cases there was no jury or regular court proceedings. The case was simply submitted to the assemblage without argument and an irrevocable voice vote was taken. Justice was swift and severe. A convicted thief might be publicly whipped, expelled from camp, and forced to forfeit all his mineral rights. A man found guilty of murder was usually hanged within the hour.[10]

Miners' courts were usually held on Sunday in the open. Miners were often pressed for time and it was not unusual to announce at the beginning of a trial that the proceedings would close at a certain time. When lawyers were used, they were not allowed to cross-examine the witnesses or make long arguments. Long disputation was usually silenced when someone yelled, "Dry up! No spread-eagle talk!" Evidence was presented in a straightforward manner. These folk tribunals had many advantages over conventional courts. There were no adjournments, no waste of time, and no mistrials. In general, the verdicts of these tribunals were rendered in good faith.[11]

If evidence against the accused was weak in a trial but suspicion strong, he was given so many hours to leave the territory before being dealt with as though the verdict had been guilty. No one begged for days of grace to make his plans to leave. Those who received the death penalty were granted one hour to one night to arrange their business affairs before execution, though to guard against a possible mistake the guilty party was nearly always allowed the privilege of hearing a second count of the assembled miners.[12] An English observer who was impressed by the behavior of the vigilantes said, "They did not seem like men, but like judges sent by Osiris from the nether world, so stern and implacable was their expression."[13]

After California became a state in 1850, its newly organized court system was little respected. Following a gruesome murder in San Francisco in the 1850s, a mass meeting was called. The mayor of the city pleaded with the mob to allow the courts to handle the case. While the mayor was still speaking, a young man named Sam Coleman mounted the platform and bellowed "To hell with your courts! We are the courts and the hangman!" His words electrified the crowd and loosed a mighty cheer.

Coleman stated that the people had no confidence in the new courts, and he suggested that those present enter the courthouse and organize their own. The prisoners would be brought before the tribunal, attorneys would be appointed for each side, and the trial would get under way by noon. He said the trial would be conducted "fairly, dispassionately and resolutely." If the prisoners were found innocent, they would be released; if found guilty, they would hang before sundown. At the close of Coleman's speech, there was a moment's silence followed by a roar of approval.

The crowd went quietly into the courtroom, leaving the guards outside. Within a few minutes the court was organized, and the prisoners were tried that afternoon. They were convicted of murder in the first degree, and they were hanged before the sun went down.[14] To the way of thinking of the vigilantes, justice had been done.

## Vigilante Hangings

Of the outlaws who were hanged by vigilante justice, a large majority committed their lawless acts in and around the gold mining areas of the frontier. However, there were outlaws hanged in other areas of the frontier, and their stories illustrate the most vivid and horrid tales of the speed by which vigilante justice was dispersed. Condemned to die, many outlaws went to the gallows with a show of the same bravado and recklessness that had characterized their criminal careers.

The trials and executions of notorious outlaws were usually tense and dramatic affairs. When George Ives was taken into custody, one of his captors shouted, "Let us raise a pole and hang him at once." Several voices expressed approval, but they were silenced by the rest of the posse. Feeling safe for the moment, Ives "chatted gaily" with his captors and gave each one a drink of whiskey.

The vigilantes selected attorneys and a jury, and the

trial got under way. An outlaw named Long John who had turned state's evidence gave testimony that Ives had killed a Dutchman and had boasted of the deed to his associates. Ives was quoted as saying, "When I told the Dutchman I was going to kill him, he asked me for time to pray." The man had knelt down, and Ives shot him through the head as he began his prayer.

Ives saw the evidence going against him throughout the trial, but he displayed no fear. He had many friends, and the vigilante committee feared they might attempt a rescue. The jury rendered its verdict after deliberating about thirty minutes: eleven guilty, one not guilty. A man in the crowd exclaimed, "Thank God for that!" Another said, "A righteous verdict!" Amid the quick click of guns, a ruffian exclaimed, "The murderous, strangling villains dare not hang him at any rate." The criminal had reason to be jubilant, for the eleven to one vote indicated a hung jury. Under normal circumstances, an accused would not be hanged without a unanimous vote of the jury.

But these were not normal times. A miner moved "that the report be received and the jury discharged"; despite some opposition of the prisoner's lawyers, the motion carried. Then someone in the crowd made a motion that the "assembly adopt as their verdict the report of the committee." This motion also carried.

The situation was getting out of hand; the prisoner might even be freed! The prosecuting attorney moved that George Ives "be forthwith hanged by the neck, until dead," and the spectators, hearing what they wanted to hear, enthusiastically adopted the resolution.

Ive's friends came forward to bid him good-bye. Some gave "way to immoderate grief." Even Ives saw that his end was near and begged for time to write his mother and sisters. No one showed the slightest sympathy for his request.

Ives then made a will leaving all his property to his associates in crime and his counsel, with nothing to his relatives. He was then forced to climb onto a platform, and a noose was fixed around his neck. When asked whether he had anything to say, he replied, "I am innocent of this crime. Alex Carter killed the Dutchman." His protests were cut short. The guard ordered, "Men, do your duty!" In a short time, the judge said, "He is dead; his neck is broken."[15]

Just before another criminal named Bill Bunton was given the drop, he asked for permission to jump off a mountain, but there was no mountain available. He would not wait for the box to be jerked from under his feet, but leaped to his death saying "Here goes it."[16]

When the vigilantes arrested, tried, and condemned George Shears to hang, he was calm and collected, knowing that death was only a few hours away. He walked to the corral with a vigilante and identified the horse he had stolen, saying that he knew his criminal career would soon come to an end but "hoped to run for another season." Shears was then taken to a barn where a rope was thrown over a beam; he saved the vigilantes the trouble of procuring a drop by climbing a ladder. When the noose had been adjusted around his neck, he said, "Gentlemen, I am not used to this business, never having been hung before. Shall I jump off or slide off?" Instructed to jump, he exclaimed, "All right! Good-bye!" and immediately leaped off. His body jerked and twirled rapidly, and all the strands of the rope untwisted and parted except one. But, even if the rope had not held, he would soon have died as his neck was broken.[17]

When William Graves—known as "Whiskey Bill"—was condemned to die, the vigilantes tied a rope to the limb of a tree. Graves was put on a horse and a noose was lowered over his head. The doomed man shouted, "Good-bye!" and dug his spurs into his horse. Whiskey Bill was jerked from the saddle and died instantly.[18]

Not all outlaws met their fate with such indifference and bravery. Two murderers, Skinner and Carter, were sentenced by a vigilante committee to die by hanging. On the way to the place of execution, Skinner broke loose. As he ran, he shouted "Shoot!" No one shot him and he was soon recaptured. While standing on the scaffold, Carter cursed his companion for his cowardice. With the noose around his neck and trembling with fear, Skinner asked for a smoke. A vigilante poked a lighted pipe between his lips. Just before the trap was sprung both criminals uttered, "I am innocent."

Another outlaw, Bob Zachery, dictated a letter to his mother while he was about to be hanged to warn his brothers and sisters to avoid drinking, card playing, and "bad company," the things which led to his criminal career. Zachery then prayed that the vigilantes be forgiven for what they were about to do, because he knew that drastic steps had to be taken to clear the country of criminals. He died without another word.

In another execution, the condemned man was

unable to walk because of a leg injury and was drawn in a sleigh to the scaffold. When a citizen attempted to place the noose around his neck, he continued to dodge it. He was commanded to hold his head still. He submitted and died without a word.[19]

A young desperado named Steve Marshland was "laid up" in his shack suffering from frozen feet and a chest wound received while attacking a wagon train. A vigilante force hot on his trail entered the cabin and began a friendly conversation with the wounded man. Seeing the condition of Marshland's feet, the men prepared supper and shared a pleasant meal with him.

Suddenly Marshland was informed that he was under arrest for participating in the wagon train robbery and was told that he could be identified by the chest wound he had received. Marshland said his breast was as sound as a dollar, but when his shirt was ripped open the bullet hole showed plainly. He could give no satisfactory explanation for it.

The vigilante leader announced that he would die for his crime. Marshland begged, "For God's sake, do not hang me. Let me go and I will trouble you no more." When his piteous entreaties failed, he confessed his crimes.

A scaffold was improvised by sticking a pole in the ground and letting it rest at an angle over the high corral fence. A rope was fastened to the end of the pole and the noose was adjusted to the prisoner's neck. "Have mercy on me for my youth!" Marshland begged. The leader told the prisoner that he should have repented long before; it was too late now. The youth was hanged, and the scent of his frozen feet attracted wolves and made it necessary to guard his body until it could be buried.[20]

One of the most dramatic of all vigilante trials and executions occurred in Virginia City, Montana, the most populous and richest of the mining towns in the territory and the stronghold of numerous lawless men. On 13 January 1863, 500 vigilantes surrounded the city; they had orders to let no one escape, as there were six wanted outlaws in the town. One of the six, Bill Hunter, eluded the pickets by crawling through a drainage ditch.

The next day, cold and cloudy, the vigilantes began taking the five remaining outlaws into custody. The first man arrested was Frank Parish, who proclaimed innocence but later confessed some of his crimes. Next was George Lane, called "Clubfoot George," who also professed innocence. Told that he must die, Lane covered his face with his hands and requested the consolation of a minister. Boone Helm and Jack Gallagher were also soon brought to the vigilantes' committee room. Helm was the most vicious of the lot, but he professed his innocence while holding his hand on the Bible. Told that he would hang, Helm showed no fear; he asked for whiskey and continued to drink until his execution.

When Helm was asked to name his associates in crime, he replied "Ask Jack Gallagher. He knows more than I do." When Gallagher, who had just been escorted into the committee room, heard Helm's remarks, he began to curse his confederate bitterly, saying, "It is just such cowardly rascals and traitors as you that have brought us into this difficulty. You ought to die for your treachery."

When Gallagher heard his sentence he sank down and began to cry, but he was back on his feet in a moment, angrily demanding to know who had brought evidence against him. Informed that it was one of his comrades who had been hanged a few weeks before, Gallagher cursed the dead man and the day of his birth. His fit of anger changed rapidly into a deep depression. He moaned, "My God! Must I die in this way!"

The fifth outlaw, Hayes Lyons, was found in his cabin eating dinner. The vigilantes ordered him to come outside and in his great fear he came out into the bitter cold in his shirtsleeves. Lyons shook violently from the cold and from fear. One of the men brought him his coat and helped him put it on. The vigilantes then took Lyons to join his convicted associates.

Preparations were then made for the execution of the five outlaws. Five ropes were hung from the central crossbeam of an unfinished log store that cornered on two of the principal streets. Under each noose they placed a dry-goods box upon which the condemned men were to stand.

As the vigilante guards were about to fasten the condemned men's arms, Jack Gallagher, with a wild look in his eyes, shouted, "I will not be hung in public." He whipped out a long knife and threatened, "I will cut my throat first." The executive officer cocked his pistol and said, "Take the knife from him . . . and tie his arms at once!" Helm gave Gallagher a sardonic glance and said, "Don't make a fool of yourself, Jack. There's no use or sense in being afraid to die." Without another word Gallagher gave the knife to the officer. Clubfoot George suddenly asked Judge Dance, "Will you pray with me?" The judge complied with the request and dropped on his knees. Clubfoot and Gallagher then knelt beside him, while the judge offered a fervent petition for the doomed man.

During the prayer, Frank Parish evinced deep remorse and asked that his hat be removed. Boone Helm, however, was irritated by the prayer, raised his sore finger, and said, "For God's sake, if you are going to hang me, I want you to do it, and get through with it; if not, I want you to tie a bandage on my finger."

When the nooses were adjusted, the chief of the committee said, "You are now about to be executed. If you have any dying requests to make, this is your last opportunity." Gallagher quickly requested and received a tumbler of whiskey. He drained the glass and said, "I hope Almighty God will strike every one of you with forked lightning and that I shall meet you all in the lowest pit of hell."

When the men seized the cord to snatch the box from under Clubfoot George, he shouted to one of his friends, "Good-bye, old fellow, I'm gone." He leaped from the box before it was removed and died quickly.

Boone Helm watched the swaying body and muttered, "There goes one to hell." Gallagher uttered an oath as the box was pulled from under him. Taking notice of Gallagher's quivering muscles and his threshing feet, Helm remarked, "Kick away, old fellow. My turn comes next. I'll be in hell with you in a minute." Just before his drop Helm shouted, "Every man for his own principles! Hurrah for Jeff Davis!" Frank Parish, as his turn neared, requested that his black necktie be draped over his eyes. He, too, died almost instantly. Hayes Lyons, the one remaining outlaw, continued his incessant entreaties for mercy. Just before he was hanged, he asked that his watch be given to his mistress and that he not be left hanging for an unseemly long time.[20]

Bill Hunter, the escaped sixth outlaw, was captured in a mountain cabin. The vigilante members treated him in a friendly manner and laughed and joked with each other while they all ate breakfast. After eating, the vigilantes held a brief consultation and decided to execute Hunter immediately.

Hunter turned pale and begged for water. He asked that his friends not be told how he had met his death. Since he had no money to pay for his funeral, he threw himself upon the mercy of his captors and requested a decent burial. The vigilantes explained that they would try to meet his request but that the ground was frozen too hard to attempt interment without proper implements. They promised to inform his friends of his death so that they could attend to the burial. Just before he was hanged from the limb of a tree, the outlaw shook hands with all the vigilantes and told them good-bye. Their work done, the vigilantes turned toward home to escape the intense cold.[22]

A vigilante committee in Bannack, Montana, arrested Henry Plummer, Ned Ray, and Buck Stinson and made plans to hang them without a trial. The evidence against the three was too strong to waste time for a trial.

On the road to the gallows, Plummer recognized the voice of the committee leader, went to him, and begged for his life. The leader said, "It is useless for you to beg for your life; that affair is settled and cannot be altered. You are to be hanged. You cannot feel harder about it than I do. . . ." Ned Ray cursed all the while and tried to fight with his captors. He made the air ring with profane and filthy expletives addressed at the posse. But, Plummer was the least composed of the outlaws and tried various arguments to save his life. With tears and sighs, he declared that he was unfit to die and needed time to settle his affairs and to see his sister-in-law.

At the place of execution an order was given to bring up Ned Ray. Just before he was dropped, Ray managed to get his fingers between the rope and his neck, which prolonged his life and his agony. Buck Stinson made no fuss and went to his death calmly.

Next, when the order was given to deal with Plummer, no one made a move. One of the vigilantes let his sympathy overrule his reason and said, "Give a man time to pray." The leader replied, "Certainly, but let him say his prayers up here." Plummer rose from his knees, slipped off his necktie, threw it over the shoulder of a sympathetic young man, and said "Here is something to remember me by." Overcome with grief, the young man threw himself on the ground and wept. The hangman raised Plummer as high as he could in order to give him the "requested good drop" and he was soon dead.

A very short time later Dutch John, another well-known desperado, was brought before the vigilante committee and was given a death sentence without delay. The German outlaw, who had bandaged, frostbitten hands, was overcome with fear. He rose from his blankets, paced the floor excitedly, and begged for his life. "Do with me as you please. Disable me in any way, cut off my hands and feet, but let me live. You can certainly destroy my power for harm without taking my life." The committee refused his request, and he was ordered to make preparations to die. All signs of weakness and fear seemed to disappear and Dutch John calmly said, "So be it, then. I wish to write my mother."

Dutch removed the rags from his frost-frozen hands and painfully wrote the letter. He told his mother that he had come from the Pacific side to deal in horses but he had fallen into evil company. While robbing a wagon, he was wounded and his companion killed. He had been sentenced to hang within the hour for his crime and he considered it a just decision. Finishing the letter, he rewrapped his discolored hands.

Dutch John's love for his mother and his grave and dignified demeanor evinced sympathy from those who escorted him to his place of execution. Standing beneath the beam, from which he soon must die, he saw the bodies of both Plummer and Stinson, one on the floor ready for burial, the other on a work-bench. He stared at the rigid corpses and asked leave to pray. He knelt and his lips began moving rapidly but no sound emerged. He then arose, gave a nod and asked, "How long will it take me to die? I have never seen a man hanged." One of the vigilantes replied, "It will be short, John, very short. You will not suffer much pain." Dutch quickly mounted the barrel and stood perfectly still while the noose was adjusted around his neck. The barrel was pulled from under him, and Dutch John's muscle spasms were soon stilled.[23]

Citizen groups did not confine hangings to murderers and thieves; they sometimes employed hanging to rid an area of a man who was too troublesome and obnoxious. John A. Slade was such a character. A native of Illinois, Slade had enlisted in the army and had won distinction for his unquestioned daring and energy. He was hired in 1859 to run an overland stage, a position he held for several years both to the satisfaction of the company and the public.

Though honest, faithful and courageous, Slade was harsh and despotic in dealing with his enemies or with criminals. He joined various vigilante groups and was instrumental in causing many men to be executed. He was always convinced that he was right and forced compliance to his will even if he had to resort to a drawn pistol.

The turning point in Slade's life came in his relations with Jules Reni, a Canadian Frenchman. The two men had many disagreements, some heated, which Slade seemed to forget but which the Frenchman remembered with increased malice. While sitting on a fence one day, they had another violent argument. Reni rushed into his cabin and Slade followed him, perhaps to apologize. Slade had walked only a short distance when someone shouted, "Look out, Slade, Jules is going to shoot you!" Slade turned quickly and a bullet grazed his body. Jules fired five more shots at his opponent in rapid succession. Seeing his opponent still on his feet, Reni reached for his shotgun and fired a load of buckshot at Slade, bringing him to the ground.

With thirteen bullets and pieces of buckshot in his body, Slade was taken by friends to the stage station and placed on a bunk to die. When Reni heard of Slade's condition, he said "When he is dead, you can put him in one of these dry-good boxes and bury him." Slade, at death's door, boasted "I will live long enough to wear one of your ears on my watchguard."

Expecting Slade to die, a posse arrested Reni. The Frenchman was led to a scaffold without trial and three times was raised by a rope around his neck until he turned black in the face. Thoroughly frightened, Reni promised to leave the territory and was released.

Slade recuperated a few weeks at the express station and then went to St. Louis for treatment. He recovered sufficiently to return to his duties with the overland stage. Reni had not kept his promise to leave the territory and was again engaged in buying and selling cattle. Slade burned for revenge, and Reni was resolved to do a better job in eliminating Slade. Reni bought a special pistol for the occasion.

When it was learned that Reni was lodging at a nearby ranch, four of Slade's friends went after him and imprisoned him in the corral. Slade followed his friends and shot Reni in the mouth the moment he saw him. The wounded man fell on his back and simulated death throes. Slade stood over his victim and said, "I haven't hurt you and no deception is necessary. I have determined to kill you, but, having failed in this shot, I will, if you wish it, give you time to make your will."

One of the men assisted Reni in writing his will. Slade then slowly aimed his pistol and shot Reni in the head. After the murder, Slade rode to Fort Laramie and surrendered. The military authorities there knew the facts of the case and discharged Slade. The stage company did not censure Slade and continued to employ him.

For the next several years, Slade remained a circumspect citizen. As division agent of the Overland Company, he was regarded as an efficient man. When the company changed its route from Laramie to the Cherokee Trail, he built a home in the Black Hills, calling it "Virginia Dale" in honor of his adored wife.

Slade gradually became insanely arrogant. Once, when a saloon keeper gave a stagecoach employee a second drink in violation of the rules of the company, Slade riddled the saloon with bullets and emptied a large amount of whiskey into the street. On another occasion while he and his friends were passing through Fort Halleck, they seized control of the sutler's store and raised so much hell that the officers of the garrison decided to punish Slade. They followed Slade to Denver, arrested him, and held him prisoner until the stage company agreed to fire him.

Out of work, Slade became a miner, and his violent temper, accentuated by heavy drinking, passed beyond control. Hardly a week passed without his being involved in some violent dispute. Even so, Slade remained a determined businessman, bent on success. When a steam-

162

boat was stranded by low water in the Missouri River, Slade with the aid of several men successfully hauled the goods seven hundred miles overland through unmarked country inhabited by hostile Indians.

But Slade's behavior grew intolerable, and the vigilante committee of which he was a member convened when he was not present and decided Slade must be executed. Slade was called in and informed that the committee had decided upon his execution and told that if he had any business to settle, he must attend to it immediately. Overwhelmed with disbelief, he cried, "My execution! My death! My God! Gentlemen, you will proceed to no such extremities. The committee could not have decreed this!" The executive officer remarked, "It is so and you had better at once give the little time left to arranging your business."

Slade began to disintegrate emotionally. He fell on his knees, clasped his hands and shuffled about the floor from one person to another and begged for his life. Slade cried, "My God! My God! Must I die! Oh, my dear wife! Why can she not be sent for?" His request to see his wife was denied because the committee feared that this strong woman might attempt to free her husband.

A scaffold improvised in the gateway of a corral was soon ready. Slade was stood on a dry-goods box and the noose was lowered into place. Several of his friends came up to bid him good-bye. One man pulled off his coat, doubled his fists and swore that Slade would die only over his dead body. A hundred rifles were aimed at Slade's defender and he retreated. Slade was then hanged, and his body was taken to the Virginia Hotel.

Slade's wife was overcome with grief. "He should never have died by the rope of the hangman," she cried. "No dog's death should have come to such a man."

Slade's body was placed in a metal coffin which was filled with alcohol to preserve it. The casket was taken to his ranch, where it was kept for several months. In the spring, it was hauled to Salt Lake City and given a decent burial.[24]

## UNUSUAL OUTCOMES

Punishments by vigilante rule were designed to meet the nature and situation of the crimes. Some appear to be strange and unusual by today's standards, but one must remember that life on the frontier was not typical.

There were times when the verdicts had humorous overtones, at least to an observer. One irresponsible, trifling fellow who deserted his family for long periods and came occasionally to San Felipe, Texas, to enjoy a prolonged drunken spree, made such a nuisance of himself that a citizen's committee finally arrested him and formed a kangaroo court to try him. The sheriff kept himself busy during the trial by whetting a big machete in the most menacing manner. The prisoner's horse was brought up fully saddled, and the defendant's counsel gave him a significant wink. The accused instantly mounted his horse and sped away, never to return to San Felipe.[25]

A thief named Brannon was arrested on the Zanesville Trace for stealing clothes. The committeemen tried Brannon and found him guilty. His bizarre sentence gave him two alternatives: He could elect to receive ten lashes on his bare back; or he could ride his horse led by his wife through the small town, and, as he passed each door, he would cry aloud "This is Brannon, who stole the big coat, handkerchief and shirt." Brannon, amid the laughter of the citizens, carried out the latter sentence.[26] In another instance, an outlaw was much surprised when the committee gave him fifteen minutes to leave town instead of the expected death sentence. The man's friends provided him with a mule and the rascal mounted the animal and said, "Fifteen minutes! Gentlemen, if this mule doesn't buck, five will do!" He lashed the mule's flanks and loped away amid the shouts and laughter of the committeemen.[27]

In Dubuque, Iowa, in 1835, public lands were not on the market, and the only claim to land consisted of occupancy. Conflicting claims over valuable lead-ore lands often terminated in killings. In one of these quarrels a man by the name of Massey was shot dead by two men, a father and son named Smith. The men were indicted for murder and committed to prison. It was later found that the court had no jurisdiction over the case and the prisoners were released. The people were incensed and called a mass meeting to try the father, who had actually done the shooting. Smith managed to escape before he was hanged.

During the ensuing winter, Smith returned to the mines and was gunned down by a brother of the slain man. This Massey easily made his escape since no one cared to pursue him. Smith's son returned to the mines later and he was shot by Massey's younger sister. The bullet struck Smith's pocketbook and he was only wounded, but Miss Massey's attempted murder was considered justifiable, and no charges were brought against her.

Sometimes even in cases of homicide, vigilantes took no action. A dispute once arose between two men over a lead mine claim and ended in a gunfight in which one of them was killed. Since both men had been armed and the deceased was in a position to fire when he received the fatal shot, the committee made no arrest. A short time later, a sister of the dead man walked into a store and shot and injured the killer. Again, the vigilante committee did nothing because they regarded the sister as a brave and daring woman with justification for her action.[28]

During one session of a court in Indiana, the accused kept interrupting the trial procedure with his remarks. At the suggestion of the prosecuting attorney, the judge ordered the accused to keep quiet. When the man continued to disturb the court, the judge ordered, "sheriff, take this man to jail and keep him there until ordered to release him." The sheriff answered, "There ain't no jail, judge." To this remark, the judge said, "Then take him beyond the hearing of this court and bind him to a tree until this case is closed." The sheriff executed the order and the trial was speedily concluded.[29]

The absence of jails gave rise to other odd means of temporarily restraining prisoners. After an ugly-tempered husband had flogged his wife and driven her from home, the wife appeared bleeding and weeping before Justice Tongs of the Northwest Territory for redress. The justice wrote an affidavit, it was duly signed and sworn to, and a constable was ordered to bring the offender before justice.

The culprit was found and the papers served, but the constable, because of the man's great strength, was unable to take him before justice. Whereupon the constable was ordered to parley with the accused and convince him to surrender.

Behaving like an unruly ox, the wife-beater remained adamant until a burly hunter came along and aided the officer in seizing and escorting the offender to the squire's office. There was still trouble however, for the witnesses to the case were not present and there was no jail. The justice could not retain the prisoner without the aid of both the constable and the hunter, so he improvised a plan to keep the prisoner until witnesses were found. He pried up the corner of his eight-rail worm fence two or three rails from the bottom and forced the prisoner's head through the enlarged crack. The pry rod was then removed and the wife-beater was securely imprisoned. His head was on one side of the fence and his body on the other. The infuriated prisoner squirmed and twisted and occasionally bawled out, "Choke trap! Damn! Take your choke trap!"

Just before sunset, the constable returned with the necessary witnesses. The prisoner was removed from the fence, tried, and sentenced to pay a fine and serve three hours in jail. Since there was no jail within a hundred miles, the prisoner was returned to the fence and confined for the stipulated period. At ten o'clock, after arranging to pay the court costs and fine, the prisoner was released with an admonition to leave his wife Betsy alone in the future or suffer the consequence of another "choke trap."[30]

Pierre, in the Dakota Territory, was especially isolated during the deep snow of the winter of 1880-81, and a vigilante committee was formed to control lawless characters. This organization was aimed mainly at one rascal named Arkansas. Arkansas frequently amused himself by emptying his gun along the streets and by going out on the roads leading into Pierre and terrorizing all he met by shooting over their heads or at the ground directly in front of their feet. He was a good man when sober, and the vigilantes informed him that he was welcome to stay in the town as long as he refrained from molesting its citizens. When Arkansas was drunk, he had no fear of the citizen group. One day when Arkansas was drunk, he attempted to hold up a dance hall. The vigilantes suddenly appeared and, rather than arrest the drunken culprit, riddled his body with bullets. This drastic measure had good effects on other law-breakers and Pierre passed the remainder of the winter in quiet. Arkansas's skull later became one of the relics in the museum at the capitol building in Pierre.[31]

In one area, a family named Driscoll which included a father and several grown sons who had recently escaped from the Ohio Penitentiary was ordered by Regulators to leave. Determined not to be driven away, the family and several of their confederates held a meeting and plotted the assassination of a man named Campbell, the captain of the Regulators, and other members of the organization. The Driscoll men went to Campbell's home on Sunday evening just after the family had returned from church. Pretending to be strangers who had lost their way, the Driscolls induced Campbell to come into the yard, where they shot him to death in the presence of his wife and children.

News of the cold-blooded murder caused the Regulators to scatter over the whole country in search of the Driscolls. Driscoll and two of his sons were captured and taken to Washington Grove, in Ogle County Illinois for trial. Three hundred Regulators, some of whom were magistrates and ministers of the gospel, conducted a trial that was both serious and solemn and which lasted most of a day. Driscoll and one of his sons were sentenced to be shot to death within an hour. Immediately after the trial, a minister offered the condemned men the consolations of religion. Then the men were blindfolded and placed in a kneeling position. All three hundred of the men fired their rifles into Driscoll and his son so that no man could be called as a witness. One hundred of the Regulators were later arrested and tried for the murder of the Driscolls but all were acquitted.[32]

Regulator committees sometimes used ingenious methods of hunting criminals. In the vicinity of Monroe, Louisiana, a man with a considerable sum of money was murdered. A committee assembled to gather evidence. One of the members suddenly suggested that all present form a line and march in single file over the body. Solemnly, the settlers began walking one after another over the corpse. It was noted that one of the men walked uncommonly erect and firm, and, when stepping over the corpse, raised his feet higher than the rest. "There," said the man who made the suggestion, "is the murderer." The posse examined the suspect's feet and found that his moccasins, especially the knot that was tied at the heel of one of them, matched perfectly some tracks found near the corpse. The stunned man confessed the murder, and the committee hanged him nearby.[33]

## HORSE STEALING

Of all the criminal acts on the frontier except murder, horse stealing was the most detestable. If a man's horse was taken, he was deprived of his means of travel and transportation and his livelihood.

Two men once came to a tavern in Ohio to inquire about horses that were stolen from them. When asked what they would do if they overtook the thieves on the road, one of them said, "Oh, shoot them off their horses." Although most of the men at the tavern thought this a harsh means of executing justice, they nevertheless believed it was the only thing to do.[34]

Before the American revolution, in the back country of South Carolina, horse stealing became a special problem.[35] The only legal authorities were justices of the peace who lived near the seacoast. When thieves were caught on the frontier, they had to be taken to Charleston, about two hundred miles away. The long trip gave the thief a good opportunity to escape, and witnesses also had to travel the great distance to Charleston in order to win a conviction. Thus, the settlers often banded together to apprehend horse thieves and they punished them as they saw fit.

In Georgia in 1793, the punishment for horse stealing was death "without benefit of clergy." As late as 1809, the first offense for horse stealing was thirty-nine lashes on the bare back and confinement to the pillory one hour each day for from twenty days to one month. The penalty for a second offense was death.[36]

Horse stealing was considered more serious in some areas than in others, and the punishment for the crime varied. When Reverend John Stewart's horse disappeared while he was riding one of his circuits, nine men organized a committee and went in search of the thief. They soon learned that the felon was a man named Baker. They overtook Baker at a stream where he had stopped to let his horse drink. The posse rode calmly forward and two of the men flanked Baker. One of them grabbed the thief and the other the stolen horse. They tied Baker's hands and started back. On the way, the posse stopped at a roadside blacksmith shop and had Baker placed in irons. Just before entering the village, one of the men took off his red flannel shirt, tore it into strips, and fixed them to sticks. The captors rode dramatically into town with flying colors.

They placed the prisoner in jail and then ate dinner at the tavern. They next searched for Reverend Stewart but could not find him. Since the local jail was so poorly constructed and the prisoner might escape during the night, the citizens resolved to give Baker the "benefit of an immediate trial and summary punishment." The court quickly found Baker guilty of horse stealing and sentenced him to fifty lashes on his bare back. Eight of the men were to lay on five stripes, the ninth man, ten.

At midnight, the committee took the prisoner about a mile out of town and stripped him to the waist. They forced Baker to embrace a tree and securely tied his hands. With a knife in one hand and a candle in the other, the sheriff stood by the prisoner and reminded him of his crime and of the punishment in store for him. The sheriff told him that if he made "any ado" his throat would be cut from ear to ear.

The first man in the whipping order stepped forward and delivered five lashes which caused one of the men to exclaim, "Well done, your elbow must have been well greased." On delivering his five, the second member of the court was applauded for a job well done. Baker, writhing in pain, had drawn his body partly around the tree to gain partial protection from a sapling that grew nearby. The third man stepped forward and struck the victim such a severe blow with the cowhide that he lost his hold on the tree and fell to his feet. The sheriff did not count this lick and allowed the third man to deliver five more. After the thief had received thirty-one lashes, the rope came loose and he ran bleeding through the dark forest. The sheriff ordered the men to let Baker go; he had received sufficient punishment.

The next morning the court visited Baker's two uncles whom they suspected of being connected with a ring of horse thieves and counterfeiters. Baker's uncles were ordered to leave the country within ten days or suffer the same fate as their nephew. The improvised citizens' group had thus returned the preacher's horse to him: the thief was thoroughly punished, and two other undesirables were banished.[37]

**VIGILANTES VERSUS THE LAW**

Some frontier citizens opposed Regulator justice on the grounds that all men had the right to be tried by a court. They claimed that the Regulators were often too quick and rash in meting out justice. But territorial governors and judges were unable to execute the laws and often winked at the Regulators or even encouraged their activities.

In many areas where courts were well established, the citizens believed that justice was improperly administered and took the law into their own hands. In Natchez, Mississippi, the townspeople became infuriated when the court declared a reprobate named Foster innocent. When Foster walked from the courthouse a free man, the citizens' group knocked him down, bound his arms behind him, bandaged his eyes, and took him to a ravine outside of town. There they bound the prisoner to a tree and tore his clothing from his back. The crowd took turns in flogging the victim until the flesh of his back hung in ribbons. The vigilantes next poured hot tar over Foster's lacerated body and showered him with a sack of feathers. He was then forced to lead a parade through the streets of Natchez with a drummer at his heels. Foster managed to march to the center of town, but, weakened by his long confinement and severe flogging, he then collapsed. The mob then put him in a wagon with his back to the horse's tail and proceeded toward the jail. The drummer all the while played "The Rogue's March." During his second night in jail, the vigilantes allowed Foster to escape but they warned him that if he returned to Natchez, he would be shot. During this altercation, the law enforcing agencies of Natchez dared not lift a hand. They knew that the vigilantes backed by public sentiment were stronger than the law itself.[38]

The citizens of Vicksburg, Mississippi, also soon saw the ineffectiveness of law, and so they organized to administer justice in accordance with their own concept of "right." The immediate cause for this vigilante movement was the invasion of the town by a sordid group of lawless "river rats." This gang established themselves in various low taverns and began luring impressionable young men to join in their wicked activities. Armed with deadly weapons, these despicable characters roamed the town, insulting, robbing, attacking and terrorizing at will. The few law officers could not stop them.

When a gangster named Cabler struck a citizen at a public dinner, the vigilantes immediately turned on Cabler and made him flee to his confederates. Cabler returned to the dinner in the company of several of his associates and boldly declared that he was going to kill all those who had expelled him. The vigilantes then seized and disarmed Cabler, and took him to the woods. His friends escaped, but Cabler was tarred and feathered and ordered to leave town.

The irate citizens of Vicksburg—including the vigilante committee—soon after adopted a resolution stating that all gamblers must leave Vicksburg within twenty-four hours. To begin enforcement of the resolution, a group of citizens with the vigilante committee as its nucleus, went to one of the gamblers' haunts, the home of a man named North. The front of the house was garrisoned, so the citizens tried to enter by a back door. Shots from within rang out. The vigilantes returned the fire but one of their most valuable leaders, Dr. Hugh S. Bodley, was killed. Enraged by the tragedy, the citizens stormed the house and captured five desperados, one of whom was badly wounded.

The prisoners were given no trial and no time to confess. A gallows was immediately prepared, and a large part of the town's population participated in the execution of the five men. The corpses were left to swing in the breeze from the limb of a tree until next morning.

Public opinion outside the state did not fully condone this citizen action, but public opinion in Mississippi sustained the hangings. The citizens of Vicksburg later wrote an elaborate justification for their conduct. The document compared society to the climatic elements and stated that the air often could be purified only by a storm. Despite arguments against the vigilantes, it was hoped that the people of Vicksburg would not relax the code of punishment which they had enacted against the unprincipled and evil class of society. Vicksburg invited Natchez, Jackson, Columbus, Warrentown, and other sister towns of the state "in the name of . . . insulted laws, of offended virtue, and of slaughtered innocence" to join in driving vice from the land. No one censured either their acts or the manner in which they were performed, since both the town and country folk were decidedly in favor of the course pursued. Public opinion was nearly unanimous on this subject, and this gave the law enforcing officers more confidence.[39]

In Illinois as late as 1841, serious problems of law

enforcement developed, especially in Ogle, Winnebago, and DeKalb Counties. Criminals there used several methods to evade conviction. Sometimes their friends and sympathizers served on the juries; at other times witnesses were induced to give perjured evidence. Another method involved changing the venue of a case from one county to another, thus delaying court procedure and the increasing inability and often indifference of state witnesses to attend the trials.

On the night preceding a trial of several criminals in Ogle County, their sympathizers set fire to the new courthouse. They believed that the prisoners would be removed from the nearby jail during the fire to save their lives and that they could easily escape. The plan failed. The prisoners were kept in jail. During the trial, three of the prisoners were convicted and sent to the penitentiary for one year. One of their confederates serving on the jury was informed by the eleven other members that unless he agreed to a verdict of guilty, he would be lynched right there in the jury room. The other four prisoners succeeded in securing a change of venue and escaped while being moved.

In Massac and Pope Counties Illinois in the 1840s, horse thieves, counterfeiters, robbers, and other objectionable characters had so long infested the areas that punishment by legal means was virtually impossible. The incident which precipitated the organization of a citizens' group came when a number of desperadoes entered the home of an aged citizen in Pope County and robbed him of a considerable sum of gold. One of the robbers left behind a knife that had been made in the neighborhood blacksmith shop and was easily traced to its owner. The robber was arrested and tortured by his neighbors. He not only confessed his part in the crime but also named his twelve confederates. When these men were apprehended and tortured, they confessed and named a long list of criminals in several counties.

In the late summer, the citizens reorganized their association of Regulators and prepared to drive all suspected criminals from the country. In the local elections in Massac County in August 1846, the lawless characters voted as a block for candidates who opposed the Regulators. John W. Read, one of the candidates for sheriff, received about 300 out of 500 votes cast. The defeated candidates for sheriff and clerk of court believed that the winners would not enforce the law, and they became the leaders of the Regulators of Pope and Massac Counties. Under the new leaders, the Regulators captured and punished a number of criminals and drove a number of others from the area. Every suspect was ordered to confess his crimes and reveal the names of other lawbreakers or else submit to torture. Stubborn outlaws were held under water or had their ribs crushed by a rope until they agreed to confess.

Reprisals against the Regulators were soon taken. Warrants were issued for their arrest, but when they were put in jail they were quickly released by their friends. Since the sheriff, the clerk of the court, and the magistrate were highly sympathetic with the criminals and may even have been members of the gang of robbers, the association ordered the three officials to leave the country or stand liable for corporal punishment.

The sheriff requested the governor to send militia to Massac County in August 1846 to maintain constitutional authority. As the territorial capital was 250 miles away and as the governor knew little of the situation, he ordered Brigadier General John T. Davis of Williamson County to investigate and use the militia to restore order if necessary. General Davis called the two warring factions together and got them to reach an amicable settlement.

Davis had hardly departed when violence broke out anew. The Regulators swarmed into Massac County and drove out the sheriff, the clerk of court, the representative-elect to the state legislature, and other officials. Some were whipped and all were threatened and warned never to testify against the Regulators.

Within a few days, the circuit court convened in Massac County. Judge Scates delivered a strong charge against the Regulators to the grand jury and indictments were filed against a number of them. Some arrests were made and several of the vigilantes were given jail sentences. In retaliation, the Regulators assembled at Metropolis City, the county seat, and threatened to release the prisoners and to lynch Judge Scates if he ever again attempted to hold court in the county. They ordered the grand jury and all witnesses to leave without delay or suffer dire punishment. The sheriff summoned a posse to secure his prisoners and to resist the Regulators. Most moderates feared that they would be given the same punishment as horse thieves by the vigilantes and refused to cooperate with the sheriff. Only sixty or seventy men, some of them returning rogues who had previously been driven out, joined the posse.

The Regulators were far more numerous than the sheriff's forces and moved first. Before any violence broke out, a discussion was held and the sheriff and his party agreed to surrender after they had been assured they would not be molested. The Regulators took possession of the jail and released their friends. They reneged on their promise and carried off several of the sheriff's posse, some of whom were drowned in the Ohio River. The sheriff and his other supporters were then driven from the area.

These exiles raced to consult with the governor, who was in Nauvoo in Hancock County with a military force trying to establish order between the Mormons and the Protestants. The governor hesitated to intervene because he was within twenty days of the end of his term of office and did not want to saddle his successor with a policy of which he might not approve. The governor reluctantly ordered Dr. William J. Gibbs of Johnson County to call upon the militia officers in some of the neighboring counties for a force to protect the sheriff and other county officers including "the magistrates, the grand jury, . . . witnesses . . . and the honest part of the community." The doctor proceeded instead directly to Massac County and summoned two justices of the peace to assist him. Dr. Gibbs requested that the Regulators appear before him to help him decide who were rogues and who were not. The Regulators refused. Gibbs then declared that no criminals resided in the county and that everyone was entitled to protection against the Regulators.

Dr. Gibbs proceeded to call the militia from Union and other adjoining counties to come to Massac County to restrain the Regulators. The militia refused the doctor's orders. They knew that there were many criminals in the county and had no intention of helping to protect them. The Regulators remained in undisputed authority and quickly took a number of suspected criminals into custody and tried them by committee. Some of the captives were acquitted, but others were whipped, tarred and feathered. These new actions caused the Regulators to lose the support of most of the moderates. It was at this time that the vigilante opposition came to be called "Flatheads."

The situation in Massac County became even more chaotic when some twenty Regulators went to the home of an old man named Mathis to arrest him and force him to testify against certain persons in the community. The old man and his wife unexpectedly resisted arrest. Unusually strong and active, the old woman felled two of the Regulators with her fists. A rifle was pointed at her breast and she was warned to make no further resistance. She grabbed the rifle, shoving it downward, and was accidently shot in the thigh. Next the old lady was struck over the head with the rifle and knocked to the floor. Her husband was then taken away, and since he was never seen again, it was assumed that he was murdered.

Soon after this episode, the old lady filed charges against her attackers. The Regulators were arrested and imprisoned in Metropolis City. An effort was made to find old man Mathis, who was wanted as a witness, and rumors spread over the country that the Flatheads intended to put the Regulator's prisoners to death if they were not convicted. This report prompted a large number of Regulators to march to Metropolis City to rescue the prisoners, where the sheriff agreed to release them. Before departing, the Regulators seized several of the sheriff's guards and turned them over to a group of Kentucky Regulators. The Kentuckians rode away with their hostages and later wrote that the captives had gone to Arkansas; this was their way of saying they had been drowned in the Ohio River by the Regulators and their bodies allowed to float toward Arkansas.

In December 1846 the Regulators again forced the sheriff and certain other Massac County officials to leave. The legislature, in an attempt to establish order, passed a law authorizing the governor to call a special court when he was convinced that a crime had been committed by twenty or more persons. The purpose of this law was to institute a change of venue in such criminal cases so they could be tried in more distant and stable communities. Law and order eventually returned to Massac County, Illinois, but what happened there illustrates that extra-legal associations sometimes gave rise to more chaos than stability.[40]

Without doubt, vigilante organizations played an important and useful role in frontier life by helping to bridge the gap between barbarism and civilization. Most members of these associations did their work with serenity of soul, motivated by the belief that they were doing a necessary service for mankind. In Owen Wister's *The Virginian*, Judge Henry justified the lynching of Wyoming cattle thieves and the general use of lynch law on the frontier by saying that the law originated from ordinary citizens. It was they who made the laws and they who created the first courts. Ordinary people put the law in the hands of these citizen committees. In using lynch law, the people were only using privileges they had seen delegated to trusted law officials elsewhere. The people were, after all, the original root of all laws. Whatever the evils of the system might be, the good accrued outweighed them. Folk law was the "fundamental assertion of self-governing man, upon whom our whole social fabric is based."[41]

174

# 11

# Acquiring Land

Although there was a vast amount of land available on the frontier, pioneers often found holding onto land difficult. They not only had to cope with government policy but were constantly confronted by claim jumpers and men who would try to take their land away. But as land provided the means of livelihood for the pioneers, they were more than willing to obtain and protect what they thought was rightly theirs.

## GOVERNMENT INVOLVEMENT

The United States Government acquired vast land areas by cession of the original states, by treaty, and by purchase. Congress attempted from time to time to regulate its survey, sale, and occupation, but not all acts were in keeping with frontier needs. Congress enacted a law in 1807 "prohibiting any and all persons from taking possession of, surveying, marking off, or occupying any portion of the lands ceded or secured to the United States by any treaty made with a foreign nation or by a cession of any state." Though the President was authorized to use force if necessary in ejecting trespassers, the Act was never enforced since it was both impracticable and impossible to keep settlers off the Public Domain. Even before passage of the general Preemption Act of 1841, Congress encouraged violation of the Act of 1807 by granting preemption privileges to some settlers who had made improvements on their land.

Jefferson's philosophy of land disposal prevailed and gave the United States a liberal land policy. Beginning with the Harrison Land Act of 1800, land was sold in plots of 320 acres at two dollars per acre, providing the price was not raised through competitive bidding. A buyer had to pay only one-fourth of the purchase price down and the remainder within four years. In 1804, the minimum amount one buyer could purchase was reduced to 160 acres on the same terms, and by 1817, a person could buy a tract as small as 80 acres. But in 1820, the credit plan was abandoned and everyone had to pay the entire amount at the time of purchase, though the minimum price was reduced to $1.25 per acre. This act was in effect until 1862 when the Homestead Act granted free land to settlers.

## SQUATTERS

Most settlers ventured onto the frontier without knowing exactly where they would live. They knew they would have to build their dwelling—a log cabin if in a woodland, or a sod house or dugout if on the Great Plains. Sometimes there were houses abandoned by others, but there were none to rent or buy. Even when a family found a tract of land they liked, they usually could not buy it. Either they had no money, or the land belonged to the Indians, or it had not yet been surveyed by the United States Government. So they often decided to build their home without a deed of any type. These people were "squatters" and were without legal right to the land.

A squatter who wished to buy a tract of unsurveyed land was faced with many difficulties. Except for blazing trees or using a natural boundary such as a stream, he had no way to establish the boundaries of the property, and he realized that when the land in his area was officially surveyed and offered for sale, he would likely not be able to buy it. Competitive bidding would usually raise the price beyond his financial means. A squatter in this situation could do nothing except live in his crude dwelling, eke out a livelihood, and sustain the hope that conditions might change so that he would be able to acquire his homestead.

Quite often such hopes were false. The government would eventually survey the land and put it up for sale. But, with few outlets to markets for his produce, a squatter would not have accumulated enough money to buy his tract at even the minimum price. Unable to borrow money, homesteaders usually did not even attend the auctions. They lived in dread of the time that the man who had bought their land would come to take possession, for they would then have to leave and squat elsewhere.

Not long after the government auction, a man one day would knock on the squatter's door and announce that he was the new owner and wanted the land vacated immediately. The squatter had come to regard the land as his own in a vague sort of way. He had built his cabin and barn, cleared the land and accumulated a few livestock. Squatters were often strongly attached to their property and were sometimes determined that the new owner should pay for the improvements.

Reverend John Mason Peck visited a squatter family in Missouri who had moved several times when the land on which they lived was bought out from under them. At the time of Peck's visit, the family had lived in their cabin for about three years and feared that their land would be sold very soon. The family planned to move to a less populous area where they could live a few years, and where they hoped to accumulate enough money to buy it themselves when it was put up for sale.[1]

Peck rode into another settlement several days later and was surprised to meet this squatter family again. They had an old wagon loaded with household goods, a pair of steers, and two old horses, which the women and children rode. Peck learned that the day he had left the family an immigrant had bought their land. The family was on its way to Black River, where a few squatters, mostly bear hunters, were beginning a settlement.[2]

It was good common sense for the "rale" owner to "pony up well" with the squatter. If the new landlord did not give satisfactory pay for all improvements, he usually could expect reprisals from the squatter. The new owner's house and barn might be burned, his fences torn down, and his livestock killed. In some instances, the new landlord was murdered.[3]

Customary though it was for the new owner to pay a squatter for improvements, they sometimes received nothing. While journeying across Missouri, James Stuart, an Englishman, met a family named Brown who had purchased a tract of land from the government on which a squatter named Eastwood had lived for several years. Eastwood had made many valuable improvements, but Brown refused to pay Eastwood for improving the land and the squatter continued to live on it.

A violent dispute developed between the two men since each in his own way believed he was "right." It was difficult for the Englishman to determine which family could out-shout the other, because both families hurled such oaths and curses as Stuart had never heard. The Englishman rationalized that Eastwood's contentions were not without justification; the squatter had had no opportunity to buy the land, because he was not informed that the land was up for sale. Stuart believed that when the homestead was bought out from under him, the new owner should have paid Eastwood for the improvements, but he left the area before learning the outcome of the dispute.[4]

Some squatters were more fortunate. A few pioneers lived close to markets for their produce and were able to save enough money to buy their tracts at the minimum government price when they were put up for sale.

Immediately after the Black Hawk War, an Illinois man with his family occupied a quarter section of government land. While living in a temporary camp, in and under his wagons, he and his sons broke forty acres of sod, planted corn, and built a fence around the field. They harvested 700 bushels of corn and sold 500 bushels for one dollar per bushel. With his earnings the squatter bought 160 acres of public land from the government at the minimum price of $1.25 per acre.

The following spring, after building a cabin, a barn, and other out-buildings, he sold this farm for $2000 and used the money to buy 640 acres nearby at the minimum price. Here he built a new house, a stable, a granary, and fences and cultivated 160 acres. Not long after his crop was gathered, he sold the entire farm for $4000, keeping his valuable livestock. With the proceeds he bought another section of government land. He continued to prosper and prepared to educate his children before they settled for life.[5] This example was an exception; the family had chanced to "squat" on land that was near good market outlets. Most squatters remained wretchedly poor, possessed few goods, and had almost no money. They were hardly ever able to buy land, and they continued to migrate every three or four years.

**SQUATTERS' LAW**

Although there were many claim clubs, the vast majority of pioneers were not members. In the northern part of Illinois many people had established homesteads before the government survey. Some settlers claimed four or five hundred acres on which they had made valuable improvements. Several villages of six or eight hundred people, were located therein. Without a claim club, the people accepted an obligation to protect each other's land rights.

In this area a number of "mean men" disregarded conventions and jumped their neighbors' claims. The majority of the inhabitants were from sedate New England, and they resolved to protect their interest from the unscrupulous men, even though it meant mob rule and violence. Disputes arising from land claims led to physical brawls in every neighborhood, and the staid Puritans unhesitatingly walked into battle in defense of their neighbors' rights. Here land claims were discussed more than all other subjects combined.[6]

Many squatters were not members of a formal claim club but entered into verbal agreements among themselves concerning the right of each individual to buy a given area of land when it came up for auction. Writing about a public land sale in Indiana, Sandford C. Cox said that the customers were mainly from the southern part of the state, but some were from Ohio, Kentucky, Tennessee and Pennsylvania. The squatters arranged matters among themselves before the sale began. When two men wanted the same tract, each asked the other what he would pay not to bid against him. If they could not strike a bargain, they cast lots to see which one would have the privilege of taking the bid.

If a speculator tried to bid against such a squatter, he suddenly found the whites of a score of eyes snapping at him, making him crawfish away from the crowd at the first opportunity. As there was enough land to go around, the squatters emphatically warned everyone that they should not bid on land they already occupied and wished to buy.[7]

Reverend Alfred Brunson asked a group of squatters in the 1830s why their lands had not been bought up by speculators. They said that the common sense of the country, equivalent to law, obligated each settler to protect the others against speculators. At land auctions, if a speculator dared bid on a settler's farm, he was knocked down and dragged out of the office. If the aggressor was prosecuted and fined, the other settlers paid the expense by common consent among themselves. But, before a fine could be assessed, the case had to be presented to a jury made up of the squatters, and they were pledged to render a verdict of "not guilty."

Brunson also learned that if a squatter refused to abide by majority will in purchasing land, he was in deep trouble. If the nonconformist came into a home at mealtime, he was not asked to eat. He was socially ostracized. If the man did not leave the community voluntarily, he would be ordered to do so and helped in his departure. If he refused to leave or to relinquish the land he had bought, he might be murdered.[8] The gentlemen's agreements among squatters were often as binding and effective as any claim club by-law.

Although preemption laws affecting frontier areas were enacted before 1841, Congress in that year passed a comprehensive preemption act, giving general recognition to squatters' claims. Despite this law, squatters' claims were not always secure. Many settlers' land boundaries were vague, determined only by blazed trees and stakes, and squatters were often lax in recording their land with the government. Thus, before and after the enactment of the preemption law there was need for claim organizations.[9]

## CLAIM CLUBS

A vast number of homesteaders who squatted on land before it was surveyed and sometimes even before the Indians' claims were voided began to organize "claim clubs" or associations. They knew the Indians would eventually be forced off the land, and they also realized that the government would eventually run a survey and sell the land. Faced with common problems—the Indian menace, order among themselves, and above all, a desire to buy a tract of government land—they formed their claim clubs and recorded their claims.[10]

Each pre-survey claim club drew up a constitution setting forth the requirements for making a claim and the amount of land each member could possess. In Illinois when land was plentiful, one association allowed each member to claim 640 acres of prairie and 160 acres of woodland. When land became less plentiful, the association reduced the amounts to 320 acres of prairie and 80 acres of woodland. The club bound each settler to stand by all the rest, for if anyone failed to fulfill his part of the mutual contract, other members would be encouraged to do the same and the club would lose public acceptance.

After signing the club constitution, each member was required to stake out his tract so that the boundaries were clear. He was then expected to cultivate a portion of it —twenty acres or more—fence it, and build a suitable house. His claim was not considered valid unless he lived on the land or placed an agent on it. Dishonest agents sometimes claimed the land for themselves.

The squatters had no legal claim to the land until they had actually bought it from the government. The associations only made it easier for them to buy their chosen tract from the United States Government at the minimum price.[11]

Before a claim club member could buy land from the government in certain parts of Wisconsin, he had to take an oath in the presence of witnesses swearing that to his knowledge there were no lead deposits on the land. The temptation to buy government land that contained lead caused many men to swear falsely. There were instances when prospective customers led witnesses blindfolded across the lands so that they could swear they had seen no lead. Squatters who were not members of a club cooperated with each other in securing lead-bearing lands. One man would buy a section in his name and then subdivide the mineral tract to share with the men who had pooled their money to make the purchase.[12]

The claim clubs, land leagues, and associations in various parts of the Iowa Territory had the same fundamental features as the Illinois organizations and differed only in minor details. They specified the amount of land one could claim, in some instances 400 acres and in others, 160 acres. Sometimes they specified what part should be in timber and what part in prairie. To hold the land, each claimant was required to make certain improvements on it. If he deserted his land for a specific time or failed to make the necessary improvements, he forfeited his claim rights. Any claimant could sell his land to another with the association's approval, but the buyer accrued both the privileges and the obligations of the seller. Provisions were made to settle the numerous disputes between claimants. Prior to an official land survey, each club member recorded his deed claim, fixing boundaries. He had no way, however, of knowing where the boundaries would be fixed by the surveyors. The survey might give a neighbor his house, fence, timber, or cleared field. These and other disputes were settled in various ways: by decisions of courts established by the association; by mass meetings; by special arbiters; or by a neighboring organization invited to review the disputes. Provisions were also made to protect claims against alien parties.

For violating the rules and spirit of the land organizations in Iowa, various punishments were meted out to both members and outsiders. In case of a difficulty, every man was pledged to do his duty, but all members were not in agreement as to what constituted their duty. Some squatters were expelled from the organizations, others were warned to leave the country, and in a few cases men were killed. After one man tried unsuccessfully to preempt a claim, he attempted to flee the country. When he was caught by several association members, he became so frightened that he tried to kill himself with his own knife. In another instance, a minister saved a settler from trouble by persuading him to renounce a widow's claim. In later years, former claim club members stated that they were present on numerous occasions when tar and feathers were administered to claim jumpers.

Distorted news of the barbaric behavior of the claim clubs trickled back to Congress and led some senators to believe that Iowa was a "wild and wooly place." Senator John C. Calhoun said he believed Iowa was inhabited by a lawless body of armed men who had divided the whole region among themselves. He also said no one was permitted to settle without being members of claim clubs and when a settler was fortunate enough to buy a plot of land he paid more for it than the United States Government charged. But at the time Calhoun made these assertions, only a small fraction of the land was under the control of the claim clubs. These associations were not groups of armed, lawless men who denied the right of settlers to make claims or collected excessive prices for it.[13]

Of all the clubs, the Johnson Claim Organization of Iowa was one of the best. This well-organized group begun on 1 March 1839 provided for a president and vice-president, a clerk who recorded and transferred deeds, seven judges of claims and boundaries, one of whom was qualified to administer the oath of affirmation, and two marshalls. Officers were elected annually by all the members. The clerk received twenty-five cents for every claim recorded and fifty cents when a claim was transferred from one settler to another. He also charged twelve and one-half cents for the privilege of examining his books. The judges and marshalls each received $1.50 for every day spent in the discharge of their respective duties.[14]

Any white male eighteen years of age or older might become a member of the Johnson Claim Association by signing the constitution. Any member could become an officer, if elected by a majority of those present. The constitution and by-laws could be altered at the semi-annual meetings by a three-fifths vote of the members. To qualify for citizenship, a person had to live in the country for two months. If one were a member of the club but not a citizen, he was required to spend the equivalent of fifty dollars in land improvements before making a claim. Those who had lived in the country before the adoption of the club's constitution were given thirty days to record their land with the club.

To claim a tract of land, a person was required to stake his tract or "blaze" it so that land lines could be easily seen. The deed had to describe the land in a practicable manner, giving the names of any bounding creeks and rivers, the names of people holding adjoining claims and the range, township, and section designations if the land had been surveyed. Each claimant also had to carve, burn, or paint his name or initials on stakes or trees at all corners of his tract. No one could claim more than 480 acres, and this could not be distributed in more than three separate tracts. The first deed nearly always took precedent over any other that might be submitted later by rival claimants.[15]

Without adequate surveying instruments and with little knowledge of starting points, it was amazing that members of the Claim Association encountered so few line problems after the government survey was run. These difficulties were partially averted because they had required detailed descriptions of each squatter's claim. For instance, Robert Moore's claim was entered in the land book as "situated on Old Man Creek, Johnson County, Territory of Iowa, about one and one-half miles in a westerly and northwesterly direction from Secord's home." His boundary began at a red oak tree marked "R. Moore" and ran in a westerly direction for about one-half mile to a marked bur oak on the bank of Old Man's Creek, thence in a southerly direction across the creek for about one mile to a marked stake. From here the line ran in an easterly direction to another marked stake. The line then ran in a northerly direction to the starting point. This tract contained about 320 acres.

The boundaries of Peter Crum's land in the same county, which contained about 320 acres, began at the northeastern corner of the supposed school section and ran one mile west to the northwestern corner of the school section. From this point it ran one-half mile north and then one mile east joining Royal & Woolcott's claims. It then ran one-half mile south to the place of beginning. Not far away from this plot Peter Crum also recorded a 120 acre tract, giving him a total of 440 acres.[16]

Any member of the Johnson Claim Association who felt his land rights had been infringed upon could take his case to one of the judges, who in turn would set a time and place for a hearing or trial. The marshalls then summoned a sufficient number of judges and witnesses. Before the trial, both the plaintiff and defendant were required to deposit enough money with the judges to defray the cost of the hearing. The verdict rendered in such cases were just as permanent and binding as if decided by the highest court. Any man who refused to abide by the Johnson Claim Organization laws was dropped from the group and henceforth denied all its benefits. At one time the club had 282 members.[17]

Once a claim club was organized and each squatter allotted his tract, members waited patiently for the government survey and public auction. The Johnson County Claim Association found itself involved in two government land sales, one in Dubuque in 1840 and the other in Marion three years later. In January 1840 President Martin Van Buren issued a proclamation stating that the first land sale would be held in Dubuque in May of that year. The announcement took the settlers by surprise; they had not thought the land would be brought to market so soon after the survey. They hurriedly held a public meeting and petitioned the government to postpone the sale for several months. Their petition was granted and the sale was delayed until 3 August 1840.

In July, prior to the auction, the claim organization convened and elected S. H. McCrory as "bidder" and Cyrus Sanders as "assistant bidder" for townships "seventy-nine, range six west of the first principal meridian and seventy-nine north, range five west of the fiftieth principal meridian."

On 30 July 1840 the settlers started for Dubuque. Although the majority had sufficient money to buy their land, some did not. The latter hoped to find men at the sale who would lend them the necessary money, even if at exorbitant interest rates. One company of forty settlers, with all necessary provisions and camp equipage, traveled to Dubuque in two horse-drawn wagons. Most prospective buyers were in town by August 1. The bidder and assistant bidder had already drawn maps of the two townships with the name of each settler and the tract he wished to buy.

When the hour of the sale finally arrived, a crier climbed upon an elevated platform and invited the bidder and his assistant bidder to take their places beside him. The crier, holding the map, began with section one, calling out each eighty-acre tract as rapidly as he could. As he read out each tract he struck his hammer down and gave the name of the man to the clerk. He took each section in numerical order and offered the two townships for sale in less than thirty minutes. While the land was being auctioned, claimants stood in a compact semicircle in front of the platform in breathless silence, not a sound being heard except the crier's voice.

Buyers were then admitted into an office two or three at a time to receive their deeds. Paying for the land was tedious to both settlers and land office officials because the government accepted no money except United States coins and notes on the Bank of Missouri. Since most land was paid for in coins, it required considerable time to count it and disregard spurious coins. On the morning of 5 August 1840 the settlers' business was complete and they started for home. They were relieved to know at last they had legal title to their lands. Three years later, after the Johnson Claim Association accomplished its goal at Marion, it was disbanded.[18]

## CLAIM JUMPERS

All claim organizations had their difficulties. One of these was caused by "claim jumpers," meaning someone who moved onto a club member's land and used it as his own. To deal with this problem, the organization first ordered the intruder to vacate the land at once. If he refused, he was forcibly ejected, even at the cost of life. Claim clubs were bound by their constitutions, by-laws, and records to enforce such action. One organization elected to eject an old man after deciding that he did not have proper claim to his land. The recalcitrant old man barricaded himself in his cabin with a loaded rifle. The armed association members failed to frighten the claim jumper and the club then made a compromise with him which was never recorded.

When conflict of interest arose between two claim clubs, the "Devil was to pay" unless cool heads could evolve a peaceful compromise. Sometimes the rival organizations resorted to violence and bloodshed.[19]

Vacating a claim for a while could give rise to trouble. After a claim organization was formed in frontier Minnesota, a young lady filed a claim to a 160 acre tract and then left for the East. In her absence a neighbor who preferred her land to his moved onto it and built a house. The association sent a committee to the claim jumper to inform him that his action was in violation of club rules. The committee offered to help the violator build a cabin on his original claim but was refused. Soon after, an armed committee rode to the unyielding violator's home, tore down his cabin, and cut many of the logs in two. The next time the committee called, they had no trouble persuading the intruder to leave. The association kept its original promise, and the members helped the man build a six-sided cabin from the short logs. Fifteen years later this cabin still stood as a rebuke to the cupidity of the trespasser and a monument to the diplomacy of the committee.[20]

Another man, determined to defy a local Kansas claim club, moved in and built a cabin on a previously recorded claim. He stated that he wanted to be shown reasons for not occupying the land. On a dark night some thirty claim club members called on the trespasser "to show him." The associates tied the man on top of two logs that were fastened together and then set him afloat in a nearby stream. Ropes were fastened to the logs so that they could pull the culprit in when he had been "sufficiently shown." The trespasser was soundly ducked several times and the claim committee finally pulled him ashore. The nearly drowned and thoroughly humbled man took an oath to leave the country and never return. The committee then burned his cabin.[21]

One quarter section of land in Nebraska Territory was jumped five times. During one of the violations, the legal claimant physically challenged the usurper. These two Civil War veterans fought each other, one armed with a pitchfork, the other with a gun. One man rammed his pitchfork through his adversary's body and mortally wounded him. The dying man shot and killed his opponent.[22]

In another instance, a settler lost his head and killed a newcomer who had jumped his claim. The man went to the local justice of the peace, told his story, and was exonerated. According to the unwritten code, a man could defend his land and home in whatever manner was necessary.[23]

Disputes over claims sometimes occurred between members of the same claim organization. Reverend William H. Goode told of a father and son who became involved in a claim dispute. They both soon after mysteriously disappeared "under the operation of squatter law." The fate of the two men was never known, but it was generally believed that members of the association had killed them and had thrown their bodies into the Missouri River. Public sentiment would not allow an inquiry, and the event was scarcely noticed beyond the locality.[24]

Land clubs exerted a great deal of influence and power but were not always in complete control of claims. In Nebraska in 1857, when claim troubles were "fearful," a claim association served notice on two brothers that they must either relinquish the eighty acre tracts they had usurped or leave the country. The brothers did neither. They continued to occupy their claims and later bought them from the government at the minimum price. Evidently this association was poorly organized.[25]

Limiting the amount of land any man could claim, especially land of exceptional value, was another function of the association. In one area of Minnesota, settlers organized an association to limit land holdings near a waterfall to eighty acres. This agreement was strictly adhered to and the organization administered such law, justice, and punishment as were necessary to keep it that way. As there were no courts or judges in the region, the association also served as a court and rendered decisions on many things in addition to land.[26]

Claim clubs served many purposes. Their primary function was to give the squatter a good deed to his land at the lowest possible cost. To maintain order among themselves, they arbitrated many disputes. Problems discussed in such organization meetings were similar to those taken up in New England town meetings. The settlers left to themselves had once again evolved an institution in response to their needs.

# 12

# The Frontier Preacher

Ministers throughout the frontier era had influence on the lives of most pioneers, for they were the ones who gave the pioneers hope when faced with their difficult life situation. Many frontier ministers were bombastic, conceited, arrogant, crude, and illiterate; they were products of their times. Despite their odd traits of character, they had a humanizing effect on the pioneers. Their theology, which intellectually speaking "may be damned to hell," gave settlers faced with adversity on every hand a real hope. The fact that the preachers received relatively strong support from the people indicates that they fulfilled a need of the congregations.

## ITINERANT PREACHERS

In the fight for survival, formal religion was often relegated to the background. Frontiersmen with few social pressures from either the church or their neighbors adopted a nonchalant attitude toward formal religious activity. Long distances to church and the lack of proper dress kept many parishioners away from church. Places of worship—log cabins, sod houses, barns and the open air—discouraged attendance in bad weather. Were it not for the itinerant or traveling preachers many areas of the frontier would have been without any religious activities.

To communicate effectively, the average frontier minister learned to use figures of speech in keeping with the life conditions of the people. A minister might say in describing a confused person that he was "badly brushed"—an expression derived from the difficulty of riding or walking through the brush or woodlands. The metaphors, "He'll do to tie to," "He won't do to tie to," and "He won't do to tie to in a calm, let alone in a storm," were

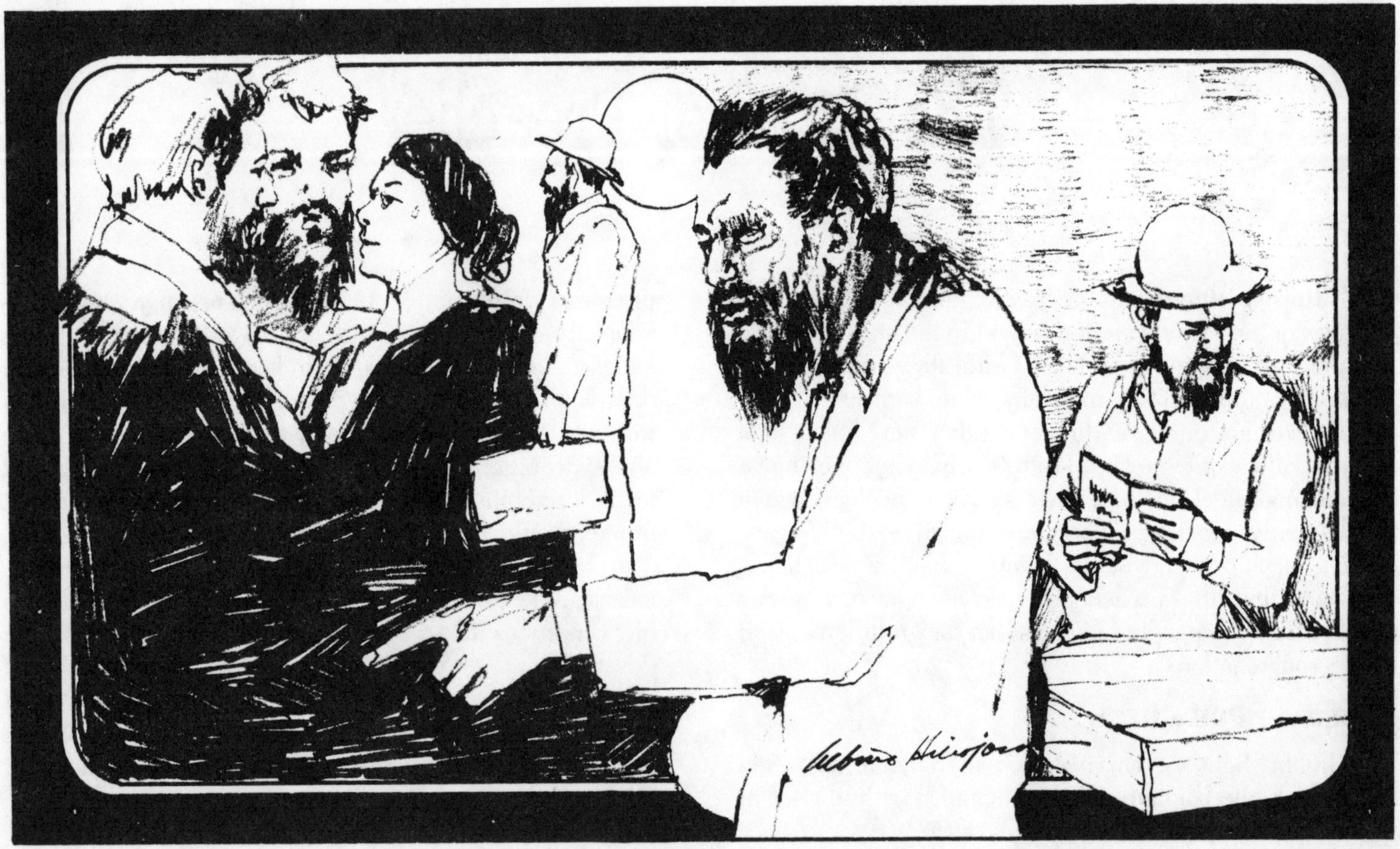

borrowed from flatboatmen who used these figures of speech when thinking of tying their boats to some secure object on shore. Ministers often said, "He'll make the trip" or "He won't make the trip," when they were expressing their confidence or lack of it in someone. Their expression "setting to her" was derived from bird hunting and it meant that a man was courting a lady. When a lady rejected her suitor, the minister said that "she kicked him," words used by people who handled livestock. When one bested his rivals and won a lady's heart and hand, the minister said that the "tallest pole took the persimmons," for settlers often procured persimmons by the use of a long pole. When a church rendered a decision pleasing to the minister, he sometimes said, "Brethren my decision is that you are all ahead of the hounds."[1] A frontier minister who knew how to "speak the people's language" and preach a sermon they appreciated was almost forced to be an itinerant, whether his church designated him as one or not.[2]

Of all the travelers of the frontier, itinerant ministers, regardless of religious affiliation, were the most highly appreciated guests since they informed the people about many things. They reported facts pertaining to Indian raids; outlaws; the price of land, skins, whiskey, wagon masters and steamboats; political affairs; diseases in other localities; conversations they had witnessed; and themselves. They often talked for hours, sometimes far into the night, answering questions and satisfying people's curiosity and need for news.

A minister was also welcomed for other reasons: to dispose of a quarrel or feud between families; to perform a marriage ceremony for a couple whose children were becoming numerous and grown; to preach an overdue funeral service; and to bring the word of the Lord to the people. Though the people were unpolished and usually illiterate and had little regard for formal Christian observance, they usually were willing and anxious to hear a sermon and a prayer—a "message of hope" in a primitive world.

An itinerant preacher was often a jack of all trades and provided other indispensable aid to the backwoodsmen. In his itinerary in the Dakota Territory, Reverend G. S. Codington found that he was needed not only as a spiritual leader but also as a teacher and counselor. Settlers came to him for advice on many subjects, from breaking the prairie land to establishing a school. Codington believed a minister needed to be as versatile as possible, as he might be asked for advice on matters ranging from housebuilding to the mechanism of a mousetrap.[3]

Though itinerants endured hardships traveling the rough and raw terrain, experience justified their belief that "the Lord will provide"; almost every pioneer family received them as cordially as they would any traveler. At the beginning of his ministerial career, Reverend Hamilton Pierson offered to pay when leaving a family with whom he had spent the night and eaten a meal or two. After learning that such an offer tended to offend, he adopted a formula that protected his host and exonerated his own character from all suspicion of trying to avoid payment of bills. Upon leaving, he simply said "I am indebted to you for a night's entertainment." To this the general reply was, "Not at all, Sir. Come and stay with us again, whenever you pass this way."

Once while traveling near sundown over a bad road through a heavy forest about a dozen miles from the Mississippi River, Pierson came to an area where the underbrush had been cut and burned and the trees had been girdled and killed. He rode his horse over a footpath that led him as near a cabin as a tall rail fence would permit. A pack of barking, snarling hounds made the preacher realize that it would be rash to dismount. He called, "Hello there!" in a loud voice. A woman, barefoot and wearing a rough woolsey dress, came to the door and said, "Howdy, sir, light sir! Light sir!" Before dismounting, Pierson replied that he was tired from his day's ride and that he wished to spend the night. The woman promptly answered, "Oh yes, if you can put up with our rough fare. We never turn anybody away." Given this hearty welcome, Pierson dismounted and walked among the now friendly dogs to the barn where he bestowed affectionate care on his horse.

Inside the house, the minister proceeded to satisfy the curiosity of his hostess by telling her his name and that he was a Presbyterian minister employed by the American Bible Society. He learned that his hostess and her husband had emigrated from a place several hundred miles to the east where Pierson had visited several times, and he was able to give her much information concerning her old friends and neighbors. The woman listened with intense interest and she gave her guest a renewed welcome to her home. Her husband, who had been working, returned home and likewise welcomed him.

Just before bedtime, the host secured a Bible and hymn book, laid them on the dining table and asked, "Will you take the books and conduct a devotion?" Completing the ceremony, Pierson said, "Madam, I have ridden a long distance and am very tired." The hostess replied, "You can go to bed at any time you wish, Sir. Just take the left-hand bed." Pierson immediately went behind their turned backs, laid his garments down, retired facing the wall, and slept soundly.

The next morning after an early breakfast, Pierson again led the family devotion. Then, thanking the family for their kindness, he bade them good-bye. Though the family gave him repeated invitations to return and spend the night, he never again saw them in his travels.[4]

In his *Journal*, a Baptist minister named James Huckins told of meeting an aged woman in the Republic of Texas who had not heard a sermon in three years. When Huckins told her that he was a preacher, she was deeply affected and requested that he spend the day and night with her family.

On another occasion while traveling through a sparsely populated area of Texas, Reverend Huckins came to a little hut which bore the marks of hasty and recent construction. In the yard he met a man who was making a bedstead with a mallet and chisel. After exchanging formal greetings, the minister remarked that the settler was far removed from his neighbors. The Texan replied that misfortune would drive a man anywhere. A moment later a woman stepped outside the cabin and asked, "A minister, did you say, Sir?" Receiving a positive reply, the lady, with tears gushing forth, reached out her hand and exclaimed, "Allow me to call you 'Brother.' I am a Baptist and I trust a Christian. Husband is a Baptist, also." Again Huckins was offered food and lodging.[5]

If a preacher made a favorable impression with one of his sermons, he was often called upon to preach other sermons in the vicinity. On one occasion after Reverend Nathan Bangs had arrived at a cabin, his hospitable landlord rode his horse for ten miles, proudly notifying settlers that preaching services would be held at his cabin at ten o'clock the following morning.

Immediately following his sermon preached to a large concourse of settlers, an elderly man approached Bangs, offered his hand, and asked him whether he had ever known Bishop Asbury. When Bangs replied that he had, the man said that while living in New Jersey he had entertained many ministers, including Asbury. The old man added that during the several years since he had been on the isolated frontier he had been totally deprived of Gospel ordinances, as there was no preacher of any order in the region.

Bangs consented to preach at the old man's home that afternoon. One of the man's sons was immediately sent riding ahead to inform other settlers. After riding ten miles, Bangs arrived at his new friends' home and found a house full of people waiting.

The preaching was well received and Bangs accepted another invitation from a German Baptist who lived about twenty miles away to preach at his home the next day. Bangs later rode to the home of an Indian woman, the widow of a French Canadian, where he again preached. The widow, in gratitude, gave him a dollar.

Another minister, Reverend John Mason Peck, rode his horse all day over a dim road without seeing a single dwelling, and for the second night in succession had nothing to eat. Sighting a curl of smoke and then a house, he galloped his tired horse to a settler's door, where he was given a cordial invitation to spend the night. Peck was soon seated at the backwoodsman's supper table. As he was eating, the hostess remarked, "I reckon that you have had no dinner today. I hope you will find something that will answer." The minister replied, "I propose, madam, to eat my breakfast and dinner first, and then I will talk about supper." While he ate "hog and hominy," he gave the settlers a sketch of his adventures during the past two days. They listened with rapt attention. The next morning after breakfast Peck continued his journey, never to see the kind people again.[6]

Hospitality was so ingrained in the minds of the people that it was considered proper, particularly for ministers, to enter a dwelling and enjoy such conveniences as there were even when the family was away. One day about sunset Reverend Joseph Smith had been unable to find lodging for the night, and he came to a cabin where no one was at home and the door was barred. Rather than force an entrance, he continued to travel. When he found no other house, and as the night was dark and rainy, he returned to the barred dwelling. He unsaddled his horse and turned him into a corn field. The minister then climbed a wall and entered through a hole in the roof, which served as a vent for smoke from a fireplace built near the center of the earthen floor. He opened the door, brought in his saddle, kindled a fire, lay down, and slept well. The next morning, after riding a short distance, Smith met the owner, who was not angry but pleased that the minister had lodged in his home. The settler directed Smith to another house where he was given breakfast.[7]

Peter Cartwright once rode up to a cabin and found no one at home. He opened the unlocked door, entered, ignited a banked fire, and began looking for something to eat. Great was his joy when he found a pan of fresh baked cornbread in a small crudely made cupboard. He broiled some dried venison that hung near the wooden chimney and had a good meal which lacked only coffee. Searching the cupboard he found no coffee but discovered some honey in the comb. He mixed honey with water and enjoyed a refreshing drink. Finished with his meal, he went to bed. The next morning he prepared and ate breakfast. Cartwright saddled his horse and rode away without ever knowing in whose home he had lodged and eaten two meals.[8]

Backwoodsmen were generally polite, usually direct, but sometimes crude in talking to a minister. When Reverend Cyrus R. Rice introduced himself to a Kansas settler, the man remarked, "You are the first preacher that has been in these diggins." After the evening meal, Rice seated himself by the light of a candle and began studying a book in preparation for a sermon he was to deliver the next day in the settler's home. In a short time the host said, "I suppose, Parson, you will want to pray before we go to bed. If so, pray now and we'll go to bed and you kin read as long as you want to." Used to the ways of the frontier life, the itinerant had learned to take such behavior in stride.[9]

Some frontiersmen had special means of expressing their gratitude toward visitors, ministers in particular. Reverend Elnathan Gavitt and a colleague preached periodically at a small isolated tavern run by a man who was not a member of any church while traveling their circuit. After preaching during the day, they spent the night with the tavern keeper. On the morning after the first night's lodging, the ministers asked for their bill. The landlord replied that he preferred to settle with the itinerants at the end of the year.

Near the close of the year, the ministers again requested their account. The innkeeper said before presenting the bill that the preachers had some credits in their favor and that he would check the bills carefully.

On the first page of the ledger, the charges for board and lodging were quite reasonable, better than the ministers had anticipated. On the second page he credited them with every sermon, blessing, and devotional service. For long sermons he gave twenty-five cents; for short ones, fifty cents; for short prayers, twenty-five cents; for long ones, twelve and one-half cents; and for their other religious activities he credited them in like manner. After looking over his ledger, the landlord revealed that the older minister, who was more talkative, was in debt. However, considering the benefit the preachers had brought to his family and the settlers, he balanced the account and called it settled, provided both itinerants called on him the following year. The benign landlord then presented each of the surprised preachers with five dollars.[10]

It was often loneliness rather than a desire to hear the Gospel that caused settlers to treat ministers with such cordiality. Stopping for the night in a sod house in Nebraska, Reverend A. Dresser continued the conversation with his host and his family long after they were all in bed and the light had died in the fireplace. Recalling better days of the past with old friends and acquaintances, the mother cried. The minister thought his visit served as an emotional release for the mother and father, both of whom would gladly have returned to their old home in the East, if they could have done so.[11]

A missionary in Indiana had a similar reaction from settlers whom he visited. Traveling through rain, sleet, and snow and over muddy and almost impassable roads, the minister succeeded in visiting all but one family in his congregation, as well as many other settlers who never attended his church. Without exception, every family received him kindly and gave him the best they had in food and lodging. He was convinced that his visits were even more valuable than his public sermons. The people not only liked to listen to him but also wanted to talk. They all seemed to have problems and all seemed lonely.[12]

At religious gatherings hospitality was much in evidence. At the close of an afternoon religious service, people living near the meeting ground invited those who had traveled a considerable distance to spend the night with them. Some men mounted stumps and logs to urge anybody and everybody, regardless of where they lived, to come home with them. Then, if not satisfied with the response, they jumped down and mingled with the dispersing crowd offering more personal hospitality. At one such assembly a man addressed himself to the presiding elder, a circuit rider and a class leader, "I should be glad to have you all stay with me, but I can't take care of your horses. I have plenty of house-room, but my stable is full." A neighbor standing nearby said, "I have room for you all. I shall be glad to have you go with me." However, this man was only able to get the presiding elder as his guest, as someone else claimed the itinerant and the class leader.[13]

Although their dwellings were small—often barely large enough to accommodate their large families—pioneers were usually delighted to entertain guests, even total strangers. Traveling from Pennsylvania to Wisconsin in 1735, Reverend Alfred Brunson chanced to lodge in a cabin not over eighteen feet square with a bedroom attached to it in which he and thirty-nine other people spent the night.[14] In one cabin in Illinois that measured twelve by sixteen feet, a family made sleeping arrangements for nineteen people, including the guests. At bedtime, the men were asked to step outside the door while the beds were made, which consisted of blankets and buffalo robes spread on the floor. Before the men entered, the ten women got under the cover, the married ones in the center. When the men were called into the room, each husband lay down by his wife and the single men lay outside. Under such cramped conditions, one said "spoon" when he wished to turn and all turned at the same time.[15]

Reverend Hamilton W. Pierson and his preacher colleagues experienced a similar situation. At bedtime one of the ministers "took the books" at the request of the host and led the evening devotion, after which the men walked outside to allow the ladies to retire in privacy. In response to a prearranged signal, the gentlemen walked into the bedroom and found the women completely covered with blankets. Immediately, the men undressed as though the blankets covering the ladies were thick walls, and went to bed on pallets. The next morning the group engaged in conversation until someone suggested that it was time to arise. The women covered their faces until the men dressed and left for the stable to feed their horses.

At the barn, young Reverend Pierson remarked that the preceding night was new in his experience, as he had never slept in such proximity to the opposite sex. Another minister looked at Pierson curiously and said, "You haven't!" implying that Pierson must be unfamiliar with frontier behavior.[16]

Not all pioneers were willing and eager to invite itinerants and other travelers into their homes to lodge and dine. After one sermon, Reverend Cyrus R. Rice realized that he had not pleased his congregation because few worshippers came forward to speak to him and because no one asked him home to dinner. Rising to the situation, he announced that he boarded at a certain place (one which did not exist) and if any of them came that way, he would be glad to give them a meal. Suddenly a woman came forward and said, "I enjoyed your preaching, but I do not believe a word you said about Christ being God. However, if you will go home with me and my boys, we will give you a dinner, the best we have." The minister quickly accepted the single invitation.[17]

Reverend Joseph Tarkington and his new wife received less hospitality than Cyrus. Two days after their marriage they set out on a long horseback ride of about one hundred miles through a new and sparsely settled area to visit the young minister's father. During the first two days and nights, they had little trouble obtaining food and lodging, though the reception they received was less than cordial. On the third day, when the minister asked for food and lodging, the owner said that he could not accommodate the travelers as he had virtually no food for his own family. With a show of compassion, the settler told the newlyweds that they might have better luck at cabins ahead of them.

They did not. At the next cabin, a woman said that her husband had gone for bread-stuffs, and, as she had no place for their horses, she could give them neither food nor lodging. At a second dwelling the couple found the family short of food and also ill. At a third cabin the family was in the same condition as the first.

Darkness approached and Tarkington had almost lost hope of finding a place to lodge, other than out in the open along the side of the road. To save his wife such an ordeal, he decided to ride back to the first of the four cabins where he had asked for accommodations. The man there seemed kinder than the rest, or at least his voice sounded kind.

Tarkington had evaluated the settler's feelings correctly. When he arrived at the dwelling after dark and described his predicament, the backwoodsman invited them into his house. The minister took his horses to a salt lick a considerable distance from the cabin, fed the animals, and built a fence around them. Back at the dwelling, young Tarkington read from the Bible, prayed, and preached a short sermon, all of which was well received, especially by the mother, who said she had not heard a sermon since leaving her old home in Kentucky. Before bedding down for the night, the travelers silently divided and ate their last biscuit.

The next morning, the Tarkingtons rode away without breakfast. When they finally arrived at their destination that afternoon, they ate their first meal in more than twenty-four hours.[18]

Reverend John Johnson drove to a cabin while traveling by wagon with his family in Kentucky and asked the owner for food and lodging. The settler refused and said that it was not far to the next dwelling. Johnson pointed out that it was a late hour to travel and that his wife and children were tired and hungry. The landlord reluctantly invited them inside.

The minister found a "dozen or twenty" people gathered in the cabin, all of whom manifested "some token of distress." After the Johnsons had supper and had gone into their room, a gentleman both "inquisitive and communicative" entered and said that the people were gathered for a wake. On the previous day a neighbor's son had attended a horse-race where he became intoxicated, got into a fight, and was killed.

The next morning the Johnsons, mortified at the cold and heartless reception they had received, left early without breakfast. Their son Thomas told of having slipped into the room where the strangers were assembled and of hearing disparaging remarks about his father. One man said he did not know what to think of a man, able to work as the preacher was, "dragging a big family around over the country to sponge a living off honest people. . . ." Methodist preachers, he observed, were an imposition on society, and when people submitted to their demands, they "never knew when to stop." According to Thomas, all the people were in agreement with the man's opinion.[19]

Other ministers not held in high esteem received little hospitality from the settlers. One stormy night Reverend Thomas Ware stopped at a cabin and asked for the privilege of spending the night. The owner replied that neither he nor his neighbors had "any great liking for priests of any kind" and that the minister should move on. Ware responded that, although there might be differences in their religious views, there was a debt of humanity which all men owed to each other and that if he had "any flesh in his heart," he would not deny shelter to a human being in a storm. "Young man, if thou would'st follow some honest calling, honest men would make thee welcome. There is neighbor Hodge, whose wife is old and ugly. He may give thee lodging," the settler replied.

Ware rode on through the storm to the home of "neighbor" Hodge, an apostate Quaker, who permitted the minister to stay provided he turned his horse into the woods and took his lodging on the cabin floor.

After the preacher had cared for his horse and changed his wet clothes, he took a seat by Hodge's side in front of the fire. Ware placed his hand on Hodge's knee and said, "Father, you have not, I presume, lived to this good old age without having serious thought on the subject of religion." This statement, which would have prompted a polite answer from nearly any other man, brought an angry scowl to his host's face. The old man vehemently stated that he believed "all professors he had known were hypocrits; the preachers, a set of rascals, no better than pick-pockets." Emphasizing that Ware was no exception, Hodge also said, "We don't want no more of ye here." Hodge then ordered his wife to "bear a hand" and give him his supper. When the meal was served, the two ate alone and completely ignored their guest. The minister slept on the floor and left early the next morning without anything to eat and with a feeling that he had never before encountered such rude and inhospitable backwoodsmen.[20]

Reverend Joseph Tarkington and a colleague had a similar experience. Stopping at a cabin for the night during a rainstorm, they dried their clothes by the fire and went to bed on the bare floor without supper. With little prospect of breakfast and believing they were not being treated respectfully as ministers, the itinerants saddled their horses and rode ten miles to a settler's dwelling where they were received kindly and given their "breakfast and dinner," as they called it.[21]

## MINISTERIAL SUPPORT

As a whole, frontier ministers were not missionaries and preached and rendered all service free of charge. Few frontiersmen entered the ministry as a profession, and few devoted their entire time to the calling or lived off donations from their parishioners. Once called to preach, a minister did so whenever and wherever he had an audience and earned his living as other settlers did.

To enter the ministry for any motive other than to save souls and raise moral standards was not in keeping with the spirit of the frontier. As one Illinois Baptist preacher termed it, "Judas was the first minister to receive pay." A Presbyterian missionary, receiving a regular salary from the American Home Missionary Society, said that local preachers preached for nothing and thanked people for coming to hear them.[22] Reverend George G. Smith of Georgia claimed there were "no paid preachers in those days," as the rank and file of the settlers doubted whether ministers should be compensated. Money for all religious purposes was spoken of timidly.[23] Asked whether he ever approached his churches on the subject, another pastor replied that he did not. The people would not "bear it and would call him a money preacher."[24] When one settler was called on to contribute to the support of a circuit rider, he refused to give anything. He indignantly "blessed God that his religion was free." He had been a Christian for fifteen years and his religion had cost him only one bit, twelve and one-half cents. Public sentiment so strongly opposed ministerial pay in some areas that merchants were threatened with loss of customers, politicians with loss of votes, and physicians with loss of practice if they supported the idea.

The attitude settlers adopted concerning ministerial support stemmed largely from their economic conditions. Without markets for their produce, they could hardly afford to give money to any religious cause. A Missouri settler said he could get practically nothing for anything he sold. Although he had plenty of oats, corn, hay, pork, and other farm products, he had little or no money. Unable to sell three thousand pounds of pork, he was forced to salt it down. Other farmers a little more lucky were forced to sell their pork for one dollar per hundred pounds and some for seventy-five cents per hundred. There was little demand for wheat. Wheat was sometimes hauled fifteen or twenty miles to market at a cost of twenty-five center per bushel. There was almost nothing that could be exchanged for hard cash, and the pioneers would have been without the benefit of the gospel if they had had to pay for it.[25]

Settlers did present their ministers with homemade gifts. Women frequently gave a beloved pastor socks, shirts, trousers, hats, and even shoes, all made with their own hands. A few ministers were given fine horses, homemade saddles, saddle blankets, bridles and reins. Renowned preachers such as Peter Cartwright, James B. Finley and a host of others who had learned to "speak the people's language" were hardly ever short of necessities, but they received little or no money.

The members of one church agreed to pay their pastor in produce, each donor receiving credit for the amount contributed at the market price. After a particularly good sermon this preacher received in pledges the following commodities: five bushels of corn, valued at one dollar; twenty-five bushels of corn, valued at five dollars; ten bushels of corn, valued at two dollars; four pounds of butter, valued at one dollar; and fifty cents worth of peaches.[26] Reverend E. C. Gavitt was frequently paid in forest products: "red-root, blood-root, crow-foot, craine's bill, star-root, yellow-root, prickly ash buds, and dried slippery elm bark," all of which were used as money.[27] In one four-week circuit, Reverend Aaron Wood preached an average of one sermon a day and merchants gave varying amounts of sugar to him and his family.[28]

In time, markets improved and settlers began selling more produce. They then paid favorite pastors small sums of money. In one church, members negotiated with a minister to preach one sermon each month on a Sunday for one dollar a sermon. A few members thought this sum excessive; but taking into consideration that the preacher had to leave home on Saturday and that he had to furnish his own means of travel, the congregation finally agreed to the bargain. The same man later preached in other churches, but none of them ever paid him a larger amount.[29]

Having preached at a church for twenty-one years, another minister said the largest amount he had ever received for a year's work was twenty dollars, and he had received as little as ten. Some ministers were paid more. Reverend Hamilton Pierson met a boy riding a mule while traveling. Pierson asked the boy how much his church paid its preacher. Proudly the youth replied, "Oh! They pay the one they have got now right smart. They give him a dollar and a half a Sunday."[30] This minister was more fortunate than most. Many preachers expected nothing from the people except a bed, meals, and food for their horse, all of which was usually gladly given.

Ministers who expected remuneration for their services soon learned that they could profit most by charging for each sermon rather than accepting a yearly stipend. If they failed to receive the agreed amount for a sermon, they were not obligated to meet with the congregation again. Preaching for a yearly salary was financially unwise, for a minister might receive only part pay and possibly none at all. During the year, half the contracting congregation might move to other areas and be replaced by new people who either could not afford to pay or would not. Reverend Jacob Bower was once hired by a Baptist church for one year. At the end of that time, the congregation—largely a new one—voted to pay him nothing.[31]

## FIGHTING MINISTERS

The lack of decorum of congregations was one of the greatest burdens the frontier minister was forced to bear. In California, one preacher found it impossible to continue his sermon because of the disorder in his disrespectful congregation. Suddenly a gold miner jumped up, drew his two pistols and fired several shots into the air. Turning to the minister, the miner said in a commanding voice, "Parson, sail in! Give 'em hell! I'll back you." A dead silence fell over the stunned congregation.[32] Not all ministers received such strong backing, and they were forced to rely on other tactics. The ability of a preacher to maintain order depended to a large extent upon his courage and experience, as well as the cooperation he received from those who wished to maintain proper decorum.

Some ministers encountered serious troubles when they were inadvertently caught in a squeeze play between rival factions. Reverend Thomas Ware had experienced wickedness in his long itinerant career that would have induced weaker men to renounce their calling. He once became entangled in a dispute between the governor of Kentucky and Colonel John Tipton. Tipton opposed the enforcement of certain laws in his district. Arriving one unbearably cold afternoon at the home of Captain Turner, where he was scheduled to hold a religious service, Reverend Ware found a company of drunken and fully armed men present. The armed mob tried to persuade all who had come to worship to join with them in an attack against Colonel Tipton, who had fortified himself in his house. Not realizing the gravity of the situation, the minister begged the group not to resort to violence. Immediately his remarks were interpreted to mean that he was a friend of Tipton. The enraged mob wanted to dispatch Ware at once. A few men rushed to save the minister's life but others suggested that Ware be sent before the governor and tried as a spy. While the mob was discussing his fate, Ware slipped out a back door, mounted his horse, and rode out of danger.[33]

Reverend Nathan Bangs was sometimes plagued by a

few church members who talked incessantly and loudly during the entire period of worship. One young lady laughed continuously during one of his sermons, despite the fact that he strongly reprimanded her several times. Bangs paused again in his sermon and gave her a solemn warning. The emotional young woman rushed from the assembly and was immediately seized with a disease which led to her death within a few days. A short time later when Bangs preached at the same church, the congregation was again noisy and disruptive. Bangs reminded the people of the girl's strange death and intimated that it was punishment from the Lord. The communicants fell silent and many began to weep. A great reformation prevailed, which led to the formation of a Methodist society.[34] Bangs did not, however, always enjoy as much success with his unruly flocks.

Reverend Bangs even had trouble with rabble-rousers while he was going to and from his appointments. On his way to preach in a log cabin, he was once overtaken by three men riding in a sleigh. Bangs turned his horse to let them pass. The men stopped and loosened a torrent of blackguard language at the minister. Bangs attempted to pass them on the narrow road and they blocked his way and continued to hurl vile insults at him. Eventually the men tired of the game and drove on.

That night when Bangs rose to preach, the three tormentors stood in the cabin door and obstructed the entrance. The minister requested the men to take their seats and two of them did; the third kept his place. Bangs began a powerful sermon against the settlers' intemperate drinking habits. He said that some were not content to drink in taverns and in their own homes, but took bottles of rum in their pockets wherever they went. The man standing in the doorway drew out a bottle, shook it at the minister and exclaimed, "You are driving that at me." The cabin owner and two other men walked toward the offender with the intention of throwing him out. Bangs feared there would be bloodshed and so requested the men to keep their seats. The intemperate man was then so enraged that he redoubled his insults.

As a last resort, Bangs called on God "Who delivered Daniel from the lions" to intervene and deliver him from the lion-like sinner. The prayer produced an instant response. The three miscreants left the house.

At the close of the service, the minister's friends feared that he might be waylaid on his way to his lodging place and persuaded him to spend the night with a family nearby. It was well that he did, for that very night a man traveling the road was stopped by three rowdies who thought he was the preacher. The traveler prepared to fight and the ruffians, seeing their mistake, fled.[35]

The troubles of Reverend Bangs were mild in comparison with those of Reverend James Finley. Desperadoes led by Mike Fink set out to wreck Finley's religious services. While he preached, they stood outside the church and yelled so loud that the worshippers were unable to hear the service. Finley paused, laid down his Bible, pulled off his coat, and said "Wait for a few minutes, my brethren, while I go and make the Devil pray."

Finley walked up to the ring leader and said, "Mr. Fink, I have come to make you pray." Sharp words were exchanged and Fink attacked the preacher. The brawling outlaw and the powerful minister struggled and rolled in the dirt. Finley got his strong fingers around the outlaw's throat and he squeezed until Fink's face turned purple. Finley slackened his hold and inquired, "Will you pray now?" When the bully replied that he did not know how to pray, the minister told him to repeat the Lord's Prayer with him. At the conclusion of the prayer, the other ruffians gave three boisterous cheers. Fink shook hands with the preacher and declared, "By golly, you're some beans in a bar-fight. I'd rather set-to with an old he bar in dog-days. You can pass this 'ere crowd of nose-smashers, blast your pictur!" There was no further disturbance for the remainder of the service.[36]

At a camp meeting attended by Reverend Finley, hell-raisers brazenly went to the pulpit to abuse the preachers. When one of the ministers tried to persuade the villains to leave, they refused. One of the trouble makers drew a pistol and aimed it at a preacher. A member of the congregation caught the gun, threw the bully on his back, and dragged him into the preacher's tent. A magistrate took him into custody and the rest of the ruffians dispersed without posting bond for their companion.[37]

In anticipation of disorder at another camp meeting, the meeting ground was fenced with hemlock bushes. According to camp rule, at the sound of the trumpet, all campers were to go to their tents and those without lodging facilities were to leave the worship area. In defiance of this rule, a rabble gathered after dark led by a captain who wore a piece of white paper in his cap and carried a white club in his hand. Trouble was bound to come and Reverend Finley blew his trumpet.

The captain of the banditti refused to leave and Finley ordered a constable to arrest him. When the leader threatened to whip the officer, Finley grabbed the bully, threw him to the ground, subdued him, and turned him over to the constable. The disorderly group, seeing the fate of their leader, left quickly. The prisoner was released after promising faithfully never again to engage in disorderly conduct. The men of the encampment feared that the rowdies might return and kept watch every night, but there was no further trouble.[38]

Finley's frequent encounters with tough characters steeled his courage and made it possible for him to meet nearly any situation. On one occasion while preaching in a courthouse, mostly to barroom people, he opened his sermon with the words, "Awake, thou that sleepeth, and arise from the dead, and Christ shall give thee life." During the first few minutes the rough congregation was noisy and disrespectful. With undaunted courage, Finley raised his voice to preach until he received perfect attention. For thirty minutes he told the assembly they were on the road to hell and were as insensible of their danger as if they were in a deep sleep. He ended his sermon and rode to a brother's house, where he soon afterwards received a message stating that if he returned to the courthouse he would be "roasted." Finley ignored the threat and preached at the same place the following day.[39]

Wise ministers often resorted to their wit to maintain order. Reverend Francis Asbury was small in stature, weighed only about one hundred pounds, and could not match physical prowess with his hecklers. During one of his sermons, he was disturbed by several unprincipled young men. In a booming voice he warned the bedeviled fellows that they might be in great danger. Methodists were not a fighting people, he said, but they could be provoked just so far. If violence did erupt, the disturbers would likely get the worst of the battle as they were in a minority. Asbury then told the congregation that he had recently attended a meeting in which there was a similar situation. A fight broke out, and a Methodist hit a rowdy with his cane and cut his head to the skull. The victim had been expected to die but he miraculously recovered. This story made a profound impression on the assembly and Asbury finished his sermon in peace.[40]

On a Saturday night at a camp meeting attended by Francis Asbury, about a score of lewd, intoxicated fellows vowed they were going to break up the religious service. One of the preachers went to the leader of the mob and begged him to leave. The leader became so enraged that he struck the minister in the face and knocked him down. This attack precipitated a violent fight between rowdies and men of order. One man possessed of giant strength seized the rascal who had struck the preacher and crashed him between two benches. When one of the rowdies tried to rescue his leader, he soon found himself flat on his back. Within a few minutes the strong man aided by others completely subdued the troublemakers. When the sheriff and his force arrived, they arrested twelve of the rowdies and took them before a justice who fined them heavily.[41]

Reverend Richardson was not easily frightened. He was a brawny giant of a man, seemingly without a trace of fear, and stood ready to face even the Devil himself. Richardson was asked to preach in a Methodist district from which a Reverend Chambers had recently been driven. The minister proceeded to the county seat, which consisted of two log cabins—one a courthouse and the other a tavern. He lodged in the tavern and preached in the courthouse.

His first sermon proceeded without difficulty and Richardson returned to his room. While he sat in a sturdy chair of home manufacture reading his Bible, four young men burst into his room and declared that they were going to flog him and drive him from the country as they had Chambers. Richardson tried without success to reason with the ruffians. He explained that he was an unoffending stranger and wanted no trouble. As the brawlers advanced menacingly toward him, Richardson got up and held the chair between him and his assailants. One of the men walked to the minister's right side, another to his left. Suddenly, Richardson swung the chair to his left and knocked one man down and quickly swung it to his right and floored the other. The minister next moved forward brandishing his heavy chair toward the two bullies in his front. A powerful, fighting minister was more than they expected, and they quickly backed out the door and fled. The two on the floor scrambled painfully to their feet as soon as they recovered and rushed from the tavern.[42]

Later, when Richardson arrived at a cabin to preach in the same district, he found a house full of women and a yard full of men. Many of the men were more interested in seeing the minister licked than in hearing his sermon. As Richardson removed his saddle bags, five young men walked up to him and one of them asked, "Are you the preacher?" When Richardson stated that he was substituting for the preacher, the surly youths told him they were honest people and did not allow horse-thieving, counterfeiting preachers to come among them. The young man then told Richardson that he knew he could not preach but they would let him try and would then run him off as they had done the other fellow. The visiting minister calmly replied that he was a man of peace and that fighting was not in his line, but that if compelled to fight, he would be a dangerous opponent.

Richardson strode through the unruly crowd of men into the cabin and commenced the service, using his hymn book and Bible. The women ceased their lively gossiping and listened intently. The men drew up in a solid square outside. During the sermon, the power of God caused many indoors to fall as if shot down in battle. Among the fallen were the five young bullies who had so recently threatened to whip the preacher. At the end of the sermon, Richardson passed on his knees through the house and yard, exhorting and praying. Around midnight, Richardson formed a class of probationers for church membership, and stated the terms of admission. Among the many who came forward to join were the five chivalrous blades who had suffered the other minister to preach only for fun before giving him a drubbing.[43]

Few frontier ministers made more effective use of "muscular Christianity" than did Peter Cartwright. During a night service at one of his quarterly meetings, a number of unprincipled men who arrived drunk and armed with dirks, clubs, knives, and horse-whips swore they would break up the meeting. Cartwright managed to preach his sermon but on the following Sunday morning the hell-raisers appeared in even greater numbers to start a general riot. As Cartwright neared the half-way portion of his sermon, two fine-dressed young men with weighted whips in their hands entered the church. Without removing their hats, they stood on seats on the ladies' side near the preacher's stand and began to laugh and talk. Cartwright asked the young men to stop their misbehavior and to get down off the seats. The two dandies cursed Cartwright and told him to mind his own business. Cartwright promptly asked several magistrates to take the intruders into custody. The law officers were afraid and refused to make the arrests. Determined to restore order, Cartwright advanced with fire in his eyes toward the brawlers. One of the men tried to hit him on the head with his whip but Cartwright closed in on his assailant, jerked him from his feet, and held the man flat on the ground. Cartwright warned the man that if he did not remain quiet he would pound in his chest. Inspired by the minister's bravery, most of the magistrates rushed forward to help restore order, and friends of the rowdy young dandies joined in the melee to free them. However, one drunken magistrate approached the fighting minister and demanded that he release his prisoner or be knocked down. "Crack away," replied Cartwright. He then requested a friend to hold his prisoner while he subdued the intoxicated official. The magistrate swung, but Cartwright parried the blow, seized the drunk by the collar and the hair of the head, jerked him forward to the ground, and jumped on him, telling him to behave or suffer the consequences. Although Cartwright was holding his own, the mob grew more riotous by the second. Already seven magistrates, several preachers and many others in the congregation had been knocked to the ground. The adrenalin poured into his bloodstream and Cartwright prepared to fight as he had never fought before. He turned his second prisoner, the drunk magistrate, to another man and threw himself in front of the friends of order. The mob leader swung wildly at the fighting preacher but missed him. Cartwright saw an opening, hit the leader on the burr of his ear, and knocked him down. At that moment, according to Cartwright, hundreds of people rushed the mob, knocking them down in every direction, and in a few minutes order was restored.

Religious services were cancelled until evening. That night not a single preacher on the campground was willing to preach. Cartwright told the presiding elder, "I feel a clear conscience, for under the necessity of circumstances we have done right, and now I ask you to let me preach." To this the elder replied: "Do, for there is no other man of the ground who can do it." Soon thereafter the preaching arena was lighted with huge bonfires and pine torches. The trumpet blown, and the courageous minister preached his sermon. His text was "The gates of hell shall not prevail."

As a result of the fight thirty men were arrested, marched to a vacant tent, and placed under heavy guard until the following Monday morning. They were then tried and fined a total of three hundred dollars. The drunken magistrate was fined twenty dollars and carried to his office.[44]

During another sermon, a young bully stood defiantly on a seat reserved for the ladies. Cartwright sharply reproved him, "I mean that young man there, with the ruffled shirt on. I doubt not that ruffled shirt was borrowed." The young man, flushed with anger, swore that he would whip the minister for insulting him.

Cartwright strolled around the encampment and came upon the young troublemaker who was still declaiming to the large company gathered around him that he was bound to whip the preacher before he left. Cartwright said, "Gentlemen, let me in here to this fellow" and the bystanders did so obligingly. Cartwright invited the fellow to go with him to the woods where they could fight without disturbing the congregation, and off the two marched. To reach the woods they had to cross a rail fence enclosing the campground. The younger man jumped quickly to the other side but, as Cartwright leaped over, he sprained his ankle. A sharp pain ran up the preacher's leg and he put his hand to his left side to steady himself. His antagonist shouted at him "D--n you, you are feeling for a dirk are you?" Cartwright was unarmed but quickly decided to trick the aggresive young ruffian. "Yes, and I will give you the benefits of all the dirks I have," he declared as he hobbled rapidly toward his opponent. Fear overcame the bully and he sprang over the fence and ran. Members of the congregation gave chase, caught him, and ducked him in a pond of water until nearly drowned.[45]

Cartwright continued to meet the challenge of his malefactors. At another camp meeting fight, Cartwright and some of his "brethren marched a deputy sheriff and fourteen others to the magistrate who fined them all to the tune of good order." Trouble still brewed, however, because a short distance away a wild drinking party was in session every night. Since the constable was afraid to arrest the well-armed leader, Cartwright was again forced to be master of the situation. Just before dawn he crept to the wagon in which the leader was sleeping, reached over into the bed, and picked up the man's gun and ammunition. He then struck the wagon, yelling "Wake up! Wake up!" The sleeper grabbed hopelessly for his gun and sprang to his feet. In a loud, commanding voice, Cartwright said, "You are my prisoner; and if you resist, you are a dead man!" The leader begged not to be shot and promised that he would leave peaceably. The minister ordered the frightened ruffian to harness his team, while he poured his prisoner's powder on the ground and fired his musket into the air. The subdued rowdy whipped his team and rode away and disturbed the meeting no more.[46]

While serving in the legislature in 1828, Cartwright was instrumental in getting two laws restricting the sale of whiskey enacted. One made it illegal for a saloon or drinking house to be located within one mile of Jacksonville, the only college seat in the state. The other prohibited a bar or liquor store from locating within one mile of a camp meeting.

In 1833 Cartwright helped to enforce the latter law in Fulton County Illinois. While a camp meeting was getting under way, a man set up a huckster's stand nearby where he sold whiskey and tobacco. Cartwright warned the man that it was against the law to sell liquor within one mile of the campgrounds. The huckster, supported by a few friends, ignored Cartwright and proceeded to sell his merchandise. The culprit was arrested and quickly brought to trial; Cartwright served as prosecuting attorney although he had no license to practice law. The huckster was found guilty and fined ten dollars, but refused to pay. The court then ordered the constable to take him to jail. The constable hesitated because he feared that the man's friends would intervene in his behalf but the iron-willed Methodist minister forced the cowed constable to deputize him and two other churchmen to help enforce the court's order. This done, one of the churchmen went into the woods and cut three stout hickory canes, one for each deputy. The three then hoisted the whiskey salesman on a horse and started for jail.

During the ride to jail, the prisoner was still hopeful that his friends would release him and frequently turned his head to see whether they were coming. They did not come and when the party came within sight of Lewiston, the county seat, the huckster paid his fine. The incident not only raised the prestige of Cartwright as a lawyer and law enforcement officer but probably also contributed to the success of the revival in which "ninety souls were converted."[47]

Keeping the women and men segregated at camp meetings and in church was deemed necessary by many ministers. They believed that better order could be achieved by having women sit on one side and men on the other. This separation policy was widely accepted but often led to disorder.

During one church service, Reverend Alfred Brunson saw two men on the women's side of the church and went to them and said, "Gentlemen, we wish the men to occupy the other side of the house. Will you please do so?" One of the men said that he was trying to find his wife so that they could go home. Brunson replied, "Very well, you can do so." The other man took offense at the mild rebuke and said that he had a right "to take care of his wife wherever he pleased." Testily, Brunson replied, "Well, if you are afraid to trust your wife among the women you had better take her and go home." His pride injured, the bully stepped into the aisle, drew back his fist and shouted, "Come down here and I'll give it to you."

Brunson summoned all of his strength, grabbed the man by his clothing and ran him out the door. The preacher slammed the door and held his foot against it. Later the evicted man's wife came and asked permission to leave. "Certainly if you wish to," Brunson replied as he opened the door. Immediately afterward two good stout brethren offered to guard the door during the remainder of the service.

The next day the troublemaker threatened to have the minister arrested for assault and battery but Brunson had the ruffian arrested for disturbing the peace. Brunson failed to record the court's decision.[48]

At another time and another place Reverend Brunson had trouble with a man who was large and stout. Disregarding the entreaties of the door guard, he showed signs of violence as he edged his way to the women's side. Brunson rushed at the offender, caught him by the elbow, and gave him a whirl towards the men's side saying "That is your side. I put these men here to keep the men upon their own side of the house." Surprised at the minister's sudden attack, the rowdy moved rather sullenly to his place. As Brunson turned toward the minister's stand, the bully tried to hit him with his fist. Another man caught his arm just in time and warned the troublemaker that if he did not behave himself he would have to leave. Concluding that discretion was the better part of valor, the man took his seat peacefully.[49]

Even the renowned Francis Asbury was frequently annoyed with this seating problem. At one camp meeting, a young man took his seat with the ladies and refused to move. The presiding elder began ejecting the nonconformist, and three young men came to the culprit's aid. One of them threw a punch at the preacher but missed his mark. Another bully was arrested and charged with "Sabbath breaking, drunkenness, and fighting." Counter-charges were lodged and the presiding elder was charged with striking one man and then running away. Asbury feared that he might be arrested and was not on the campground when the officers arrived.[50]

## IMPOSTER PREACHERS

Because of their naivete and ignorance, settlers were often harassed by various imposters, particularly preachers. In August 1828 in the Leatherwood Circuit of Ohio, a camp meeting was held under the auspices of the Salesville Congregation of the United Brethren and the Temple. On the last day of the meeting, attendance was unusually large, with people coming from as far away as twenty miles. Presiding Elder Reverend John Crum through his eloquence had stirred the congregation's emotions to an intense pitch. A solemn silence pervaded the entire assembly. Suddenly a loud voice shouted, "Salvation!" and was followed by a strange noise similar to the snort of a frightened horse. The minister stopped preaching; all heads turned toward the spot from whence the sound came. There they beheld an odd character whose countenance was of marked solemnity and who continued to make awesome sounds. Seized with fear, some people jumped to their feet. Women shrieked and every cheek blanched. Several minutes passed before the minister could proceed with his sermon, but no one listened for the entire congregation was absorbed in staring at the mysterious man, who was none other than Joseph C. Dylks, the legendary "Leatherwood God."

Dylks was around fifty years old, about five feet eight inches tall, straight as an arrow, and a little heavy about the shoulders. He wore a black, broadcloth suit, a frock coat, a white tie, and a yellow beaver hat. His manner of dress made him appear quite eccentric in a day of linsey-wool hats and hunting shirts. The strange man seemed even more mysterious since no one had seen him slip into the congregation.

After the congregation was dismissed, many people sought to meet with the mysterious, dignified, and grave visitor. Though some whispered that he was God, he professed to be nothing but an humble Gospel teacher.

The Leatherwood God began to hold religious services. He used only one hymn, the beginning line of which was, "Plunged into a gulf of dark despair, we wretched sinners lay." With his simple preaching mode he soon made many converts but divided the community against itself. Family was set against family, parent against child, and husband against wife. Dividing and conquering, the imposter continued until the church was almost overwhelmed.

As virtually all were ardent followers of Dylks, the congregation decided to dedicate the church to the "New Dispensation." The imposter preached the dedicatory sermon to a packed house. At the beginning of his discourse he was slow and cautious; gradually he became bolder and bolder, professing that he was "God and Christ united." There was no salvation except through belief in him. All who trusted him would never die and would live forever in the New Jerusalem he was about to transfer from Heaven to Earth.

The service turned into bedlam. Some people shouted, "We shall never die." Women screamed and uttered prayers to the storming and snorting Leatherwood God, begging him to have mercy on their souls. As Dylks descended from the pulpit, a local minister remarked, "Behold our God!" and many believers fell on their knees before him. When partial order was restored the imposter announced that the next meeting would be held one week later. He then dismissed the congregation.

The lofty pretensions of the avowed God were soon put to crucial test. He was challenged to produce evidence of his omnipotence. Realizing the need to substantiate his claims, Dylks promised to make a seamless garment, provided the cloth was furnished him. He failed to perform this feat. Dylks' prestige rapidly began to wane, but he preached according to plan on the next Sunday night—an occasion marked with greater decorum than his previous one. Several women, however, fell on their knees and worshipped him.

On another night when the Leatherwood God was expected to preach, many attended, not out of awe and respect, but because it was rumored that he was going to be mobbed. Just before the service, while the people waited and watched in silent expectancy, a certain Reverend Briggs rose, looked over the congregation for a full minute, and said, "This is all a fal lal lal." Dylks' disciples sprang to their feet, cried, "He is my God" and stormed from the meeting. They hurried to the home of Michael Brill where the avowed God was in hiding from his enemies.

A few days later a mob seized Dylks but did no harm. Perceiving that his day of greatness was over in the neighborhood, he left for another community. He evidently gained little fame there, for he next journeyed to Philadelphia, where he soon disappeared into obscurity.

In after years some people in the Leatherwood Circuit continued to profess their faith in Dylks, and the harm that he had done during his brief reign so completely disorganized the church that it could not be reorganized until newcomers moved into the area in sufficient numbers to build it all anew.[51]

There were many other instances of imposter preachers. When Reverend Thomas Ware went to Albany, New York, to assume duties as a circuit rider, he was met by a preacher who seemed much embarrassed. The preacher asked Ware for his credentials because a short time before another Thomas Ware had visited in the area, supposedly sent there by Bishop Asbury. To gain the people's sympathy this other Thomas Ware had claimed that he had become overheated and had contracted a violent cold, which affected his voice so adversely that he was unable to preach or pray. Since Ware's name was frequently seen in church minutes and since the man had such a decent appearance, the people saw no reason to ask to see his credentials. The settlers even made a collection in his behalf and directed him to another minister's home, where he remained for several days. A short time later the minister had asked Ware for his credentials, and became suspicious of the man who was unable to speak. The minister later learned that the false preacher had gone to another area after accepting a final collection and had palmed himself off on the people there in similar manner.

Ware told the local preacher that he too had heard of the imposter. The man had lived in one place under the name of Ware for some time without being detected. On another occasion the swindler had chanced to meet a man who knew the real Ware and who threatened to have the adventurer prosecuted. The imposter quickly mounted his horse, put the whip and spurs to him, and escaped.

The lengthy conversation between the two men terminated in a sympathetic understanding between them. The settlers soon accepted Reverend Ware and found him a dedicated circuit rider.[52]

Peter Cartwright at one time lived in a two-room log cabin in Kentucky and he too entertained a false preacher. Late one afternoon, a man calling himself a Baptist preacher and his son rode up to Cartwright's home and asked for lodging. Though Cartwright did not have a stable, he helped the men dispose of their horses and invited the two men into his house.

Immediately after supper, the strangers stepped into the room where they were to sleep and returned in a few minutes smelling strongly of whiskey. The host refrained from saying anything about it.

Just before bedtime, Cartwright brought his Bible and said, "Brother, it is our custom to have family prayer. Take the book and lead prayer." When the elder guest declined the invitation, Cartwright took the book, read, sang, and prayed, but neither of the visitors participated in the religious service. The next morning the strangers again declined to participate in the family devotion. At the completion of the morning ceremony the elder guest went into his room and returned with a bottle of whiskey and offered his host a dram. Cartwright refused.

After breakfast the elder man said, "Perhaps, Brother, you charge." Cartwright remarked, "Yes, all whiskey-drinking preachers that will not pray with me, I charge." The guest said that it looked "hard for one minister to charge another." Cartwright remained firm in his demand. He pointed out that he had no evidence that the man was a preacher at all, but was likely a vile imposter whom he took pleasure in charging the full price. Rather than press the subject further, the "Baptist minister" reluctantly paid his belligerent and muscular host.[53]

William F. Pope wrote in his book *Early Days in Arkansas* of the sensation created in Little Rock in the Fall of 1832 by Alfred W. Arrington, a preacher, imposter, lawyer, politician, and author who was made pastor of the Methodist church. Arrington came from Indiana, was over six feet tall, and had big powerful hands, light blue eyes, and flaxen colored hair. Although secretly a moral leper, he was brilliant in diverse callings—"resistless in eloquence and convincing in logic." Hundreds of people flocked to hear his sensational sermons. One woman of another denomination in describing his delivery said he "seemed to reach up and grasp the stars and set them on his brow."

For reasons unknown the people of Little Rock eventually became convinced that Arrington was an imposter. His prestige waned rapidly and he was forced to resign. He went to Missouri where he soon became involved in a scandal that compelled him to relinquish the ministry entirely. He next turned to a career in law at Fayetteville, Arkansas, where he became a renowned attorney. His status as a lawyer enabled him to enter politics and he was elected a representative to the state legislature on the Whig ticket. Two years later, after being appointed a National elector on the Whig ticket, he resigned from the party because be was convinced that the Democrats were right in advocating the annexation of Texas. From Arkansas, Arrington next went to Texas and was elected a circuit judge. He later resigned this position to avoid impeachment resulting from gross misconduct. This talented but erratic character made his next appearance as a lawyer in Chicago. Here he later published a book entitled *The Desperadoes of the Southwest*. This book clearly showed his contempt for the frontier society which had long been more than hospitable to him.[54]

No part of the frontier was safe from imposter preachers. One fraudulent minister preached with great zeal and approbation one Sunday morning in Galena, Illinois, and was found drunk that afternoon at a gambling table in a low public house, spending the money he had collected from his morning congregation. In another Illinois community, an escaped European convict posed as a minister for a year and a half. Finally his congregation learned "from what college he was promoted to the ministry," and they fired the criminal imposter.[55] A few years later, two men entered a small village in Illinois and loudly proclaimed that they possessed the power of communicating with the dead. They asserted that for a small fee anyone might have correct answers from their departed friends. A neighborhood minister preached on the subject and logically demonstrated to settlers the absurdity of the claim. The fake divines were unmasked. The expected audience failed to show up and the imposters received no money for their preposterous scheme.[56]

In March 1821, *The Missionary*, a Methodist publication, warned Christians of Georgia to beware of a man named Parker Williams. Going from place to place in the state posing as a Methodist preacher, Williams frequently solicited donations. *The Missionary* claimed he was not a church member and definitely not a preacher. Friends of religion who had sufficient regard for church honor and discipline should discountenance the fake.[57] The Georgia Baptist Association also found it necessary in 1832 to adopt a resolution disclaiming any connection with a certain Joseph Stephens, who was traveling about under the guise of a Baptist minister. Another imposter Baptist minister named Musgrove became so troublesome in Tennessee, South Carolina, Alabama, and Georgia that church members from these states petitioned *The Christian Index*, a Georgia periodical, to expose the hypocrite to the public. Musgrove, an anti-missionary and abolitionist, had thrown a number of church organizations into confusion. The *Index*, responding to the petitions, published articles in several issues warning churches to be on their guard and take heed whom they received and bid God's speed.[58]

To lessen the influence and activities of fake preachers in the vicinity of Houston, Texas, in 1837, a committee of vigilantes consisting of six ministers was organized. To prevent imposters from gaining the confidence of the people, the committee inserted a notice of its organization and its functions in the *Telegraph*, a local newspaper. The notice stated that no minister who came to Texas would be recognized by the committee until he had exhibited unmistakable credentials of authority from his denominations.

The specific instance that gave rise to this preachers' vigilante committee was the appearance of an imposter in Washington, Texas. In the absence of Reverend Z. N. Morrell, its regular pastor, the stranger preached at a Baptist church. At the end of the sermon the guest preacher stated that he was badly in need of monetary assistance and he convinced someone in the congregation to circulate a subscription. After collecting the money, the fake man of God left for parts unknown. This incident so angered and humiliated Morrell that he initiated the vigilante movement to counteract fake preachers.[59]

In time, frontier people evolved an integrated and compact society and adopted more uniform concepts of right and wrong. As the various frontiers came to an end, people became more decorous at religious services. Churches became better organized and more available to people. Preachers focused greater attention on religion and righteous living, and a more moral and dedicated ministry evolved. Religious observation became more serene and better accepted. Bonds of social control became stronger and religious decorum became accepted. The frontier preacher changed as an organized society took over the frontier.

212

# 13

# Emotional Religion and Frontier Sermons

Overt emotional reactions to religion on the frontier were varied. The spirit of personal freedom permeated every phase of the backwoods and made people relatively free to think, speak and act as they desired in most situations. When one became an exponent of a new way of living, the voice of the community lacked force of custom and was generally not sufficiently strong to shout one down. Bold, reckless, and even revolutionary, one missionary observed that settlers had an air of self-assurance bordering on cockiness which was manifested in both church and state and in saint and sinner. Pioneers pronounced judgments on subjects which had long perplexed the wisest of men. Frontiersmen can be compared with a high pressure boiler on a steamboat which had vast propelling power but lacked a prudent captain and a sober crew. They were like a great kettle that ever and now overflowed.[1]

This frontier freedom made the people changeable in character—ready to shoot you or shoot for you, and ready to worship Paul and Barnabus today and stone them tomorrow. Deeply religious one week, they might the next become proprietors or patrons of a vile dance house or gambling hall. They often had little regard for law and morality and made the first to suit themselves while neglecting the second to a surprising degree.[2] On the frontier, where bonds of social restraint were lifted, people were free to act as they pleased.

Frontiersmen were emotionally starved and welcomed any excitement, religious or otherwise. Even a murder had its rewards, as it afforded a topic for conversation and a place to go—to the wake and to the cemetery. At a wedding, funeral, working, hanging, or frolic, settlers sought emotional release in wild outbursts of laughter or in tears. When unsophisticated people went to a camp meeting or traveled many miles to hear a much discussed and famed minister, they were more susceptible to suggestion—to the sermon, singing, prayers, and the unstable behavior of the congregation.

Religious services usually produced an air of excitement. Persuasive songs and heart-rending prayers put congregations in a receptive mood for the sermon. The minister, regardless of education, had usually mastered the art of knowing what to say and how to say it in order to obtain maximum response. Somewhere in his sermon, after relating humorous incidents, a minister would usually change to a serious mood to depict the horrors of hell and bliss of heaven. The audience would stare at the minister and enter into a hypnotic state. The preacher was swaying the congregation; the congregation was influencing the minister; and each one in the assembly radiated his mood to others. In the words of Charles Cooley, "Each to each a looking-glass, reflects the other that doth pass." Suggestion and imitation passed swiftly, impulsively, and without resistance, as in the united action of a lynching mob or a political revolution.[3] It was inevitable that frontier people without customary bonds of social restraint would either become uncontrollably sad and moody in realization of their sinful and lost condition or completely enraptured at the sight of pearly gates.

Frontier people adopted various theories concerning emotional exercises. Some believed that they were a sign that the world was coming to an end soon. Others believed that they signaled that the judgment of God was coming upon them in the form of a dreadful calamity. Some maintained that odd behavior was the work of the Devil, who came unchained for a season and assumed the guise of an angel of light to deceive both ministers and the saved. Still others believed that these exercises gave evidence that a great spiritual awakening was in the making, which would cover the earth, as the waters cover the sea, and gather the nations into one united body.[4]

In its frontier setting the hysterical reaction of the people to religion was not abnormal. The settlers were generally naive and backward and were subjected to harsh living conditions; they sought emotional release and easily gave vent to their feelings. There was little or no social censure. It was impossible for most of them to refrain from such activity. Preachers attempted to achieve a favorable response to their prayers and sermons, even though they caused half their congregations to take the jerks, to fall to the floor or ground, or to moan and cry in agony to find the way to heaven. Those ministers who were best able to arouse high emotional response were usually regarded as prophets of the Lord, and neither distance nor privation kept people from hearing them. When the frontier passed so did the exercises.

Emotional response fed upon the overt act of those who had the least self-control. Everyone was prone to imitate the behavior of the congregation as a whole or in part. Once emotional control began to slip, there was no way of predicting what extremes of behavior might be manifested.[5]

## FALLING

The most common physical manifestation of emotional religion was falling. During one religious gathering while some of the people were earnestly engaged in prayer, the preachers' stand was crowded with a group of giddy and talkative young people. One of these, a gaily attired girl, was making fun of those who were praying. One of the ministers on his knees laboring with a convicted woman suddenly rose and exclaimed in a clear and commanding voice, "My God, knock that young woman down!" These words were repeated three times, and suddenly the girl fell "as if pierced by a rifle ball." Turning to the lady who was kneeling near him, the preacher tapped her on the shoulder and said, "Sister, that is what I call taking them between the lug and the horn." The incident had its good effect. The girl, after a long hard struggle, was "powerfully converted."[6]

At the camp meeting held at Cabin Creek, Kentucky, in 1801, falling was without parallel. Those who tried to run away were frequently stricken down or impelled to return. Even obstinate sinners found no shelter except under the protection of prejudiced and bigoted professors. On the third night of the meeting, to prevent the fallen from being trampled under foot by the multitude, they were picked up and laid side by side on two squares in a nearby church. Inasmuch as many people from Caneridge, Concord, and Eagle Creek were attending this gathering, this strange phenomenon soon spread to these places.[7]

The number who fell at other religious gatherings was fantastic. In Ohio hundreds fell within a few minutes, including nearly all the adults in the congregation. In the early hours of morning after one such congregation had been dismissed, Reverend James B. Finley was called from his tent to pray for eight families, most of whom had fallen on the floor of the church building and were crying for mercy.[8]

While Reverend M'Kendree was preaching, the power of God fell on the congregation and the preacher himself was so spiritually overcome that he sank down into the arms of another minister who was sitting in the pulpit behind him. M'Kendree was raised to his feet; his face beamed with glory; and he began to shout. An "electric shock" ran through the congregation, and many people began falling to the floor as if slain in a field of battle. Another minister at this meeting was employed night and day without interruption for seventy-two hours, administering to the fallen.[9]

Falling became so commonplace that the success of a revival was often measured in terms of the number so affected. Many "professors of religion" began to believe that up to the time of their "spill," they had never really experienced a spiritual rebirth. Many were strengthened in their faith after experiencing a falling. One man who had professed his religion for twenty-five years fell and lay motionless for hours, overwhelmed with a sense of ingratitude toward God. Two Presbyterian ministers became convinced while lying in a helpless state that their condition was due to divine goodness. Most victims of falling were happy, but a few were dejected, saying that they had no hope of salvation.[10]

Two physicians examined a young man and woman who had fallen to ascertain their physical states. The young man apparently had "no connection in his joints" and the woman seemed to have "no joints at all." Their pulses remained regular and normal, but their breathing was extremely low, no "oftener than once a minute, or nearly so." The muscular state of the two mystified the doctors—one had relaxed muscles, the other rigid.[11] Although most victims of falling lay helpless for a period of time ranging from a few minutes to twenty-four hours or longer, some experienced graphic visions and were conscious all the while to the happenings about them. Most felt no pain, though many struck against objects in their convulsive falling movements.[12] Curious to learn whether a stout man lying on his back was a mere pretender, one minister dropped some hartshorn or ammonium carbonate into the man's nostrils. To the minister's surprise, the man was completely insensible to the pungent stimulant. However, not all who fell were in such an advanced hypnotic state, since they convulsed, writhed, and screamed while lamenting that they were lost sinners but proclaiming they had hope through Christ.

The psychological power of suggestion no doubt helped to bring on falling. Those most susceptible to suggestion were its victims. One elderly lady who heard of the strange disorder believed it was "put on" and went to see for herself. While sitting in a church where the phenomenon had been prevalent, she wondered who would be the first affected. In this mental state, she all at once felt something sweet as honey in her throat and fell helplessly to the floor. Her breathing became so labored that she feared for her life. To conceal her fear she began laughing uncontrollably. When her condition subsided, the woman arose somewhat chagrined. She believed her malady was real. She never realized that she had hypnotized herself.[13] Another woman who had frequently fallen at religious services often fell while seated at her spinning wheel. Asked why she did so, she replied that it was the result of reflecting on the glory of God.[14]

While one minister was preaching in a cabin, an elderly gentleman became so happy that he whistled and fell from his chair in a helpless state. The brethren lifted him from the floor and laid him on a bed, where he remained motionless and apparently lifeless until the next morning at eight o'clock. At that time he awoke and said he was as happy as could be.[15]

Two men attended a sacramental meeting to investigate falling. They became separated in the mass of humanity but met after the service. One affirmed that this unusual behavior was the work of the Devil; scarcely had he spoken when he fell headlong from the log on which he was standing. On another occasion, a husband, bitterly exasperated with his wife for remaining at a meeting house all night, went to the religious service and ordered her home. When she refused to go, he angrily returned home and soon after fell powerless to the floor. Witnessing a series of fallings at a church, one man condemned the behavior as madness. The following day, while at work in his field, he began thinking about what he had seen at church and fell to the ground where he lay until found by his family during the night.[16]

No one seemed immune to falling once they had witnessed the phenomenon. A doctor of many years experience and supposedly inured to physical and psychological disorders, suddenly felt that he was about to fall out of his church seat. He tried to leave but was able to walk only a few steps before he fell. He cried out in anger, "Carry me away!" Several men picked him up and took him a short distance from the congregation. The doctor's mind remained rational, but his limbs trembled so violently that he was unable to support himself. "What does this mean? I have cut off limbs, and taken up arteries with as steady a hand as any man ever had. Now I cannot hold these hands still if I might have a world."[17]

Another physician was curious to examine the phenomenon and accompanied a young lady to a religious assembly. Before arriving, each agreed to watch over the other, if either should fall. During the service, the physician saw many people falling all around. Suddenly a strange feeling entered his body and he began to run for the woods. He proceeded only a short distance before he fell and lay immobile "for some time."[18] The doctor was another victim of suggestion.

## JERKS

The jerks was another psychological reaction to frontier religion. This condition was characterized by a violent twitching of muscles of the neck, arms, and legs, and often of the entire body. The seizure sometimes caused a victim's head to jerk so forcibly from front to back and from side to side that the neck was in danger of being dislocated or broken. In his *History of Giles County, Tennessee,* James McCallum tells of women who jerked so violently that their long hair, when unbraided, cracked as loud as a whip.[19] A drunken man at a camp meeting began cursing the jerks. Instantly his body was afflicted with violent bodily contortions. He tried to escape, but he jerked so furiously that he could not run very far. The intoxicated man stopped among some saplings, took out a bottle of whiskey and swore he would "drink the damn jerks to death." His muscular system became so convulsive that he was unable to hold the bottle to his mouth. He suddenly began to jerk so violently that his neck snapped. He fell to the ground and died moments later.[20] Other drunkards attempting to ward off the jerks found themselves unable to hold bottles to their lips. The spasmodic movement of their arms, head, and legs caused them to drop their flasks to the ground or to break them against the surrounding trees.[21]

When women and girls contracted the jerks, men rushed forward to hold them so that they would not injure themselves. This was no easy undertaking. Girls so affected often became so strong that they could not be controlled by two men.[22]

Seized with this "illness," one generally staggered around until dashed to the ground, where the spasm continued for varying lengths of time. If one sat down, one's muscles tended to quiet. Others gained relief by jumping and dancing around, inducing their bodies somehow to relax. According to Peter Cartwright, when one "caught" the jerks it was best to adopt a passive state of mind, if possible.[23]

Evidently no one was safe from this malady, especially if one responded easily to suggestion. Reverend Lewis Garrett had seen both people who made no pretense of being religious and those of eminent piety take the disorder. If deeply moved by a "warm" song or a very persuasive sermon, either saint or sinner might be seized. If one tried to stop, the jerking might become worse. One inquisitive woman went to church to witness the strange behavior and soon found herself jerking and rolling in mud.[24] Another woman who had been afflicted many times said she could usually avoid the phenomenon by shouting praises to God. If she tried to restrain her emotions, she usually contracted the jerks.[25]

The number who were affected by the jerks is almost incredible. On one occasion in Tennessee, about 150 people had jerking exercises.[26] Peter Cartwright contended that in large gatherings he had seen as many as 500 persons jerking at one time.[27] Saplings were often cut off breast high to provide stump supports for the people to jerk by. One eyewitness reported that after a jerking exercise the ground around a grove of trees was kicked up as though horses had been stamping flies.[28]

During a religious service in a home, a young girl contracted the jerks and fell to the floor. Two young men tried to control her to keep her from rolling in the fire. A wicked man who assumed her condition to be pretension told the men to leave her alone. Later, when this evil man walked into the yard, he too began to jerk, which nearly frightened him out of his senses.[29] At another assembly, when two sisters became afflicted with the ailment during one of Peter Cartwright's sermons, their brothers threatened to horsewhip the preacher. Cartwright warned the men to beware or he would give them the jerks. The brothers ran away in great fear.[30]

Reverend James McGrady told of a young man who faked an illness one Sunday rather than go to a camp meeting with his family. While lying in bed, he began thinking of occurrences at a recent meeting, especially the actions of an excited woman. To his astonishment, his body began to jerk violently. He fell from the bed and began to exercise all around the floor. He began to pray and soon he found relief. He returned to bed, but his mind again returned to the scenes of the religious meeting. Once again the sickness returned. After gaining control, he dressed and walked into the yard to remove the hair from a dogskin. He drew the skin from the soaking vat and laid it on a beam, but when he raised the scraping knife he again was seized. Jerking backward and forward and to the sides, he was unable to keep the knife from falling to the ground. Again, earnest prayer calmed his nerves. Angrily, he tried again to scrape the skin but could not—the ailment returned. This time he was thoroughly frightened because prayer gave him no relief. After ordering a slave to return the skin to the vat, he walked to his room, jerking all the way. When his family returned, they found the young man in bed crying for mercy.[31]

In areas where jerks were a common occurrence, men in taverns were sometimes affected. They suddenly began to throw glasses and liquor to the ceiling, much to the amusement and alarm of others. While pouring coffee, some women were seized and they threw pot, cup, and saucer from their hands. Such incidents became the general topic of conversation. Some attributed the seizures to the Devil, others to God.[32]

Even sober and respected ministers were not immune

to the jerks. Once when a Cumberland Presbyterian preacher went into the woods near a church to attend a devotional meeting, he became so stirred by testimonials, prayers, and songs that he contracted the jerks. To keep himself from falling he caught hold of a sapling. While holding to the tree, his head jerked back violently and he emitted a sound similar to that of a barking dog. A rogue who witnessed the spectacle later reported that he had found the minister barking up a tree.[33]

Reverend Doke, another Cumberland Presbyterian, was often afflicted with the infirmity. This alarmed both his family and his congregation. Seized while standing in the pulpit, he sometimes jerked so hard and rapidly that many feared he would break his neck or dislocate his joints. During his convulsions, he laughed uncontrollably, hallooed at the top of his voice, and occasionally leaped from the pulpit and ran into the woods, screaming like an insane man. When the jerks subsided, he returned to preach, rational and calm as ever.

A third preacher who before his conversion and entry into the ministry had been a dancing master was another victim of the strange seizures. Stationed in a Methodist circuit where jerks were prevalent, he resolved to preach them out of existence. He pursued the task with great zeal and high expectations, but before long he became a victim of the jerks. As he was seized he would shout, "Ah, yes! Oh, no!" and then would use his hands and arms as if playing a fiddle. Once the disorder seized him while on horseback. He dropped the reins and his horse carried him onward to a picket fence in front of a house. The preacher dismounted and caught hold of the top portions of two pickets. His shaking and jerking became so violent that he pulled the pickets from their fastening. The lady of the house rushed to his aid. To escape from the embarrassing situation, the preacher ran toward an orchard, with a pack of barking dogs at his heels. Frightened by the dogs, he circled back, ran into the house, and jumped into a bed. There he lay until his convulsion subsided. Unable to rid himself or his circuit of the jerks, the minister eventually relinquished his charge and retired from the ministry.[34]

Ministers could cause or prevent the jerks and other irrational emotional behavior. If a minister voiced disapproval at the first appearance of excess excitement in his congregation, he could usually calm the people. One Baptist preacher saw a man begin to jerk, paused in his sermon, and in a loud and solemn tone shouted, "In the name of the Lord I command all unclean spirits to leave this place." The suggestion immediately relieved the man of his disorder. Ministers who preached from such texts as, "Bodily exercises profit little" and "Let all things be done decently and in order" were sometimes effective in keeping emotions in check. Wiser ministers, who were opposed to the exercises, said little or nothing about them and preached sermons of a less soul-stirring nature.[35]

One Presbyterian minister tried an experiment to determine what conditions gave rise to such emotional displays. He noted that while he preached in a smooth, melodious voice his audience remained calm. When he raised the pitch and loudness, or injected emotion and provoking ideas, scores of people made a "suppressed noise similar to the barking of a dog." One very pious woman, a previous victim of the "exercises," instantly began to jerk. Sitting in another area, an enthusiastic man interrupted the impassioned sermon by singing a lively tune. Several young men then began to jerk violently. The hysterical jerkers and the song raised the emotional level and induced many others to jerk, the preacher noted.[36]

Some ministers intentionally preached sermons to induce members of their congregations to jerk. A Methodist named Reverend Jacob Young, preaching to a group of "Old School Presbyterians" who opposed emotional exercises, deliberately tried to make the congregation jerk. Alluding to the Presbyterians' opinion of the jerks, he said, "Now the Methodists are a pack of hypocrites, and could refrain from shouting if they would." Pausing, he shouted at the top of his voice, "Do you leave off jerking if you can?" Instantly "more than five hundred commenced jumping, shouting, and jerking." The preaching came to an abrupt halt. An old lady later admonished Young for preaching in order to set them to jerking.[37] The woman's analysis was correct. Young had preached as he did to defend the Methodists' point of view and to satisfy his own personal desire to evoke great emotional response.

## PULPIT BEHAVIOR

Frontier preachers were expected to make use of "long, loud, and violent declamations."[38] Reverend William Burke began one of his sermons in a voice which was like the crash of thunder, but within an hour it was as weak as an infant's.[39] Another minister felt somewhat insecure at the beginning of his sermon and explained to his congregation that he was not the man he once was because he had only one lung. As he warmed to the message, he preached grandiloquently "with forty lung power." A group of boys in the back of the church nearly fell off their seats with laughter. What would the preacher have done with two lungs?[40]

Many ministers did not use their accustomed speech patterns while preaching. They drawled out their sentences from beginning to end, and this manner of speaking was generally acceptable. Pitching their voices so high, they were able to make small variations in sound. When their lungs were exhausted, they caught their breath with repeated "ahs." Reverend Pierson wrote that he once heard a minister near the close of his sermon, whose voice organs were wearied with exhaustion and face was in painful contortions, who spoke less distinctly and repeated "ah" more frequently. According to him, the preacher said, "Oh, my beloved brethren—ah, and sisters—ah, you have all got to die—ah, and be buried—ah, and go to the judgment—ah, and stand before the great white throne—ah, and receive your rewards—ah, for the deeds—ah, done in the body—ah." Apparently he decided what he would say next while catching his breath and saying "ah." The settlers, however, regarded this man as a great preacher.[41]

Elijah Whitten, called the "stormer," usually began his sermons standing behind a chair when preaching in a home. As he became more animated, he stood in the split-bottom chair and it soon had a hole stamped in it.[42] William McGee, a prominent minister of the Kentucky revival, would stand or lie in the dust and exhort so energetically that his body became exhausted and his eyes streaming with tears. He could only moan, "Jesus! Jesus!"[43]

One young minister named Simpson, President of Asbury University, because of his youth and plain dress did not seem to have the making of a great preacher. Eventually he developed an unusual ability to excite people's emotions. During his sermons, when his heart was "set on fire," many in his congregations shouted and cried so loudly that they drowned out his voice. At a high point of one of his discourses, an intelligent woman not given to excitement jumped to her feet, waved her hands, and exclaimed, "Sun, stand thou still, and let the moon pass by!" After she repeated the statement a second time, the congregation began to sing, during which time the hysterical woman was taken from the building. As a result of his stirring sermons, the Methodist Church eventually voted Simpson orator of the year.[44]

During the buildup of emotional excitement during a sermon, Reverend Jonathan Shaw had the habit of standing on tip-toe and stretching his arms above his head. Then he would suddenly bend his body forward and spring from one end of the pulpit to the other. On one such occasion, he jumped completely from the podium and down into the surprised congregation, landing on his hands and knees. Another minister remarked, "Well! Well! That's what you get for running around so much." Shaw picked himself up and proceeded with the sermon as though nothing had happened.

Reverend Johnson was also most effective in eliciting strong emotional response from his congregations. Once while his wife sat holding her baby near the outskirts of a camp meeting, she heard a wild and profane young man say that he would bet fifty dollars that her husband "would get up a shaking among the dry bones." Johnson, true to the young man's prediction, preached with "uncommon liberty and power," though not more than fifty minutes. At the end of the sermon, half of the congregation were bathed in tears and at least fifty persons were shouting the praises of God at once.[45]

Portraying torments of hell, one minister soon had the sinners crying for mercy. Suddenly he exclaimed, "A center shot, my Lord; load and fire again." A group of people wandering around outside began making their way down the church's center aisle. The preacher saw the group, stood on his tiptoes, raised his hand forward, and pointed a finger at them, exclaiming, "Here they come now, my Lord; shoot them as they come." Instantly those striding down the aisle either fell to the floor or sank into a seat. Thereafter, this minister held the congregation at his will.[46]

Exotic emotional behavior in the pulpit was exhibited by many ministers. For more than an hour during his sermon at Turtle Creek, Kentucky, a Reverend Thompson danced around the pulpit in perfect time as he murmured over and over in a loud whisper, "This is the Holy Ghost—glory!" At another meeting in a Kentucky church, a Reverend William McGee once fell unconscious to the floor and his brother John trembled so violently that he could not preach. This resulted in a violent uproar among the congregation, some of whom fell unconscious, while others only grunted and groaned. Addicted to holy hopping and dancing, a few preachers stopped their sermons and pranced and swayed around the pulpit and up and down the aisles. One minister stopped his sermon, shouted that God was in the house, and then he began to squeal like a pig. He constantly interrupted himself with cries of "Oink! Oink! Oink!" and then fell to the ground. His friends had to prevent him from rooting his nose to the ground like a hog.

Peter Cartwright was another master who played freely with the emotional strings of his congregations. One night Cartwright sat impatiently watching an educated minister read a sermon in an unplastered frame building by flickering candle light. He performed poorly, balking, hemming, and coughing before a restless congregation who were anxious to give vent to their feelings. The "book" preacher finished in about thirty minutes, and then Cartwright began delivering a moving exhortation, urging the sinners to come to the mourners' bench.

A solemn power rested on the congregation, and many accepted the invitation. The educated minister, however, did not know how to cope with the situation, at least in Cartwright's opinion. Talking with sinners, the sermon-reading preacher asked if they did not love Christ, the "lovely Savior." It was easy to be a Christian, he assured the repentants, one had only to resolve to do so.

Disgusted with this soft approach, Cartwright stepped to the preacher and said, "Brother, you don't know how to talk to mourners. I want you to go out into the congregation and exhort sinners."

He tried, but the educated minister was out of his element in trying to console sinners. A back-slidden Christian, a large man weighing about 230 pounds, stood near the mourners' bench crying for mercy. The visiting minister walked to the sinner, tapped him on the shoulder and said, "Be composed. Be composed." The suggestion was futile and Cartwright moved toward the distressed man and commanded him to "Pray on, brother, pray on. Brother, there is no composure in hell."

As the congregation had jammed the aisle, Cartwright ordered them to stand aside so that he could get the sinner to the bench. Immediately as the aisle opened "The Lord spoke to the back-slider," inducing him to cry aloud, "Glory to God." Ecstatically the converted sinner blindly reached to take Cartwright into his arms, but instead accidentally caught the visiting minister. Being a strong man, he lifted the preacher from the floor and jumped from bench to bench, knocking people against one another, right and left, front and rear. With outstretched arms and legs, the frightened minister expected every moment to be his last. Cartwright later said he had an urge to tap the scared preacher on the shoulder and command him to be composed.

When the hysteria had subsided, the educated minister departed as quickly as propriety would allow. He had failed, but Cartwright had given the people what they wanted—emotional release.[47]

James McGrady, an outstanding member of the Kentucky revival movement during the first part of the nineteenth century, was unusually effective in using fear as a tool of repentance. In one of his sermons entitled "The Character, History and End of the Fool," he said that when a fool died, black flaming vultures of hell began to encircle his soul on every side and all the horrid crimes of his past life stared him in his face in all their glowing colors. While in this miserable state, remembrance of sermons and sacramental occasions flashed like streams of forked lightning through the fool's tortured soul, causing him to reflect, as though a poison arrow were piercing his heart, that he had rejected the mercy of God. As the fiends of hell dragged him into the eternal gulf, the sinner screamed and yelled like a Devil. In this everlasting hell the sinner's conscience "stings and gnaws his soul like a never-dying worm." Through the blazing flames of hell, the fool sees the heaven he has lost—a heaven in which his relatives are living in sublime peace and joy.

In hell the fool is presented a dictionary which gives the meaning of daily expressions such as "I'll be damned," and "God damn his soul." The fool now knows the full meaning of these terms for God has damned his soul. Inasmuch as he is damned in hell forever and ever, he is constrained to confess emphatically that he is, indeed, a "damned fool."[48]

McGrady could so array hell before the wicked that they would tremble and quake, imagining a lake of fire and brimstone yawning to overwhelm them. While preaching in South Carolina, he caused so much excitement among one congregation that he was accused of "running the people distracted" and of interfering with necessary vocations. The opposition to him there grew so strong that his pulpit was torn away and burned and a threatening letter written in blood was sent to him.[49]

McGrady and other frontier ministers used many psychological devices to save souls. Some were successful, others were not. McGrady, for instance, once drew up a solemn covenant binding all who signed it to offer special prayer every Saturday evening and Sunday morning for one year that there might be a revival in Logan County Kentucky as well as throughout the world. Another preacher in western New York, faced by an unresponsive congregation, suddenly gave sinners the choice of publicly accepting Christ or rejecting Him. The surprised audience made no move. The minister stared long and hard at the congregation and then pronounced its doom: "You have made your choice, you have rejected Christ; your sins are on your head." He then abruptly walked from the pulpit and the building, leaving an awe-stricken congregation.[50]

On another occasion, while a minister was preaching a sermon on "The Last Judgment," a young man became so excited that he began running around the pulpit. The minister immediately began telling the agitated youth how he could reach salvation. Three men who were not Christians begged the minister to leave the young man alone, and they prepared to take him home. The preacher protested; he argued that the sinner should get religion in his own way. Desirous of saving all lost souls, he asked the three men if they would permit the congregation to pray for them for thirty minutes. He assured the three that at the end of that time if they were not "happily writhing on the floor," they could take their friend home. The bargain was made; the skeptical sinners took seats in front of the pulpit; and the preacher, while holding a watch in one hand, raised the other toward heaven as a signal for praying to begin. The entire congregation prayed so loud that they soon shook the building. When the preacher shouted, "Fifteen minutes of the time are gone!" two of the doubters fell unconscious to the floor. Later, when he screamed, "Twenty minutes!" the third collapsed. All three were soon "gloriously converted" and joined the Methodist Church. It is hoped that the excited youth also made his peace with God.[51]

In his *Journal*, Francis Asbury frequently alluded to emotional responses from his congregations. On a tour of Kentucky in 1790, he preached on one occasion mainly to a group of women, many of whom "lay prostrate, overpowered with the Divine presence" at the close of the service. At the peak of emotionalism, a venerable old man stood ramrod straight, his eyes closed, in grave silence.[52] In another place in his *Journal*, Asbury recorded: "Lord's day, 14. Preached at Bohemia. There were but few people but it was a melting time." During the sermon, looking wherever he would, he saw nothing but streaming eyes, and heard nothing but groans and strong cries after God and the Lord Jesus Christ."[53] At another place the groans and prayers of his congregation were so loud that Asbury's voice was lost. In an enraptured mental state, Asbury sat down and said, "This is none other than the house of God! This is the gate of heaven!" For more than an hour he wrestled vainly with the agitated congregation. He tried to speak and to get the assembly to sing. As night drew near, it was with difficulty that he finally persuaded the people to go home.[54] Speaking to yet another assembly, a number began "to fall and shake." The next day the "Methodist Saint" preached at "Rowe's place" where another shaking took place. "Many were pierced to the heart" and others wept and cried.[55] During one protracted service which lasted from noon until midnight, fifteen people were converted. One sinner was stricken so powerfully that he could not hold a joint still and roared for mercy. Asbury began to pray and the congregation increased its lamentations. When the prayer was finished, the stricken man gained enough self-control to jump to his feet and praise God with a countenance so altered that those who beheld him were filled with astonishment.[56]

Salvation came hard to many sinners. One distressed sixteen-year-old girl had fits and lost her reason for three days. At the end of this time she was "justified by faith" and made peace with God, although she remained weak in body for about five weeks—a period in which she fasted, prayed, and sang.[57]

Prayer at a religious service was often unplanned. Often no one in particular was called upon to pray. The class leader or minister simply said, "If any of you feel like taking up the cross and delivering your mind, do so." In response, three or four communicants might rise to their feet and commence talking and praying at once. This practice was carried over into the preaching service. Several people might stand and begin to express themselves on diverse subjects, some of which had nothing to do with religion.[58]

The use of testimonials was quite common, especially in small congregations. These impassioned confessions often reduced an entire congregation to tears. One backwoodsman in telling of his experiences with sin and religion said that his sinful career had been checked by the death of his lovely daughter. For a time after her death he had walked the straight and narrow path, living close to God. But within a short while he longed for "flesh-pots of sin" and returned to the beggarly elements of the world. God then took another of his little daughters unto Himself, inducing the sinner to be a more consistent Christian for a few months. After a time, however, the backwoodsman again became a captive of the Devil, and God then took his third and last child "home to glory." Now stricken low, he again lived righteously and close to his Maker for a while. But in the course of time worldy temptations led him once again over the line into the "Devil's dominions." This time God called him into repentance by taking his beloved wife, leaving the sinner bereft of wife and children and alone in the world. He said in a tearful voice that he was striving to meet his family again in the City of God.

This tragic account of the sinner's personal experiences rapidly turned the meeting into an emotional orgy. However, one man reacted adversely to the testimony. This skeptic jumped to his feet and shouted that God had managed the backslider's case poorly. He had killed one good woman and three innocent children to save an old "humbug" from hell, whom the Devil would probably get in the end anyway. "The next time he gets drunk and goes to pieces generally, there will be no wife or beloved little children to kill, and how will God ever get him straight anymore?" The doubter said that if God had been in charge of the situation, He would have killed the old fraud with a bolt of lightning rather than the first child and sent him to glory before he had a chance to backslide. The expressed doubts calmed the congregation and brought some measure of sanity back to the group.[59]

Inexperienced ministers faced with wild emotional displays often became easily upset. At one Presbyterian camp meeting when several families began to pray and shout loudly, the minister reprimanded them and told them that they were making too much noise. He said his church back East would have disowned them, as it was a "stickler" for peace and order. This castigation cost the young preacher acceptance by the congregation.[60]

Another minister, a Methodist, became unpopular in much the same way. Following a benediction at an evening service in Kansas, some of the people refused to retire. Since the sermon had failed to produce sufficient emotional outlet, they began to sing. Several became quite happy, one brother even "shouting lustfully." Listening to the emotional revelers as long as his patience would bear, the minister went to demand that they should get some rest. "It was not best to expend all their ammunition in the first charge," the preacher said. Though they courteously agreed, the communicants were soon again praying, singing, and shouting before the minister could get to sleep. Once more the preacher beseeched them to be quiet so that others could get sleep. If they did not get their rest, there would be a sleepy preaching and a sleepy congregation the next day. All were finally quiet, but some of the revelers became irritated and grumbled that the preacher was "cold-hearted and formal."[61]

Neither ministers nor church organizations needed to be present for settlers to display an emotional response to religion. With no organized sabbath worship available in a remote part of Georgia, two women who lived six miles apart decided to meet each other half way and hold a devotional service one Sunday morning. A curious hunter hearing their female voices in the wilds went to see what was happening. Meeting the women, he invited them to hold their next meeting at his cabin, with the understanding that settlers in the adjoining area be invited also.

On the following Sunday, one of the women read a chapter from the Bible and then led in the singing of a hymn. Next, the woman prayed and led another song. The other woman then told so dramatically of her conversion that loud cries for mercy rang forth in the cabin. Several people fell to the floor and a few rushed from the cabin in great consternation. The settlers continued to hold religious services in the backwoodsman's cabin, with some people traveling from as far as forty miles to attend. Eventually, a minister heard of the enthusiastic devotionals begun by the two women and came to the cabin to conduct a revival. This service was so successful that it spread to outlying settlements and a circuit was formed.[62]

Peter Cartwright was truly a master of the art of swaying a congregation. One evening in Illinois he began a discourse with a "loud and beautifully modulated tone . . . that rolled on the serene night air like successive peals of . . . thunder." For ten minutes he made commonplace remarks, then suddenly changed his tactics. His face reddened and his eyes grew bright, his gestures became as "animated as the waftures of a fierce torch, and his whole countenance changed into an expression of inimitable humor . . . Now his wild waggish, peculiar eloquence poured forth like a mountain torrent." Some of the sour faced clergymen and maidenly saints groaned with anguish at this desecration of the "evangelical desk." So effective were his shafts of ridicule and side-splitting anecdotes that every word seemed to be a finger tickling the ribs of the congregation. The more one attempted to control himself the more disposed one was to burst into loud and uncontrolled laughter. Cartwright's humorous discourse lasted for thirty minutes and left the encampment in convulsions of laughter; he caused the sternest features to relax into smiles and the coldest eyes to melt into tears of irrepressible merriment.

Suddenly Cartwright changed the mood of his presentation. He began sketching the "joys of a righteous death . . . and the winged raptures in the starry home of beautiful angels." So picturesque and magnetic were his words that the entire congregation rose to its feet, as if to look upon the magnificence of heaven the minister so vividly described.

At this opportune moment Cartwright called mourners to come forward to the altar. And they came, 500 in number, many of whom had been infidels until that hour.

The backwoods preacher aroused so much religious fervor on this night that the meeting continued for two weeks. "Two thousand additions to the church" were won, and Cartwright's prestige as a frontier minister soared to new heights. His success as a minister was due largely to his inimitable wit and masterly eloquence. His efforts caused Methodism to become the largest denomination in Illinois.[63]

Most sermons were tirades against the sins of gambling, drunkenness, horseracing, fighting, and Sabbath breaking. Some sermons beseeched worldly women to put their sins behind them and walk in the paths of "righteousness for His name's sake." Others sought to persuade young men to renounce their ungodly ways and attend church, speak in love feasts, and pray in the bosom of family and church. All ministers stressed the importance of conversion—a spiritual rebirth—as a prerequisite for entering the Kingdom of God.[64]

All sermons were not alike. The frontier was composed of heterogeneous cultural elements and had nearly all shades of learning and all types of people. Reverend Nathan Bangs, a Methodist who was well familiar with the ways of frontier people, told how he conducted himself before an unfamiliar congregation in a log cabin meeting. A complete stranger, he told them his name, from whence he had come, the year of his conversion and when he had become a minister. Bound for the heavenly city, Bangs said he was there to persuade as many as possible to go with him. He explained that in conducting a service he stood while singing and preaching and he knelt while praying.

Taking for his text, "Repent ye therefore, and be converted, that your sins may be blotted out when the time of refreshing shall come from the presence of the Lord," Bangs received a most favorable response. He believed that even remote as he was from civilization, God was with him "in truth and power."

After the sermon, Bangs informed the settlers of the Methodists' manner of presenting the Gospel, the amount of quarterage the ministers received, and how it was collected. Those who wanted to hear more preaching were asked to stand, and to the minister's delight, all stood. Bangs promised that he would preach there again in two weeks. Using similar techniques in other parts of the area, he organized a new circuit.[65]

What a frontier minister might do or say in the pulpit was unpredictable. While Reverend James Axley was standing behind a chair, preaching in a dwelling, two young ladies wearing low-necked dresses entered the room and took seats covered by two large handkerchiefs immediately in front of the minister. Unable to keep his mind on his sermon, Reverend Axley asked the young ladies to stand. He picked up the two handkerchiefs, handed them to the arrivals, and requested that they cover their bosoms.[66]

Some ministers even chewed tobacco while they preached. For instance, one preacher stepped before his congregation, turned the back of the chair toward him, leaned his hands on the top part, and spat amber to his right and left during his two-hour discourse entitled, "Live in Hope."[67] In Ohio, another minister stopped his sermon, stepped down from the pulpit, and asked a man on the front row of the congregation for a chew of tobacco. After "taking a mouthful," he continued his discourse with renewed fervor.[68]

Such behavior was not singular, however, inasmuch as many men chewed tobacco during a sermon and women often left the congregation to smoke their pipes or to dip snuff. Traveling with a minister in a circuit known as Brush College, Reverend Pierson noticed a twelve-year-old boy carrying a brand of fire and swinging it through the air to keep it alive. Although the month was July, Pierson learned that the fire was used to kindle a stump near the meeting ground so that both men and women could light their pipes. When the communicants had assembled, many stood around the stump, smoking their pipes or enjoying tobacco in other forms. When some brethren started a song, all extinguished their pipes and participated in the service.

During the lengthy sermon, a group of women began poking one another with their elbows. They arose from their log seats, went to the burning stump, and lit their pipes. While smoking, each was attentive to the sermon, saying nothing to each other.[69] The use of tobacco during religious services was not as odd as it might at first seem. The settlers were only acting in accordance with time and place.

## FUNERAL SERMONS

Frontier people attached great importance to funeral sermons, because they believed all deceased persons should have the benefit of a funeral and because the minister usually revealed the fate of the deceased's soul. When a Tennessean who had moved to Texas wrote his friends a letter stating that he was dangerously sick, his Tennessee friends were convinced that the Texan was dead. They selected a minister and a number of people were assembled. The preacher began the funeral oration by saying, "The last time we heard from him he was very sick, an' seein' as how he's never writ anymore, the brethering, friends and relatives consider onsafe to wait any longer about the funeral, an' so the time has arriv, a-cordin' to previous a-p'intment, to preach the funeral." What the minister meant by "onsafe" is not quite clear, but the case illustrates the importance people attached to funerals.

A woman on her death bed requested that a certain minister who had once lived in the community preach her funeral. After she died, her family offered the minister fifty dollars and traveling expenses to come and conduct the service. Living in another state, he did not accept the offer. Since the woman had mentioned no other minister, the funeral was never preached.[70]

Frontier ministers usually revealed any dying confessions or last messages of the deceased to the congregation. The deceased sometimes left messages of advice and rebuke for relatives, friends, and even enemies. The minister in his eulogy skillfully wove in all such matters. He usually commended those who were of the same faith and order as the deceased and in full fellowship and good standing with their church. Pointing the way to the "true church," he gently reminded those of other denominations of their heresy. To those without God he lectured against their waywardness and warned them of their danger.

When skillfully and tactfully presented, a funeral sermon made a profound impression on a congregation, for many people believed that they were listening to a message from an unseen world. Because the preacher was regarded as a man called to the ministry, the people considered it impossible for him to make a mistake in his sermon about the destiny of the deceased. They considered him responsible for the fate of the soul and believed it within his power to preach one into heaven or hell. However, when he preached one into the lower regions, he almost invariably aroused the indignation of the deceased's friends. If the minister sent a questionable character to heaven, he invited silent contempt and sometimes ridicule. Thus, the preacher was often caught "between the Devil and the deep blue sea," and he had to accept the consequences.[71]

On the death of a young man who had been notoriously and desperately wicked to his dying hour, his family requested Reverend John Johnson to preach the funeral. The minister, not personally acquainted with the man, reluctantly agreed to do so. In his sermon he drew a sharp distinction between the godly and ungodly, and in conclusion said, "I was not personally acquainted with the deceased. You who knew him can best tell to which class he belonged in life and in death. The great interest with us is, so to live and so to die that God himself may say it is well with us." After the sermon, a few friends of the deceased voiced displeasure with the address because the minister had failed to mention any of his virtues.[72]

The main speaker at another funeral invited other ministers of his denomination to sit with him in the pulpit, as was the custom. One of these local preachers, who wore red cowhide shoes and homespun clothes and who had walked a long distance through the dust and heat, was asked to open the "meetin'" by offering a prayer and conducting a song. When the old backwoodsman arose with hymn book in hand, he looked over the audience and said, "breethering, as bein' as I'm here I'll open the meetin' for brother Buncomb, an' then he'll preach the funeral sarmit accordin' to previous a-p'intment. But, while I'm before you, I want to say as how my main business over her is huntin' of some seed peas, an' if anybody has got any to spar', I'd like to know it after meetin'!"[73]

## OFFBEAT SERMONS AND ECCENTRIC PREACHERS

Many ministers represented the rank and file of the population and were largely illiterate. One minister, a poor reader, preached for months from a few leaves of an old Bible. Still another, who was unable to read correctly but was fond of controversy, requested Robert William Patterson to read the proof texts for him and he "followed the reading with his comments and arguments, which proved a somewhat tedious process to both parties." Patterson knew of one minister who preached from the part of Revelation concerning the man "who had a pair of balances in his hand," but who misread the Scripture as "the man who had a pair bellowses in his hand." He boldly interpreted this to mean that the wicked would "finally be blown to perdition."[74]

Another minister in a reference to the "great white throne" from Revelation 20:11, read "throne" as "thorn." In his sermon he enlarged on the difficulty of holding a steady seat on top of a thorn tree.[75] For his text one minister used the words: "The name of the Lord is a strong tower: The righteous runneth into it, and is safe." He described these towers as places of safety and preached from various passages of the Old Testament. In his discussion of the New Testament he said the world then was in a bad condition, because there were no more towers of safety. Fearing that some people might not think his interpretation of the Bible was correct, since he had little learning or knowledge of history, he said that since the Bible was true, he had no need for "histories." "Here it is," the preacher said, "straight from the Bible: 'For Peter, preaching on the day of Pentecost, commanded the people to save themselves from this untowered generation.'"

When the minister preached another sermon along this line, an old brother told him that he had made a mistake. "Mistake!" replied the preacher, "What is it?" The brother explained: "Why, that about the 'untowered generation.' It is not 'untowered.' It is 'untoward.' It is 'Save yourselves from this untoward generation.'" The preacher dropped his head and after a moment said, "There can't be any mistake about that. Why, I've preached that way more than a dozen times." When the preacher arrived at the old gentleman's house for dinner, they procured a dictionary and a Bible that rendered a verdict spoiling a favorite sermon.[76]

Backwoodsmen gained strange impressions from sermons and preachers that pleased them. If the minister quoted numerous Biblical passages, though none had more connection with his text than the pages of a dictionary, he was lauded as a Scripture preacher. Describing him, many would say that he was "not a larnt man, but a real Scripture preacher."[77]

"We have this treasure of the Gospel in earthen vessels," began one preacher and he never alluded to it again. He began quoting Scripture back and forth from Genesis to Revelation with no connection between the Scriptural passages, except that some word in one verse would serve as a catchword to remind him of another. Bellowing and blowing, the minister shed no more light on the quoted passages than the roar of artillery does upon our Declaration of Independence.

After the sermon, two women began discussing its merits. One said that it was the greatest ever preached in the place. The other woman remarked, "Yes, but I don't like these yankee preachers. They are always proving things, just like lawyers."[78]

Many preachers used texts which they had borrowed from another without knowing where they were found in the Bible, stating that it was found "somewhere betwixt the lids of the good book." Not only did they frequently misquote texts, but often used an adage not found anywhere in the Bible, such as, "Make hay while the sun shines" and "Every tub shall stand on its own bottom." If a congregation member, in reading the Bible at random, chanced to find a text "just adzactly as how the parson said it read," he was often convinced that the sermon was correct, despite its actual content.

Errors in pronunciation sometimes distorted the meaning of texts and made them more usable in the sermon plan. One minister quoting from 2 Peter 2:1, read it as "shall bring in damnable heresays." He then aimed his entire sermon at an old woman whose loose tongue had caused strife in the community by repeating and enlarging on what she had heard about others.[79]

One minister said in his sermon that "some folks come to Christ—I don't just remember who—to axe him questions." These people, the minister said, "wanted to trap Him; but they couldn't come it. The Old Fellow was too smart for 'em." Making use of interrogations, a preacher frequently clinched his arguments by saying, "I answer in the negative, yes!" The frequent appearance of this expression in sermons confirmed that it was not a slip of the tongue. Knowledge of history was limited; one preacher proudly announced that the 4th of July was to celebrate the Battle of New Orleans. While reading the minutes of his association to an audience of less than 100, the pastor asked someone to read the "statistics," as he himself was not versed in figures.[80]

Another minister used the text, "Wright, Blessed are the dead, . . .," supposing "Wright" to mean "right," while preaching the funeral services for a child. He endeavored to comfort the parents by exclaiming that it was "right" to suffer affliction and "right" that their children had become ill and died, for the Lord's dealings with his people were "right."

A few local ministers hastily gathered a small group of people together at a home. Since they had not prepared a formal sermon, the preachers decided that each would read a portion of Scripture and then make appropriate comments. One preacher read a chapter so poorly and mispronounced so many words that it was difficult to understand it, but his interpretation of the scripture was well received and no one questioned him.[81]

The local preachers of Iowa were little above the general cultural level of the people; they were ignorant, superstitious, and even fanatic, reported one missionary. One minister took his text from Shakespeare, thinking it was from the Bible. Another Iowan apologized to his congregation for not citing the book, chapter, and verse where his text was found and explained that he had not had time to check the reference before beginning his sermon. At any rate, he said, it would not hurt anyone to search the Scripture to find it.

An ignorant coal miner turned preacher began his discourse on the creation by stating that the Lord at first created a little world the size of hay stacks. The population increased, and the world "growed" to its present size. It was his belief that both coal and rocks "growed" and "pushed their way along in the earth, just as sweet potatoes do in the ground." On and on the minister went with his theory of creation and development. Simplistic as he was in his thinking, he had a strong following among the people. Such ministers were usually regarded by their flocks as men of intelligence, wisdom, and learning.[82]

Questions asked of ministers frequently revealed their lack of Biblical understanding. In conversation with a Hillerite minister, a missionary asked him whether he and his people believed that Christ had no existence previous to His incarnation. After pausing a moment the preacher replied, "Sir, I s'pose you are a learned man. I don't know what that means. You've got a huckleberry over my persimmon." When asked the meaning of the expression, "I am the root and the offspring of David," the Hillerite replied, "Why he was the root of what he was sent to do!" Another Hillerite said in a sermon that "Christ, it 'peared like, spit on the ground and made a kind of paste, and 'ointed the eyes of the blind man, and told him to go and wash in the Pool of Sillum, and it 'peared like, if he hadn't went and washed in the Pool of Sillum, he would have never saw."[83]

An eastern missionary wrote that he had listened intently to an Arian minister deliver a two hour discourse on the importance of being baptized. The minister read extremely poorly and it was rumored that he could not write his name. On another occasion when a backwoods preacher was asked to close a service, the missionary observed that the preacher read "badly" and pronounced "strangely." A few months before, this local divine had been struggling to learn simple division.[84]

Traveling through various frontier areas, Hamilton Pierson found that the "denser the ignorance of the people, the greater was the number of preachers." Men who were almost completely unlettered had pressed their claims on a church in order to secure their license and ordination.[85] Writing from Iowa in 1855, Reverend John D. Strong said he had never yet found a place in the West where there was not a large supply of ministers; in some neighborhoods he could hardly enter a house without stumbling upon one. Nearly all of the men possessed only the merest rudiments of an English education and were engaged in secular pursuits, living very much as their neighbors did.[86] In one village of thirty families there were five ministers of the same denomination with two more expecting to receive the call, and it was anticipated that still another minister would soon move to the area. All these men could barely read.[87]

Frontier life spawned some rather eccentric preachers, one of whom was Lorenzo Dow, known as "Crazy Dow." His odd behavior and extensive travels both in America and abroad brought him much publicity and fame. As a fortune teller; seer; miracle worker; professor of calamities, births, deaths, and illnesses; and interpreter of dreams; he was one of the most discussed and controversial preachers of his day. He could preach on virtually any subject and damned nearly everyone and everything. At times he shocked his congregations by preaching from obscene and sadistic portions of the Old Testament.

Tall, slender and spare of frame, with sloping shoulders and just a hint of a stoop, Dow's physical appearance normally would not have seemed forbidding, except for the fact that his matted and unkempt hair hung almost to his waist; much of it hung down his back and on his shoulders, but some of it fell forward over his face and full beard. With a grave countenance and piercing eyes, he "glanced reproofs wherever he looked" and caused the hardest sinners to flinch. He was emaciated from lack of proper food and sleep, and he knew little about the benefits of a bath. He went hatless and shoeless, wearing torn and shabby clothes. Dow presented an odd sight even to the backwoodsmen.

When he came in possession of any money, which was rare, he soon lost it to a swindler. When he bought a horse, it was usually a spavined, ill-looking brute, scarcely able to totter along the trails and roads. Trusting in God to send angels and ravens to feed him, he usually begged for food from door to door. Rumor said that when unable to find food, he ate grasshoppers. Dow had hidden powers of endurance.[88]

Dow's voice sounded more female than male, not loud but trenchant. He often dragged some of the syllables of his words to painful lengths making them disgusting and disagreeable to delicate ears. While preaching for several successive days at Pittstown, New York, some of the members of his congregation thought that he was either crazy or possessed of the Devil. After hearing the strange man preach, many people cursed and swore, partly because of what he said, but mostly because of his peculiar speech and odd demeanor. Most people detested him—some believed he was saucy and deserved to be knocked down.

Eccentric in the extreme, Dow eventually evolved techniques through trial and error that often made him a very effective preacher. One Sunday morning while Reverend Jacob Young was preaching at a camp meeting, Dow lay sick in a tent nearby. At the close of Young's sermon the sick minister rose from his bed and walked up to the pulpit. Standing there in a stooped position, looking over his right shoulder, his back to the congregation, he said, "There is a notable robber in this country, who has done a vast deal of mischief, and is still doing it; and, in order that the people may be on their guard, I intend to give you a full description of his character and the instrument by which he carried on his work." The congregation was often plagued by outlaws and became alarmed. Some people thought that Dow was referring to a Baptist minister who had been a Tory and a thief during the American revolution. This man had fled to escape punishment after the war to Spanish territory where he supposedly had become a respectable citizen.

But, this was not so. Dow was only trying to grab the attention of the congregation. He turned his face toward the assembly and began talking slowly in a dark and mysterious manner, eventually giving the robber's name in Hebrew, in Greek, and in English. The evil one was none other than the Devil. For the remainder of his sermon, Dow preached to a rapt audience and many conversions were gained.[89]

In closing one sermon, Dow said, "If there is any gentleman in the congregation who has any objection to my sermon, let him come forward, take the stand and make it known." There were five Calvinist ministers in the congregation and Dow expected a rebuttal, but none came.

After standing silently for a few moments, Dow continued, "Now, gentlemen, I am going to leave the country, and, if you do not come forward and defend your doctrine while I am present, but attempt to contradict my sermon when I am gone, someone may compare you to the little dog that does not have the courage to bark at the traveler when he is opposite to the gate, but will run along and bark on his track after he is gone!" Dow closed the meeting with a prayer and left unceremoniously.[90]

When Dow arrived at one camp meeting ground, several settlers moved toward him shouting in satisfaction that the "wild man" was coming. Dow did present a bizarre appearance. He wore a tarpaulin hat cocked on his head, a tattered green military coatee without its shiny ornaments, and a pair of knee breeches that did not conceal his knees. Dow was in a hurry and he was laden with a bundle of tracts and handbills. On each bill was printed in large letters the following words: "Hush! Hark! This afternoon at three o'clock, Lorenzo Dow will preach under the Federal Oaks." Dow rushed past one man without giving him a handbill. He stopped abruptly and appeared to search the innermost recesses of his soul for guidance, after which he handed out the first tract. He passed several other people ignoring them as if they lived on another planet. He continued this unusual and scattered distribution until all his bills were gone.[91]

Although Francis Asbury believed Dow demented, he wisely never interfered with the miracle worker. In time, when Asbury believed that Dow was not exercising a good influence on the people east of the Appalachian

Mountains, he sent him to the western frontier. In the thinly populated western areas, Dow gained unusual fame and became venerated as a prophet of the Lord.[92]

It did not take long for a preacher on the frontier to learn the importance of emotional release to the frontier people. The successful ministers were able to sway the behavior of the congregation in ways which today would appear unusual. Falling and jerking were common. Because the frontiersmen were themselves an odd lot by today's standards, some eccentric preachers were quite acceptable on the frontier. Unusual pulpit behavior and offbeat sermons often resulted. But, as the frontier disappeared and organized churches moved into an area, it gradually became less acceptable for ministers to move their congregations to such physical and emotional levels.

# 14

# Conclusion

Pioneers lived in a state of nature, faced with deadening loneliness, drabness, and adversities difficult to imagine. Despite varied geographic conditions, they lived under similar economic conditions. They had ready access to the use of the land whether it belonged to them, to the government, or to the Indians. They lived in small cabins or sodhouses and possessed a limited number of livestock. They owned guns and crude hand tools, but had little or no money. Even when a man owned more land and livestock than others around him, he was not an aristocrat, for each family did its own work. There was little inducement to produce more goods than could be used at home since people were cut off from most markets. The economy was primitive; each family produced its own food, clothing, and household fixtures and most of its own medicine. Except for cooperative enterprises such as house raisings, corn huskings, quilting bees and log rollings, the family was a self-sufficient unit. With no bank accounts, rents, stocks or bonds, frontiersmen could not afford to be idle for even one season. In hardly any society was wealth more evenly divided or were the people subjected to such uniform economic conditions.

Settlers were satisfied with the common necessities which were available to all who were willing to work for them. The work ethic was deeply ingrained in frontier thought. In private conversations and in public discourse the subject of work was ever present. In preaching a funeral sermon a minister could pay the deceased head of a family no higher compliment than by saying, "He was a good provider for his family and was willing to work longer than from sun to sun."[1] Pioneers imagined God in their own image, "a mechanic, the greatest in the universe."[2]

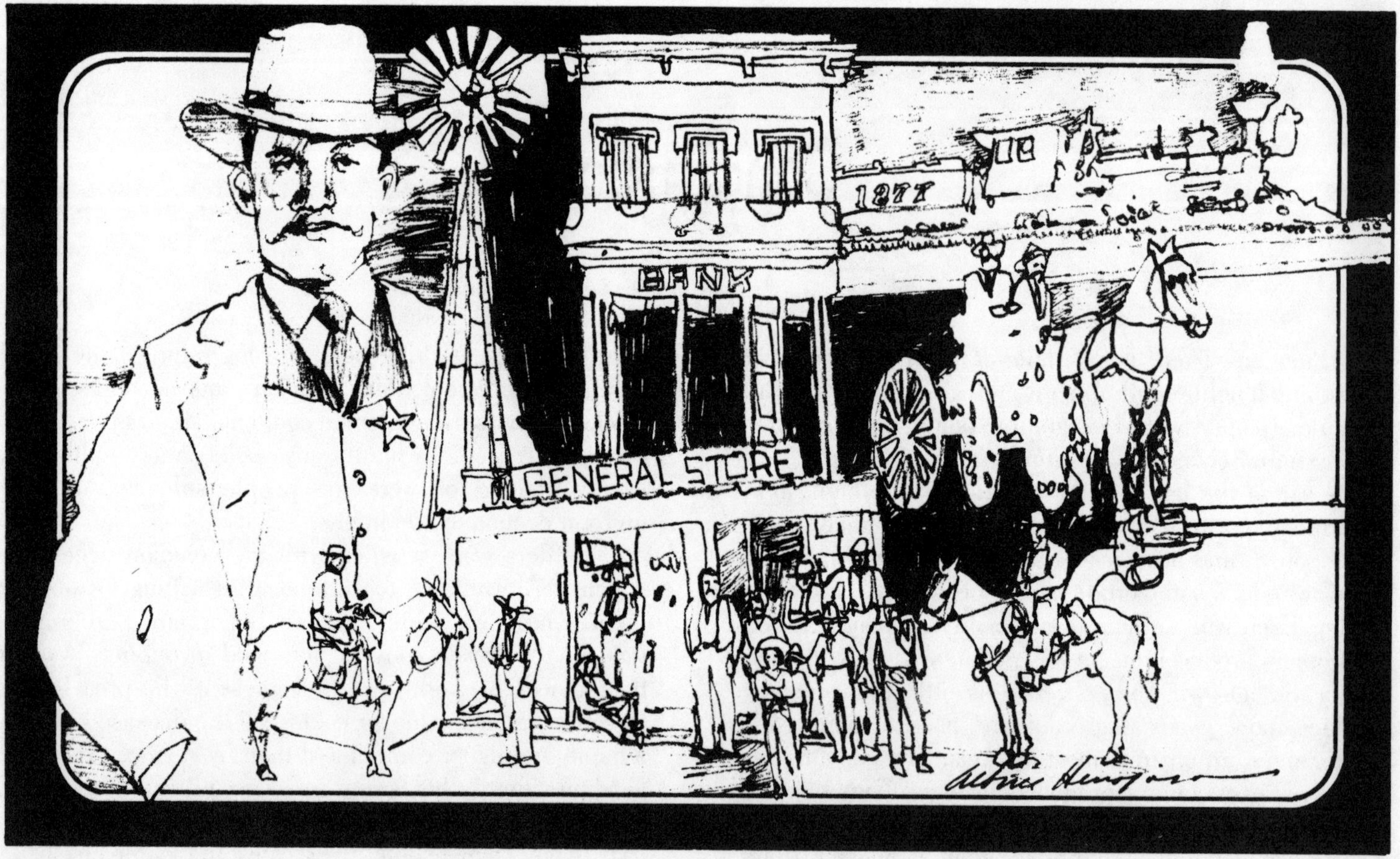
BANK
GENERAL STORE

Everyone had to work and there was little emphasis placed on specialization because little division of labor was possible. Both men and women were "jacks of all trades." It was not uncommon for a man to be a farmer, hunter, trapper, fisherman, trader, carpenter, furniture maker, butcher, veterinarian, undertaker, gravedigger, barber, shoemaker, wheelwright, brewer, distiller, gunsmith, lawman, doctor and minister. A woman was often a midwife, doctor, nurse, and counselor and an aid in many other respects to her neighbors; at home she was housekeeper, cook, carder, weaver, seamstress, tailor, hat-, shoe-, soap-, and candlemaker. She usually did the gardening, milked the cow, and helped her husband slaughter and prepare meat for the table. She was often her husband's part-time field hand, hunter, and trapper, and she assisted him as a carpenter and furniture maker. Although the words "No load too heavy to lift, no burden too great to bear" are largely empty and meaningless in an organized society, they were a reality to frontier people. They had to learn "what worked" in their primitive environment, and they were forced to perform all types of work, including many tasks that were performed by specialists in more integrated societies. Work acted as a social leveler on the frontier.

Each backwoodsman exhalted individualism, the reliance on one's own personal strength and wisdom. In an organized society, where the concept of "man as he should be" had become more or less established, individuals had little chance to make decisions that ran counter to the common accepted pattern. However, pioneers lived in an embryonic social state and had unprecedented freedom, but they did not always have security. For the sake of survival, they had to be self-reliant. They had to find and make necessary adjustments to their hostile environment or perish. In making these adjustments, they could not always rely on time-honored precedents; they often had to improvise, originate, and work out their own solutions.

Economic equality fostered social equality. Morris Birkbeck, an Englishman, found the bulk of frontier inhabitants similar to the lowest English peasantry. The American settlers, however, had a proud independence of mind that was in sharp contrast to the humble, poor, and apologetic countrymen he had left behind, grovelling in ignorance and want. Birkbeck would have rejoiced if these Englishmen could have been transplanted to the boundless regions of the American frontier.[3] Another Englishman, John Bradbury, noted that contempt of one person for another, which was quite evident in Europe, was virtually unknown on the frontier. One would likely search in vain there for a contemptuous feeling in man for man. Europeans visiting in America should realize, Bradbury warned, that they could not abuse waiters or hostlers at inns, for these people were full-fledged citizens and considered their role in society as important as any other. People everywhere demanded that they be spoken to not as servants, but with civility and cheerfulness.[4] As Benjamin Franklin said, it was not advisable to come to America if one had no other quality to recommend him but one's birth.[5]

There were many other examples of the prevalence of the spirit of equality on the frontier. For example, while on a tour of Ohio in the 1790s, Francis Baily saw what seemed to him a most odd situation when dinner was served at a doctor's home. The hired hands who had been working in the fields were called to eat. Instead of taking seats in servants' quarters, the sweating workers sat at the same table with the doctor and his guest. Baily condenscendingly noted they even partook of the same provisions as himself. Baily further noted that the workers treated their employer and everyone at the table with the same degree of familiarity.[6] Another English tourist, Thomas Anburey, was entertained in the large, beautiful home of John Randolph while touring Virginia in the eighteenth century. One day three country peasants burst unannounced into the drawing room. The uninvited guests took chairs near the fire and began spitting tobacco and pulling off their boots. After the intruders had made themselves comfortable, they informed Randolph they had come to grind wheat at his grist mill. After the crude men departed to tend to their business, Anburey remarked to his host that they had certainly taken great liberties. Randolph calmly replied that every so-called "peasant" considered himself in every respect his equal.[7]

A final illustration of the spirit of equality can be gleaned from an account of the reception Peter Cartwright once gave to General Andrew Jackson. The celebrated minister was delivering a sermon to a large congregation one day when the General entered the meeting. Jackson walked up the aisle and leaned against a post while searching for a seat. "Brother Mac," a visiting preacher who was sitting behind Cartwright, noticed the General. Mac tugged at Cartwright's coat and whispered a "little loud, 'General Jackson has come in! General Jackson has come in!'" To his surprise, Cartwright loudly exclaimed, "Who is General Jackson? If he don't get his soul converted, God will damn him as quick as He would a Guinea Negro." Brother Mac turned red with embarrassment, tucked his head, and hunched downward in his seat. The entire congregation laughed heartily.

After the meeting, Brother Mac informed Cartwright that although he admired his courage he was sure that the volatile Jackson would chastise him. Cartwright calmly retorted that two could play the game. Mac, however, feared for his stubborn friend and went to Jackson's room to apologize. Later, when Cartwright chanced to meet Jackson, the General said, "Mr. Cartwright, you are a man after my own heart. I am very much surprised at Mr. Mac, to think he would suppose that I would be offended at you." Indeed, said Jackson, he approved of Cartwright's independence, for a minister should love everybody and fear no one. If he had a few thousand fearless men—as fearless as Cartwright—Jackson said he could take England.[8]

This feeling of equality helped promote the growth of democracy on the frontier. Democracy has been defined as a government that carries out the will of the majority of the people, but in a broader sense it is a social philosophy governing the whole of human relations, personal and collective.[9] Democracy as an ideal is a social condition in which the individual has social, political and economic equality as well as personal freedom. Such an ideal condition has never been fully attained and perhaps never will be, but the democratic ideal was more nearly achieved on the American frontier than in any other place on earth.

Frontiersmen were courageous. To cut free of the benefits of an old society and journey into unknown lands to hack out a new life required daring men and women whose courage outweighed all their other attributes. Surrounded by the perils of nature and of men, they met the test or died. Their adversities steeled and moulded their characters. The frontier was truly the "land of the brave."

There is no doubt that the frontier played a major role in making American society more dynamic and fluid. Social relations on the frontier were in a constant state of flux and the vagrant habits of the people constantly altered frontier life patterns. European immigrants melded with American migrants there and helped eventually to produce a society unlike any other.

It has been said that the frontier served as a safety valve for older populated areas. The theory has been argued for years, with advocates and opponents often going to extremes. There is, however, undeniable evidence to support the idea. The poor, the downtrodden, the persecuted, the malcontents, the social misfits, the outcasts, and land-hungry left eastern society and found a niche in the West. Thomas Macaulay was prompted to write: "As long as you have a boundless extent of fertile and unoccupied land, your laboring population will be far more at ease than the laboring population of the Old World."[10] The land was there and they went out to take it.

The abundance of land and its rich resources in a comparatively favorable climate provided an opportunity for economic expansion, which is the lifeblood of the capitalist system. Capitalism itself was not part and parcel of the frontier; it was one step behind it with its transportation systems, industries, and credit institutions. The process of spanning a continent gave rise to a unique and high civilization without parallel in the history of man. In science, literature, and art—all indexes of a dynamic culture—America has made contributions of enduring value. With all its problems, it remains in an even deeper sense than the French statesman Robert Turgot meant it, "the hope of the human race."

# Notes

### Chapter 1
### From Romance to Reality

1. Samuel Eliot Morison and Henry Steele Commager, *The Growth of the American Republic* (New York: Oxford University Press, 1962), I of II, p. 26.
2. Ibid., p. 35.
3. Ibid., p. 38.
4. Ibid., pp. 40-41.
5. Thomas A. Bailey, *The American Spirit* (Lexington, Massachusetts: D. C. Heath and Company, 1963), p. 64.
6. The term society means a consensus, or more appropriately, "a group of human beings living in a cooperative effort to win subsistence and to perpetuate the species." William Graham Sumner and Albert Galloway Keller, *The Science of Society* (New York: Yale University Press, 1927), I of IV, pp. 6-7.
7. Ibid., p. 1.
8. Albert Galloway Keller, *Societal Evolution* (New York: The MacMillan Company, 1931), pp. 53-54.
9. In nearly all parts of the frontier, the settlers, for the sake of survival, made use of Indian customs in extracting a living from the land, causing some to say that pioneers became "Indianized."
10. Andrew Burnaby, *Travels Through the Middle Settlements of North America in the Years 1759-1760* (London: Printed for T. Payne, 1775), pp. 152-153.
11. Francis Asbury, *Journal* (Cincinnati: Jennings and Pye, 1821) III of III, p. 451.
12. John Bradbury, *Travels in the Interior of North America in the Years 1809, 1810, and 1811* (London: Sherwood, Neely and Jones, 1819), p. 291.
13. Samuel J. Mills and Daniel Smith, *Report of a Missionary Tour Through that Part of the United States which Lies West of the Alleghany Mountains* (Andover: Flagg and Gould, 1815), p. 19.
14. Lyman Beecher, *A Plea for the West* (Cincinnati: Trumen and Smith, 1835), pp. 16-17.
15. Collins Brumitt Goodykoontz, *Home Missions on the American Frontier* (Caldwell, Idaho: Caxton Printers, 1939), p. 19.

16. Ibid., p. 20.
17. W. W. Hall (St. Charles, Missouri, 12 April, 1833), Letter to American Home Missionary Society, University of Chicago Library.
18. Daniel Nelson (Lawrence, Kansas, 13 June, 1859), Letter to American Home Missionary Society, University of Chicago Library.
19. James A. B. Scherer, *Life in Old San Francisco* (Indianapolis: The Bobbs-Merrill Company, 1939), p. 69.
20. Charles Lyell, *Travels in North America* (London: J. Murray, 1845), II of II, p. 76.
21. Morris Birkbeck, *Notes on a Journey in America* (Philadelphia: Caleb Richardson, Publisher, 1817), II of II, p. 76.
22. Ibid., p. 139.
23. John Wood, *Two Years' Residence in the Settlement on the English Prairie in the Illinois Country*, in Reuben Gold Thwaites, *Early Western Travels, 1748-1846*, X of XXXII, pp. 30-31.
24. Ibid., pp. 31-32.
25. A. J. Beveridge, *The Life of John Marshall* (New York: Houghton-Mifflin Company, 1916), I of IV, pp. 14-17.
26. William Graham Sumner, "An Unpublished Manuscript," in A. G. Keller, *Societal Evolution*, pp. 53-58.
27. Charles Darwin, *The Origin of Species* (London: J. Murray, 1859), p. 412.

## Chapter 2
## The Hard Life

1. William Henry Perrin, *History of Cass County, Illinois* (Chicago: O. L. Baskin & Co., 1882), pp. 32-33.
2. James B. Finley, *Autobiography* (Cincinnati: Methodist Book Concern, 1854), pp. 150-151.
3. Hamilton W. Pierson, *In the Brush* (New York: D. Appleton Co., 1881), pp. 47-48.
4. John Stewart, *Highways and Hedges* (Cincinnati: Hitchcock & Walden, 1870), pp. 35-36.
5. Francis Baily, *Journey of a Tour in the Unsettled Parts of North America in 1796, 1797* (London: Baily Brothers, 1856), pp. 136-137.
6. Pierson, *In the Brush*, pp. 60-61.
7. Cyrus R. Rice, "Experiences of a Pioneer Preacher," *Collections of the Kansas State Historical Society*, XIII, (1913-1914), pp. 284-285.
8. *The Home Missionary*, L, No. 11 (April 1878), pp. 284-285.
9. Ibid., pp. 285-286.
10. John Farris Edger, *Pioneer Life in Dayton and Vicinity, 1796-1840* (Dayton, Ohio: W. J. Shuey, 1896), pp. 52-53.
11. Finley, *Autobiography*, p. 69.
12. Joseph Badger, *A Memoir* (Hudson, Ohio: Sawyer, Ingersoll & Co., 1851), p. 42.
13. Ibid., pp. 134-135.
14. Solon Justice Buck, *Illinois in 1818* (Springfield: The Illinois Centennial Commission, 1917), p. 132.
15. Ibid., p. 136.
16. Harvey Lee Ross, *The Early Pioneers and Pioneer Events of the State of Illinois* (Chicago: Eastman Brothers, 1899), pp. 21-23.
17. Finley, *Autobiography*, pp. 87-88.
18. John Bach McMaster, *A History of the People of the United States* (New York: D. Appleton Company, 1931), V of VIII, pp. 155-156.
19. *The Home Missionary*, L, No. 11 (April 1878), pp. 286-287.
20. John George Nicolay and John Hay, *Abraham Lincoln* (New York: The Century Co., 1886), I of X, pp. 40-41.
21. G. W. Featherstonhaugh, *Excursion Through the Slave States* (New York: Harper and Brothers, 1844), pp. 92-93.
22. Walter W. Jennings, *A History of Economic Progress in the United States* (New York: The Thomas Y. Crowell Co., 1926), pp. 78-79.
23. Herbert L. Osgood, *The American Colonies of the Eighteenth*

*Century* (New York: Columbia University Press, 1924), II of II, p. 384.
24. William Cooper Howells, *Recollections of Life in Ohio from 1813 to 1840* (Cincinnati: The Robert Clarke Co., 1895), pp. 78-79.
25. Thomas Anburey, *Travels Through the Interior Parts of America in a Series of Letters* (London: Printed for William Lane, 1789), I of II, pp. 353-356.
26. F. D. Srygley, *Seventy Years in Dixie, Recollections, Sermons and Sayings of T. W. Caskey and Others* (Nashville: Gospel Advocate Publishing Co., 1891), pp. 80-82.
27. Seymour Dunbar, *A History of American Travel* (New York: Tudor Publishing Co., 1937), pp. 421-423.
28. Finley, *Autobiography*, p. 152.
29. William Newham Blane, *An Excursion Through the United States and Canada During the Years 1822-1823* (London: Baldwin, Cradock and Joy, 1824), p. 175.
30. Ibid., p. 176.
31. Elmer C. Griffith, "Early Banking in Kentucky," *Proceedings of the Mississippi Valley Historical Association,* Edited by Benjamin F. Shambaugh (Cedar Rapids, Iowa: The Torch Press, 1909), I of II, p. 168.
32. Featherstonhaugh, *Excursion Through the Slave States*, pp. 81-82.
33. Finley, *Autobiography*, p. 273.
34. Everett Dick, *The Sodhouse Frontier* (Lincoln, Nebraska: Johnson Publishing Co., 1937), p. 90.
35. Ibid., p. 92.
36. Thomas Ford, *A History of Illinois* (Chicago: S. C. Griggs & Co., 1854), pp. 221-223.
37. George Wood (Palmyra, Missouri: December 23, 1834), Letter to American Home Missionary Society, University of Chicago Library.
38. F. R. Gray (Missouri: March 18, 1840), Letter to American Home Missionary Society, University of Chicago Library.
39. *The Pioneer Record*, II, No. 1 (Verdon, Nebraska: August 1894), p. 26.
40. Perrin, *History of Cass County, Illinois*, pp. 75-76.
41. Harriet Munro Longyear, "The Settlement of Clinton County," *Michigan Historical Collections*, Lansing, 1915, XXXIV, p. 261.
42. Morris Birkbeck, *Notes of a Journey in America* (Philadelphia: Caleb Richardson, 1817), pp. 141-142.
43. George Washington Ewing Griffith, "My 96 Years in the Great West," (Los Angeles: Published by the Author, 1929), pp. 46-47.
44. Elnathan Corrington Gavitt, *Crumbs from My Saddle Bags* (Toledo, Ohio: Blade Printing and Paper Co., 1884), pp. 150-152.
45. Jakob Schramm, *Letters of Jakob Schramm and Family to Germany in 1836* (Hanover, N.H.: The Dartmouth Printing Company, 1851), p. 78.
46. Harvey Lee Ross, *Lincoln's First Years in Illinois* (Elmira, N.Y.: The Primavera Press, 1846), pp. 12-13.
47. George R. Carroll, *Pioneer Life in and Round Cedar Rapids, 1839-1849* (Cedar Rapids, Iowa: Times Printing and Binding House, 1895), p. 15.
48. Caroline Von Huneubar, "Life of German Pioneers in Early Texas," *The Quarterly of the Texas State Historical Association*, II, (June 1898 to April 1899), pp. 229-231.
49. John Turner, *Pioneers of the West* (Cincinnati: Jennings and Pye, 1903), pp. 66-67.
50. G. R. McKeith, *Pioneer Stories of the Pioneers of Fillmore and Adjoining Countries* (Exter, Nebraska: Press of Fillmore County News, 1915), p. 7.
51. *The Home Missionary*, XLV, No. 6, October 1872, p. 138.
52. Edna Nyquist, *Pioneer Life and Lore of McPherson County, Kansas* (McPherson, Kansas: The Democratic-Opinion Press, 1932), pp. 51-53.
53. Ibid., p. 55.

54. McKeith, *Pioneer Stories of Fillmore and Adjoining Counties*, pp. 18-19.
55. Joseph Smith, *Old Redstone* (Philadelphia: Lippincott, Grambo and Co., 1854), p. 96.
56. Ibid., pp. 93-95.
57. Finley, *Autobiography*, pp. 150-151.
58. Perrin, *History of Cass County, Illinois*, pp. 75-76.
59. Stewart, *Highways and Hedges*, pp. 35-36.
60. Birkbeck, *Notes on a Journey in America*, pp. 141-142.
61. Edgar, *Pioneer Life in Dayton and Vicinity, 1796-1840*, pp. 52-54.
62. Von Hinueber, "Life of German Pioneers in Early Texas," *Southwestern Historical Quarterly*, IV (1900-1901), pp. 229-231.
63. Edgar, *Pioneer Life in Dayton and Vicinity 1796-1840*, pp. 52-54.
64. D. W. Wright, *Pioneer Sketches, Nebraska and Texas* (Hico, Texas: Hico Printing Co., 1915), pp. 4-5.
65. Von Hinueber, "Life of German Pioneers in Early Texas," *Southwestern Historical Quarterly*, IV (1901-1902), pp. 230-235.
66. Birkbeck, *Notes on a Journey in America*, pp. 141-142.
67. Badger, *A Memoir*, p. 44.
68. Lucius G. Pisher, "Pioneer Recollection of Beloit, Wisconsin," *Wisconsin Magazine of History*, I, No. 3, March 1919, p. 13.
69. Francis Asbury, *Journal* (Cincinnati: Jennings & Pye, 1787), I of III, p. 488.
70. Badger, *A Memoir*, p. 71.
71. Featherstonhaugh, *Excusion Through the Slave States*, p. 106.
72. *The Home Missionary*, XLV, No. 1 (May 1872), p. 10.
73. Ibid., XLV, No. 6 (October 1872), p. 138.
74. William Shakespeare, *As You Like It* (New Haven: Yale University Press, 1919), p. 43.
75. Statement by Randolph Meriot, retired peach brandy distiller, Ruston, Louisiana, 1924.
76. Lorin Gray, "Experiences in Southwestern Minnesota," *Collections of the Minnesota Historical Society*, XV (1915), p. 437.
77. Ross, *Lincoln's First Years in Illinois*, pp. 28-29.
78. McKeith, *Pioneer Stories of Fillmore and Adjoining Counties*, p. 22.
79. Dick, *The Sod House Frontier*, p. 225.
80. Nyquist, *Pioneer Life and Lore of McPherson County, Kansas*, p. 35.
81. Nicolay and Hay, *Abraham Lincoln*, pp. 18-19.
82. Ross, *Lincoln's First Years in Illinois*, pp. 27-29.
83. Simon A. Ferrell, *A Ramble of Six Thousand Miles Through the United States of America* (London: Historical Publications Co., 1832), p. 522.
84. Theodore Rodolf, "Pioneering in the Wisconsin Lead Region," *Wisconsin State Historical Society*, XV (1900), p. 356.
85. John Carroll Power, *Early Settlers of Sangamon County, Illinois* (Springfield: Wilson & Co., 1876), p. 173.
86. McKeith, *Pioneer Stories of the Pioneers of Fillmore and Adjoining Counties*, p. 22.
87. Wright, *Pioneer Sketches, Nebraska and Texas*, pp. 4-5.

## Chapter 3
## Marriage and Sex

1. Adam Smith, *The Wealth of Nations* (London: Methuen & Company, 1830), I of II, p. 81.
2. Ibid., pp. 72-81.
3. T. R. Malthus, *An Essay on the Principle of Population* (London: Ward, Lock and Co., 1826), pp. 3-4.
4. John Bernard, *Retrospections of America 1797-1811* (New York: Harper and Brothers, 1887), pp. 246-248.
5. James R. Masterson, *Tall Tales of Arkansas* (Boston: Chapman & Grimes, 1943), p. 131.
6. Edna Nyquist, *Pioneer Life and Lore of McPherson County*,

*Kansas* (McPherson, Kansas: The Democrat-Opinion Press, 1932), p. 157.
7. Arthur W. Calhoun, *A Social History of the American Family from the Colonial Times to the Present* (Cleveland: The Arthur H. Clark Co., 1917), I of III, p. 163.
8. Noah J. Major, "The Pioneers of Morgan County," *Indiana Historical Society Publications*, V, No. 5 (1915), p. 287.
9. Auguste Carlier, *Marriage in the United States* (Boston: De Vries, Ibarra & Company, 1867), pp. 44-45.
10. Arthur W. Calhoun, *A Social History of the American Family from Colonial Times to the Present*, I, p. 163.
11. Andrew Burnaby, *Travels Through the Middle Settlements in North America in the Years 1759-1760* (London: T. Payne Printer, 1765), pp. 84-85.
12. Thomas Anburey, *Travels Through the Interior of America* (London: Printed for William Lane, 1789), I of II, pp. 40-41.
13. William J. Campbell, *Travels in the Confederation* (Philadelphia, 1791), pp. 100-101.
14. John Bernard, *Retrospections of America, 1797-1811*, p. 246.
15. Thomas A. Bailey, *The American Spirit* (Lexington, Massachusetts: D. C. Heath and Company, 1968), p. 76.
16. Arthur W. Calhoun, *A Social History of the American Family from the Colonial Times to the Present*, I, pp. 131-132.
17. Ibid., pp. 130-131.
18. Harvey Lee Ross, *Lincoln's First Years in Illinois* (Springfield, Primavera Press, 1946), p. xiv.
19. Robert M. Coates, *The Outlaw Years* (New York: The Literary Guild of America, 1930), pp. 46-47.
20. Z. N. Morrell, *Flowers and Fruits from the Wilderness* (Boston: Gould and Lincoln, 1872), pp. 168-172.
21. George E. Howard, *History of Matrimonial Institutions* (University of Chicago Press, 1904), II of II, pp. 422-423.
22. Z. N. Morrell, *Flowers and Fruits from the Wilderness*, p. 78.
23. J. L. McConnell, *Western Characters* (New York: Redfield Press, 1853), pp. 128-129.
24. Arthur W. Calhoun, *A Social History of the American Family from Colonial Times to the Present*, II, p. 34.
25. S. F. Nuckolis, "Letters to J. W. Pierson, President of the Old Settlers' Association, Salt Lake City, Utah, June 10, 1874," *Nebraska State Historical Society*, I (1885), p. 33.
26. John George Nicolay and John Hay, *Abraham Lincoln* (New York: The Century Company, 1886), I of X, p. 56.
27. Arthur W. Calhoun, *A Social History of the American Family from Colonial Times to the Present*, II of III, pp. 35-36.
28. James B. Finley, *Autobiography* (Cincinnati: Methodist Book Concern, 1854), p. 72.
29. Cyrus B. Rice, "Experiences of a Pioneer Preacher," *Kansas Historical Collections*, XIII (1915), pp. 302-303.
30. James R. Masterson, *Tall Tales of Arkansas*, p. 143.
31. Joseph Doddridge, *Notes on the Settlement and Indian Wars of the Western Parts of Virginia and Pennsylvania* (Albany: Joel Munsell, Publisher, 1876), pp. 157-158.
32. Ibid., pp. 156-157.
33. James R. Masterson, *Tall Tales of Arkansas*, p. 143.
34. James B. Finley, *Autobiography*, pp. 71-72.
35. Joseph Doddridge, *Notes on the Settlement and Indian Wars of the Western Parts of Virginia and Pennsylvania*, p. 156.
36. Estwick Evans, *A Pedestrious Tour of Four Thousand Miles Through the Western States and Territories in 1818* (Concord, N.H.: Printed by Joseph C. Spear, 1819), p. 310.
37. W. B. Parker, *Notes Taken During the Expedition Commanded by Captain L. R. Marcy, U.S.A., Through Unexplored Texas, 1854* (Philadelphia: Hayes & Zell, Printers, 1856), p. 43.
38. Arthur W. Calhoun, *A Social History of the American Family from Colonial Times to the Present*, I, p. 166.
39. H. M. Brackenridge, *Journal of a Voyage Up the Missouri River in 1811* (Baltimore: Coale & Maxwell Publishers, 1815), pp. 129-130.
40. Ibid., pp. 130-131.
41. Benjamin Franklin, *The First Civilized American* (New York:

Brentano's Publishers, 1935), p. 136.
42. Thomas A. Bailey, *The American Spirit*, pp. 75-76.
43. Theodore Roosevelt, *The Winning of the West* (New York: G. P. Putnam & Sons, 1889), I of II, p. 129.
44. Arthur W. Calhoun, *A Social History of the American Family from Colonial Times to the Present*, II of III, pp. 33-34.
45. Nathaniel Pitt Langford, *Vigilante Days and Ways* (Chicago: A. C. McClurg and Company, 1931), pp. 50-51.

## Chapter 4
## Health and Medical Practices on the Frontier

1. Edgar Lee Masters, *Spoon River Anthology* in *Modern American Poetry*, Edited by Louis Untermeyer (New York: Harcourt Brace and Company, 1962), p. 143.
2. Charles Francis Adams, *Three Episodes of Massachusetts History* (Boston: Houghton, Mifflin & Co., 1893), II of II, pp. 800-801.
3. James R. Masterson, *Tall Tales of Arkansas* (Boston: Chapman & Grimes, 1943), pp. 78-79.
4. G. W. Featherstonhaugh, *Excursion Through the Slave States* (New York: Harper & Brothers, 1844), pp. 92-93.
5. Statement by Martha Jackson, widow, in a personal interview, Ruston, Louisiana, 1919.
6. James Bradley Finley, *Autobiography* (Cincinnati: Methodist Book Concern, 1854), p. 107.
7. *The Home Missionary*, XII, No. 8 (November 1839), pp. 149-150.
8. Adiel Sherwood, *A Gazetter of the State of Georgia, 3rd Edition* (Washington City: Printed by P. Force, 1837), p. 82.
9. *The Home Missionary*, XXII, No. 8 (December 1850), pp. 180-189.
10. John Mason Peck, *A Guide for Immigrants* (Boston: Lincoln and Edmands, 1831), p. 253.
11. Sandford C. Cox, *Recollections of the Early Settlement of the Wabash Valley* (Lafayette, Indiana: Courier Steam Book & Job Printing, 1860), p. 79.
12. Logan Esarey, *A History of Indiana from Its Exploration to 1850* (Indianapolis: B. F. Bowen & Co., 1918), I of II, p. 491.
13. Joseph Latrobe, *The Rambler in North America* (London: R. B. Seeley and W. Burnside, 1836), I of II, p. 253.
14. Harvey Lee Ross, *The Early Pioneers and Pioneer Events in the State of Illinois* (Chicago: Eastman Brothers, 1899), p. 82-85.
15. Ibid., pp. 80-84.
16. Noah J. Majors, *Memoirs* (Indianapolis: Edward J. Hecker, 1915), pp. 206-208.
17. Charles Giles, *Pioneer: A Narrative of the Nativity, Experience, Travels and Ministerial Labors of Reverend Charles Giles* (New York: G. Lane and P. Sandford, 1844), pp. 226-227.
18. O. H. Smith, *Early Indiana Trials and Sketches* (Cincinnati: Moore, Wilstach, Keys & Co., 1858), pp. 12-13.
19. Jacob Young, *Autobiography of a Pioneer* (Cincinnati: L. Swormstedt, 1857), pp. 315-316.
20. F. D. Srygley, *Seventy Years in Dixie, Recollections, Sermons and Sayings of T. W. Caskey and Others* (Nashville: Gospel Advocate Pub., 1891), p. 106.
21. A segment of Dr. Goodwin's lecture, "Twenty-five Great Americans," University of Texas, Summer, 1932.
22. Ross, *The Early Pioneers and Pioneer Events of the State of Illinois*, pp. 86-88.
23. Henry Boehm, *Reminiscences, Historical and Biographical of Sixty-Four Years in the Ministry* (New York: Carlton & Porter, 1865), p. 445.
24. Young, *Autobiography of a Pioneer*, pp. 320-324.
25. Cox, *Recollections of the Early Settlement of the Wabash Valley*, pp. 20-21.
26. Srygley, *Seventy Years in Dixie*, pp. 97-103.
27. Ross, *The Early Pioneers and Pioneer Events of the State of Illinois*, pp. 87-88.
28. Ibid., pp. 89-92.

29. Boehm, *Reminiscences, Historical and Biographical of Sixty-Four Years in the Ministry*, p. 448.
30. Jacob Bower, "Autobiography," *The Baptists*, Ed., William Warren Sweet (New York: Henry Holt and Co., 1931), p. 206.

## Chapter 5
**Perils of Travel**

1. Nearly all settlers lived near Indians whose society was, in most instances, well organized. But, because of extreme cultural differences and hostilities between the races, frontiersmen were often unable to make effective use of Indian institutions.
2. Samuel E. Morison and Henry S. Commager, *The Growth of the American Republic* (New York: Oxford University Press, 1962), I of II, p. 59.
3. Edmund Burke, *On Conciliation with the American Colonies* (Boston: Sibley and Co., 1905), p. 27.
4. Harold Underwood Faulkner, *American Economic History* (New York: Harper & Brothers, 1960), p. 105.
5. Andre Michaux, *Journal of Andre Michaux, 1793-1796* American Philosophical Society, 1889), p. 161.
6. Susannah Johnson, *Recollections of the Reverend John Johnson and His Home* (Nashville: Southern Methodist Publishing House, 1869), p. 24.
7. William W. Goode, *Outposts of Zion* (Cincinnati: Poe & Hitchcock, 1863), p. 202.
8. Seymour Dunbar, *A History of Travel in America* (New York: Tudor Publishing Co., 1937), p. 660.
9. G. W. Featherstonhaugh, *Excursion Through the Slave States* (New York: Harper & Brothers, 1844), p. 104.
10. Alfred Brunson, *A Western Pioneer* (Cincinnati: Poe & Hitchcock, Printers, 1879), p. 51.
11. Hamilton W. Pierson, *In the Brush* (New York: D. Appleton Co., 1881), pp. 184-188.
12. Ibid., pp. 184-185.
13. Sanford Cox, *Recollections of the Early Settlements of the Wabash Valley* (Lafayette: Courier Steam Book and Job Printing, 1860), p. 12.
14. George R. McKeith, *Pioneer Stories of the Pioneers of Fillmore and Adjoining Counties* (Exeter, Nebraska: Press of Fillmore County News, 1915), pp. 16-17.
15. Ibid., pp. 22-24.
16. Ibid., p. 38.
17. Richard Irving Dodge, *The Great Plains of the Great West and Their Inhabitants* (New York: C. P. Putnam's Sons, 1877), pp. 47-50.
18. McKeith, *Pioneer Stories of the Pioneers of Fillmore and Adjoining Counties*, p. 28.
19. Jacob Burnett, *Notes on the Early Settlement of the Northwest Territory* (New York: D. Appleton Co., 1847), pp. 72-73.
20. Abel Stevens, *Life and Times of Nathan Bangs* (New York: Carlton & Porter, 1863), pp. 146-147.
21. Goode, *Outposts of Zion*, p. 50.
22. John Mason Peck, *Forty Years of Pioneer Life* (Philadelphia: American Baptist Publication Society, 1864), p. 104-105.
23. Elnathan Corrington Gavitt, *Crumbs from My Saddle Bags* (Toledo: Blade Printing & Publishing Co., 1884), p. 164.
24. William Henry Perrin, *History of Cass County, Illinois* (Springfield, O. L. Baskin & Co., 1856), pp. 65-67.
25. Some men caught in extremely cold weather killed their horses, disemboweled them, and thrust themselves into their cavities as a last resort to save their lives.
26. John Carroll Power, *Early Settlers of Sangamon County, Illinois* (Springfield: A. E. Wilson & Co., 1876), pp. 65-67.
27. Ibid., pp. 27-30.
28. Joseph Badger, *A Memoir* (Hudson, Ohio: Sawyer, Ingersoll & Co., 1851), pp. 70-71.
29. John George Nicolay and John Hay, *Abraham Lincoln* (New York: The Century Co., 1886), I of X, pp. 47-48.

30. Cyrus R. Rice, "Experiences of a Pioneer Preacher," *Collections of the Kansas State Historical Society*, XIII (1915), pp. 304-305.
31. William Rhodes, *Recollections of Dakota Territory* (Pierre, South Dakota, 1931), pp. 35-36.
32. Walter Prescott Webb, *The Great Plains* (Dallas: Ginn & Co., 1931), pp. 109-110.
33. Andy Adams, *The Log of a Cowboy* (New York: Houghton, Mifflin & Co., 1903), pp. 63-64.
34. Wagon wheels often needed to be soaked in water to hold the rims and spokes in place.
35. Cox, *Recollections of the Early Settlers of the Wabash Valley*, p. 14.
36. Jacob Burnett, *Notes on the Early Settlement of the Northwest Territory*, pp. 65-68.
37. Peter Cartwright, *Autobiography* (Nashville: Cranston & Curtis, 1856), p. 330.
38. Gavitt, *Crumbs from My Saddle Bags*, pp. 150-152.
39. Harvey Lee Ross, *Lincoln's First Years in Illinois* (Chicago: Eastman & Brothers, 1899), pp. 28-29.
40. Francis Baily, *Journal of a Tour in the Unsettled Parts of North America in the Years 1796 and 1797* (London: Baily Brothers, 1856), pp. 145-146.
41. George R. Gilmer, *Sketches of Some of the First Settlers of Upper Georgia* (New York: Appleton and Co., 1855), p. 332.
42. Baily, *Journal of a Tour in the Unsettled Parts of North America in the Years 1796 and 1797*, p. 229.
43. Thomas Ford, *A History of Illinois* (Chicago: S. C. Griggs, Publisher, 1854), pp. 122-123.
44. Richard Irving Dodge, *The Plains of the Great West and Their Inhabitants* (New York: C. P. Putnam's Sons, 1877), pp. 418-419.
45. Ibid., p. 147.
46. *Time*, Vol. 93, No. 3 (17 January 1969), p. 76.
47. Dodge, *The Plains of the Great West and Their Inhabitants*, p. 147.
48. Ibid., p. 20.

## Chapter 6
## Odd Ideas

1. George Gilmer, *Sketches of Some of the First Settlers of Upper Georgia* (Americus, Georgia: Americus Book Company, 1926), pp. 128-141.
2. John Mason Peck, *A Guide for Immigrants* (Boston: Lincoln and Edmands, 1831), p. 243.
3. James L. Batchelder, *The United States, the West and the State of Ohio as Missionary Fields* (Cincinnati: David Anderson, Printer, 1848), p. 13.
4. *The Home Missionary*, VI, No. 3 (1 July 1833), p. 56.
5. Christiana Holmes Tillson, *Reminiscences of Early Life in Illinois* (Library of Congress typewritten copy, 1871), p. 71.
6. F. D. Srygley, *Seventy Years in Dixie, Recollections, Sermons, and Sayings of T. W. Caskey and Others* (Nashville: Gospel Advocate Publishing Co., 1891), pp. 101-102.
7. Hamilton W. Pierson, *In the Brush* (New York: D. Appleton Co., 1881), pp. 60-81.
8. Tillson, *Reminiscences of Early Life in Illinois*, pp. 61-62.
9. *The Montanian* (Virginia City, Montana Territory), V, No. 24 (31 December 1874).
10. Henry Benjamin Whipple, *Southern Diary, 1843-1844* (New York: Da Capo Press, 1968), pp. 44-45.
11. Gilmer, *Sketches of Some of the First Settlers of Upper Georgia*, pp. 240-246.
12. Beverley W. Bond, *The Civilization of the Old Northwest* (New York: The MacMillan Co., 1934), pp. 184-185.
13. J. L. McConnel, *Western Characters or Types of Border Life in the Western States* (New York: Redfield, Pub., 1853), p. 133.
14. Robert Wilson Patterson, *Early Society in Southern Illinois* [A paper read before the Chicago Historical Society, October 19, 1880], (Chicago: Fergus Printing Co., 1881), pp. 24-25.
15. G. W. Featherstonhaugh, *Excursion Through the Slave States*

*from the Washington on the Potomac to the Frontier of Mexico* (New York: Harper and Brothers, 1844), p. 14.
16. *The Mirror*, II, No. 74 (February 1799).
17. Jacob Bower, "Autobiography," *The Baptists*, Ed., William Warren Sweet, (New York: Henry Holt & Co., 1931), p. 191.
18. Joseph Tarkington, *Autobiography* (Cincinnati: Press of Curtis, 1889), p. 67.
19. Bower, "Autobiography," pp. 196-198.
20. Carl Sandburg, *Abraham Lincoln* (New York: C. Scribner's Sons, 1940), I of VI, pp. 65-66.
21. Joseph Doddridge, *Notes on the Settlement and Indian Wars of the Western Parts of Virginia and Pennsylvania, from 1763 to 1783, Inclusive* (New York: Joel Munsell, Publisher, 1876), pp. 64-65.
22. Sandburg, *Abraham Lincoln*, I, pp. 63-66.
23. Logan Esarey, *A History of Indiana from 1850 to the Present* (Indianapolis: B. F. Bowen & Co., 1918), II of II, pp. 65-67 and 682-683.
24. Sandburg, *Abraham Lincoln*, I, pp. 65-67.
25. Samuel E. Morison and Henry S. Commager, *The Growth of the American Republic* (New York: Oxford University Press, 1962), I of II, pp. 785-786.
26. Washington Irving, *Knickerbocker History of New York* (New York: C. P. Putnam's Sons, 1809), pp. 110-111.
27. Ibid., p. 112.
28. Ibid., pp. 114-115.
29. Doddridge, *Notes of the Settlement and Indian Wars of the Western Parts of Virginia and Pennsylvania, from 1763 to 1783, Inclusive*, p. 160.
30. Ibid., pp. 180-181.
31. Estwick Evans, *A Pedestrious Tour of Four Thousand Miles Through the Western States and Territories During the Winter and Spring of 1818* (Concord, New Hampshire: Joseph Spear, Printer, 1819), p. 148.
32. Featherstonhaugh, *Excursion Through the Slave States*, p. 14.
33. Doddridge, *Notes of the Settlement and Indian War of the Western Parts of Virginia and Pennsylvania, from 1763 to 1783, Inclusive*, p. 160.
34. Thomas Anburey, *Travels Through the Interior of America* (London: Printed for William Lane, 1789), I of II, pp. 51-53.
35. Irving, *Knickerbocker History of New York*, p. 300.
36. Andre Michaux, *Journal of Andre Michaux, 1793-1796* (American Philosophical Society, 1889), p. 48.
37. Isaac Weld, *Travels Through the States of North America* (London: Library of Congress, 1807), pp. 171-172.
38. Alfred Brunson, *A Western Pioneer* (Cincinnati: Hitchcock and Walden, 1879), II of II, pp. 29-30.
39. Gilmer, *Sketches of Some of the First Settlers of Upper Georgia*, p. 200.
40. A. A. Parker, *Trip to the West and Texas* (Boston: William White, 1836), p. 147.
41. Tillson, *Reminiscences of Early Life in Illinois*, p. 96.
42. Featherstonhaugh, *Excursion Through the Slave States*, p. 14.
43. Margaret Van Horn Dwights, *A Journey to Ohio in 1810* (New Haven: Yale University Press), p. 9.
44. Whipple, *Southern Diary, 1843-1844* (New York: Da Capo Press, 1968), p. 133.
45. Francis Asbury, *Journal* (Cincinnati: Jennings and Pye, 1821), II of III, p. 295.
46. Cyrus R. Rice, "Experience of a Pioneer Preacher," *Kansas State Historical Society*, XIII (1915), p. 303.
47. Evans, *A Pedestrious Tour*, p. 126.
48. Andrew Burnaby, *Travels Through the Middle Settlements of North America in the Years 1759-1760* (London: Printed for T. Payne, 1775), pp. 82-83.

## Chapter 7
**Barbarous and Unorthodox Behavior**

1. John George Nicolay and John Hay, *Abraham Lincoln* (New York: The Century Co., 1886), I of X, pp. 53-54.
2. Vincent Otto Nolte, *Fifty Years in Both Hemispheres* (London:

Trubner and Co., 1854), p. 282.
3. John Reynolds, *My Own Times* (Belleville, Illinois: B. H. Perryman and A. L. Davison, 1855), p. 69.
4. Harriet Munroe Longyear, "The Settlement of Clinton County," *Michigan Historical Collections*, XXXIX (1915), pp. 361-362.
5. J. S. Williams, *Old Times in West Tennessee* (Memphis: W. G. Chenney, 1873), pp. 153-154.
6. John Carroll Power, *Early Settlers of Sangamon County, Illinois* (Springfield: E. A. Wilson & Co., 1876), pp. 38-39.
7. Reynolds, *My Own Times*, pp. 76-68.
8. Statement by Martha Jackson, widow, in a personal interview, Ruston, Louisiana, 1922.
9. Ibid.
10. Thomas Ford, *History of Illinois* (Chicago: S. C. Griggs & Co., 1854), pp. 39-41.
11. Peter Cartwright, *Autobiography* (New York: Carlton & Porter, 1856), pp. 60-63.
12. Reynolds, *My Own Times*, pp. 15-17.
13. Maxwell Pierson Gaddis, *Footprints of an Itinerant* (Cincinnati: Methodist Book Concern, 1863), pp. 42-43.
14. George Gilmer, *Sketches of Some of the First Settlers of Upper Georgia* (New York: D. Appleton & Company, 1855), pp. 233-234.
15. Susannah Johnson, *Recollections of the Reverend John Johnson and His Home* (Nashville: Southern Methodist Publishing House, 1869), pp. 22-23.
16. Nicolay and Hay, *Abraham Lincoln*, I of X, p. 33.
17. John Mason Peck, *Forty Years of Pioneer Life, or, Memoirs of John Mason Peck* (Philadelphia: American Baptist Publication Society, 1864), pp. 120-124.
18. Johnson, *Recollections of the Reverend John Johnson and His Home*, pp. 24-29.
19. A. A. Parker, *Trip to the West and Texas* (Boston: William White, 1836), pp. 75-76.
20. Alberton Moore, *History of Alabama* (Tuscaloosa: University of Alabama Press, 1934), pp. 142-145.
21. *The Christian Index* (Washington, Georgia), VI, No. 43 (November 1933), p. 677.
22. Charles Dickens, "American Notes," in Allen Nevins' *American Social History* (New York: Augustus M. Kelley, 1969), p. 26.
23. John Melish, "Travels," in Allen Nevins' *American Social History* (New York: Augustus M. Kelley, 1969), p. 74-75.
24. John Bach McMaster, *A History of the People of the United States* (New York: D. Appleton & Co., 1930-1937), VII of VIII, pp. 234-235.
25. Gilmer, *Sketches of Some of the First Settlers of Upper Georgia*, pp. 240-241.
26. Frances Trollope, *Domestic Manners of the Americans* (New York: Dodd, Mead, and Co., 1904), p. 15.
27. G. W. Featherstonhaugh, *Excursion Through the Slave States* (New York: Harper and Brothers, 1844), pp. 35-39.
28. A. L. Child, "A Justice Court of Cass County in 1857," *Centennial History of Plattsmouth City and Cass County, Nebraska* (Plattsmouth, Nebraska, 1877), p. 72.
29. Thompson Gaines Onstot, *Pioneers of Menard and Mason Counties* (Forest City, Illinois: T. G. Onstot, 1902), p. 126.
30. Johnson, *Recollections of the Reverend John Johnson and His Home*, pp. 30-31.
31. John P. Wright, *Sketches of the Life and Labor of James Quinn* (Cincinnati: Methodist Book Concern, 1851), p. 226.
32. Johnson, *Recollections of Reverend John Johnson and His Home*, p. 30.
33. Charles Giles, *Pioneer: A Narrative of the Nativity, Experience, Travels, and Ministerial Labors of Reverend Charles Giles* (New York: G. Lane & P. P. Sandford, 1844), p. 175.
34. Onstot, *Pioneers of Menard and Mason Counties*, p. 122.
35. Peter Cartwright, *Fifty Years as Presiding Elder* (Cincinnati: Hitchcock & Walden, 1871), pp. 64-65.
36. Cartwright, *Autobiography*, pp. 187-189.

37. Cartwright, *Fifty Years as Presiding Elder*, pp. 70-73.

## Chapter 8
## Frontier Fights

1. J. E. Alexander, *Transatlantic Sketches* (Philadelphia: Key & Biddle, 1833), p. 252.
2. Thomas Anburey, *Travels Through the Interior of America* (London: Printed for William Lane, 1789), pp. 161-162.
3. Joseph Smith, *Old Redstone* (Philadelphia: Lippincott, Grambo & Co., 1854), pp. 106-107.
4. *The Montanian* [Virginia City], V, No. 24 (31 December 1874).
5. Thomas Ford, *A History of Illinois* (Chicago: S. C. Griggs & Company, 1854), pp. 81-82.
6. John George Nicolay and John Hay, *Abraham Lincoln* (New York: The Century Company, 1886), I of X, p. 172.
7. Frederic Austin Ogg, *The Reign of Andrew Jackson* (New Haven: Yale University Press, 1921), pp. 20-21.
8. James Parton, *Life of Andrew Jackson* (Boston: Houghton, Mifflin & Company, 1887), pp. 380-382.
9. Ogg, *The Reign of Andrew Jackson*, pp. 20-21.
10. William Henry Perrin, *History of Cass County, Illinois* (Chicago: O. L. Baskin & Co., 1882), pp. 77-79.
11. Ibid., pp. 77-79.
12. John Bach McMaster, *A History of the People of the United States* (New York: D. Appleton & Co., 1937), II of VIII, pp. 14-15.
13. James Parton, *Life of Andrew Jackson* (Boston: Houghton, Mifflin & Co., 1887), pp. 380-382.
14. Nicolay and Hay, *Abraham Lincoln*, I, p. 79.
15. McMaster, *A History of the People of the United States*, II of VIII, pp. 96-97.
16. Lucian Carr, *Missouri, A Bone of Contention* (Cambridge, Mass: Riverside Press, 1894), p. 131.
17. James Hall, *Letters from the West* (London: Henry Colburn, Printer, 1828), p. 229.
18. William Newham Blane, *An Excursion Through the United States and Canada During the Years 1822-1823* (London: Baldwin, Cradock & Joy, 1824), p. 136.
19. Alexander, *Transatlantic Sketches*, p. 252.
20. Ibid., pp. 251-252.
21. Isaac Weld, *Travels Through the States of North America* (London: Library of Congress, 1807), pp. 143-144.
22. Augustus B. Longstreet, *Georgia Scenes* (New York: Harper and Brothers, 1848), pp. 9-11.
23. Weld, *Travels Through the States of North America*, pp. 143-145.
24. John Palmer, *Journal of Travels in the United States of North America and Lower Canada* (London: Sherwood, Neely and Jones, 1818), pp. 131-132.
25. Anburey, *Travels Through the Interior of America*, pp. 161-162.
26. John Melish, *Travels in the United States of America in the Years 1806, 1807, 1809, 1810, and 1811* (Philadelphia: T & G Palmer, Pub., 1812), p. 206.
27. The name of the victim was John Butler, a Carolinian, who apparently had been dared into the combat by a Georgian. The first eye gouged out was "for the honor of the state in which the men respectively lived." Charles William Janson, *The Stranger in America, 1793-1806* (New York: The Press of Pioneers, 1835), pp. 307-308.
28. Sinslow C. Watson, *Men and Times of the Revolution* (New York: Dana & Co., 1856), p. 47.
29. Ibid., pp. 32-33.
30. Anburey, *Travels Through the Interior of America*, pp. 347-349.
31. Thomas Ashe, *Travels in America, Performed in 1806* (London: William Sawyers and Co., 1808), pp. 58-59.

32. James Masterson, *Tall Tales of Arkansas* (Boston: Chapman and Grimes, 1943), pp. 53-54.
33. James Bradley Finley, *Autobiography; or, Pioneer Life in the West* (Cincinnati: Methodist Book Concern, 1857), pp. 33-34.
34. Orville A. Park, "The History of Georgia in the Eighteenth Century," *Georgia Bar Association*, XIII (1888), pp. 141-142.
35. Seymour Dunbar, *A History of Travel in America* (New York: Tudor Publishing Co., 1937), pp. 636-637.
36. Longstreet, *Georgia Scenes*, pp. 53-64.
37. Charles William Janson, *The Stranger in America, 1793-1806* (New York: The Press of the Pioneers, 1835), p. 310.
38. Alexander, *Transatlantic Sketches*, p. 203.
39. Anburey, *Travels Through the Interior of America*, pp. 161-162.
40. Janson, *The Stranger in America, 1793-1806*, pp. 308-309.
41. Anburey, *Travels Through the Interior of America*, pp. 347-349.
42. Dunbar, *A History of Travel in America*, pp. 677-678.
43. Thomas J. Dimsdale, *The Vigilantes of Montana* (Virginia City: Madison Publishing Co., 1921), pp. 35-36.
44. Nathanial Pitt Langford, *Vigilante Days and Ways* (Chicago: A. C. McClurg & Co., 1931), pp. 176-178.
45. George Combe, *Notes on the United States of North America in 1838, 1839, and 1840* (London: Maclachlan, Steward & Co., 1841), pp. 53-95.
46. John Robert Godley, *Letters from America* (London: J. Murry, Printer, 1844), I of II, pp. 46-47.
47. T. G. Onstot, *Pioneers of Menard and Mason Counties* (Forest City, Illinois: T. G. Onstot, Printer, 1902), pp. 133-134.
48. Statement by Randolph Merritt, retired peach brandy distiller, in a personal interview, Ruston, Louisiana, 1928.
49. Ibid.
50. Ibid.
51. Ashe, *Travels in America*, p. 90.
52. Harvey Lee Ross, *The Early Pioneers and Pioneer Events of the State of Illinois* (Chicago: Eastman Brothers, 1899), pp. 143-145.
53. Timothy Flint, *Recollections of the Last Ten Years* (Philadelphia: Adam Waldie, 1835), p. 177.
54. G. W. Featherstonhaugh, *Excursion Through the Slave States From Washington on the Potomac to the Frontier of Mexico* (New York: Harper and Brothers, 1844), p. 97.
55. Don C. Seitz, *Famous American Duels* (New York: Thomas Y. Crowell Co., 1929), pp. 152-157.
56. Statement by Martha Merchant, widow, in a personal interview, Ruston, Louisiana, 1918.
57. Ibid.
58. David Ramsey, *History of South Carolina* (Charleston: David Longworth, Pub., 1809), pp. 216-217.
59. Beverley W. Bond, *The Civilization of the Old Northwest* (New York: The Macmillan Co., 1934), pp. 502-503.

## Chapter 9
## Outlaws

1. William Findley, *History of the Insurrection in the Four Western Counties of Pennsylvania* (Philadelphia: Samuel Harrison Smith, Printer, 1796), pp. 60-88.
2. Thomas Ford, *History of Illinois* (Chicago: S. C. Griggs & Co., 1844), pp. 88-92.
3. William Warren Sweet, *Religion on the American Frontier: The Congregationalists* (Chicago: The University of Chicago Press, 1939), III of III, pp. 182-183.
4. H. L. Griffin, "The Vigilante Committees of the Attakapas County, or Early Louisiana Justice," *Proceedings of Mississippi Valley Historical Association*, VII-VIII (1913-1914), pp. 148-149.
5. Ibid., pp. 149-153.
6. *Silver Bend Reporter* [Belmont, Nevada], I, No. 5 (20 April 1867).

7. Richard Lee Mason, *Narrative of Richard Lee Mason in the Pioneer West* (New York: Charles Fred Heartman, 1809), pp. 40-42.
8. Nathaniel Pitt Langford, *Vigilante Days and Ways* (New York: A. C. McClurg & Co., 1890), pp. 441-446.
9. Mason, *Narrative of Richard Lee Mason in the Pioneer West*, pp. 43-50.
10. G. W. Featherstonhaugh, *Excursion Through the Slave States* (New York: Harper & Brothers, 1844), pp. 87-88.
11. Langford, *Vigilante Days and Ways*, pp. 74-76.
12. J. E. Alexander, *Transatlantic Sketches* (Philadelphia: Key & Biddle, 1833), p. 250.
13. Judge Hall, *Letters from the West* (London: Henry Colburn, 1828), pp. 265-282.
14. Alexander, *Transatlantic Sketches*, p. 282.
15. Robert M. Coates, *The Outlaw Years* (New York: The Literary Guild of America, 1930), p. 82.
16. Thomas Ashe, *Travels in America* (London: William Sawyers & Co., 1808), pp. 226-227.
17. J. S. Williams, *Old Times in West Tennessee* (Memphis: W. C. Cheeney, Pr., 1873), pp. 203-205.
18. Alexander, *Transatlantic Sketches*, pp. 248-249.
19. Tyrone Power, *Impressions of America During the Years 1833, 1834, and 1835* (Philadelphia: Carey, Lea & Blanchard, 1836), II of II, pp. 125-126.
20. Frances Wright D'Arusmont, *Views of Society and Manners in America* (London: Longman, Hurst, Rees, Orne & Brown, 1821), pp. 295-296.
21. James McCallum, *A Brief Sketch of the Settlement and Early History of Giles County, Tennessee* (Pulaski, Tennessee: Printed by Pulaski Citizens, 1828), pp. 84-85.
22. Theodore Roosevelt, "Frontier Types," *The Century*, XXXVI, No. 6 (May-October 1888), pp. 838-839.
23. C. C. Rister, "Outlaws and Vigilantes of the Southern Plains, 1865-1885," *Proceedings of the Mississippi Valley Historical Review*, XIX (June 1932-March 1933), p. 549.
24. Roosevelt, "Frontier Types," pp. 831-843.
25. Horace Greeley, *An Overland Journey from New York to San Francisco in the Summer of 1859* (New York: C. M. Saxton, Barker & Co., 1860), p. 163.
26. Thomas J. Dimsdale, *The Vigilantes of Montana* (Virginia City, Montana: Madisonian Pub. Co., 1921), pp. 31-34.
27. Ibid., pp. 364-368.
28. Dimsdale, *The Vigilantes of Montana*, pp. 25-26.
29. Frances Trollope, *Domestic Manners of the Americas* (New York: Dodd, Mead, and Company, 1832), pp. 108-112.
30. Joseph Tarkington, *Autobiography* (Cincinnati: Press of Curtis, 1889), pp. 108-109.
31. John Carroll Power, *Early Settlers of Sangamon County, Illinois* (Springfield: Edwin A. Wilson and Company, 1876), p. 40.

## Chapter 10
### Vigilante Committees

1. David Ramsay, *The History of South Carolina* (Charleston, David Longworth Publishing, 1809), pp. 119-122.
2. Frederick Jackson Turner, *The Significance of Sections in American History* (New York: Henry Holt and Co., 1932), pp. 98-99.
3. James Stuart, Esq., *Three Years in North America* (London: Whittaker and Co., 1833), II of II, pp. 212-213.
4. J. L. McConnell, *Western Characters or Types of Border Life in the Western States* (New York: Redfield Publishing Co., 1853), pp. 24ff.
5. *The Kentucky Gazette*, No. 4 (1 September 1787), p. 1.
6. C. C. Rister, "Outlaws and Vigilantes of the Southern Plains, 1865-1885," *Proceedings of the Mississippi Valley Historical Review*, XIX (June 1933), p. 554.
7. *The Kentucky Gazette*, Vol. XIX (June 1932), pp. 553-554, The Library of Congress.

8. William N. Blane, *An Excursion Through the United States and Canada, 1822-1823* (London: Baldwin, Cradock and Joy, 1824), pp. 234-235.
9. John Bach McMaster, *A History of the People of the United States* (New York: D. Appleton & Co., 1938), VII of VIII, p. 609.
10. Charles Howard Shinn, *Mining Camps* (New York: A. A. Knopf, 1948), p. 126.
11. Nathaniel Pitt Langford, *Vigilante Days and Ways* (Chicago: A. C. McClurg & Co., 1931), pp. 139-141.
12. Ibid., pp. 139-141.
13. William T. Coleman and James A. Schener, *The Lion of the Vigilantes* (Indianapolis: The Bobbs-Merrill Company, 1939), pp. 121-123.
14. Ibid., pp. 101-103.
15. Langford, *Vigilante Days and Ways*, p. 300.
16. Thomas J. Dimsdale, *The Vigilantes of Montana* (Virginia City: Madison Publishing Company, 1921), pp. 81-82.
17. Ibid., p. 82.
18. Langford, *Vigilante Days and Ways*, pp. 397-399.
19. Ibid., pp. 397-399.
20. Ibid., pp. 389-391.
21. Ibid., pp. 274-288.
22. Ibid., pp. 402-404.
23. Ibid., pp. 371-373.
24. Ibid., pp. 441-462.
25. Ross Klebert, "Early Experiences in Texas," *Southwestern Historical Quarterly*, Vol. 1 (July 1898-April 1899), p. 171.
26. W. W. Strickland, *Pioneer Life in the West* (Nashville: Methodist Book Concern, 1854), p. 110.
27. Langford, *Vigilante Days and Ways*, pp. 139-141.
28. Alfred Brunson, *A Western Pioneer* (Cincinnati: Hitchcock & Company, 1879), pp. 41-42.
29. Logan Esarey, *Courts and Lawyers of Indiana* (Indianapolis: Federal Publishing Company, 1916), I of II, p. 69.
30. Ibid., p. 69.
31. William Rhodes, *Recollections of Dakota Territory, Fort Pierre, South Dakota* (No Publisher, 1931), pp. 28-29.
32. Thomas Ford, *A History of Illinois* (Chicago: S. C. Griggs & Company, 1854), pp. 246-249.
33. Thomas J. Dimsdale, *The Vigilantes of Montana*, pp. 81-82.
34. William Cobbett, *A Year's Residence in the U.S.* (London: Clayton & Kingsland, Printers, 1818), p. 16.
35. Theodore Roosevelt, "Frontier Types," *The Century*, Vol. XXXVI, No. 6 (May 1888), pp. 839-840.
36. Orville A. Park, "The History of Georgia in the Eighteenth Century," in *Annual Report of the Georgia Bar Association* [Macon, Georgia] (June 3, 1921), p. 46.
37. Peter Cartwright, *Autobiography* (Nashville: Abingdon Press, 1956), pp. 24-25.
38. Marion Michael Null, *The Forgotten Pioneer: The Life of Davy Crockett* (New York: The Vantage Press, 1954), pp. 314-317.
39. G. W. Featherstonhaugh, *Excursion Through the Slave States* (New York: Harper & Brothers, 1844), pp. 135-139.
40. Thomas Ford, *A History of Illinois*, pp. 437-445.
41. James Y. Leyburn, *Frontier Folkways* (New Haven: Yale University Press, 1935), pp. 217-218.

## Chapter 11
### Acquiring Land

1. John Mason Peck, *Forty Years of Pioneer Life* (Philadelphia: American Baptist Publication Society, 1864), pp. 146-148.
2. Ibid., pp. 101-103.
3. Christiana Holmes Tillson, *Reminiscences of Early Life in Illinois* (Library of Congress typewritten copy, 1871), pp. 6-7.
4. James Stuart, *Three Years in North America* (London: Whittaker & Co., 1883), II of II, pp. 303-304.
5. Alfred Brunson, *A Western Pioneer* (Cincinnati: Hitchcock & Walden, 1872), II of II, pp. 46-47.

6. N. C. Clark (DuPage, Illinois: April 1835), Letter to American Home Missionary Society, University of Chicago Library.
7. Sandford C. Cox, *Recollections of the Early Settlement of the Wabash Valley* (Lafayette, Indiana: Sourier Steam Book and Printing House, 1860), pp. 17-18.
8. Brunson, *A Western Pioneer*, II of II, pp. 33-34.
9. Charles James Ritchey, "Claim Associations and Pioneer Democracy in Early Minnesota," *Minnesota History*, IX (1928), pp. 85-86.
10. Claim Association of Johnson County, Iowa, *Constitution and Records of the Claim Association of Johnson County, State Historical Society of Iowa*, 1894, Library of Congress, pp. 10-13.
11. A. D. Jones, *Illinois and the West* (Boston: Weeks, Jordan & Co., 1838), pp. 224-227.
12. Theodore Rodolf, "Pioneering in the Wisconsin Lead Region," *Wisconsin State Historical Society*, XV (1900), p. 365.
13. Jesse Macy, *Institutional Beginnings in a Western State, Iowa* (Baltimore: Johns Hopkins University Press, 1884), pp. 14-15.
14. Claim Association of Johnson County, Iowa, *Constitution and Records of the Claim Association of Johnson County, State Historical Society of Iowa*, 1894, Library of Congress, pp. 3-6.
15. Ibid., pp. 5-7.
16. Ibid., pp. 22-24.
17. Ibid., pp. 8-10.
18. Ibid., pp. 16-19.
19. John A. MacMurphy, "Early Nebraska," *Centennial History of Plattsmouth City and Cass County, Nebraska* (Plattsmouth, Nebraska: A. L. Child, 14 July 1876), p. 82.
20. Charles James Ritchey, "Claim Associations and Pioneer Democracy in Early Minnesota," *Minnesota History*, IX (1928), pp. 610-611.
21. S. H. Fairfield, "Getting Married and the Ague," *Collections: Kansas State Historical Society*, XI (1909-1910), pp. 604-608.
22. G. R. McKeith, *Pioneer Stories of the Pioneers of Fillmore and Adjoining Counties* (Exter, Nebraska: Press of Fillmore County News, 1915), pp. 20-21.
23. Edna Nyquist, *Pioneer Life and Lore of McPherson County, Kansas* (McPherson, Kansas: The Democratic Opinion Press, 1932), p. 48.
24. William H. Goode, *Outposts of Zion* (Cincinnati: Poe and Hitchcock, 1863), pp. 270-271.
25. Thomas Thomas, "Early Days in Nebraska," *Centennial History of Plattsmouth City and Cass County, Nebraska* (Plattsmouth, Nebraska, 1877), p. 71.
26. Frank C. Coolbaugh, "Reminiscences of Early Days of Minnesota, 1851-1861," *Collections of the Minnesota Historical Society*, XV (1915), p. 487.

## Chapter 12
## The Frontier Preacher

1. Hamilton W. Pierson, *In the Brush* (New York: D. Appleton and Co., 1881), pp. 251-252.
2. Abel Stevens, *Life and Times of Nathan Bangs* (New York: Carlton and Porter, 1863), pp. 135-139.
3. *The Home Missionary*, XLVII, No. 2 (June 1874).
4. Pierson, *In the Brush*, pp. 47-57.
5. *The Christian Index*, XIII, No. 41 (1 October 1840), pp. 664-666.
6. John Mason Peck, *Forty Years of Pioneer Life* (Philadelphia: American Baptist Publication Society, 1864), p. 29.
7. Joseph Smith, *Old Redstone, or Historical Sketches of Western Presbyterianism* (Philadelphia: Lippincott, Grambo and Co., 1854), p. 181.
8. Peter Cartwright, *Autobiography* (New York: Cranston and Curtis, 1856), pp. 229-232.
9. Cyrus R. Rice, "Experiences of a Pioneer Preacher," in *Collections of the Kansas State Historical Society*, XIII (1915), p. 301.

10. Elnathan Corrington Gavitt, *Crumbs from My Saddle Bags* (Toledo: Blade Printing and Paper Company, 1894), pp. 152-153.
11. *The Home Missionary*, XLV, No. 1 (May 1872), p. 10.
12. *The Home Missionary*, XX, No. 3 (July 1847), p. 63.
13. Pierson, *In the Brush*, pp. 60-61.
14. Alfred Brunson, "A Methodist Circuit Rider's Horseback Tour from Pennsylvania to Wisconsin," in *Wisconsin State Historical Society*, XV (1900), p. 221.
15. Harvey Lee Ross, *Lincoln's First Years in Illinois* (New York: Premavera Press, 1846), pp. xviii-xix.
16. Pierson, *In the Brush*, pp. 61-81.
17. Rice, "Experiences of a Frontier Preacher," p. 307.
18. Joseph Tarkington, *Autobiography* (Cincinnati: Press of Curtis, 1889), pp. 192-193.
19. Susannah Johnson, *Recollections of the Reverend John Johnson and His Home* (Nashville: Southern Methodist Publishing House, 1869), pp. 192-193.
20. Thomas Ware, *Sketches of the Life and Travels of Reverend Thomas Ware* (New York: G. Lane and P. Sanford, 1842), pp. 145-146.
21. Tarkington, *Autobiography*, pp. 118-119.
22. George Wood (Mount Prairie, Missouri, October 1832) Letter to American Home Missionary Society, University of Chicago Library.
23. George G. Smith, *The History of Georgia Methodism from 1786 to 1866* (Atlanta: A. R. Caldwell, Publisher, 1913), pp. 110-111.
24. *The Christian Index*, IV, No. 17 (15 May 1836), p. 261.
25. A. H. Cox, Houston, Missouri, December 1842, to American Home Missionary Society.
26. *The Home Missionary*, XLV, No. 11 (1873), pp. 259-260.
27. Gavitt, *Crumbs from My Saddle Bags*, p. 152.
28. Aaron Wood, *Sketches of Things and People in Indiana* (Indianapolis: J. M. Olcott, Publisher, 1883), p. 12.
29. Pierson, *In the Brush*, pp. 254-256.
30. Ibid., pp. 256-260.
31. Jacob Bower, "Autobiography," *The Baptists*, Ed. William Warren Sweet (New York: Henry Holt and Co., 1931), pp. 254-255.
32. James G. Leyburn, *Frontier Folkways* (New Haven: Yale University Press, 1935), pp. 227.
33. Thomas Ware, *Autobiography* (New York: G. Lane and P. Sandford, 1844), p. 175.
34. Stevens, *Life and Times of Nathan Bangs*, p. 148.
35. Ibid., pp. 154-158.
36. James B. Finley, *Autobiography* (Cincinnati: Methodist Book Concern, 1854), pp. 327-329.
37. Ibid., p. 267.
38. Ibid., pp. 290-291.
39. Ibid., p. 229.
40. Jacob Young, *Autobiography of a Pioneer* (Cincinnati: Swormstedt and Poe), pp. 295-296.
41. Finley, *Autobiography*, p. 252.
42. Peter Cartwright, *Fifty Years as Presiding Elder* (Cincinnati: Hitchcock and Walden, 1871), pp. 83-84.
43. Ibid., pp. 84-86.
44. Ibid., pp. 90-92.
45. Ibid., pp. 131-133.
46. Ibid., pp. 376-379.
47. Harvey Lee Ross, *The Early Pioneers and Pioneer Events of the State of Illinois* (Chicago: Eastman Brothers, 1846), pp. 188-189.
48. Alfred Brunson, *A Western Pioneer, or, Incidents in the Life and Times of Reverend Alfred Brunson* (Cincinnati: Hitchcock and Walden, 1872), I of II, pp. 305-307.
49. Ibid., p. 304.
50. Francis Asbury, *Journal* (Cincinnati: Jennings and Rye, 1821), III of III, p. 260.
51. Richard Henry Taneyhill, *The Leatherwood God* (Cincinnati:

R. Clark, 1870), pp. 10-50.
52. Ware, *Sketches of Life and Travels of Reverend Thomas Ware*, pp. 200-207.
53. Cartwright, *Autobiography*, pp. 157-158.
54. William F. Pope, *Early Days in Arkansas* (Little Rock: F. W. Allsopp, 1895), pp. 140-141.
55. *The Home Missionary*, XX, No. 3 (July 1847), p. 57.
56. *The Home Missionary*, XXV, No. 11 (March 1853), pp. 259-260.
57. *The Home Missionary*, II, No. 45 (March 1821), p. 179.
58. *The Christian Index*, VII, No. 29 (July 1839), pp. 452-453.
59. Z. N. Morrell, *Flowers and Fruits from the Wilderness* (Boston: Gould and Lincoln, 1872), pp. 206-207.

## Chapter 13
### Emotional Religion and Frontier Sermons

1. *The Home Missionary*, New York, XXIV, No. 6 (October 1951), pp. 131-132.
2. *The Home Missionary*, New York, XLIII, No. 11 (March 1881), pp. 259-260.
3. Frederick Morgan Davenport, *Primitive Traits in Religious Revivals* (New York: The Macmillan Company, 1917), pp. 4-5.
4. James B. Finley, *Autobiography* (Cincinnati: Methodist Book Concern, 1854), pp. 240-241.
5. Davenport, *Primitive Traits in Religious Revivals*, p. 3.
6. Noal J. Major, "The Pioneers of Morgan County, or Memoirs," in *Indiana Historical Society Publications*, V, No. 5 (1915), pp. 339-340.
7. Richard M'Nemar, *The Kentucky Revival* (New York: Edward O. Jenkins, printer, 1846), p. 124.
8. Finley, *Autobiography*, p. 270.
9. Ibid., pp. 83-84.
10. Davenport, *Primitive Traits in Religious Revivals*, pp. 72-75.
11. Alfred Brunson, *A Western Pioneer* (Cincinnati: Hitchcock and Walden, 1872), II of II, p. 21.
12. Catherine Caroline Cleveland, *The Great Revival of the West, 1797-1805* (Chicago: University of Chicago Press, 1914), pp. 96-98.
13. Susannah Johnson, *Recollection of the Reverend John Johnson and His Home* (Nashville: Southern Methodist Publishing House, 1869), pp. 27-28.
14. Joseph Badger, *A Memoir*, (Hudson, Ohio: Sawyer and Ingersoll Co., 1851), p. 50.
15. M. M. Ludlow, *Brother Mason, The Circuit Rider* (Philadelphia: Quaker City Publishing House, 1855), p. 26.
16. Cleveland, *The Great Revival of the West, 1797-1805*, pp. 116-117.
17. Badger, *A Memoir*, pp. 51-52.
18. Barton Warren Stone, *Autobiography* (Cincinnati: J. A. and U. P. James, 1847), pp. 39-42.
19. James McCallum, *A Brief Sketch of the Settlement and Early History of Giles County* (Pulaski, Tennessee: Published by Pulaski Citizens, 1876), pp. 77-78.
20. Peter Cartwright, *Autobiography* (New York: Carlton and Porter, 1856), pp. 50-51.
21. Abel Stevens, *Life and Times of Nathan Bangs* (New York: Carlton and Porter, 1863), pp. 149-150.
22. Joseph Tarkington, *Autobiography* (Cincinnati: Press of Curtis, 1889), pp. 72-73.
23. Cartwright, *Autobiography*, pp. 46-50.
24. John B. McMaster, *A History of the People of the United States* (New York: D. Appleton and Co., 1930-1937), II of VIII, p. 582.
25. Tarkington, *Autobiography*, pp. 72-73.
26. Davenport, *Primitive Traits in Religious Revivals*, pp. 78-79.
27. Cartwright, *Autobiography*, pp. 51-54.
28. McMaster, *A History of the People of the United States*, II, p. 582.
29. McCallum, *A Brief Sketch of the Settlement and Early History*

*of Giles County*, pp. 77-78.
30. Cartwright, *Autobiography*, pp. 39-45.
31. Cleveland, *The Great Revival of the West, 1797-1805*, p. 126.
32. Jacob Young, *Autobiography of a Pioneer* (Cincinnati: L. Swormstedt and A. Poe, 1857), pp. 135-138.
33. Stone, *Autobiography*, pp. 45-49.
34. Young, *Autobiography of a Pioneer*, pp. 140-144.
35. Ibid., pp. 160-163.
36. Cleveland, *The Great Revival of the West, 1797-1805*, pp. 150-152.
37. Young, *Autobiography of a Pioneer*, pp. 156-158.
38. Thomas Ford, *History of Illinois* (Chicago: S. C. Griggs, 1854), p. 40.
39. William Henry Milburn, *The Pioneers and People of the Mississippi Valley* (New York: Denby and Jackson, 1860), pp. 358-359.
40. George R. McKeith, *Pioneer Stories of the Pioneers of Fillmore and Adjoining Counties* (Exter, Nebraska: Press of Fillmore, 1915), p. 24.
41. Hamilton W. Pierson, *In the Brush* (New York: D. Appleton & Co., 1881), pp. 61-81.
42. Tarkington, *Autobiography*, p. 119.
43. Cleveland, *The Great Revival of the West, 1797-1805*, pp. 44-45.
44. Tarkington, *Autobiography*, pp. 18-19.
45. Ibid., p. 140.
46. Major, "The Pioneers of Morgan County, or Memoirs," pp. 340-341.
47. Cartwright, *Autobiography*, pp. 370-372.
48. James McGready, "Posthumous Works," in *The Great Revival of the West, 1797-1805* (Chicago: University of Chicago Press, 1914), pp. 45-46.
49. Cleveland, *The Great Revival of the West, 1797-1805*, pp. 39-45.
50. Calvin B. Goodykoontz, *Home Missions on the American Frontier* (Caldwell, Idaho: Caxton Printers, 1939), pp. 136-137.
51. Herbert Asbury, *A Methodist Saint: The Life of Bishop Asbury* (New York: Alfred A. Knopf, 1927), p. 260.
52. Francis Asbury, *Journal* (New York: Eaton & Mains, 1821), I of III, p. 65.
53. Ibid., II, p. 65.
54. Ibid., II, p. 227.
55. Ibid., I, p. 210.
56. Ibid., I, p. 220.
57. Ibid., I, p. 77.
58. Finley, *Autobiography*, pp. 286-288.
59. F. D. Srygley, *Seventy Years in Dixie, Recollections, Sermons, and Sayings of T. W. Caskey and Others* (Nashville: Gospel Advocate Publishing Co., 1891), pp. 236-237.
60. B. W. P. Strickland, *The Life of Jacob Gruber* (New York: Carlton & Porter, 1860), pp. 43-44.
61. James Shaw, *Early Reminiscences of Pioneer Life in Kansas* (Atchison, Kansas: Haskell Printing Company, 1886), pp. 118-119.
62. James Bradley Finley, *Sketches of Western Methodism* (Cincinnati: The Methodist Book Concern, 1857), pp. 531-535.
63. Finley, *Autobiography*, pp. 322-325.
64. George G. Smith, *The History of Georgia Methodism from 1786 to 1866* (Atlanta: A. R. Caldwell, Publisher, 1913), pp. 110-111.
65. Stephens, *Life and Times of Nathan Bangs*, pp. 134-139.
66. Tarkington, *Autobiography*, p. 74.
67. Frances Trollope, *Domestic Manners of the Americans* (New York: Dodd, Mead and Company, 1927), pp. 105-109.
68. James G. Leyburn, *Frontier Folkways* (New Haven: Yale University Press, 1935), pp. 202-203.
69. Pierson, *In the Brush*, pp. 175-177.
70. Johnson, *Recollections of the Reverend John Johnson and His Home*, p. 238.

71. Srygley, *Seventy Years in Dixie*, pp. 193-195.
72. Johnson, *Recollections of the Reverend John Johnson and His Home*, p. 235.
73. Srygley, *Seventy Years in Dixie*, pp. 196-200.
74. Robert Wilson Patterson, "Early Society in Southern Illinois" [A lecture read before the Chicago Historical Society, 19 October 1880] (Chicago: Fergus Printing Company, 1881), pp. 28-29.
75. Robert W. Malcolm, "Scotch Settlers of Oakland County," *Michigan Historical Collection*, XXXIX (1915), p. 368.
76. Pierson, *In the Brush*, pp. 251-252.
77. Ibid., pp. 250-251.
78. Flavel Basion, "Autobiography," in *Religion on the American Frontier, The Congregationalists*, by William Warren Sweet (Chicago: The University of Chicago Press, 1939), III of III, pp. 258-259.
79. Srygley, *Seventy Years in Dixie*, pp. 90-92.
80. *The Home Missionary*, XXII, No. 1 (May 1849), p. 16.
81. Pierson, *In the Brush*, pp. 244-250.
82. *The Home Missionary*, I, No. 7 (November 1838), p. 168.
83. *The Home Missionary*, XXIII, No. 12 (April 1850), p. 283.
84. *The Home Missionary*, XIV, No. 4 (August 1841), pp. 78-79.
85. Pierson, *In the Brush*, pp. 238-239.
86. *The Home Missionary*, XXVII, No. 1 (May 1855), pp. 8-9.
87. *The Home Missionary*, XIV, No. 4 (August 1841), pp. 78-79.
88. Asbury, *A Methodist Saint: The Life of Bishop Asbury*, pp. 227-229.
89. Young, *Autobiography of a Pioneer*, pp. 236-237.
90. Ibid., p. 239.
91. Alfred M. Lorrain, *The Helm, the Sword and the Cross* (Cincinnati: Poe and Hitchcock, 1867), p. 171.
92. Asbury, *A Methodist Saint: The Life of Bishop Asbury*, p. 231.

## Chapter 14
## Conclusion

1. Statement by Martha Merchant, widow, in a personal interview, Ruston, Louisiana, 1918.
2. Benjamin Franklin, *Two Tracts* (London: John Stockdale, Printer, 1784), pp. 5-9.
3. Morris Birkbeck, *Notes on a Journey in America* (London: Severn and Co., 1818), p. 139.
4. John Bradbury, *Travels in the Interior of America in the Years 1809, 1810, and 1811* (London: Sherwood, Neely and Jones, 1819), pp. 291-293.
5. Franklin, *Two Tracts*, pp. 5-9.
6. Francis Baily, *Journal of a Tour in the Unsettled Parts of North America in 1797-1798* (London: Baily Brothers, 1856), p. 199.
7. Thomas Anburey, *Travels Through the Interior of America* (London: Printed for William Lane, 1789), II of II, pp. 370-371.
8. Peter Cartwright, *Autobiography* (New York: Cranston and Curtis, 1856), pp. 192-193.
9. Louis Wasserman, *Modern Political Philosophies and What They Mean* (Garden City: Halcyon House, 1944), p. 12.
10. Max Lincoln Schuster, *A Treasury of the World's Great Letters* (New York: Simon and Schuster, 1914), p. 333.

# Index

Abilene, Texas, 144
Adams, Andy, 75
Adams, Charles Francis, 51
Adams, Mrs. John (Abigail), 52
Alabama, 43
Alexander, J. E., 107, 118
America, discovery of, 1-3
American Home Missionary Society, 197
Anburey, Thomas, 41, 107, 113, 116, 240
Arizona, 144
Arrington, Alfred W., 210
Asbury, Francis, 4, 30, 59, 76, 91, 202, 207, 209, 224-25, 235
Ashe, Thomas, 116
Attakapas County, Louisiana, 131
Austin, Stephen F., 132
Axley, James, 228

Babcock family, 68
Badger, Joseph, 59
Badmen, 143-48
Baily, Francis, 11, 240; quoted, 76
Baker, Henry, 59

Balboa, V. N. de, 1, 3
Bale, Abraham, 104-5
Bangs, Nathan, 191, 199-200, 227-28
Bank of Missouri, 183
Banks, 19
Bannick, Idaho, 144-45
Barataria Island, 142
Barrett, George, 12
Barter, 15-16
Bates, William, 145
Beard, Thomas 32
Beds, 30-31
Beecher, Lyman, quoted, 5
Belmont, Nevada, 131-32
Benefield and Sapp fight, 120-21
Benton, Jesse, 110
Benton, Thomas Hart, 110
Bering, Vitus, 3
Bernard, John, 41
Berry, James, 103
Bettie County, North Carolina, 118
Beveridge, A. J., 8
"Bilious fever", 52-53

Birkbeck, Morris, 7, 239
Bissell, Dr., 120-21
Black Hawk War, 77
Blue Ear River (Minn.), 76
Boatmen, 113 (see also, river pirates)
Bodley, Hugh S., 169
Bolin brothers, 143
Bossier, E., 125
Boston, 52
Bower, Jacob, 61, 199
Bozan, Jesse, 81
Bradbury, John, 239; quoted, 5
Bradford, William, quoted, 63
Braintree, Mass., 52
Brant, Molly, 46
Bridgman, L., 15
Brunson, Alfred, 65, 90, 178-79, 194, 206-7
Bundling, 39-42
Bunton, Bill, 155
Burke, Edmund, quoted, 63
Burke, William, 220
Burnaby, Andrew, 4
Burnett, Judge, 75

263

Burr, Joseph S., 56
Bush, Mirim, 38
"Butcher Knife Boys", 130-31

Cabin Creek, Ky., 215
Calhoun, John C., 181
California, 153-54
Calomel doctors, 55-56
Cameons, Luis de, 2
Camping, 69-72
Carrhart, George, 120, 121
Carroll, William, 110
Carter, Alex, 155
Cartwright, Peter, 75, 97-98, 192, 197, 203-6, 209, 218, 222-23, 226-27, 240
"Cave-in-Rock", 140
Cavendish, Thomas, 2
Cherokee Bob, 49
Chewing tobacco, 100-102
Childbirth, 54
Childers, Mr., 134
Children, need for, 37-39
Chinn, Thomas T., 56
Cholera, 53
*Christian Index*, 100, 211
Circuit riders, 187-96
Citizens Associations, 151
Claiborne, William C. C., 142-43
Claim associations, 151
Claim clubs, 151, 179-83
Claim jumpers, 183-86
Clarksville, Ohio, 149-50
Clary Grove Boys, 113
Cleveland, Jack, 144
Clothing, 13-15
Codington, G. S., 189
Coleman, Sam, 154
Coleridge, Samuel, 2
Colt revolver, 120
Columbus, Christopher, quoted, 1
Comanches, 77
Concordia Parish, La., 125
Concordia Sandbar affair, 125

Cooley, Charles, quoted, 214
Cooper, William, 16
Corn, 9-11
Coulter, Mrs. Hugh R., 54
Courts/politics, violence and, 109-13
Courtship, 38-39
Cox, Sandford C., 178
Crawford, William, 79
Crockett, David, 119-20
Crum, Peter, 182
Crum, John, 207
Curiosity, 89-92

DaGama, Vasco, 2
Darwin, Charles, quoted, 8
Davis, Jefferson, 105
Davis, John T., 171
Deer killing/butchering, 14-15
Defoe, Daniel, 2
Dentists, 57-59
DeSoto, Hernando, 3
*Desperadoes of the Southwest* (Arrington), 210
Dewees, W. B., 132
Dickens, Charles, 101
Dickinson, Charles, 124-25
Diseases, 51-53
Doddridge, Joseph, 88, 89
Dodge, Irving, 79
Dodge, Richard, 68-69
Dodge City, Kansas, 144
Doke, Rev., 219
Donelson, Rachel, 124
Douglas, Stephen A., 8
Dow, Lorenzo, 233-36
Drake, Sir Francis, 1
Dresser, A., 26, 193
Driscoll family, 166
Dubuque, Iowa, 164, 182-83
Duelling, 121-27
Dugouts, 25-26, 29
Dupray family, 119
Dutch Fred, 135
Dutch John, 159-60

Dwight, Margaret Van Horn, 92
Dylks, Joseph C. "Leatherwood God", 207-8

*Early Days in Arkansas* (Pope), 210
Easely, Mrs., 54
Economic interdependence, 37
*Eddy Grove Songster*, 99
Education and teachers, 97-100
Edward, B. F., 61
Edwards, Jonathan, 41
Elizabeth I, 1
Emotionalism in religion, 213-36
England, 1-2
Epidemics, 51-53
Equality, economic/social, 239-41
Ethnic diversity of the frontier, 4-5
Executions, public, 148
Eye gouging, 114-18

Falling, 214-17
Featherstonhaugh, G. W., 15, 18, 30, 52, 88, 101-2, 103, 134
Ferrel, S. A., 33
Fighting ministers, 199-207
Fights and violence, 107-27
Fink, Mike, 200-201
Finley, James B., 11, 13, 27-29, 43-44, 52, 53, 59-61, 117, 197, 200-201, 215
Finley, John, 29
"Flatheads", 172
Florida, 3
Food, 9-13
Ford, Thomas, quoted, 19
Fort County, Ark., 44
Fort Scott, Kansas, 44
Fort Stoddard, Ala., 43
Fountain & Son, 53-54
Franklin, Benjamin, 47, 92, 239
Franklin County, Ark., 18
Frontier: badmen, 143-48; camping, 69-72; chewing tobacco, 100-102; churches, 5; clothing, 13-15; curiosity, 89-92; dentists, 57-58; diseases, 51-53; duelling, 121-127;

equality, 239-41; ethnic diversity, 4-5; fighting preachers, 199-207; food, 9-13; gang fighting, 113-14; home furnishings, 27-31; illiteracy, 81-84; imposter preachers, 207-11; Indian atrocities, 76-79; itinerant preachers, 187-96; land rights, 175-86; log cabins, 19-23, 27-29; loneliness/ isolation, 64-65; marriage and sex, 37-49; medical treatment, 53-61; ministerial support, 197-99; murderers, 132-38; neighbors, 31-35; politics, 96-97; practical jokes, 93-96; religion/revivalism, 213-36; river pirates, 138-43; sanitary conditions, 29-30; social chaos, 3-8; social life, 31-35; sod houses, 23-27; superstitions, 84-87; table manners, 102-3; teachers/education, 97-100; trade/barter, 15-19; travel perils, 63-79; unenforceable laws, 129-33; U.S. early, 3; weather conditions, 72-76; weddings, 42-46; witchcraft, 87-89; work, 239
Fuel, 22
Fulton County, Ill., 205-6
Funeral sermons, 228-30
Furnishings, 27-31

Gaddis, Maxwell, 98
Gaiennie, François, 125
Galena, Ill., 210
Gallagher, Jack, 157-58
Gang fighting, 113-14
Garrett, Lewis, 217-18
Gavitt, Elnathan C., 22, 70-72, 76, 192, 198
Georgia, 167
Georgia Baptist Association, 211
Gibbs, William J., 171
Gilbert, Sir Humphrey, 2
Giles, Charles, 61
Giles County, Tenn., 143
Gilmer, George, 90, 99
*Golden Hind*, 1
Gold field courts, 153-54
Goode, William W., 64, 184
Government land policy, 175-76
Graves, William "Whiskey Bill", 156

Great Plains, 23-27, 29, 32, 67-69
Greeley, Horace, 144

Hall, W. W., 5
Hamilton, Alexander, 129
Harpe, Micajah, 136-38
Harpe, Wiley, 136-38
Harrison Land Act of 1800, 175
Hathaway, J., 68
Hays City, Kansas, 144
Helm, Boone, 135-36, 157, 158-59
*History of Giles County, Tennessee* (McCallum), 217
Holmes, Oliver Wendell, 54
Homestead Act of 1862, 176
Horse stealing, 167-68
Houston, Texas, 211
Huckins, James, 190-91
Hudson, Henry, 2
Humble, James, 123
Hunter, Bill, 157, 159
Hyer, Henry, 145

Illiteracy, 81-89
Illinois, 32-33, 72, 83, 130-31, 132, 169-73, 179; State Legislature, 109; Territorial Legislature, 127
Imposter preachers, 207-11
Incas, 1
Indians, 5, 46-47, 69; atrocities, 76-79; medicine men, 59
Individualism, 239
Institutions, frontier, 4
Iowa, 180-81
*Iowa Republican*, 39
Irving, Washington, 89
Itinerant preachers, 187-96
Ives, George, 120, 154-55

"J", 136
Jackson, Andrew, 59, 110, 112, 124-25, 136, 143, 240
Jackson, Martha, 52
Jefferson, Thomas, 110

Jefferson County, Ill., 18
Jerks, the, 217-20
Johnson, Francis, 32
Johnson, John, 195-96, 222, 230
Johnson, Thomas, 196
Johnson, William, 46
Johnson County (Ia.) Claim Association, 181-83
Jones, A., 61
*Journal* (Asbury), 76, 224
*Journal* (Huckins), 190
*Justice Form Book*, 151

Kansas, 43, 74, 184
Kentucky, 5, 110-11; Regulators, 172

Lafitte, Jean, 142-43
Lake Ponchartrain, 123
Land rights: claim clubs, 179-83; claim jumpers, 183-86; government policy, 175-76; squatters, 176-78; squatters' law, 178-79
Lane, George, 157, 158
Latrobe, Charles, 54
Law-and-Order Men, 151
Laws, unenforceable, 129-33
Leatherwood Circuit (Ohio), 207
"Leatherwood God" (Joseph Dylks), 207-8
Leon, Ponce de, 3
*Life of John Marshall* (Beveridge), 8
Lindsey, Eli, 103
Lincoln, Abraham, 8, 87, 109-10
Lincoln, Tom, 87
Little Rock, Ark., 210
Log cabins, 19-23, 27-29
Logan County, Ky., 224
Loneliness/isolation, 64-65
Long John, 155
Louisiana, 31, 131, 142-43
Lucas, Jarvis, 118
*Luciads* (Cameons), 2
Lynch Law, 151
Lyons, Hayes, 158-59

Macaulay, Thomas, quoted, 241

McCallum, James, 217
McClellan, Hugh, 99
McConica, Rev., 84
McCrory, S. H., 183
McGee, John, 222
McGee, William, 220-21, 222
McGrady, James, 218, 223-24
McKendree, Rev., 215
McMaster, John B., 111
M' Millan family, 27
McNairy, Judge, 110
Maddox, Thomas, 125
Magellan, Ferdinand, 1, 2
Major, Noah N., 52
Marigny, Bernard, 123
Marion, Iowa, 182
Marshall, John, 8
Marshland, Steve, 157
Mason, Richard Lee, 132-34
Mason gang, 138
Massac County, Ill., 170-72
Massachusetts, 16
Masters, Edgar Lee, quoted, 51
Mather, Cotton, 87-88
Mayfield, Bill, 49
*Mayflower*, 2
Medicinal treatment, 53-61
Medicine men, 59
Melish, John, 101, 116
Merriman, Tom, 114
Methodists, 104-5
Metropolis City, Ill., 171, 172
Midwives, 54
Mills, Samuel J., 5
Mining areas, 144-45
Mining law and order, 153-54
Ministerial support, 197-99
Ministers as physicians, 59-61
Minnesota, 31, 184, 186
Minnesota Historical Society, 31
*Missionary*, 210
Mississippi River, 3, 138
Mississippi Valley earthquakes (1811), 84

Moffitt, Joseph, 56
Money, 15-19
Monson, Judge, 18-19
Montgomery County, VA., 112
Moore, Robert, 182
More, Sir Thomas, 2
Morrell, Z. N., 43, 211
Mortality rate, 39, 51
Murderers, 132-38
Murray, Joe, 39
Murrell, John A., 140

Napier, 89
Narvaez, Panfilo de, 3
Natchez, Miss., 140-42, 168
Natchez Trace, 138
Natchez-Under-the-Hill, 140-42
Nebraska, 19, 21, 184, 186
Neighbors, 31-35
Nevada City, Calif., 145
New England, 15, 88
New Mexico, 144
New Netherlands, 89-90
New Orleans, 113, 142-43
New Salem, Ill., 113
New York, 88
North Carolina, 16

Ogle County, Ill., 170
Ohio, 5-7
Old Man's Creek (Johnson County, Ia.), 182
Onstot, T. G., 103
*Origin of Species* (Darwin), 8

Pacific Ocean, discovery of, 3
Palmer, John, 115
Parish, Frank, 157, 158-59
Parker, A. A., 90-91, 100
Patterson, Robert William, 230
Pecan Bottom circuit (Ill.), 12
Peck, John Mason, 70, 81, 100, 176-77, 191
Pennsylvania, 4
Penrise, Thomas, 118

Perkins, Jeff, 145
Peters, Samuel, quoted, 41
Physicians, 54-61
Pierre, South Dakota, 165-66
Pierson, Hamiltin W., 11, 12, 30, 65-67, 82, 97, 100, 189-90, 194, 198-99, 220, 228, 233
Piggot, Joseph, 70
Pioneer era, 3
Pitt County, North Carolina, 119
*Pittsburgh Gazette*, 130
Pittstown, N.Y., 234
Pizarro, Francisco, 1
*Plea for the West* (Beecher), 5
Plummer, Henry, 144-46, 159, 160
Politics, 96-97
Pope, William F., 240
Pope County, Ill., 170
*Poor Richard's Almanac*, 47
Power, Tyrone, 142
Practical jokes, 93-96
Prayer, spontaneous, 225
Preachers, eccentric, 231-36
Preemption Act of 1841, 175
Presbyterians, Old School, 220
Primitive fighting tactics, 119-20
Pulpit behavior, 220-28

Quakers, 104
Quinn, James, 104

Raccoon (Indian chief), 14
Randolph, John, 240
Ray, Ned, 159
Read, John W., 170
Regulators, 151, 168, 170-72
Reilly, Goliah, 121
Religion, 103-6, 187-236
Reni, Jules, 160-61
"Restoration Francaise", 54
Rice, Cyrus R., 12, 44, 74, 92, 192, 194
Richardson, Rev., 202-3
*Rime of the Ancient Mariner* (Coleridge), 2
River pirates, 138-43

Robinson, A. A., 144
*Robinson Crusoe* (Defoe), 2
Rodolf, Theodore, 33
Roosevelt, Theodore, quoted, 143, 144
Root doctors, 56
Ross, Harvey Lee, 14
Ross, Ossian M., 23; quoted, 42
Ross, Thomas, 54
Russell, Jack, 120-21
Ruzan, Mrs. Jesse, 91

St. Charles, Missouri, 5
Salesville (Ohio) Congregation, 207
Sanders, Cyrus, 183
Sanders, John, 18
San Felipe, Texas, 163
Sangamon County, Ill., 146-48
Sanitary conditions, 29-30
Sawyer, John York, 95
Scates, Judge, 171
Schramm, Jakob, 23
Scott family, 76-77
Sermons, 220-28; funeral, 228-30; off-beat, 230-36
Sevier, John, 110
Sexual irregularities, 46-49
Shakespeare, William, 2; quoted, 31
Shaw, Jonathan, 221
Shawnee Village, Ark., 140
Shears, George, 155-56
Shelbyville, Minn., 76
Shoot, Littlebury, 135
Shuler, Laurence S., 57
Simpson, Rev., 221
*Sketches of Some of the First Settlers of Upper Georgia* (Gilmer), 90, 99
Skinner, Cyrus, 120
Smith, Adam, quoted, 37
Smith, David, 5
Smith, George C., 197
Smith, Joseph, 191-92
Smith, Oliver H., 65
Social life, 31-35

Sod houses, 23-27
South Carolina, 125-27, 149, 167
*Speech of Polly Baker* (Franklin), 47
*Spoon River Anthology* (Masters), 51
Squatters, 176-78; law, 178-79
*Squirrel*, 2
Stade, John A., 160-63
Staked Plain (Texas), 77
Stallions, Billy, 119
Stephens, Joseph, 211
Stevens, J. D., 53
Stevenson, Robert Louis, quoted, 5
Stewart, John, 11, 167
Stinson, Buck, 159, 160
Strong, John D., 233
Stuart, James, 177
Superstitions, 84-87
Swan, Thomas, 110

Table manners, 102-3
Tarkington, Joseph, 195, 196
Teachers/education, 97-100
*Telegraph* (Houston), 211
*Tempest* (Shakespeare), 2
Tennessee, 33
Testimonials, religious, 225
Texas, 42-43, 46, 77, 90-91, 152, 190-91
Thomas family, 74
Thompson, Rev., 222
*Three Episodes of Massachusetts History* (Adams), 51
Tiffen, Edward, 59
Tillson, Mrs. Christian Holmes, 82
Tillson family, 91-92
Tipton, John, 199
Tombigbee River (Alabama), 43
Tonkaway Indians, 77
Tongs, Justice, 164
Trade/barter, 15-19
*Travels* (Anburey), 116
*Travels Through North America* (Weld), 90
*Trip to the West and Texas* (Parker), 100
Trollope, Frances, 102-3

Turgot, Robert, 241

Union church (Tennessee), 32
Union County, Ky., 138
*Utopia* (More), 2

Vagrancy, 7
Van Buren, Martin, 182
Vickburg, Miss., 169
Vigilante committees, 149-73; hangings, 154-63; versus the law, 168-73
Virginia, 16, 112
Virginia City, Montana, 157
*Virginian* (Wister), 172
*Vittoria*, 1

Wampum, 15-16
Ware, Thomas, 196, 199, 209
War of 1812, 142-43
"Warning to Thieves in Hill Country" (Texas), quoted, 152
Washington, George, 16, 130
Washington Grove, Ill., 166
Watson, Elkanah, 116
Wayne County, Ga., 83
Weather conditions, 72-76
Wedding ceremonies, 42-46
Weld, Isaac, 90
Wells, Samuel, 125
West, Bill, 39
Weymouth, Mass., 51
Whetstone, Pete, 52
Whip duels, 122
Whipple, Henry B., 92, 102
Whiskey Rebellion 1794, 129-30
Whitten, Elijah, 220
Wilcox, J., 52-53
Wilkes County, Ga., 81, 83
Williams, Parker, 210
Wilson gang, 140
Winchester, Va., 4
Winters, frontier, 72-75
Wisconsin, 33, 43, 52, 179

Wister, Owen, 172
Witchcraft, 87-89
Wood, Aaron, 198

Wood, George, 21
Woodlands, 19-23
Wright family, 29, 35

Young, Jacob, 56-57, 220, 235

Zachery, Bob, 156